ALSO BY EVAN THOMAS

The Very Best Men
Four Who Dared
The Early Years of the CIA

The Man to See
Edward Bennett Williams
Ultimate Insider; Legendary Trial Lawyer

The Wise Men
Six Friends and the World They Made
(with Walter Isaacson)

Robert Kennedy
His Life

John Paul Jones

SAILOR, HERO, FATHER OF
THE AMERICAN NAVY

EVAN THOMAS

Simon & Schuster

New York   London   Toronto   Sydney   Singapore

SIMON & SCHUSTER
Rockefeller Center
1230 Avenue of the Americas
New York, NY 10020

SIMON & SCHUSTER and colophon are registered trademarks
of Simon & Schuster, Inc.

Book design by Ellen R. Sasahara
Maps and illustrations copyright © 2003 by David Cain

For information regarding special discounts for bulk purchases,
please contact Simon & Schuster Special Sales
at 1-800-456-6798 or business@simonandschuster.com

Manufactured in the United States of America

5   7   9   10   8   6

Library of Congress Cataloging-in-Publication Data

Thomas, Evan—date.
John Paul Jones : sailor, hero, father of the American Navy / Evan Thomas.
p. cm.
Includes bibliographical references and index.
1. Jones, John Paul, 1747–1792. 2. Admirals—United States—Biography. 3. United States. Navy—
Biography. 4. United States—History—Revolution, 01775–1783—Naval operations. I. Title
E207.J7T48 2003
973.3'5'092—dc21
[B]   2003042411

ISBN 0-7432-0583-9

To my mother
Anne D. R. Thomas

CONTENTS

"Every officer in our navy should know by heart the deeds of John Paul Jones."

—PRESIDENT THEODORE ROOSEVELT, *April 24, 1906*

John Paul Jones

"My Desire for Fame Is Infinite"

*J*OHN PAUL JONES, the captain of the Continental Navy ship *Bonhomme Richard*, first sighted his Brittanic Majesty's Ship *Serapis* at 3 P.M. on September 23, 1779. The *Serapis* was about ten miles away. The wind was light, a gentle southwest breeze, and in the rush of the tide off of Flamborough Head on England's east coast, the two ships crept toward each other. No captain of an American navy ship had ever defeated and captured a British man-of-war of any real size or strength. Jones ached to be the first. He had about four hours to contemplate his chances for immortality.

At 5 P.M., drummers marched the deck of the *Bonhomme Richard*, beating a rattling cadence. The ship was cleared for action: bulkheads, chairs, tables, bunks, any objects that were portable and wooden, were stowed in the hold, in part to reduce the risk of flying splinters that could impale a man. The decks were sprinkled with sand to keep them from becoming slick with blood. Down in the dim cockpit, far belowdeck where the surgeons worked, tubs were put out for discarding amputated limbs. At each gangway, marines were posted to stop cowards from fleeing below. For courage, the men were issued an extra ration of rum.

Jones could see, through the light haze, two warships, one large—a heavy frigate, perhaps—and one small, probably a sloop-of-war. Captain

Jones's squadron comprised four ships: the *Bonhomme Richard*, forty guns; the *Alliance*, thirty-six guns; the *Pallas*, thirty-two guns; and the *Vengeance*, twelve guns. Their combined firepower could hurl more than a thousand pounds of metal in a single broadside. The odds heavily favored Jones. He could squeeze the larger British ship in a vise, hammering her from both sides, or run along in line of battle, discharging broadside after broadside before the enemy could reload.

The British warships were protecting a convoy of more than forty British merchantmen, fat prizes. They were carrying lumber, canvas, and cordage from Scandinavia, crucial raw materials for Britain's "wooden wall," the Royal Navy that commanded the seas. Taking these ships would make Jones wealthy, but he cared far more that victory would make him famous.

At 6 P.M., Jones ordered an officer to run up three flags, blue up the foremast, blue up the mainmast, blue-and-yellow up the mizzen. The flags signaled "Form Line of Battle."

Jones could see the flags stirring in the dusk. This was the greatest moment of his life, the reckoning for any naval commander, that rare chance for true fame. Jones looked out at the other three ships in his little fleet and saw . . .

Nothing. No response. The other captains simply ignored Jones's command. The *Alliance* sheered away. The *Pallas* continued on her previous course. The *Vengeance* hung back.

In those few moments, the odds radically shifted. The larger British warship swung open her gun ports and showed her teeth as a two-decker with a full lower gun deck of heavy cannon. Jones's ship was old and slow; many of its very mixed lot of cannon were old and of dubious reliability. The British man-of-war was faster and brand-new.

Jones was on his own, though not for the first time. He may have sighed, he may have sworn, but more likely his face was a coldly impassive mask. By now, he was accustomed to gross insubordination. Before going into his first decisive single-ship action, against HMS *Drake*, his crew had almost mutinied. Jones had bullied and cajoled the men into obedience.

On this cruise, one of his captains, an irascible, addled Frenchmen named Pierre Landais, had been flouting orders at every turn. At one point, Jones and Landais had nearly dueled.

Jones had a temper, but now he held it. Or rather, he aimed it. He steered the *Bonhomme Richard* right for the enemy.

Low on the eastern horizon, a full harvest moon was just beginning to rise. The water was still, almost glassy. The two ships, bristling with cannon, their slow matches eddying smoke in the zephyrs, slowly glided toward each other. One hundred yards. Fifty yards. Twenty-five yards, the range, Jones later recorded, "of a pistol shot."

A BRUSH WITH GLORY, then oblivion. Then he rose again. On a brilliant summer's afternoon in July 1905, a casket bedecked with the American flag and bearing the body of John Paul Jones was paraded down the avenues of Paris. A squadron of French cuirassiers, in glittering helmets and breastplates, led the way, followed by a column of 500 U.S. Navy bluejackets. The American sailors in the honor guard were chosen, according to one contemporary account, for their height (all were over six feet) and "manly" good looks. "Quels beaux garçons!" whispered the French ladies in the vast, cheering crowd, which surged against the barricades. Down the Champs-Elysées, across the grandly ornate Pont Alexandre, the cortege made its way. At Les Invalides, before the gilded dome of the tomb of Napoleon, stood a pavilion hung in royal purple velvet adorned with martial emblems and battle-axes. There Jones's casket rested while the diplomats and statesmen made speeches to the glory of his name.

A U.S. Navy squadron of cruisers awaited at Cherbourg to take him to America. The squadron—*Brooklyn*, *Tacoma*, *Galveston*, and *Chattanooga*—steamed westward across the Atlantic, to be met by seven battleships, passing through the Virginia capes, up the Chesapeake Bay to the U.S. Naval Academy at Annapolis. On July 24, the casket was carried past rows of midshipmen, standing to attention along the seawall, while the academy band played Chopin's funeral march and cannon boomed a salute.

The homecoming had been long delayed. Jones had died, lonely and feeling forgotten, in Paris in 1792. His casket had been interred for over a century in a graveyard so obscure that it had been paved over. It had taken the United States ambassador to France, General Horace Porter, several months just to find Jones's remains, buried beneath a laundry on the outskirts of the city.

Jones had been resurrected in part because Teddy Roosevelt needed a hero. The young President, an avid naval historian, was eager to make the United States a great naval power at the turn of the twentieth century. Roosevelt wanted to celebrate Jones's legacy with appropriate pomp. On a clear and cool day, April 24, 1906, special trains carried the President and various dignitaries down from Washington to the Naval Academy at Annapolis. The Baltimore Oratorio sang "The Star-Spangled Banner" and "How Sleep the Brave." Jones's casket was draped with the Stars and Stripes and upon it rested a wreath of laurel, a spray of palm, and the gold-mounted sword presented by King Louis XVI to Commodore Jones for his exploits. In his remarks, President Roosevelt wanted to make sure that the lessons of Jones's life were not lost to his countrymen and its future leaders. "Every officer in our navy should know by heart the deeds of John Paul Jones," the President decreed. From then on, all midshipmen were required to memorize Jones's purported pronouncements on the correct training and proper manners of an officer and a gentleman. Beneath the transept of the Naval Academy Chapel, Jones was laid to his final rest in a marble sarcophagus modeled after Napoleon's own crypt. "He gave our Navy," reads the inscription on the tomb, "its earliest traditions of heroism and victory."

How Jones would have loved it. "My desire for fame is infinite," Jones once admitted in a letter to the French Minister of the Marine. He craved—too much, he knew—the trappings of glory. During his life, Jones had commissioned the drawing of three increasingly elaborate coats of arms (his real family had none). He spent hours designing uniforms for the fledgling Continental Navy; he preferred the more dashing white waistcoats of the British Royal Navy to the dowdy red ones required by the Continental Congress. He was very pleased when the court of Louis XVI awarded him the Ordre du Mérite Militaire, which allowed Jones to wear a ribbon and a cross and to call himself "le Chevalier." Angry when Congress would not give him flag rank, he was gratified to be named a rear admiral in the Russian navy ("Kontradmiral Pavel Ivanovich Dzhones"). As time went on, he was bitter that he had not received more public recognition in America.

Still, over the years, his popular legend grew. In cheap penny chapbooks, British children in the late eighteenth century read about the terrifying "Pirate Paul Jones" who had plundered their seacoast. Throughout the nineteenth century, authors with a romantic bent—Alexandre Dumas, James Fenimore Cooper, William Thackeray, Rudyard Kipling—made him a character in biography and fiction. He was exalted as "an audacious Viking" in a fictionalized telling of his triumphs (*Israel Potter*) by Herman Melville. Teddy Roosevelt's cousin Franklin was entranced by the legend. In the mid-1920s, FDR wrote a perfectly awful screenplay treatment of Jones's life. (At a strategy meeting during World War II, FDR's aide, Harry Hopkins, had to interrupt the President as he digressed into a debate over Jones's tactics against the *Serapis* with the British Prime Minister, Winston Churchill.) In 1958, to the delight of schoolboys (including this one), Hollywood finally did discover Jones. In *John Paul Jones*, actor Robert Stack bellowed from the burning deck at the climax of Jones's epic sea battle, "I have not yet begun to fight!" (stirring words Jones probably never said, though he did shout out a refusal to strike his flag).

Today, Jones has largely vanished from high school history books, and his glory in life did not begin to match his outsized dreams. He never did fulfill his ambition to become a great blue-ocean fleet commander. He imagined America as a mighty sea power long before the country had the capacity or the will to become one. He showed astounding flashes of fortitude and ingenuity in battle, but he endured long bleak spells of brooding over opportunities missed or denied. He could inspire with brave words and dash, but his narcissism sometimes cost him the affection of his men. Though he blamed others and suffered more than his share of bad luck, his edgy character caused much of his misfortune.

Jones was not what he wished to be. Even so, he was a warrior his new nation sorely needed. He was one of the few members of the revolutionary generation who really knew how to fight. His boldness and resourcefulness stand out against the sorry record of the Continental Navy.

Jones was memorable for more than his martial accomplishments. His life offers a window into the nation's founding. Jones was the quintessential striver. He was, in the purest American sense, a self-made man whose raw drive and talent broke through his era's walls of class and place. His rise mirrors that of his adopted country and its restless people, the ascendancy of the New World over the Old. Herman Melville saw the identification: "Intrepid, unprincipled, reckless, predatory, with boundless ambition, civilized in externals but a savage at heart," Melville wrote, "America is, or may yet be, the Paul Jones of nations."

JONES LIKED TO SAY that he drew his sword, not for hire, but "in defense of the violated rights of mankind." To be sure, he was willing to fight for other, less noble reasons. Eager for action and fame after the end of the Revolutionary War, he went (with Congress's blessing) into the service of one of history's great despots, Catherine the Great of Russia. Yet he was a true-blue patriot. At his first meeting with the Russian Tsarina in 1788, he handed her a copy of the new Constitution of the United States. He was proud that he was the first naval officer to hoist the American flag over a warship, at Philadelphia in January 1776. Jones saw himself as a romantic, larger-than-life figure, and though he was a huge egotist, he was not self-deluding. He had a dreamy sense of destiny: "Our marine," he wrote about the ragtag American navy in 1778, "will rise as if by enchantment, and become, within the memory of persons now living, the wonder and envy of the world."

Jones earned the respect, if not always the friendship, of many of the

Founding Fathers. General George Washington recognized Jones's immense talents and all too singular achievements in the Continental Navy with praise that made Jones preen. Benjamin Franklin was an avuncular figure to Jones, who named his ship, the *Bonhomme Richard*, after Franklin's *Poor Richard's Almanack*. Franklin valued Jones's drive and naval genius, though he scolded him for his self-absorption. During a tour as American minister to Paris, Thomas Jefferson performed one of the habitual duties of that post: handling Captain Jones's tangled love affairs. (On one occasion, Jones asked Jefferson to pass private letters to one of his mistresses, reputedly an illegitimate child of King Louis XV. Jefferson dutifully acted as go-between, but backed off when the woman asked him for a loan.) Notwithstanding Jones's dalliances, Jefferson had high praise for the Captain. In 1788, Jefferson wrote a friend, "I consider this officer to be the principal hope of our future efforts on the ocean." At Monticello, Jefferson displayed Jones's bust alongside those of Washington, Franklin, and Lafayette.

John Adams, a great proponent of American sea power and shrewd judge of men, was fascinated by Jones's ego. In 1780, after dining with Jones, Adams observed:

> This is the most ambitious and intriguing officer in the American Navy. Jones has Art, and Secrecy, and aspires very high. You can see the Character of the Man in his uniform . . . variant of the Uniforms established by Congress. Golden buttonholes, for himself—two Epaulets. . . .
>
> Eccentricities and Irregularities are to be expected from him— they are in his Character, they are visible in his Eyes. His voice is soft and still and small, his eye has keenness and Wildness and softness in it.

Adams's wife, Abigail, was struck by the unexpected softness in Jones's demeanor. After encountering the naval hero in a Paris salon in 1784, Abigail wrote playfully to a female relative, "I daresay you would be as much disappointed in him as I was. . . . I expected to have seen a rough, stout, warlike Roman. Instead of that, I should sooner think of wrapping him up in cotton wool and putting him into my pocket, than sending him to contend with cannon ball[s]. He is small of stature, well-proportioned, soft in his speech, easy in his address, polite in his manners, vastly civil." Abigail noted, with some surprise, that Jones knew "the etiquette of a lady's toilette as perfectly as he does the masts, sails, and rigging of his ship. . . . He knows how often the ladies use the baths, what colors best suits a lady's complexion, what cosmetics are most favorable to the skin. We do not often see," she whimsically observed, "the warrior and the abigail thus united."

Jones may have been part "abigail" (a seventeenth-century literary expression for a lady's maid) in the drawing room, but his tenderness vanished on the quarterdeck. He was, without question, a great sea warrior. The tiny, patchwork Continental Navy that put to sea (or, in many cases, stayed in port) against the mighty Royal Navy was pitifully overmatched. On the rebel side, the sea story of the War of Independence is largely one of bumbling and futility.* Jones was a powerful exception. Admiralty records show the British sea lords at Whitehall in London working late into the night and on Sunday to try to catch "the Pirate Jones," whose daring raids were causing a popular uproar along the English coast.

As a strategist and commander, Jones was well ahead of his time. In the eighteenth century, warfare was notable for its restraint. Battles were contained, hot and fierce when the forces clashed but rarely free-wheeling or marauding. With some infamous exceptions, civilians were not targeted. The officer class valued personal bravery. Naval commanders disdained protective armor and—like Nelson, wounded fatally at the Battle of Trafalgar—wore their shining decorations as they stood on the quarterdeck, exposed to grapeshot and musket ball. Yet an unwritten code al-

---

*Of the fifty-seven ships that sailed under the flag of the Continental Navy, thirty-four were taken or sunk by the British or destroyed to avoid capture; four were lost at sea; fifteen were sold or decommissioned; and four cannot be accounted for. The Continental Navy captured approximately thirteen Royal Navy ships, almost all of them small vessels.

lowed a sea captain to break off an engagement before it became an outright or senseless slaughter.

While he dearly wished to be seen as a gentleman officer, Jones was determined to fight to the death. He fought one three-hour battle that was a bloodbath by eighteenth-century standards. Fully half the combatants were killed or wounded in large part because Jones stubbornly refused to surrender, even though his ship was battered, burning, and sinking. When one of Jones's petty officers did try to haul down the ship's flag to halt the carnage, Jones threw a pistol at his head. Jones's all-out drive for victory, no matter the odds, no matter the cost, was a harbinger of the concept, all too familiar in modern times, of total war. Jones posed (especially for the ladies) as a chivalric knight, but his tactics at times more closely resembled those of the people's armies of the nineteenth and twentieth centuries than the aristocratic set-piece combat in the seventeenth and eighteenth centuries. He excoriated the British for putting some colonial towns to the torch, and he was disgusted when his Russian allies burned to death their Turkish captives, yet he wanted to hold hostage whole British cities for the release of American prisoners. For all his avowals of principle, Jones was an opportunist. He was cunning. He understood the power of psychological warfare, that the civilian population could be terrorized by attacks on their homeland.

It pained Jones that his new nation did not try harder to win mastery of the seas. "Without a respectable Navy—alas America!" he wrote. He constantly agitated to create an officer class based on merit, not cronyism, and to create a naval establishment that would choose shipbuilders for their ability, not their political connections. "I wish to have no connection with any ship that does not sail *fast*," he wrote a French patron who was trying to find him a suitable warship, "for I intend *to go in harm's way*." He never got what he wanted. He fought his greatest battle in an old slow tub.

Jones complained about his lot—endlessly. His hundreds of letters and extensive campaign journals are exhaustive in their self-justification. In his self-pitying moments, he could be a tiresome crank. Yet Jones was not blind to his shortcomings. He had a vision of a better self—modest, humble, and true—and he struggled, manfully if with mixed success, to adjust his nature to his ideals. He lamented that war was eclipsing his more tender feelings and wrote flowery poetry to prove it. He was loyal to his friends, if not his mistresses. While prim and touchy about his reputation, he could be exuberant, even outrageous, especially in battle when he had outfoxed his enemies. But, always, he was seized with ambition.

John Adams once described Jones as "leprous with vanity." Forever on guard against shows of conceit (especially his own), Adams despairingly wrote, "Titles, Ribbons, Stars, Garters, Crosses, Keys, are the important Springs that move the ambition of Men in high life. How poor! How mean! How low! Yet how true." True for Jones, certainly. The Chevalier Jones was vainglorious. But then so were Lord Horatio Nelson ("if it be a sin to covet glory," Nelson wrote Lady Hamilton, "I am the most offending soul alive"), General George S. Patton with his pearl-handle revolvers, General Douglas A. MacArthur with his sunglasses, and any number of strutting great military geniuses and warriors. It can require an enormous ego to lead men to their deaths. Real-life heroes are rarely like "Lucky Jack" Aubrey, the sunny, bluff, big-hearted sea captain of Patrick O'Brian's novels of the British Age of Sail. Jones's temperament—prickly, self-absorbed, and easily wounded—makes him a dead ringer for the real Jack Aubrey: Lord Thomas Cochrane, the Royal Navy captain whose actual exploits were the model for the dramatic, against-the-odds sea battles described in O'Brian's first Aubrey-Maturin novel, *Master and Commander.*

John Paul Jones's ambition—ever present, all-consuming, and limitless—was his most defining characteristic, his goad and his vice. It was a trait he shared with many of the leaders of the American Revolution—and a good thing, too. The Founders were the original self-made men, hungry for advancement and recognition. Their gentlemanly concern for honor feels old-fashioned, almost feudal, with one critical difference: they understood that honor might be inherited, but fame must be *earned.* In their scramble for glory, for lasting fame, they launched an enduring republic.

Jones and other sons of liberty came of age in a time and place when the old order and the old certitudes were cracking. For centuries, status had been largely determined by birth. But, at least in some quarters and for some classes, an Age of Enlightenment had arrived. Diverse philosophers were suggesting that virtue was not bestowed by the Almighty, but could be learned. Human nature was not immutable but could be improved, even perfected, by a liberal education. It is more than an interesting coincidence that most of the Founding Fathers were first-generation college graduates.

The son of a landscape gardener who labored for the landed gentry, Jones could not wait to improve his place. He studied gentlemen in order to become one. He had to catch up: his threadbare upbringing in Scotland included no dancing and fencing lessons, but he made himself literate. He could quote Pope and Shakespeare and write romantic verse—though sometimes, admittedly, the same verse to two different ladies. He admired other strivers. His friends included an African-American poetess, Phillis Wheatley, who had been discovered by the smart set in London and Boston. For a sweet month of May in 1780, Jones was the darling of Paris society.

Jones won titles and decorations and other marks of respect and recognition, but they were never enough. Ultimately, Jones's life was less heroic than tragic. He exulted in his moments of battle, appearing almost light-hearted at times of great peril, but then his habit of brooding would return. His many insecurities would begin to gnaw; he would pout and lash out. His temperament was self-defeating, and he knew it. He knew that he was too proud and abrasive, and yet he could not help himself. His flickers of self-awareness would vanish, replaced by theatrical posturings. He wanted to be a gentleman of the Enlightenment, able to use reason to tame his inner demons, but he never succeeded, at least for long.

Jones had much in common with another flawed genius and revolutionary climber, Alexander Hamilton. A bastard immigrant of Scottish descent, Hamilton would have sooner died than wind up, as he put it, as a "grov'ling" clerk. Both dandies wrote poetry and preened for the ladies. Both Hamilton and Jones knew the surest way to get ahead. "I wish there was a war," Hamilton wrote when he was fourteen years old. Jones found his war as soon as he could, as the first commissioned lieutenant in the Continental Navy, six months before the Declaration of Independence.

Jones was his own invention. He had arrived in America without even a name. He was traveling "incog.," he wrote—incognito, under a false identity. He had killed a man. He was on the run.

CHAPTER ONE

"You Meet a Gentleman"

HIS REAL NAME WAS JOHN PAUL, inherited, along with a chip on the shoulder, from his father. John Paul Sr. was a proud and talented man. Today, he would be called a landscape architect. In eighteenth-century Scotland, he was a gardener. He had been hired—indeed, recruited all the way from Leith on Scotland's east coast—to lay out the gardens at Arbigland, a 1,400-acre estate in the soft and wildly beautiful countryside that rims the Firth of Solway, the body of water that divides England and Scotland on Britain's west coast. John Paul Sr.'s profession was at a kind of apex: the mid-eighteenth century was a great age of landscape gardening. Abandoning the constrained formalism of the Continent, English landscape gardeners like Capability Brown created romantic vistas, ponds, glades, groves, hillocks, and glens and dales for the local gentry who hired them. At Arbigland, Paul Sr. turned nature's gifts into murmuring brooks and fragrant ponds with lily pads and gently overhanging willows. Luxuriant flowers and foliage spilled across mossy paths that wound through a sweet-smelling wonderland. As a little boy, John Paul Jr. wandered in a man-made enchanted forest that would suddenly and breathtakingly open to the sea. Walking through the gardens John Paul Sr. laid out more than two centuries ago, it is easy to understand how John Paul Jr. formed the softer sensibility that inspired the romantic poetry and "fine feelings" he espoused.

John Paul Sr. was a manager as well as an artist. The household staff at Arbigland was enormous, over a hundred maids, grooms, cooks, game-keepers, and gardeners, and as head gardener Paul Senior's rank roughly equaled that of head butler. But he was still a member of the servant class, required to tip his forelock to his master, Mr. Craik. The world was still stratified in 1750. Each man was supposed to know where he stood in the Great Chain of Being, the immutable social order, fixed by God. (If he didn't, notes historian Gordon Wood, there were guidebooks. Young George Washington, growing up in the colony of Virginia, copied out in-structions on how to pull off one's hat to "Persons of Distinction" and how to bow "according to the custom of the better bred and quality of the person" in order to "give every person his due title according to his de-gree.") The Scottish lived with another level of subservience. From time to time, English kings subdued Scottish uprisings. One of the most sto-ried rebellions was crushed about a year before young John Paul was born. In April 1746, on Culloden Moor, an English army defeated the forces of Charles Edward Stuart, "Bonnie Prince Charlie," Jacobite pretender to the crown.

William Craik, the master of Arbigland and John Paul's employer, was not a Jacobite. He cast his lot with the ruling English. Craik was a domi-neering figure, "ardent to make himself completely master of whatever he took in hand," according to his daughter, Helen. He understood Latin, Greek, Hebrew, French, and Italian; he made "some little progress in Spanish," was a "tolerable architect," "fond of chemistry," and "read much on learned subjects." He had been a willful hell-raiser as a young man. "In hard drinking, hard riding, and every other youthful excess, few could equal his notoriety," wrote his daughter. And he was a hard man who brooked no disrespect or dissent. Social tensions ran high on Scottish es-tates after landlords began driving tenants off the land in the early eigh-teenth century. There were riots as "levelers" fought back. Craik ordered his tenants to conform to the new rules of agriculture or face jail instead. Toward his gardener Craik was more respectful, but John Paul was sup-posed to do what he was told.

John Paul bristled against Craik's overbearing authority, but he did so quietly, using an edge of sarcasm to undercut his deference. His sullenness showed in an odd way. Symmetry in architecture was all the fashion in the mid-eighteenth century. It appears that Craik, who was building a manor house in the classical style, insisted on building not one but two summer houses in the garden. John Paul, raised a frugal Scotsman, thought the second summer house was extravagant, a point he made in peculiarly subversive fashion. Upon catching a man stealing fruit, John Paul Sr. locked him in one of the summer houses. Then he locked his little boy John Jr. into the other summer house. Craik found this peculiar, and asked why the boy had been locked up. John Paul Sr. drily replied in his brogue, "for the sake of symmetry."

John Paul Sr. may have resented more than his laird's extravagance. For many years after John Paul Jones became famous as an American navy captain, it was rumored in Kirkbean and the small towns around Arbigland that John Paul Jr. was really the bastard son of William Craik. It is true that John Paul's mother, Jean McDuff, worked as a housekeeper for Mr. Craik. She married John Paul Sr. the day before Craik married a neighboring lady, a coincidence that raised eyebrows in the village. Scottish lairds not uncommonly enjoyed sexual favors from the household help and sometimes had the progeny to show for it. Craik did have at least one illegitimate son (interestingly, in later life he became George Washington's personal physician). Was young John another? John honored his nominal father. He had built in the Kirkbean graveyard a large crypt, inscribed "John Paul Senior who died at Arbigland the 24 October 1767 Universally Esteemed. Erected by John Paul Junior." But he may have questioned his parentage. A sensitive boy, he could not have missed the tension between his proud father and the lordly Mr. Craik, especially when he was sitting locked in the summer house, wondering why he had been put there. John Paul Jr. observed his father's seethings and vowed not to cringe himself. John Paul Jones's sense of resentment and wounded pride were never far from the surface in later life. He came by them naturally.

From the day of his birth, July 6, 1747, John Paul Jr. lived with his brother, three sisters, and both parents in a tidy, two-room cottage. Cramped and stuffy inside, it overlooked a magnificent vista, a field running down to the Firth of Solway. Playing along the shore, with its pungent salty smell, John Paul Jr. could imagine Viking ancestors who had landed there centuries before. On clear days, he could see across to the English coast and the mountains of the Lake District. On most days of his childhood, he could watch the great ships slipping down the firth to the Irish Sea beyond, bound for distant lands.

Young John was an eager, bossy boy. Mr. Craik's son Robert recalled watching John Paul Jr. standing high on a rock at the edge of the shore, yelling orders at his playmates in a shrill voice as they paddled about in rowboats. He was pretending to be a fleet admiral, staging a sea battle. John Paul turned twelve years old in the "Glorious Year" of 1759 when the Royal Navy under Admiral Hawke defeated the French at Quiberon Bay on the Brittany Peninsula. Hawke's flagship captain, John Campbell, hailed from Kirkbean, a small town just outside the gates of Arbigland, where John Paul attended the parish school. He heard the story of how Admiral Hawke sent the British fleet tearing in after the French, ignoring the danger of a lee shore on a stormy day, ordering his captains not to open fire until they were, as close range was then commonly measured, "within pistol shot."

John Paul wanted to join the Royal Navy. "I had made the art of war at sea in some degree my study, and had been fond of the navy, from boyish days up," he wrote Benjamin Franklin many years later. The navy could be a social ladder for some poor boys. Captain James Cooke, the great South Sea explorer, had been a laborer's son, and Horatio Nelson was born in a modest parsonage. But entering the navy's officer class by obtaining a midshipman's berth—as a "young gentleman"—usually required the right social connections. The Pauls had none. The best John Paul Jr. could do was sign on as an apprentice aboard a merchant ship. John Paul could hope— after seven years of servitude—to rise above the level of an ordinary seaman. But the social prestige and chance of glory for a first mate or even a master aboard a merchantman did not approach that of a naval officer.

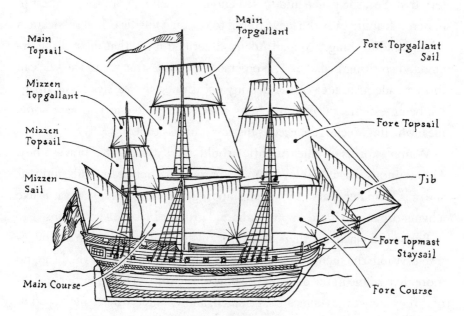

Main Topgallant

Main Topsail

Fore Topgallant Sail

Mizzen Topgallant

Mizzen Topsail

Fore Topsail

Mizzen Sail

Jib

Fore Topmast Staysail

Main Course

Fore Course

A Typical Three~Masted Ship

Jones swallowed his disappointment at not winning a naval commission, but not his ambition.

Young boys sometimes catch sea fever. In the eighteenth century, many boys went to sea by the age of thirteen. If they waited any longer, the philosopher of the age, Dr. Johnson, once observed, they wouldn't go. No right-minded adult would volunteer to go to sea. Shipboard life was too awful.

In 1760, when John Paul turned thirteen, he boarded a two-masted brig out of Whitehaven, a British port across the Solway (where he would return eighteen years later as an American naval officer, intending to burn the place). The *Friendship* was about eighty feet long and could carry less than 200 tons; she would barely qualify as a "tall ship" today. In the wintery Irish Sea, she rolled and tossed enough to send all but the hardiest of her crew leaning over the leeward rail to vomit. Melville called seasickness "that dreadful thing." Abigail Adams described it as "that most disheartening, dispiriting malady. . . . No person, who is a stranger to the sea, can form an adequate idea of the debility occasioned by sea-sickness." Imagine being extemely drunk and hung over all at once and you have some idea: whirling, reeling, nauseous distress and lassitude.

Winter storms in the Atlantic would terrify even the bravest boy. Mountainous seas could lay a small ship over on her beam ends and tear the sails from her spars. A wooden ship rigged with rope and canvas is like a living organism: it creaks and sighs and groans. In a gale, it screams.

Belowdecks in all weathers, the ship stank from unwashed men and bilgewater. While the men were supposed to relieve themselves at the head, no more than a hole in the deck off the bow of the ship, in bad weather and illness they sometimes defecated, urinated, and vomited where they stood or slept. The water that collected in the bilge, full of excrement and rot of one kind or another, was unspeakable. In the abundance of Arbigland, John Paul had milk, butter, fresh vegetables. Aboard the *Friendship*, he dined on salt beef, dried peas, and biscuit, day after day. The beef, pickled in brine, savored vaguely of fish, and the biscuits were so full of weevils that they moved. The peas were like bullets; the butter, when it wasn't rancid, tasted like oil sludge. The water, carefully rationed (no bathing—saltwater had to do) was covered with a coat of slime after a few weeks. The damp was inescapable: wool clothes, caked with salt, held moisture for days.

Like everyone else, young John Paul was given a ration of alcohol. Typically, seamen were allowed a half pint of rum or a half gallon of beer a day (or a pint of red wine, which they disdained and called "black strap"). Four ounces of rum, served twice a day cut with water and made into "grog," was a pretty powerful cocktail. And naturally, the men hoarded and stole rations and smuggled liquor aboard to get drunker. Drunkenness was the number one cause of discipline problems and no small cause of accidents.

A slightly tipsy—or "groggy"—man could miss a step as he climbed the rigging or lose his footing as he edged out along a spar.

John Paul didn't develop a taste for grog. In all his years at sea, he never touched hard spirits. His "steady drink," recalled one of his midshipmen, was lemon or lime juice laced with sugar and, in good weather, three glasses of wine after dinner. He liked to be in control of himself and, insofar as possible, his world. Too many times he had witnessed the damage caused by indulgence.

Like all new hands on a square-rigged ship, John Paul was sent aloft to learn how to reef and furl the sails. Creeping out along a single rope far above the deck and leaning over to gather wet and sometimes frozen canvas flailing and snapping in the wind was not for the fainthearted. Anyone who has climbed a mast on a ship as it rolls and bucks at sea can attest to a frightening law of physics: the higher you go, the wider (and wilder) the swings. Men, especially the inebriated ones, often fell. If they were unlucky, they hit the deck and shattered bones and skulls. If they were more fortunate, they glanced off a rope or the belly of a sail and landed in the ocean. Some were rescued in time, but a large, square-rigged sailing ship is cumbersome to turn around, and ocean water temperature in the northern latitudes could freeze a man in a few minutes. Many drowned because they could not swim; few seamen in those days could.

Some men fell from sheer exhaustion. The *Friendship* carried a crew of twenty-eight, large for a merchantman but far fewer than the ship's company aboard a man-of-war of comparable size. Merchants tried to squeeze every last penny out of their ships. Carrying the bare minimum of crewmen and stinting on food were standard practices in the merchant marine. Aside from a large winch, called a capstan, and various blocks and pulleys to take off some of the strain, eighteenth-century sailing ships relied on brute man power. The work could be perilous: men had to haul on rigid and icy ropes as they slipped and slid on slanting and shifting decks, in storms and rain and in utter darkness. The most common medical hazard was hernia, or rupture. (During the eight years from 1808 through 1815, the Royal Navy handed out an amazing 29,712 trusses.) It has been estimated that about one in seven British seamen in the navy busted a gut, literally.

Misery excited John Paul's ambition. The position of master or first or second mate aboard a merchantman may not have been nearly so grand as that of a naval officer, but it was better than ordinary seaman, in part because the first or second mate was rarely required to work aloft or heave on a rope.

John Paul's deliverance from the hardship of the lower deck was a brass instrument called an octant. His ascent began the moment the master of the *Friendship*, Captain Robert Benson, summoned him to the rail of the quarterdeck one day when the sun was at its zenith, pointed to the horizon, and handed him the tool navigators used to find their way on the trackless sea.

Jones's own octant, possibly his very first, sits in the museum of the U.S. Naval Academy. Curved (an eighth of circle, hence "octant"), fixed with small mirrors and etched by degrees, an octant can tell a mariner the angle of the sun to the horizon at high noon. From these readings, taken repeatedly for accuracy, a mariner who knows a little math and has the right tables can calculate his ship's latitude, his distance from the equator. Navigation was still crude in the mid-eighteenth century. Navigators could fix their place on a north–south axis by knowing their latitude (at least when the sun was not clouded over), but they still couldn't precisely measure longitude, their position along the east–west axis. Finding one's way was still to a frightening degree a matter of guesswork—dead reckoning.

And yet elemental navigation was considered sorcery in the wrong hands. A sailor who could navigate made a much more dangerous mutineer. In the navy, the officer class did not want ordinary seamen to be able to find their way if they mutinied. The merchant marine

was not quite so fearful about sailors rising above their station. As an apprentice, John Paul could entertain some hope of learning the skills required of a deck officer, though perhaps not right away, since his apprenticeship was expected to last seven years. A quick learner, eager to please, he apparently won the attention and support of the master, Captain

Benson.* Before long, he was mastering all the intricacies of seamanship and ship handling, the proper set and trim of the sails, the uses of all the myriad ropes and spars that festooned the masts of a square-rigged ship.

He accomplished his tasks efficiently and surely but not joyously. John Paul was a self-described romantic, but not about the sea. He did not wax on about the beauty or mystery or power of the oceans, except in one batch of letters written after a particularly fearsome storm, and then only to comment that "the awful majesty of the tempest . . . surpassed the reach even of poetic fancy and the pencil." If John Paul was touched or awed by the majesty of nature on his first cruises across the ocean, he failed to record those feelings. His greater concern was with self-improvement.

John Paul discovered aboard ship a place to excel. In any age, seamanship demands certain qualities of character. It rewards the careful and deliberate and punishes the loose and sloppy. The uncoiled line lying about the deck can quickly be transformed into a snare or a whip in bad weather; the sleepy lookout nodding off as the ship approaches a hidden reef is criminally negligent. In his manner and bearing, John Paul was neat to the point of primness. As a sailor he was constantly, almost exasperatingly, fastidious, incessantly fiddling with the rigging and trim to eke out more speed and make his craft more seaworthy. He may not have loved the sea, but he was very good at sailing upon it.

JONES HAD TO stoop low to climb up. In 1764, after he had crossed the Atlantic eight times in three years aboard the *Friendship*, hard times forced

---

*He must have learned just enough math at the little parish school he attended in Kirkbean. At a small museum in Dumfries, near Kirkbean, John Paul's original geometry book, *Euclide's Elements: The Whole 15 Books, Compendiously Demonstrated with Archimedes Theorems of the Sphere and the Cylinder*, is preserved with John Paul's bold, round thirteen-year-old signature in the flyleaf. Scottish schools were unusually good at that time, and many boys won scholarships to university at Glasgow, Edinburgh, and Aberdeen. The spirit of scientific inquiry was strong in the Scottish lowlands at mid-century: two other low-born Galwegians who made good, Thomas Telford, the bridge builder, and John McAdam, inventor of macadam road, were roughly the same age as John Paul.

the sale of the ship. Released from his apprenticeship, he found a wretched job as the third mate aboard a slaver, the *King George*, out of Whitehaven, a "black birder" in the cruel jargon of the time. Black birders were known for a stench so strong that ships downwind bore away to avoid it. John Paul served for two years aboard the *King George* and was made first mate of another slave ship, the *Two Friends*. No more than fifty feet long, she carried a crew of six and, chained in the hold, according to one manifest, a cargo of "77 Negroes from Africa." John Paul sailed the infamous "middle passage" between Africa and the slave plantations of the Caribbean. "Slaves were stowed, heel and point, like logs," Melville wrote, "and the suffocated and dead were unmanacled, and weeded out from the living every morning." John Paul Jones never wrote a word about his time on a slave ship, but after three years he had apparently had enough of duties like "weeding." When the *Two Friends* returned to Jamaica from a voyage to "the windward coast of Africa" sometime in 1767, John Paul asked to be paid off.

In Kingston, the unemployed John Paul ran into the captain of a brig, the *John*, out of Kirkcudbright, a small Scottish port some thirty miles from Arbigland. The captain, Samuel McAdam, offered John Paul free passage home. On the voyage, both the captain and the first mate died of fever, which was rampant in the West Indies. John Paul was the only man aboard who could navigate. When he brought home the *John* safely, the owners rewarded him with command. At the age of twenty-one, he was the master of a ship. A very small one, to be sure: sixty tons, about sixty feet long, with a crew of half a dozen men. But John Paul had crossed the line from servant to master.

John Paul was not an easy captain. He was fastidious and demanding. His standards of neatness and precision were closer to those aboard a man-of-war than on a merchant ship. His rigor and exactitude did not necessarily make him unpopular with the crew. The hands of a square-rigged ship, a fragile and complex mechanism, depended on their captain to survive. They usually distrusted captains who were slack or sloppy. Taut ships were happy ones if every man knew his duty and the captain showed steadiness and good seamanship. Captain Paul was a superb seaman whose confidence seemed to rise in dangerous moments, and he was usually mild and soft-spoken. But there was a scratchy, fussy side to him that was off-putting and which, over time, worked to undermine his authority. Jones had a temper, and he could not abide disrespect. He was bound to clash with sailors who did not know their place or challenged his.

On John Paul's second voyage aboard the *John*, from Scotland to the Windward Islands, he tangled with a carpenter's mate named Mungo Maxwell. The son of a prominent local family in Kirkcudbright, the *John*'s home port on the Firth of Solway on Scotland's southern coast, Maxwell was cocky, entitled, and in no mood to take orders from someone who was the son of a gardener. Captain Paul had him flogged.

It has been said that ship captains were more powerful than the King of England in the eighteenth century, because the crown could not order a man flogged. Harsh physical discipline was a fact of life aboard ship. The lash was part of the "ancient custom of the sea." The age was violent, and not just at sea. Public hangings were spectator sports, where refreshments were served. In the Royal Navy, floggings were morality plays, staged on Sunday after church.

Floggings were less ritualistic or commonplace on merchant ships like the *John*, but the lash was still an effective tool against an unruly crew. Mungo Maxwell tested John Paul's shallow well of patience, mouthing off at him, shirking duty, and doing his work sloppily, which particularly incensed the meticulous Captain Paul. His "mildness" quickly spent, John Paul ordered Maxwell triced by his wrists to the rigging and subjected to the traditional tool of punishment, the cat-o'-nine-tails.

The "cat," nine tightly wound and knotted strands of cord attached to a piece of wood, was usually stowed in a red baize bag and never used twice. One stroke on the back would raise bright red welts, two or three would break the skin. A dozen, the usual sentence, would leave a human back looking like "roasted meat burnt nearly black before a scorching fire," according to one contemporary account. The flogger would sometimes pause to wipe the chunks of bloody flesh from the knotted strands, or to change hands to make sure each stroke counted.

Aboard a British man-of-war, the spectacle would be staged with all hands standing at attention, watched by marines in red coats, the seagoing soldiers who kept order. On John Paul's little brig, the scene was simpler and drearier. The captain stood on the quarterdeck, trying to look stern and wise despite his age, glaring at the mate who wielded the cat to make sure he swung hard enough. A sullen clump of crewmen watched the blood run from Maxwell's back, then after a dozen strokes let him down and tended, as best they could, to his wounds.

They probably grumbled and called Captain Paul brutal, but sailors of the age generally put up with flogging. Miscreants at sea fared no worse than those on land, maybe better. A thief aboard ship might get twelve lashes; ashore he could be hanged, branded, or exiled to a penal colony. At the same time, however, Englishmen prized "liberty" and had at least a rough sense of individual rights and the rule of law, arbitrarily imposed perhaps, yet still a British birthright. On merchant ships, it was unusual—but not unheard of—for a crewman, returning to port after a beating at sea, to go to court to sue his captain, charging assault or unjust abuse. That is what Mungo Maxwell did when the *John* reached Tobago in the summer of 1770.

An Admiralty Court was sitting at the time, and John Paul was quickly vindicated. The judge examined the wounds on Maxwell's back and found them to be neither "mortal nor dangerous." The judge ruled that the carpenter had earned the stripes across his back by his incompetence and disobedience. Captain Paul was well within his authority to have Maxwell flogged.

That might have been the end of it. Maxwell angrily quit the *John* and found passage home to Scotland on another ship. After picking up his cargo of rum, sugar, and mahogany, John Paul sailed across the Atlantic, into the mouth of the English Channel, and up the Irish Sea to the Firth of Solway. In early November, as the green pastures sloping down to the sea were just beginning to yellow in the cold gales of late autumn, Captain Paul navigated the *John* up Kirkcudbright Bay, twisting through the narrow channel between the shifting mud banks, and bringing his brig and its crew safely home.

At the quay, Captain Paul was greeted by the sheriff and informed that he was under arrest. As the town people gawked, young Paul was escorted on a walk of shame. He was marched up High Street, past Grayfriars Church and MacLellan's Castle, to the Tolbooth, the local jail. There he was clapped into irons and left, either in the "laich sellar," the low cellar where a local witch had been imprisoned before she was executed (strangled by the neck) some years earlier, or possibly in the new debtor's prison on the third floor.

John Paul was dumbfounded. Mungo Maxwell, he learned, had died on the return voyage. Rumors had flown about that the *John*'s carpenter had never recovered from a brutal and unjust flogging ordered by the ship's master. His indignant family had used its influence to get John Paul arrested and thrown in jail. The Maxwells were a powerful clan in southern Scotland. For centuries, the Maxwells had been earls of Nithsdale, living in a castle some thirty-five miles from Kirkcudbright. Mungo's father, Robert, was able to persuade the Vice Admiral of Scotland, William Earl of March and Ruglen, to issue a warrant for John Paul's arrest. In a formal deposition, Maxwell's father charged that his son had been "most unmercifully, by the said John Paul, with a great cudgel or batton, bled, bruised, and wounded upon his back and other parts of his body, and of which wounds and bruises he soon afterwards died."

John Paul was allowed to post bail and collect proofs of his innocence, even returning to the Caribbean the next year to obtain evidence. From the captain of the ship that carried Maxwell home, John Paul obtained a statement that Maxwell had seemed "in perfect health" when he came aboard but had later caught a fever and died at sea. Court papers from Tobago showed that John Paul had already been cleared by an Admiralty judge. The Maxwell suit was dismissed, and the incident appears to have blown over.

But John Paul brooded over his embarrassment. He was especially angry at the laird of the estate where he had grown up. Mr. Craik had appeared to take the side of the Maxwells, and not that of his gardener's son. Eight months after he had been released from jail and gone again to sea,

Paul was still stewing about Craik's class prejudice. He was angry that he had been forced to produce testimonials to his good character to satisfy the local gentry. "Mr. Craik's nice feelings," John Paul wrote his mother, with an edge of bitterness, "will not perhaps be otherwise satisfied." Craik had behaved coldly and scornfully toward John Paul, whom he had known ever since he was a little boy. "His ungracious conduct to me before I left Scotland I have not yet been able to get the better of," John Paul confessed to his mother and sisters. "It is true that I bore it with seeming unconcern, but Heaven can witness for me, that I suffered the more on that very account." Fitfully throughout his life, John Paul would struggle to contain his resentments. John Paul knew that the proper and prudent course was to shrug off the snubs of his father's master. But it was in his nature to brood and nurse slights.

Jones needed some kind of social armor, some way of protecting himself from the sneers of the landed gentry. He found it in the institution of Freemasonry. On November 27, 1770, shortly after he had obtained bail and set out to vindicate himself in the Mungo Maxwell case, he joined the Ancient Society of Free and Accepted Masons. Freemasonry, which had a lodge in Kirkcudbright, was spreading through Great Britain and the colonies. John Paul would find Masonic lodges wherever he went on his journeys. He used them both as refuges and stepladders.

Freemasonry was an essential social elevator in the eighteenth century. In its earliest incarnation, in London at the beginning of the 1700s, Masonry was a kind of gentleman's club with a high-minded interest in philosophy as well as fellowship. Early Masons were often aristocratic, even noble; the future George III was a Master Mason (Prince Charles and other Royals are still Masons). By the mid-eighteenth century, however, Masonry had become a path of upward mobility for the nascent middle class. New members tended to be lawyers, merchants, and sea captains.

Ever the dutiful student, John Paul studied to become a Master Mason. Freemasonry was a ritualistic, semisecret society that sought to tap the purity of the past. When John Paul entered the lodge at Kirkcudbright, he had to swear that he would not disclose their rituals "under no less penalty than to have my throat cut, my tongue taken from the roof of my mouth, my heart pluck'd from under my left breast." John Paul without doubt enjoyed the feeling of elitism, of acceptance into an exclusive order. At the same time, he was taught more than snobbery and hocus-pocus about ancient rituals of dubious authenticity. The Masons of the eighteenth century looked forward as well as back. They embraced values that today we associate with a liberal arts education: tolerance, rationality, a spirit of scientific inquiry, the virtues preached by Enlightenment thinkers whose presence was being especially felt in the Scottish universities at the time. At lodge meetings, John Paul was instructed in good manners and universal fellowship. "It makes us courteous, easy, free," went a Mason verse. "Generous, honourable, and gay;/What other Art the like can say?/We make it plainly to appear,/By our behavior everywhere." But the real prize for John Paul was expressed by the last couplet:

That where you meet a Mason, there
You meet a Gentleman.

THE MUNGO MAXWELL INCIDENT, which occurred on Captain Paul's second Atlantic crossing aboard the *John*, was an interruption in John Paul's ascent, but only a brief one. After traveling to the Caribbean in the spring of 1771 to gather evidence of his innocence, John Paul looked for a new opportunity. In his absence, the *John* had been sold; the owners had given their young captain a glowing recommendation ("he approved himself every way qualified"). Armed with this praise, John Paul had won command—as well as a guarantee of the share of the profits—of a larger ship, a three-master of some 300 tons, the *Betsy*. London was her home port. In the early fall of 1772, John Paul went to the great capital to take command of his new ship.

London was then the largest city in the Western world with almost a million inhabitants. It was also one of the most unsanitary. Depending on the wind, the stench of raw sewage carried for miles. Sailing up the

Thames, John Paul passed East London and saw the gallows at Executioner's Dock at Wapping. Pirates were hanged there at low water, their bodies left to rot through three full tides. The image of a pirate swinging at Executioner's Dock stayed with him in later years, when he was denounced in the British press and by the government itself as the "Pirate Paul Jones."

London along the docks teemed with pickpockets and prostitutes plying their trade amid the din of rattling carts, carriages, and the shrill cries of hawkers. Soot fell so heavily that rain and fog could bring darkness at noon. But in 1772 the city, like John Paul, was on the rise. The muddy streets were being paved with stones; in St. James's Park, ditches with their "stinking exhalations" had just been removed as the park was remodeled under Capability Brown, the landscape architect contemporary of John Paul Sr.

John Paul, who could appreciate such beauty from his boyhood at Arbigland, longed to be part of London society. On the more fashionable streets stretching from Charing Cross to Whitehall, shopkeepers doted on their wealthy customers. A London shopkeeper must "speak fluently, though not elegantly, to entertain the ladies, and to be the master of a handsome bow and cringe," wrote a commentator of the time. Pall Mall and St. James Street were the stomping grounds of the "macaronis," foppish young dandies who wore tight breeches, high-heeled shoes, and carried outlandish nosegays. The macaronis dyed their hair blue one day, red the next. Society women piled their hair into elaborate towers reaching as high as three feet. (The only way they could ride in a carriage was to sit on the floor.) A certain languor set the upper crust apart. At the theater, the rabble might hoot and holler, but gentlemen in the balcony could barely be moved to clap. In some circles, it became fashionable to speak in an almost unintelligible drawl.

In his desire to be recognized as a gentleman, John Paul was chasing a moving target. The closer he came, the further his goal receded. The Great Chain of Being was weakening in the 1760s. As merit and wealth began to vie with birth as determinants of the social order, a backlash set in. If a merchant or a sea captain like Jones began to forget his place, the gentry found ways to remind him. Manners, modes of speech and dress, and a certain attitude all helped keep the *arrivistes* at arm's length.*

John Paul encountered these rebuffs in ways both subtle and obvious. His closest contemporaries were Royal Navy officers. In a letter written four years later, he made passing reference to "intimacy with many officers of note in the British Navy." But he does not appear to have befriended any. As a master of a merchant ship, he was not equal in status to the lowliest navy lieutenant. "Even masters, though generally well rewarded, were professionally and socially insecure," writes naval historian N. A. M. Rodger. "With luck, a master might become a successful merchant, but he was not likely to be reckoned a gentleman." Though the most meritocratic of services, the British navy, too, by 1770 was beginning to throw up class barriers. "The officers and men of the 1750s and 1760s were perhaps the last generation of the Navy to be almost unconscious of class," writes Rodger. The naval officers John Paul met in 1772 might have been friendly, but certainly not intimate. With a social lesser, a gentleman displayed what one commentator called "a certain affability carefully modulated between reserve and familiarity."

Around naval officers, John Paul tried to be ingratiating. He was well spoken, neatly dressed and coiffed, bright and curious, and knowledgeable about the sea. But his insecurities showed through. There was an edginess about him, an overeagerness to please that mixed uneasily with his pridefulness. His intense desire to be accepted and his easily wounded ego could make him uneasy company, not just with languid fops, but with self-assured Royal Navy officers. If John Paul sensed condescension, he would bristle. Aboard ship, if he felt his authority questioned by lower ranks, he would sometimes lash out.

---

*The sharp break came at the end of the century, after the upper classes felt threatened by the French Revolution. In the early 1700s, a lady traveling with her maid and staying at a roadside inn might share the same bed, even the same chamber pot. A century later, such familiarity between ruling and servant classes would be unthinkable.

CHAPTER TWO

"That Great Misfortune"

JOHN PAUL'S TEMPER was very nearly his undoing at sea. In 1773, John Paul was well on his way to prosperity and respectability as the captain of a merchant ship, the *Betsy*, sailing between Europe and the West Indies. A merchant captain who shares in the profits could make a tidy fortune, provided he was not ruined by chance, war, or weather. In the early 1770s, a time between wars, John Paul had amassed a net worth of some £2,500. Though still a young man, he had already begun thinking about retiring. He had been dreaming about buying some land in Virginia to lead a life, as he put it, of "calm contemplation and poetic ease" as a gentleman farmer in the new world.

But bad luck struck John Paul in the summer of 1773. Making his way from London to the West Indies with a load of butter and wine, he discovered that the *Betsy*'s futtocks, the ribbing in the frame of the vessel, were badly cracked and broken. As he impatiently waited for repairs in Ireland, a "severe fever" sent him to bed for sixteen days and left him "much reduced," he wrote a friend. The butter went bad, the winter storm season was fast approaching, and John Paul's humor was poor as the *Betsy* set sail again that fall.

Arriving at the island of Tobago before Christmas 1773, Captain Paul took on some new crewmen. Among them was a malcontent who stole the captain's liquor, drank heavily, and disobeyed his orders. The man, whom John Paul described years later in a self-justifying letter to Benjamin Franklin only as "the Ringleader," was a "prodigious brute of thrice my strength," Paul wrote, who "neglected and even refused his duty with much insolence."

Most mutinies of the era started over money, and this one was no different. Captain Paul was strapped by his repairs and ruined cargo. Rather than pay advance wages to his men in Tobago, where the hands would go ashore and spend their money on drink and women, John Paul apparently decided to reinvest his money in a new cargo to take back to London. The Ringleader grumbled—"pretended," wrote Jones—that the men had not been paid in fourteen months. John Paul ignored him and went ashore to attend to business.

When he returned, the Ringleader was stirring up the crew and threatening to abscond with the ship's launch. The "brute" confronted John Paul with "the grossest abuse that vulgarism could dictate." The captain of the *Betsy* had to calculate the odds. He temporized. He offered to give the Ringleader "frocks and trousers" from the ship's supply of "slops," the evocative term used to describe the well-worn canvas and wool patchwork that served as seaman's garb.

This gift was a poor substitute for what pieces of silver would buy ashore. The Ringleader was enraged. He "swore with horrid imprecations that he would take away the boat by force," wrote John Paul. As John Paul put it, his "mildness" was now exhausted. Captain Paul marched into his cabin intending to grab a stick, but found instead his sword, he wrote (a little unconvincingly), "by chance being on the table." He meant to make a show of force, he later claimed, not to actually wield the weapon. But the Ringleader wanted a confrontation. He grabbed a "bludgeon" of some kind—probably a belaying pin, a stout wooden handle with a bulbous knob at one end—and advanced on the captain.

John Paul was "thunder struck with surprise." He had expected the man's "raving" of "disappointed rage" to "subside of itself." He did not want to duel the Ringleader. He was in a lonely and exposed position. The ship's crew clearly sided with the Ringleader, and Paul's deck officers were nowhere to be seen. John Paul suspected that his first mate would be only too happy to see the captain go down, thus allowing number two to become number one. The second mate was sick in bed.

As the *Betsy* rocked gently at her anchor, her crew stood stock-still to watch the showdown. The man took a step forward. Still facing the Ringleader, Captain Paul slowly began to back away. The Ringleader advanced, looming and menacing. As John Paul retreated, he could feel his heel strike the coaming, or edge, of a hatchway. He was cornered. One more step back, and he would plunge down the companionway, the ladder leading below. John Paul made a "sudden stop," he recorded. At just that moment, the Ringleader raised his cudgel and lunged forward. He was impaled by John Paul's sword.

As John Paul later described the incident, his action was defensive, almost passive. The Ringleader had "rush[ed] upon the sword's point." His death was an accident, not a murder, "the fatal and unavoidable consequence" of attempting to rush the captain as he stood backed up against the open hatch. It is hard to imagine that John Paul did not thrust his sword at the attacker, but we have only John Paul's inevitably self-serving account. In any case, a man lay mortally wounded at John Paul's feet.

At first, Captain Paul did not hesitate to turn himself in to the authorities. He was not arrested, but he understood that he would be summoned before a legal proceeding of some kind. His experience in the Mungo Maxwell affair gave him some confidence that the courts would ultimately vindicate him. He knew that captains were afforded great latitude to put down mutinies, at least under maritime law. Tobago was an English crown possession, and normally any legal case arising from an action aboard ship would be tried in an Admiralty Court, where the law of the sea—invariably protective of the authority of captains—prevailed. But the Admiralty Court was not sitting in Tobago at Chistmastime 1773, which meant that John Paul might have to face a normal jury trial in the local court, where he could be charged with murder. Since the Ringleader was a local, one of about 300 white men who lived on the island, John Paul looked upon a jury of his "peers" with some foreboding.

He decided to flee. He mounted a horse and rode across the island, where he hired a boat to take him away to another Caribbean port. John Paul would later insist that he was just taking the advice of his partner, Archibald Stuart, a Scottish merchant who lived on a plantation on the island. John Paul did not, he protested, intend to flee forever. The plan was to lie low on the American continent for a time, and then return to face trial before an Admiralty Court. Stuart would send John Paul money to support him while he waited for the right time to reappear. The time, and the money, never came. Stuart never sent John Paul the "remittances" he had promised, leading John Paul to suspect that he had been double-crossed, encouraged to flee by a man who had no intention of ever letting him come back. Before John Paul could muster the resources and the will to return, the American Revolution intervened.

Or so he told the story to Ben Franklin in 1779, when John Paul—by then, John Paul Jones—was a captain in the United States navy, operating out of France, and Franklin, America's ambassador to France, was effectively his boss. John Paul portrayed himself as the unfortunate victim, describing the incident as "that great misfortune of my life." John Paul almost surely was acting in justifiable self-defense when he killed the Ringleader. Nonetheless, he apparently felt guilty or at least embarrassed about the episode and tried to conceal it. He only opened up to Franklin when he believed—mistakenly—that Franklin had somehow gotten wind of it. The fact is that John Paul had killed a man. Death was common enough, and severe discipline was routine on some ships, but few captains ran through their sailors with swords. As a captain, John Paul would have a history of mutinous crews. To some degree, he was unlucky. His ship's companies, patched together with foreigners and farm boys, were surly and unruly. But other captains somehow coped with green or sullen crews without unsheathing their swords. With the Ringleader, John Paul let his low tolerance for insolence get the better of him. It is revealing that he did not trust his own officers and subordinates to back him at a public trial. John Paul's touchy rectitude was isolating.

John Paul was alone, traveling "incog.," as he put it. He had added a new last name—Jones, chosen, probably, because it was commonplace. Where did he go? Legend says that he roved the high seas for a time as a freebooting buccaneer.* More likely, he headed as directly as possible to the town of Fredericksburg in the colony of Virginia, the place where he had hoped to retire from the sea into a life of "calm contemplation and poetic ease."

He had been there before. "America was my favorite country from the age of 13, when I first saw it," he later wrote. He had been an apprentice seaman at the time, a Scottish boy making his first sea voyage. He had come to visit his older brother, who had emigrated from Scotland to Virginia and set up shop as a gentleman's tailor. With 3,000 inhabitants, the town was prosperous, a bustling port of well-cared-for houses and shady streets. "The town was constantly filled with sailors from all parts of the world," recalled a frequent visitor to Fredericksburg, Thomas Jefferson.

The boy named John Paul had arrived in May 1761, when the Rappahannock River valley was lush and verdant. But when the man named John Paul Jones returned in the winter of 1774, the Virginia countryside was cold and gray. No one came forward to offer refuge. His older brother was dead. William Paul, like his sibling, had apparently been a difficult man. He had separated from his wife, unusual in that day, and the executors named in his will refused to serve. He bequeathed nothing to his brother, John.

---

*According to one story, around the time John Paul was fleeing Tobago, a "sharp, rakish clipper-built craft, painted entirely black, with no name whatever marked upon her," dropped anchor off the island of Martha's Vineyard in Massachusetts. "The captain announced himself as Paul Jones," recalled Thomas Chase, then a boy living on the island. The crew of the black ship was "a set of Spanish and Portuguese desperadoes." Young Chase, a carpenter, was summoned to make a coffin for one of the crew, who had died in a struggle. His duty done, Chase claimed to have gone hunting with John Paul and acted as his pilot across the Nantucket Shoals. A few years later, liberated as a prisoner from a British jail during the Revolution, Chase ran into Paul Jones—now John Paul Jones, captain of the American warship *Bonhomme Richard*—and signed on to fight in his famous battle against the *Serapis*. Or so Chase claimed in his dotage. The story is probably a tall tale.

At the age of twenty-six, John Paul Jones was slender and slightly round-shouldered, short of stature at about five foot six. With a sharp, hawkish nose, a cleft chin, and thin, curved lips, his face was handsome—not warm or friendly, but strong and proud. He could bristle when he felt, as he often did, that his dignity was under siege, and yet his mien was intelligent, curious. We can guess that his appearance, despite the long journey, was neat, well kept. His hazel eyes could be soft, but they were bright, burning at times, and even, as John Adams later saw them, "wild."

He needed to make friends, and he needed a place to stay. He probably found lodging in one of several boarding houses or inns. There still stands in Fredericksburg a carefully preserved late-eighteenth century inn called the Rising Sun. The inn was not opened until a few years after Jones arrived in town, but it was typical of the accommodations available to a traveler of that era. The class divide is stark. As one enters, to the left is a wainscotted room with Queen Ann furniture where the gentlemen ate. Dinner, an ample two-hour affair, cost one shilling and six pence. A private room for the night was one shilling and three pence. To the right is the tavern room where the barkeep stood behind a wooden enclosure for protection in case the customers became violent. For a penny, a fellow could sleep above the barroom on a straw pallet in a fifteen-foot-by-eighteen-foot room with fifteen other men, who were required to give the innkeeper their boots at night to keep them from leaving without paying. The bathwater in the common room was changed every third man.

There can be no doubt that Jones would have preferred a gentlemen's lodgings. Jones had stood on the quarterdeck and slept in a captain's cabin; he had no desire to return to the dank intimacy of the lower deck, where the crew slept, their hammocks slung so close they touched. But Jones had to watch his shillings. When he fled Tobago he had £50, not an inconsiderable sum, but as it turned out, his only resources to survive for twenty months. He was "prey to melancholy and want," he later complained. Jones was determined to become a gentleman. The question was how.

*   *   *

REVOLUTIONARY CHANGE was stirring in the American colonies in the winter of 1773–74. In Boston that December, Sons of Liberty dressed as Indians had thrown hundreds of crates of tea into the harbor in protest against the British government's onerous taxes. In Virginia, young radicals like Thomas Jefferson, Patrick Henry, and Richard Henry Lee formed a Committee of Correspondence to share their views and experiences with their rebellious brethren in the northern colonies. In the following September, the First Continental Congress would meet in Philadelphia to take the initial, uncertain steps on a path that would lead, in less than two years, to a declaration of independence from the mother country.

But neither rebellious murmurings nor outright defiance of the crown meant that a social revolution was brewing, not yet. All men were not created equal in the Virginia commonwealth, certainly not in the Tidewater region of great estates along the James and Rappahannock Rivers. A squirearchy of some forty families owned most of the land and kept their lessers in thrall. Gentleman ate with silver; common folk ate with a spoon or their hands. At church, the gentry still entered as a body, after their families and the commoners were seated in their assigned pews.

John Paul Jones was not welcome as an outsider in Fredericksburg. Strangers were openly gawked at in eighteenth-century America; gentlemen from far-off places were expected to have letters of introduction. Jones didn't even have a real name. With his Galwegian brogue, Jones was particularly suspect. The landed gentry looked down on Scotsmen, who were seen as crass money-grubbers. (In 1781, Charles Lee, of the Virginia Lees, would complain that Virginia was becoming a "maccocracy," overrun by a Celtic "banditti.") Even the Scottish faith in education brought sneers: a member of the local gentry complained that, while children could learn Latin and Greek from a Scottish tutor, the "Scottish dialect . . . never can wear off."

Jones was welcomed, however, by the Masons. The Fredericksburg Lodge met regularly at a local inn or the Townhouse, a substantial brick structure at the center of town. As a member of the brotherhood, Jones was free to attend. Jones enjoyed pomp and fancy dress, a disposition shared by the Masons. In a public progression staged on St. John's Day, December 27, 1774, the Masons paraded through the streets of Fredericksburg, wearing calfskin aprons, holding their sacred texts on pillows, and carrying jewels. Cannon boomed to honor the occasion. When they retired to conduct their business, a Mason stood at the doorway holding a sword to keep away eavesdroppers. Masonry gave its members a sense of exclusivity; the blackball box of the Fredericksburg Lodge still survives, a massive ark that can only be opened by three keys.

Jones improved himself through friendship. Dr. John K. Read, who was a Grand Master of Masonry, befriended the carefully dressed stranger with a hidden past and a familiar brogue. Read would later fondly write Jones, reflecting back on "the many sentimental hours which (solitary enough) passed between us at the Grove," a plantation outside Fredericksburg. A fellow Scotsman, Dr. Read was shrewd as well as cultured: he warned Jones that he had been taken for a ride by his former trading partner in Tobago, Archibald Stuart. Dr. Read's later letters to Jones reflect his Enlightenment values. Congratulating him on his naval victories in 1779, Dr. Read wrote: "You once more taste the pleasure of affluence, and taste it with feelings that do not accompany the generality of mankind—a nice sentiment of honour and the slow, though sure reward of merit." Reward based on merit, not birth or "interest," was a central precept of the Enlightenment. It would become Jones's core ideology, just as its denial became the basis of his many grievances.

During those solitary hours spent with Dr. Read at the Grove, Jones read a great deal. He was self-educating. "Any young gentleman travelling through Virginia was presumed to be acquainted with dancing, boxing, card and fiddle-playing and the use of the small sword," wrote Philip Fithian, a Princeton graduate of the day hired to tutor the sons of the Virginia gentry. Jones had missed out on all those arts. But gentlemen also prided themselves on their classical learning, and here, by dint of study, Jones could catch up. One of his midshipmen later observed, "The learning he obtained . . . from the age of nine years, was from close application to books, of which he was remarkably fond."

Self-education, like a little knowledge, can be a dangerous thing. Without a real teacher or some other critical filter, Jones was left to his own devices. His conversations with the formally educated Dr. Read helped, but if his later efforts at poetry are any indication, Jones was not always discriminating in his taste. Even so, his efforts at learning were prodigious, and the results generally creditable. Jones's letters are far more literate than those of his contemporary sea captains and not unworthy of the lawyers and merchants who went to Philadelphia as delegates to the Continental Congress.

There was a recognized canon of literature for a well-educated man in the late eighteenth century—Thomas Jefferson once made a list, of roughly a hundred books. Jones's later correspondence reflects at least a passing familiarity with most of the greats. He quotes Shakespeare's *Othello*, with whom he clearly identified: the noble man continuously disappointed and betrayed. "I should have found within my soul one drop of patience,"* Jones wrote in 1777, exasperated with the selfishness of American privateers who sailed for gain, not glory.

Jones avidly read James Thomson, a fellow Scotsman and forerunner of the Romantic poets. Very popular in his day, Thomson touched Jones's conscience by inveighing against the wrong of slavery ("that cruel trade, which spoils unhappy Guinea of her sons") and stirred his desire for liberty in "Rule Britannia." Other nations suffered under tyrants, but Britain flourished "great and free," wrote Thomson. In *The Seasons*, Thomson's epic poem, Jones found inspiration for his own florid verse, as well as for his dream of a pastoral retirement from ocean-going command. "Let others brave the flood in quest of gain/And beat for joyless months the gloomy seas," wrote Thomson in Jones's favorite verse. "The happiest he. . . . Drinks the pure pleasures of the rural life. . . . Calm contemplation and poetic ease." Poetry sustained Jones and his revolutionary cohort on many lonely journeys. As John Adams told his son, John Quincy, "You'll never be alone with a poet in your pocket."

---

*"I should have found in my soul/A drop of patience." *Othello*, Act 4, Scene ii.

Jones savored pulpy epics of knight errantry and ancient heroism. He imagined himself in *The Poems of Ossian*, a saga of a bold but sensitive warrior. *Ossian*, which was on Jefferson's recommended reading list and described by Voltaire as "the Homer of Scotland," was a fraud: its author, James Macpherson, an obscure schoolmaster and unsuccessful poet, had "discovered" some ancient Gaelic verse about a third-century Celtic hero. But Jones also read more intellectual fare, books and plays by authors, like Joseph Addison, who preached Enlightenment virtues. Addison's popular play, *Cato*, gave Jones one of his favorite moralisms: "We cannot insure success, but we can deserve it"—a line used not only by Jones, but in the darkest days of the Revolution by John Adams and George Washington, who reportedly saw *Cato* performed again and again. Addison held out the dream of a world made better by men who had learned to behave rationally: "To make Man mild, and sociable to Man/To cultivate the wild licentious Savage/with wisdom, discipline and liberal arts."

Jones spent contented hours sitting in a glade at the Grove, talking with his friend Dr. Read and reading Addison, imbibing the virtues he would need in his ceaseless battles with his own savage soul. Addison held out the reward: what Thomas Jefferson would call "natural aristocrats," genteel men whose reputation was earned, not inherited. Jones often used the word "liberal" as Cato had used it, to mean qualities that rose above the parochial and backward-looking, that were universal and cosmopolitan. Jones wished to be, as he would write, "a citizen of the world." If he could not join those Virginia landowners, he would transcend them.

But first he wanted to marry one of their daughters. Dorothea Spottswood Dandridge was a dark-haired, dark-eyed beauty of nineteen who came from a good family. She was the granddaughter of the colony's greatest governor, Alexander Spottswood, and a cousin of Martha Washington. We do not know much about Jones's wooing of Miss Dandridge, except that it failed. Jones himself wrote only that he had relinquished "the softer affections of his heart" to go to war. He later learned that she had married the governor of Virginia, Patrick Henry. His friend Dr. Read informed him in 1777, "Miss Dandridge is no more, that is, she a few

months ago gave herself into the arms of Patrick Henry." The great orator was nearly twice Dorothea's age, but he came from a socially acceptable family. According to a biography of Henry, "neighborhood gossip
held that 'Dolly' had fancied an impecunious young sailor named John
Paul Jones, then visiting cousins on a nearby plantation, but her father
dashed her hopes in favor of the more glorious match with the governor."
(The "cousin" was in all likelihood Dr. Read; the nearby plantation was
probably the Grove.)

After a year in Virginia, Jones had exhausted his savings. He was depen-
dent on Dr. Read's kindness, and appeared to have no prospects for employment. Jones was saved from brooding about Miss Dandridge and
provided the career opportunity of a lifetime by the onset of war.

On April 22, 1775, a horseman rode into Fredericksburg with ominous
news. In the dead of the night before, British marines had removed the
gunpowder from the armory at Williamsburg, lest it be seized by rebel
troublemakers. A few days earlier, a British column marched out to destroy a rebel cache of arms in Concord, Massachusetts, and the colonists,
forewarned, resisted. Fighting broke out on Lexington Green and at Concord Bridge. On their retreat to Boston, more than 200 British redcoats
were slain by colonial militia.

Colonial rebellion against the crown, fueled by repressive colonial gov-
ernors, was boiling over. In March 1775, Patrick Henry, Jones's rival for
Miss Dandridge, had thrilled a convention of Virginia delegates by ex-
claiming, "Give me liberty or give me death!" The British government
became jittery and moved to crack down. On April 29, the streets of Fredericksburg filled with volunteers, eager to form up and do battle for "liberty." An observer recorded: "We had in this town 600 men in hunting
shirts well accoutered that if convinced would have marched to Boston."

Jones watched the growing agitation with excitement and an eye for the
main chance. He knew about British repression close to home. He had
heard the stories of Culloden, the crushing of the insurgency of Bonnie
Prince Charlie in the year before his birth. The British boot had stomped
down hard after Culloden: rebels were dragged from their homes and

shot, Highlanders were banned from wearing their native kilts. Jones's mother was a Highlander; her kin had suffered. At the Fredericksburg Lodge, the Scotsmen talked of British brutality. One of the Master Masons, Hugh Mercer, had, as a young physician back in Scotland, treated the bayonet wounds of Highlanders cut down at Culloden. More than three dozen of the Fredericksburg Masons, Jones among them, would take up arms against the crown in the months ahead.

Jones never recorded his precise reasons for enlisting. His later correspondence includes only the grandiose avowal that he relinquished his "prospects for domestic happiness" to "restore peace and goodwill among mankind." Sweeping declarations of this kind were fairly typical of his time. Jefferson and others wrote of the "universal rights of mankind." Jones's generalities obscure a more particular transformation. Jones may have been thwarted as he tried to climb into the Tidewater gentry, but he still sensed the possibilities of freedom in his new land. The prospect of war meant a great chance for Jones—to advance in ways closed to him in his prior life. True, he risked hanging as a rebel or getting killed or maimed in action. Yet he was not afraid. He had faced peril at sea. Most likely, he was thinking along the lines of John Adams, who forthrightly declared, "the more danger the greater glory."

CHAPTER THREE

"Proof of Madness"

*J*ONES HAD PLENTY to offer the American rebels: seamanship, navigation skills, experience commanding a ship. He knew something about gunnery. His first ship, the *Friendship*, had carried eighteen guns as protection against French cruisers during the Seven Years War. In the early autumn or late summer of 1775, he traveled to Philadelphia to offer his services to a navy that did not yet exist.

Philadelphia, with 30,000 inhabitants, was the largest city in the colonies, and it was alive with "martial spirit" when Jones arrived. The Second Continental Congress was raising an army and—Jones hoped—a navy as well. "Oh that I was a soldier!" John Adams, delegate from Massachusetts, had written Abigail in May. Troops, including companies of formerly pacific Quakers, were drilling in the streets. The green behind the State House was piled high with cannons and barrels of gunpowder (since the colonies made none, gunpowder had to be smuggled past the British blockade; on the Delaware River, a ship from St. Eustatius, a Dutch island in the West Indies, had dropped anchor—a floating powder keg of 49,000 pounds).

At sea, the colonies were defenseless against the British navy. George Washington, laying siege to British-occupied Boston, had put together some small armed merchantmen to waylay British supply ships, but Congress was hard put to do much more. In the fall of 1775, the colonies were casting about for the means to protect their shores from the counter-strikes of the British Empire. The rebels were woefully short of arms and ammunition. (Benjamin Franklin suggested that soldiers be equipped with bows and arrows—which, while admittedly little defense against musketry, could at least be reloaded faster.) Josiah Quincy of Massachu-setts wondered if the colonials, lacking warships, might cheaply build some rowing galleys to confront the British cruisers. On October 3, the Rhode Island delegation introduced a resolution calling "for building at the Continental expense a fleet of sufficient force, for the protection of these colonies, and for employing them in such a manner and places as will effectively annoy our enemies."

"Annoy" was the operative word. What else could the colonies hope to do against Britannia, ruler of the seas?* "It is the maddest idea in the world to think of building an American fleet," railed Samuel Chase of Maryland. "The opposition . . . was very loud and vehement," reported John Adams, a staunch advocate of naval power. "It was represented as the most wild, visionary, mad project that has ever been imagined. It was an infant, taking mad Bull by the horns."

In October, a seven-man Naval Committee appointed by Congress worked late into the night in a fog of pipe smoke, quaffing port and rum at the Tun Tavern near the Philadelphia waterfront. They discussed Roman, Greek, and British history, John Adams recalled, before crafting Articles of War along the lines of the British model, which had been in turn bor-rowed from the Romans. Discipline remained strict: a sailor could be forced to wear a wooden collar for swearing and be flogged (though usu-ally no more than twelve lashes) for numerous other offenses.

———————————

*In 1775, the British Navy numbered some 270 ships, 131 of them ships of the line carrying more than fifty guns. Proud of their tradition of winning, most recently over the French in the Seven Years War, British tars sang rousing patriotic songs like "Hearts of Oak" and made up cocksure doggerel:

Two skinny Frenchmen and one Portugee
One British sailor can beat all three

Adams hoped to inspire Yankee daring and ingenuity. He buoyantly prophesied,

> We shall take some of the [Royal Navy's] twenty-gun ships before long. We must excite by policy that kind of exalted courage, which is ever more victorious by sea and land—which is irresistable. The Saracens had it—The Knights of Malta—The assassins—Cromwell's soldiers and sailors. Nay, N[ew]. England men have ever had it hitherto. They may never yet fail in an attempt of any kind.

Others on the committee, however, took a more mercenary approach. To them, war was a business opportunity, risky perhaps, but possibly lucrative. The worst of the profiteers was Silas Deane, an avaricious, ambitious Connecticut merchant who lost no time writing a friend to say that if he moved fast, he might secure a shipbuilding contract. By the time the Naval Committee was done recommending, they had obligated $866,666 (money that Congress did not have) to build thirteen frigates. The construction was to be spread around among the colonies, to make sure everyone got a piece of the pie.

Building a fleet would take time. Meanwhile, Lord Dunmore, the loyalist governor of Virginia, was behaving as a virtual pirate, sailing off the Viginia capes and Chesapeake Bay snatching ships and terrorizing town people with shore raids. The Naval Committee needed to find a ready-made fleet to confront him. In December, they pulled together a motley collection of merchantmen and small sloops and began to fit them with cannon.

To command the ships, Congress needed officers. To find them, they turned to friends and family. As commander of the fleet, the committee chose Esek Hopkins—conveniently, the brother of the committee's chairman, Stephen Hopkins, a Falstaffian figure known as "Old Grape and Guts." As captain of the *Alfred*, the largest of the converted merchantmen, the committee picked Dudley Saltonstall—brother-in-law of committee member Silas Deane. John Paul Jones would later bitterly complain that

nepotism was a poor way to create an officer corps. But he was a benefi-
ciary of the spoils system himself.

Through the network of Freemasonry, Jones was recommended to an
influential member of the Naval Committee, Joseph Hewes. Jones would
later refer to Hewes, a North Carolina merchant, as "the angel of my happiness" for his efforts to promote Jones's career. At Hewes's recommendation, Jones was offered command of the *Providence*, a seventy-foot,
single-masted sloop.

Surprisingly—and to his later regret—he declined. He explained that
he wasn't confident he could sail the sloop, whose giant gaff-rig mainsail,
stretching along an immense boom that hung over the stern, was tricky
and dangerous to handle. Ever the studious self-improver, he thought he
could learn more by taking a post as the number two aboard a larger,
square-rigged ship.

On December 7, 1775, he was commissioned a first lieutenant. "John
Paul Jones, Esq.," reads the parchment, and that "Esq.," a gentleman's title, meant the world to Jones. Four days before he had been filled with
pride to raise the American flag aboard the *Alfred*, his new ship. The flag
was a hybrid: thirteen red-and-white-striped bars, representing the
colonies, with symbols of the British Union—the crosses of St. George
and St. Andrew—in the canton. The Stars and Stripes of the American republic were still two years off. Indeed, the Declaration of Independence
had not been written or signed. When the hostilities ended—provided
that he had not been killed or hanged—Jones expected to be a free citizen
of a still loyal British dominion.

Jones was charged with fitting out the *Alfred*. She was a slab-sided merchantman, about a hundred feet long and thirty-five feet wide, painted
black with a yellow stripe. Her figurehead was painted white "with a remarkable large Plume of feathers on his helmet," according to the report
of a British agent spying for the Admiralty. The ship's original name was
the *Black Prince;* the Continental Congress renamed her after King Alfred,
founder of the British navy. She "sails dully," observed the spy. Jones later
described her as "crank," meaning that she heeled over too easily in a fresh

breeze, burying her gun ports and making the battery on that side unserviceable. The problem came from trying to transform a merchant ship into a man-of-war. Putting thirty cannons on deck, well above the waterline, raised the ship's center of gravity, making her more tippy.

The *Alfred* was no more unsuited to war than the rest of the tiny colonial fleet. On January 3, a raw, wind-whipped day, a large crowd came to the harbor side to watch the hope of the navy sail down the Delaware, toward the sea and the enemy beyond. A fife and drum corps gaily played; the crowd cheered. There was the *Alfred*, rated thirty guns; the *Columbus*, twenty-eight guns; the *Cabot*, fourteen guns; the *Andrew Doria*, sixteen guns; and the *Providence*, twelve guns. "Was it proof of madness in the first corps of sea officers," Jones later wrote, "to have at so critical a period launched out on the ocean with only two armed merchant ships, two armed brigantines, and one armed sloop, to make war against such a power as Great Britain?"

THE AMERICAN FLOTILLA under Commodore Hopkins made it about halfway down the Delaware and got stuck in the ice. The winter of '76 was unusually cold, and weeks would pass before the ice melted. Smallpox broke out in the fleet, and men began to desert in droves. Jones tried not to become dispirited. He worked his men at exercising the cannons. "Cast loose your guns!" he ordered, time and again. "Level your guns! Take out your tompions! Load with cartridge! Shot your guns! Run out your guns! Prime! Point your guns! Fire! Sponge your guns!" The crews shoved and pushed and struggled to complete the ponderous exercise in under two minutes, the British Royal Navy standard. They could only pretend to fire. Gunpowder was too scarce to use for practice. Still, the exercise was useful. British crews routinely defeated the French in part because their disciplined gun crews fired faster. Working with the gun crews helped Jones keep his mind off his captain, Dudley Saltonstall, whom he regarded as an "ill-natured and narrow-minded" man.

The winter thaw finally came in mid-February, and the squadron, en-

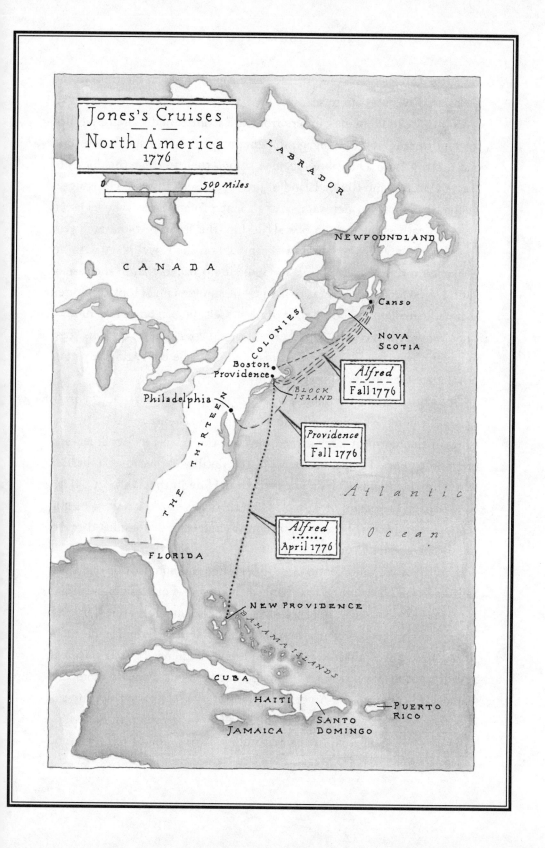

Jones's Cruises
North America
1776

0   500 Miles

LABRADOR

NEWFOUNDLAND

CANADA

• Canso

NOVA
SCOTIA

COLONIES

Boston •
Providence •

BLOCK
ISLAND

Alfred
Fall 1776

Philadelphia •

Providence
Fall 1776

THE THIRTEEN

Atlantic

Ocean

Alfred
April 1776

FLORIDA

NEW PROVIDENCE

BAHAMA ISLANDS

CUBA

HAITI

PUERTO
RICO

JAMAICA

SANTO
DOMINGO

larged by three sloops (the *Fly*, the *Hornet*, and the *Wasp*), ran down the Delaware River and out to sea.

Commodore Hopkins's orders from the Continental Congress called for him to seek out and engage the enemy off the Chesapeake—to find and destroy Lord Dunmore's loyalist ships—then to clear the coasts of North Carolina and Rhode Island of British cruisers. Instead, Hopkins set a course for safer, warmer waters. An ancient, profane figure who had seen enough death as the captain of a slave ship (the slaves revolted and were shot down), Hopkins was in no rush to take on the Royal Navy with his weakened force. He seized on a loophole in his orders that in the case of "unforeseen accident," he was to use his "best judgment." Hopkins figured that with smallpox on board four of his vessels, he had an out. "I did not think we were in a condition to keep on a cold coast," he wrote. His "best judgment" was to sail to the Bahamas and see if he could find any gunpowder for General Washington's army.

The squadron had trouble staying together. Two days out, a fresh nor'easter became a gale and a pair of sloops, the *Hornet* and the *Fly*, vanished in the storm; it later turned out that the vessels had collided and crept off to port. Finally, on March 1, the flotilla reached the sunlit blue waters of the Spanish Main, anchoring off Hole in the Wall, an old pirates' lair on the island of Abaco. The Americans seized a pair of fishing schooners and learned that gunpowder was indeed to be found at the port of Nassau on New Providence Island.

The town was undefended. A British ship and some troops had just sailed away. The two forts that flanked the town—Fort Montague to the west and Fort Nassau to the east—would be presumably manned, if at all, by civilians. Hopkins's plan was to hide some 300 marines and soldiers belowdecks in the captured schooners and send them into Nassau harbor to take the town by surprise. A fine plan, but Hopkins made an elemental blunder. He allowed the American squadron of a half-dozen ships to sail too close to the town in broad daylight. They were promptly spotted by the townsfolk. Someone fired a warning gun from one of the forts, and the sneak attack was aborted.

Hopkins called a meeting of his officers to figure out what to do. "It was I who developed the plan," Jones wrote in a memoir. As Jones told the story, Hopkins wanted to land the marines to seize the western fort, but Jones pointed out that the poor road to the town would give the citizenry too much time to rally a defense. Jones suggested instead that the flotilla sail to a small island about ten miles away and then send in the marines, under cover from two of the armed sloops, to take the eastern fort, which was closer to the town. Jones claims that he personally climbed to the masthead with the pilots to guide the *Alfred* past the reefs to its secret anchorage. The picture of Jones at the masthead, leading the way, is romantic and inspiring, but probably not true. As naval historian Samuel Eliot Morison points out, it is unlikely that the deep-draft *Alfred* would have served as lead ship in these shallow waters. Jones had a need to self-dramatize; his account may be an early example of his posing for posterity. As for strategy, he was certainly not shy about offering his opinions. Hopkins made no mention of Jones's advice in his official report. But then perhaps Jones was so officious and meddlesome that Hopkins, in irritation, churlishly denied him credit.

The Continental Marines stormed ashore—for the first time in history—while a cannonball or two whizzed by their heads. The resistance collapsed. The fort quickly fell. But then it was the marines' turn to dither. Instead of marching directly on the town, they rested for the night. While they slept, the governor of New Providence had enough time to smuggle almost all the gunpowder—162 barrels—onto a merchantman, which slipped out to sea and off to another port under British dominion. The American invasion did not come up empty-handed though. The marines seized seventy-eight cannons, fifteen mortars, and over 16,000 shells and cannonballs, as well as about twenty remaining barrels of powder, a badly needed arsenal for the rebels. The victory was not a great feat of arms— "the Americans had conquered merely by coming," wrote one historian. Yet every finger in the eye of John Bull was good for the morale of the budding war effort. In Nassau, the celebrations appear to have gotten out of hand: the booty included "part of a cask of spirits," and the drunken sailors behaved predictably. Many were laid low by "tropical fever" on the return voyage.

It was a rough as well as sickly trip, with heavy rains and gales. But the night was moonlit and calm, warm for early spring, when Commodore Hopkins's squadron approached the New England coast and engaged in the first real sea battle in the history of the U.S. Navy.

At about 1:30 A.M. on April 6, with the fleet about twenty miles off Block Island, south of Rhode Island's Narragansett Bay, a lookout spotted a ship in the moonlight. "She had all the appearance of a warlike vessel," recorded Captain Nicholas Biddle of the brig *Andrew Doria*. "No one in the fleet doubted her being an English man of war." She was the *Glasgow*, twenty-four guns, a British cruiser that had been harrassing American shipping.

"At 2 a.m. cleared ship for action," Jones recorded in the *Alfred*'s log. Pipes shrilled and drummers "Beat to Quarters," turning men out of their hammocks and on deck to their battle stations. Hammocks were stuffed in the netting along the rails, as a buffer against grapeshot. Chains were slung around the fore and man yard, to prevent the heavy wooden spars and blocks, if shot away, from falling on the heads of the crew. The lower sails were clewed-up to keep them from catching fire. (In an age when ships were made of highly flammable oak, tar, cordage, and canvas, sailors dreaded fire most of all.) The men stripped down to their trousers, so that dirty cloth would not be ground into their wounds. A tot of rum was given to all hands. (The new Articles of War authorized an extra ration of spirits "for particular occasions, such as action, extra duty, and the like.") At the powder magazine, flannel "fearnaught" curtains were hung and soaked, lest fire flash through and detonate the whole ship like a bomb. Small boys—"powder monkeys"—lined up to carry cartridges filled with powder to the guns. On the gun deck, where Jones stood, battle lanterns were hung; the whole area would be thick and dark with smoke after the first few broadsides.

Everything depended on how these tasks were accomplished—if at all—by sleepy, sickly seamen stumbling about in the dark. Few, if any, had ever fought in a sea battle. Commodore Hopkins's command presence was shaky at best. He should have signaled his squadron to "Form Line of Battle." By hitting the *Glasgow* in rapid succession the Americans could have quickly taken or sunk the British warship. But no signals flew from the flagship, the *Alfred.* Instead, "away we all went helter skelter," recorded Captain Biddle.

The brig *Cabot* was the first to confront the *Glasgow.* The British ship challenged the *Cabot* to identify herself and the other ships looming dimly in the moonlight. The *Cabot's* captain, John B. Hopkins, son of the commodore, shouted back, "The *Columbus* and *Alfred,* a 22-gun Frigate." Young Hopkins apparently was hoping to intimidate the British. He may have owed his job to nepotism, but Hopkins was brave, even rash. One of his marines hurled a grenade onto the deck of *Glasgow,* and the battle erupted. Jets of flame flared from cannon in the night. Badly outgunned, the *Cabot* was disabled by two broadsides from the *Glasgow;* Hopkins was wounded and his sailing master was killed. The *Cabot* drifted off, her rigging cut to pieces.

Now it was *Alfred's* turn to enter the fray. She unloosed a broadside at the *Glasgow* and the *Glasgow* fired back. Splinters flew as the cannonballs struck home; wounded men cried out. Belowdecks, commanding his gun crews, Jones was enveloped in smoke and clamor.

A stray cannonball—"an unlucky shot," wrote Jones—cut the rope connecting the *Alfred's* wheel to the rudder. Unable to steer, the Continental frigate wallowed helplessly while the *Glasgow* raked her—sailed across her bow and stern and unleashed broadsides that swept the length of the American ship. Biddle's *Andrew Doria,* meanwhile, was trying to manuever around the shattered *Cabot* and the wounded *Alfred* to get a shot at the British warship. The poorly trained American gun crews fired wildly. Beyond the flash of gunfire, the frigate *Columbus* sat becalmed and the sloop *Providence* dawdled, safely out of range.

Aboard the *Glasgow,* Captain Tryingham Howe decided he had pushed his luck far enough. He ordered his helmsman to spin the wheel and run for it. The battered and scattered American squadron gave chase, yawing—rounding up to present their broadsides at the fleeing *Glasgow*—but could not disable or catch her. About an hour after dawn, Hopkins signaled his flotilla to cut off the pursuit. He was afraid of sailing into the arms of a British squadron cruising off Rhode Island.

Arriving home the next day in New London, Connecticut, the Americans were welcomed as conquering heroes. "Good News for America!" announced a headline in the *Salem (Massachusetts) Gazette*. A popular ode was written to the new sea gods; one verse compared Commodore Hopkins to Neptune. But then the second-guessing began. How had five ships failed to capture one? Why hadn't the Americans used their overwhelming superiority to board and carry the *Glasgow*? The *Glasgow*'s rigging had been shot up, her sails riddled with holes. How had the chasers failed to catch her? There were some legitimate excuses. The bottoms of the American vessels were foul after the cruise to the tropics and the ships were logy, heavily laden with captured cannon. But at least one commander was honest about "the shameful loss of the *Glasgow*," as Captain Biddle put it in a letter to his brother. "A more imprudent, ill-conducted affair never happened." Biddle hooted at the accounts in the newspapers of "hot fight" that had lasted "three glasses," an hour and a half. "They must mean half-minute glasses," he scoffed. Congress ordered the inevitable inquiry. The captain of the *Columbus*, Abraham Whipple, was cleared of a cowardice charge, but the captain of the *Providence*, John Hazard, was convicted of an array of crimes, including embezzling his ship's stores.

Jones later wrote that he was "surprised" by how few men were killed and wounded in the battle. The *Glasgow*, the Americans later learned, lost only one man dead, three wounded, while the colonial ships lost ten dead, fourteen wounded. Jones bragged about the *Alfred*'s gun crews. He wrote his patron, Joseph Hewes, "I formed an exercise and trained the men so well to the great guns on the *Alfred* that they went thro' the motions of broad sides and rounds as exactly as soldiers generally perform their manual exercise." Maybe so, but the casualties aboard the *Glasgow* were caused by the musketry of the marines, not by Jones's cannon. The record suggests that Jones had less than harmonious relations with his subordinates on the gun deck. A week after the battle, Jones received an apology from the ship's gunner, James Thomas, that appears to have been extracted and possibly dictated: "Sir: As I have been for some time confined very justly for ill behavior towards you and am very sorry I should ever give any gentleman any displeasure . . ." The gunner's offense was not spelled out, but the fact that Jones compelled his chief noncommissioned officer to write a formal letter of apology raises questions. Good lieutenants are supposed to form strong bonds of trust and authority with their NCOs, not make them grovel for "giving gentlemen displeasure."

Jones labored over his report of the voyage of the *Alfred* to Hewes, his "special friend" on the Naval Committee (now called the Marine Committee), whose favor he wished to curry. Sitting in his tiny first lieutenant's cabin as the *Alfred* swung on its anchor in New London harbor, he wrote out in his neatly flowing longhand an account of the attack on Nassau and the engagement with the *Glasgow*, drawing on his entries from the ship's log. Then he reached the tricky subject of the performance of his commanding officers. He struggled to find the right words. He began, "I leave in your province to make the natural comments you see arising from the subject . . ." i.e., draw your own conclusions. He paused and began again, "I wish to avoid censuring any individuals—the utmost delicacy is necessary and highly becoming in my situation. I therefore content myself with relating facts only—and leave wiser heads the privilege of determining their propriety."

Then he crossed out those simperings. We can see from a surviving draft of his letter that he started over, this time by praising (however insincerely) Commodore Hopkins. "I have the pleasure of assuring you that the commander in chief is respected through the fleet and I verily believe that the officers and men in general would go any length to execute his orders." He paused again to contemplate Saltonstall. Jones tried to cast his resentment of Saltonstall's high-handedness in general terms, as a morality tale for the new navy: "It is certainly for the interest of the service that a cordial interchange of civilities should subsist between superior and inferior officers—and therefore . . ." Here his spleen vented: "it is bad policy in superiors to behave towards their inferiors indiscriminately as though they were a lower species."

Saltonstall may have regarded Jones, who was ten years his junior, as simply an annoying upstart, but the Brahmin captain showed his conde-scension in a way that made the thin-skinned Jones feel like a "lower species." Jones's sermonizing continued: "Such a conduct will damp the ardour of any man—would to heaven it were otherwise!—but in sad truth this is a conduct too much in fashion in our infant fleet." Jones must have thought he was getting carried away, because he struck out that last sen-tence. Instead, he reached for a lofty, as he would put it, "philosophical" view: "Men of liberal minds, who have long been accustomed to com-mand" (i.e., Jones) "can ill brook being used thus. . . . The rude ungentle treatment which they experience creates such heartburnings as are no wise consonant with that cheerful ardour and spirit which ought ever to be the characteristic of an officer." One can almost feel Jones's "heart-burn." He knows he should show "cheerful ardour" but all he feels is con-tempt for his captain.

A month later, Jones made no attempt to conceal his feelings for Saltonstall. By this time, "the unfortunate engagement with the *Glasgow*," as Jones called the battle in a letter to Hewes on May 19, had been re-vealed as a failure, and Jones was feeling the public's scorn. Hopkins had published a letter asserting that "all the officers of the *Alfred* behaved well—yet still," Jones wrote, "the public blames me among others for not taking the enemy." He castigated "the rude unhappy temper" of Captain Saltonstall but tried to show Hewes that he had risen above petty bicker-ing. "I now reflect with pleasure that I had philosophy sufficient to avoid quarrelling with him," he wrote. Seeking to stay on a higher plane, Jones defined the desired qualities of an officer with words that perfectly convey his Enlightenment values and his social ambition:

In my opinion a captain of the navy ought to be a man of strong and well connected sense with a tolerable education. A gentleman as well as a seaman, both in theory and in practice—for, want of learning and rude ungentle manners are by no means the characteristic of an officer.

Though eighteenth-century language can sound a bit stilted to the modern ear, Jones was far-seeing. If only he had been able to live by his words. He needed to see himself as an actor on a great stage, rendering grand pronouncements, fighting for a cause worthy of his nobility, self-consciously identifying his own climb with the rise of a new nation and its new navy. The scale of his ambition was wearying. He would grasp, for a moment, that he needed to be gracious and to rise above petty rivalry to get ahead, but then his resentments would flood back in.

He did, however, win at least temporary victories over his temper and burning sense of grievance. In his May 19 letter to Hewes, he observed that, despite the strains between captain and first officer aboard the *Alfred*, he had managed to obtain Saltonstall's "blessing at parting. May he soon become of an affable even disposition," wrote Jones, "and may he find pleasure in communicating happiness around him."

Jones could afford to take a more benign view because by mid-May he was no longer Saltonstall's subordinate. With the court-martial of Captain Hazard for stealing his own ship's stores, the sloop *Providence* was once more offered to Jones. This time he said yes, as much to flee Saltonstall, he acknowledged to Hewes, as to have his own command.

WHEN CAPTAIN JONES was piped aboard the *Providence* on May 10, her crew was relieved, if not overjoyed. On May 1, the sloop's crew had written Commodore Hopkins, "We are used like dogs." Captain Hazard, as well as another of the ship's officers, carried a "stick with bullets and rope ends to beat us with and we are kept from morning til night upon deck and scarcely have time to eat. . . . Cannot bear with it," the crew complained. A fellow captain described Hazard as "a stout man very vain and ignorant—as much low cunning as capacity." Though vain himself and certainly capable of imposing harsh discipline, Jones offered a refreshing contrast to his thuggish predecessor. Trim and well mannered, lofty in his sentiments, Jones saw to it that his crew was well fed and fairly treated, at least by eighteenth-century standards.

Not all the *Providence*'s officers were ogres. Jones was very lucky in his second (soon to be first) lieutenant, John Rathbun. Close in age—a year shy of their thirtieth birthdays—both men brimmed with eagerness and panache. Rathbun was deft at sailing the sloop, with her enormous and difficult-to-control mainsail. Jones, who had turned down command of the *Providence* in December 1775 in part because he wasn't sure he could handle the sloop's fore-and-aft gaff rig, was relieved to have such a skilled subordinate to show him the ship's feel and quirks. Most important, perhaps, Rathbun served as a buffer between Jones and the men, softening the captain's harsh edges and moderating his temper, without in any way lessening his authority. With Rathbun's help, Jones quickly asserted his control over his new charges. He compelled the lieutenant of marines to make peace with a fellow officer after a feud and threw another malcontent into irons until he apologized for his behavior. For the rest of the cruise, harmony reigned. In later years, Jones would look back on the crew of the *Providence* as his best ever—and his time at her command as his happiest.

The *Providence* was lightly armed but quick and manueverable, a sort of eighteenth-century PT boat. Sailing vessels cannot head straight into the wind, and square-rigged ships, in particular, did not do well to windward. Most could not sail any closer than at a 70 degree angle to the direction of the wind. With her fore-and-aft rig, the *Providence* could do better—about 50 degrees off. She could take larger and faster ships on a tacking duel, working to windward to make her escape. When she wanted to fall off and run before the wind, the *Providence* could set a "course," a full-bellied square sail, for extra speed.

Swooping to leeward and climbing to windward, Jones came to appreciate the sailing qualities of his new command. With her immense forty-foot bowsprit and an even longer mainsail boom, she could crowd on sail.

At times, too much sail: in a storm, the expanse of canvas made the sloop vulnerable to a knock-down blast of wind. Mishandled in any weather, jibing the mainsail—bringing the boom across from one side to the other as the vessel changed course running before the wind—could be disastrous. In an abrupt or uncontrolled jibe, the enormous force of the mainsail slamming across the deck could cause the sloop to broach—roll over on her side, ship water, and possibly sink. The *Providence* could carry an enormous stretch of sail for a seventy-foot, single-masted ship. A smaller topsail and light studding sails could be stretched out above and on either side of the course, like canvas wings, to catch more breeze. The different sail combinations and the danger of piling on too much canvas demanded able seamanship, but they made sloops like the *Providence* hard to catch. The sloop's design was favored by pirates.

Jones spent most of the summer of 1776 on escort duty in Long Island Sound, playing cat-and-mouse with British frigates. (He also had time to court the ladies. In a letter sent to a fellow rover, Captain Abraham Whipple, Jones chided his friend for not giving him word "about our agreeable widow, or my little affair of the heart in Providence.") In August, Jones received the orders he longed for. "You are to proceed immediately on a cruise against our enemies," the Marine Committee instructed the commander of the *Providence*. It was his "duty to seize, take, sink; burn or destroy" British vessels of all kinds. The Marine Committee admonished him to "be careful of the sloop, her stores and materials, use your people well, thereby recommending the American naval service to all who engage in it, and we also recommend humane kind treatment of your prisoners." Jones's masters recommended that he begin his hunt for prizes around "the latitude of Bermuda"—the best spot for picking off British merchantmen, laden with riches, on their return home from the West Indies. Although Jones always insisted that he desired glory, not gain, he was not unmindful that a captain on a solo cruise kept a significant portion of the proceeds (up to 10 percent) from the sale of any prize.

Before weighing anchor, Jones looked to the needs of his crew. The meals on board may not have tasted very appetizing, but they were not skimpy—on most days, each man was allotted a pound of bread and a pound of salted beef or pork, ample calories for heavy seaborne labor. There were casks of rum for the daily ration of half a pint per man, and even fresh meat and produce for the officers' wardroom, enough to last for the first several weeks at sea. Inside the ship's longboat, stowed on deck, were stored crates of chickens, while live pigs and a sheep or two were tethered to the mast. The deck of an eighteenth-century warship could sound (and smell) like a barnyard: sailors not only heard the singing of the wind in the halyards and the rush of the waves, but the clucking, bleating, and braying of animals. (At the height of his most glorious battle, against the British man-of-war *Serapis*, when Jones needed to rest for a moment, he sat on top of a hen coop.)

Jones was in Philadelphia when he received his orders. He had sailed there on the *Providence* to see Joseph Hewes and further ingratiate himself with his congressional sponsors on the Marine Committee. The city was in an uproar that summer of 1776. In July, the Continental Congress had voted to declare independence from England. On July 1, as Congress prepared to vote for the final break the following day, Hewes lifted up his hands to heaven and, as if in a trance, cried out, "It is done, and I will abide by it!" In early August, as members of the Continental Congress affixed their names to the document during those critical weeks, they were all aware of the potential consequences. "We must all hang together or most assuredly we will all hang separately," Ben Franklin warned. For the moment, narrow self-interest was forgotten. Old Stephen Hopkins, brother of Esek and the chairman of the Marine Committee, suffered from palsy, but as he picked up the pen, he said, "My hand trembles, but my heart does not." In New York, where Jones had cruised with a boatload of General Washington's soldiers earlier that spring, jubilant crowds toppled a giant equestrian statue of George III. But the crowds soon became less jubilant: in late July and August, 130 British warships and transports had sailed into New York harbor and disgorged 32,000 fully equipped, well-trained soldiers—more than the population of New York or Philadelphia. They were no more than a week's march from Philadelphia. As he sailed from Boston to Philadelphia at the end of July, Jones had seen several ships of the British armada and wisely steered clear.

The force John Paul Jones was assembling aboard the *Providence*, anchored on the Delaware River not far from the State House where the signers had pledged their "lives, their fortunes, and their Sacred Honor," seems trifling. He had seventy-three officers and men, twenty-five of them marines, including a fife and drummer—all to be squeezed aboard a seventy-foot ship. To stand on the deck of the *Providence* (a full-scale replica, based in Providence, Rhode Island, was built during the 1976 Bicentennial) is to wonder how. The men slept belowdeck in hammocks that were slung only a foot or two apart. Cramped conditions were routine: officially, fourteen inches was the space allotted each crewman of a British ship of the line. The only ventilation on the *Providence* came from a single open hatchway. While body heat was a blessing in northern latitudes, in the tropics the air belowdecks was fetid. The men became inured to their cramped conditions (interestingly, in the Royal Navy mutinies of the 1790s, overcrowding was not in the list of grievances). The marines slept between the seamen and the officers berthed in the stern—as protection from an uprising by the crew in the night. The seagoing soldiers, who were not expected to take on any sailing duties, acted as a local police force. One stood at attention outside the captain's cabin, a small—but, by comparison, palatial—chamber, roomy enough for a desk and chairs and built with wide stern windows that admitted plenty of light.

The *Providence* cleared the Delaware capes on August 26. Less than one week out to sea, the lookout spotted, just over the horizon in the brightening of an early morning, the masts of five ships. Jones's officers excitedly speculated that the largest was an old Indiaman or a Jamaican three-decker, a large merchant ship and potentially a fat prize. Jones was not so sure, but he did not think he should flatly overrule his subordinates so early in the cruise. The *Providence* plunged ahead, a dog among sheep—until she ran straight into a wolf. The Indiaman turned out to be a twenty-six-gun British frigate, the *Solebay*. Spotting the intruder, the British warship gave chase. Jones ordered his sloop to haul to windward and try to escape. Normally, the *Providence* would have had the edge because she could sail closer to the wind. But a strong cross sea was running, and the sloop pounded in the steep waves, slowing her momentum. A brisk wind was blowing, favoring the longer, heavier frigate, which could sail faster in heavy weather.

The hunt was on. As countless sea sagas have testified, time passes with agonizing slowness in a stern chase. The officers and men of the *Providence* could only watch as the *Solebay* crept closer. They could see the enemy warship rising and falling in the choppy sea, the armed British marines on deck and climbing into the tops, then the frigate's loaded guns run out as she steadily drew within range. The *Providence*'s twelve 4-pounders would be mere popguns against the *Solebay*'s twenty-six 12- and 9-pounders. Death or a prison hulk surely awaited if the *Providence* was overtaken. Jones was well aware of his own probable fate. Under the usual rules of war, officers of an enemy nation were usually paroled, given a measure of freedom on their word not to escape and then swapped in a prisoner exchange. The British government, however, had made clear that it would treat rebels as criminals and threatened to hang them. As the hours crawled by and the shadows lengthened, Captain Jones paced the quarterdeck, trying to figure a way out.

Jones was in no way paralyzed or even uncertain about a course of action. If anything, he was euphoric. Mortal peril seems to have lightened Jones's step, made him more clever and nimble. His characteristic brooding was swept away. He became clear-eyed and clever-minded, even jaunty as he faced a superior foe. In this engagement with the enemy, and in the many that followed, danger and the chance for glory appear to have had a transformative effect on Jones: the scowling countenance of a nitpicking martinet was replaced with the glow of confidence and courage.

When the *Solebay* drew within musket shot, just to leeward of the *Providence*'s stern quarter, Jones raised the American flag and ordered his gun crews to prepare to fire. The British captain tried to play a trick, a *ruse de guerre*. He, too, ordered his crew to hoist American colors. The *Solebay* fired a few guns to leeward, the international signal for "I am friendly."

Since warships looked similar from navy to navy, and indeed had frequently been captured and renamed, captains would often try to deceive each other by posing as friend not foe. Unless used to lure an enemy's ship onto the rocks, ruses were not considered unsporting.

Jones was not fooled for an instant by the *Solebay*'s knavery. He knew that the Continental Navy had no frigates of this size. "The bait would not take," he wrote in his account of the chase.

The captain of the *Providence* was plotting a gambit of his own. His one advantage was manueverability. Both ships were close-hauled, sailing as near to the direction of the wind as possible. As the *Solebay* prepared to open fire, Jones sent his men aloft to the yardarms to ready a sudden sail change. At Lieutenant Rathbun's command, they suddenly let drop the main course, the big-bellied sail used for sailing before the wind. The sail filled and the *Providence* shot forward. At once, her lightweight steering or studdingsails sprouted from the yardarm. The helmsman pulled the tiller, and the sloop's bow swiftly veered downwind. As the British men and officers gaped and cursed, the *Providence* swept right across the bow of the *Solebay* and flew by. By the time the British ship could reset her sails and swing around to follow, "I was almost out of reach of grape [shot] & soon after out of reach of cannon shot," Jones recorded.

"*Providence* at Sea in no. latd. 37 [degrees] 40 [minutes] & wt. longitude 54 [degrees] Sept. 4th 1776," Jones wrote in his precise script, as the lantern swung in his stern cabin and he recounted the chase in his formal report to the Marine Committee. He allowed himself to exult at the expense of the British captain. "Our 'hairbreadth scape' & the saucy manner of making it must have mortified him not a little," gloated Jones.

Had he foreseen this motion & been prepared to counteract it he might have fired several broadsides or double-headed and grape shot which would have done us very material damage but he was a bad marksman & tho' within pistol shot did not touch the *Providence* with one of the many shots he fired.

Jones was also pleased to report that his ship had taken the brig *Sea-Nymph*, bound from Barbados for London, stuffed with valuable cargo, including a dozen cases of "the best particular London market Madeira wine." The captured brig, Jones reported, "is new & and sails very fast so that she is a pretty good prize."

The *Providence* was a contented ship. Jones was already well on his way to recouping the fortune he had lost when his business partner swindled him after he fled the "great misfortune" of his life in Tobago. His crew was pleased to be sailing for such an enterprising and successful commander after the slovenly, cruel Hazard. Though in far smaller shares, prize money was distributed to crew members as well as officers. On deck, while the sloop gently rocked in the warm current of the Gulf Stream, seamen danced to the fiddle while they imagined how the girls would greet them when they came home with gold in their pockets. Jones's letter shows that he was still gleeful over outfoxing a British frigate. And yet, as so often would be the case for Jones, whose highs and lows bordered on the manic, there came an emotional letdown, a dose of post-combat *tristesse*.

Jones wrote a second, less ebullient letter that night of September 4, this one to Robert Morris, a member of the Marine Committee whom Jones had recently met and begun to cultivate. Jones was wise in his choice of patrons: Morris was a shrewd and very wealthy Philadelphia merchant whose services to the cause already included the donation of a ship—the *Black Prince*, the merchantman that Congress had armed and renamed the *Alfred*. Before the war's end, as the new republic ran out of money, Morris would help finance the Continental Army out of his own pocket. Jones and Morris were well matched in zeal and vision if not in status or resources, and Jones shamelessly played up to Morris. Flowery formalism was the language of the age; letters typically ended in a cascade of fawning salutations ("your humble, obedient, faithful servant," etc.). In his letter, he referred to Morris in the third person: "I esteem the honor done me by his accepting my correspondence as the greatest favor I could have aspired to." Switching into the more familiar second person, he "concluded," gingerly and discreetly, that "Mr. Hewes hath acquainted you with a very great misfortune which befell me some years ago and which brought me unto No. America." (Jones was presumably referring to killing the Ringleader at Tobago.) With a last bow, Jones wrote Morris that he had ordered the master of his prize, the captured *Sea-Nymph*, to "deliver you a turtle"—a sea turtle caught by Jones's men—which Jones prayed that Morris would accept as a token of his esteem.

Having thus cringed, he unloaded. He lectured Morris, as he would in later letters, on naval matters, borrowing from the British ("as their navy is the best regulated in the world, we must in some degree imitate them and aim at such further improvement as may one day make ours vie and exceed theirs"). Then he got to what was really eating him. When Jones was given command of the *Providence* on May 10, his orders were written on the back of his lieutenant's commission. He was thus only *acting* captain. His formal commission as captain was not dated until August 8. If Morris and the Marine Committee let this "injustice" stand, then Jones would be superseded in seniority by men of lesser experience and ability. "I esteem it a greater disgrace and severer punishment than to be fairly broke and dismissed from the service," Jones exclaimed. Quite a sullen outburst from someone who had, in a letter just written, jauntily celebrated the "saucy manner" of his "hairbreadth scape." Jones's mood swings could be severe, especially before and after battle. His joy at victory was always tempered, if not undone, by the burning question: would glory follow? Over time, Jones's wounded feelings about the injustice of the seniority list would fester and become malignant.

By mid-September, the hurricane season was approaching. The prize pickings were becoming slim, as few merchantmen would risk getting caught out in mid-ocean in an autumn storm. Jones might have sailed for home, but instead he headed north, toward Sable Island, a hundred miles off the coast of Nova Scotia, into a sea of shoals that had torn out the bottoms of dozens of ships. Jones intended to destroy the British fishing fleets there.

As she steered into the cold northern waters, the *Providence* was caught in a storm so severe that the sloop's twelve cannon had to be taken off their carriages and stowed in the hold. Jones was being prudent: a loose cannon, broken free from the ropes that anchored it, was a sailor's nightmare—two tons of metal rolling about the deck, threatening to smash through the bulkhead and anyone who got in the way. But the *Providence* weathered the two-day tempest, and on September 20 she anchored at Sable Island, a bleak outcropping in an angry sea.

Jones had just allowed his crew to drop fishing lines (with tackle that John Adams had frugally insisted upon in the Articles of War), when a British frigate, the *Milford*, appeared to windward. His Majesty's cruiser immediately bore down on the American sloop "the instant he discovered us." The threat of a more powerful but ponderous warship once more put Jones in a playful mood. He let the frigate draw within "cannon shot" and then led her on a "wild goose chase." First, he headed downwind to test the frigate's speed under full sail. Finding her a little too quick for comfort, he then hauled his sails and headed up to take advantage of the *Providence*'s superiority sailing close to the wind. Jones enjoyed baiting the British captain. To "tempt him to throw away powder and shot," Jones wrote, he shortened sail, allowing the *Milford* to draw close, but not too close. This "curious mock engagement was maintained between us for eight hours," Jones related in his later account, which he finished with a literary flourish right out of Sir Walter Scott—"'Til night with her sable curtain put an end to this famous exploit of English knight errantry."

On the quarterdeck, Jones did not conceal his delight at flummoxing the Royal Navy. The British captain, Jones wrote, "excited my contempt so much by his continual firing at more than twice proper distance that when he rounded to give his broadside I ordered my marine officer to return the salute with a single musket." Jones's euphoria was at full flood. The next day, Jones wrote, he could see the *Milford* sailing westward, toward Nova Scotia. After the British captain reached port, Jones observed, "It is not unlikely that he hath told his friends in Halifax what a trimming he gave to a 'rebel privateer' that he found infesting the coast." Jones had not misjudged his adversary's arrogance: a few weeks later, the British papers reported that the *Milford* had taken the American "privateer."

Jones suspected he might find some sailors willing to join the rebel cause in the little fishing port of Canso, so he sent his ship's boat in to investigate. It returned with "several" volunteers and some valuable intelligence. A British fishing fleet—a total of nine vessels—was not far away, anchored in two harbors off the island of Madame on the east side of the bay. "These I determined to take or destroy," Jones recounted. From the friendly local fishermen, he bought a shallop, a small sailing vessel, and sent her off with twenty-five armed men to raid one harbor. Then he sailed for the other in the *Providence*. "The expedition succeeded to my wish—so effectual was the surprise and so general the panic that numbers yielded to a handful without opposition, and never was bloodless victory more complete."

The weather was the real enemy off Nova Scotia in late September. The bite of oncoming winter could be felt in the wind, which whipped the tops off the waves and sent stinging spray sweeping across the deck of the *Providence*. Another violent gale struck that night, destroying two of Jones's prizes on the rocks. As a humanitarian gesture, Jones loaded the 300 British fishermen he had captured into two schooners and a brig and sent them back across the Atlantic, with a safe-conduct written in his hand, prohibiting "any subject of the Free States of America from offering any violence or interference at their utmost peril."

It was time to head for home. Jones was sure that the *Milford* had sounded the alarm in Halifax and that the British would soon be out hunting for him. His ship's company was badly depleted by the necessity of putting prize crews aboard captured ships (the prizes were sent back to colonial ports in order to be sold off). On September 30, as the *Providence* rode at anchor at Sable Island, Jones wrote the Marine Committee that he was all done in—though ever ready to serve:

I have had so much stormy weather and been obliged on diverse occasions to carry so much sail that the sloop is in no condition to continue long out of port. I am besides very weak-handed and the men I have are scarce able to stand the deck for want of clothing, the weather here being very cold. These reasons induce me to bend my thoughts towards the continent. I do not expect to meet with much, if any, success on my return. But, if fortune should insist on sending a transport or so my way—weak as I am, I will endeavor to pilot him safe. It is but justice to add that my officers and men behaved incomparably well.

Indeed they had. When she sailed safely into Narragansett Bay on October 7, the *Providence* could boast of a proud and profitable cruise: sixteen prizes taken, of which six reached port (the rest were burned by Jones, sunk, or retaken by the British). Jones was so heartened by his success that he was ready to turn around and go right back out to sea, the gales of autumn be damned.

CHAPTER FOUR

"Determined at All Hazards"

*T*HE REVOLUTION was not going well. In August, while Jones was sailing circles around HMS *Solebay*, British forces had invaded Long Island and battered Washington's army. The Continentals had escaped across the East River in a "providential fog," but in September the British bombarded and attacked Manhattan, and the rebel forces broke and ran. General Washington himself had stepped into the breech, swatting fleeing soldiers with his riding crop in a futile attempt to rally them. At Harlem Heights, British dragoons were said to have arrogantly sounded the fox-hunting call, "View Halloo." Washington was forced to evacuate to New Jersey, then across the Delaware to Pennsylvania to take refuge with a dwindling band of "winter soldiers," the "summer soldiers" having gone home to their farms and families.

The American Continental Navy, Jones excepted, was stuck in port in the fall of 1776. Jones intended to cruise off New York harbor near Sandy Hook, hoping to pick off British merchantmen rushing to supply the British army of occupation before winter set in. But Commodore Hopkins tugged at Jones's "finer feelings" with a more noble mission. In the coal pits of Cape Breton, Nova Scotia, the British were using at least a hundred American prisoners as slave labor. Would Jones mount an expedition to rescue them? "All my humanity was awakened," Jones wrote. He was not gushing. Jones's desire to liberate American prisoners would be a constant preoccupation. While the coal pits were particularly cruel, other incarcerations were also grim. Jones knew the story of the *Jersey*, a verminous prison hulk, a "Hell Afloat" that was moored off a mud flat in New York harbor, crammed with half-naked rebel prisoners riddled with disease. For many of the rebels consigned to the coal pits of Nova Scotia, Jones feared, winter would be a death sentence.

To accomplish his rescue mission, Jones was given a small fleet: the *Alfred*, Jones's old converted merchantman from the New Providence expedition; the sloop *Providence*; and the *Hampden*, a two-masted brigantine. The former lieutenant could now call himself commodore. The ships did not, however, come with anywhere near enough men. The *Alfred*, which normally required a crew of 200, had only thirty sailors aboard. Jones knew why: the lure of privateering was too strong.

Sailing on a privateer was at once more free-wheeling and more lucrative than serving aboard a ship of the Continental Navy. Congress and the different colonies gave "letters of marque"—license to seize enemy ships—to about 2,000 privateers during the Revolutionary War. The privateers aided the war effort, seizing so many British ships that they drove up insurance rates in London. Such were the rewards from licensed piracy that at war's end in the seaport of Salem, Massachusetts, "there were many persons dejected on the return of peace," wrote one local observer. But the privateers, employing some 20,000 men, were a drain on the Continental Navy. Captains like Jones tried to recruit with handbills and advertisements promising glory and honor and by offering inducements like rum and cash. Unscrupulous seaman would pocket the money and run off to join a privateer.

Shows of unpatriotic self-interest infuriated Jones. "Privateers entice men away as soon as they receive a month's pay," he complained to Robert Morris, his new friend on the Marine Committee, in a letter dated October 17, ten days after he had returned from his voyage on the *Providence*. The muster roll of the sloop *Providence* is dotted with the names of men with an "R," for "run," after their names, and notations like: "inveigled away." Advertisements in local papers offered rewards of $5 for each deserter recaptured. (One *Providence* deserter was described in a wanted ad as a "sly, smooth tongued fellow . . . lurking somewhere in Jersey.") Jones largely blamed the politicians in Philadelphia for creating the manpower shortfall. Strapped for money, Congress hoped to raise funds by taking half to two thirds of the profits from prizes seized by its warships. This was "penny wise and pound foolish," Jones argued. The government of Britain, he pointed out, wisely made no claim on prizes, leaving the rewards to be divvied up by the officers and men of its navy. In America, the navy was being essentially outbid by the privateers. Until its sailors made more money, Jones warned, the American navy can "never become respectable—it never will become formidable—and without a respectable navy—Alas America!" Jones's urgings were heartfelt and sensible. He heard nothing in return.

As he scrambled to find the men to man his tiny fleet, Jones was understandably impatient. He knew he was running out of time to rescue the poor prisoners in the coal pits of Nova Scotia—the winter would sock in along the Canadian coast if his ships did not make haste. He finally decided to leave the *Providence* behind and use her crew to man the *Alfred.* On October 27, he shoved off along with the *Hampden*—and never made it farther than the mouth of Narragansett Bay. The boneheaded captain of the *Hampden*, Hoystead Hacker, muddled his navigation and put his ship right onto a rock. "The noble captain doth not understand the first case of plain [sic] trigonometry!" despaired Jones. It was back to port to switch men from the wounded *Hampden* into the *Providence*—as the days shortened and the season grew late.

Now it was Jones's original congressional patron, Joseph Hewes, who got to hear the bleats of a thwarted warrior. On October 30, as he bleakly sat in his cabin while a "gale of wind at S.E. with thick weather" lashed the *Alfred* at her mooring, Jones complained about the problems besetting "our infant navy." Other captains—who, maddeningly, had been given better commands, new frigates just now sliding down the ways—held hidden interests in privateers, Jones charged. These selfish scoundrels "not only wink at, but encourage and employ deserters from the navy. What punishment is equal to such baseness?—and yet these men pretend to love their country!"

Here, Jones felt obliged to state his own principles. While delivered in an indignant huff in Jones's grandiose style, they reflect his hope for a new republic in a new age that will reward virtue and merit, not a mighty empire (like Britain) that exists to protect power and privilege ("since liberty hath chosen America as her last asylum every effort to protect and cherish her is noble and will be rewarded with the thanks of future ages").

Jones was not just spouting platitudes. He went on to make practical suggestions, like unlimited enlistment periods (so the sailors would not just vanish after their tours of duty), an impartial Board of Admiralty to run the navy (rather than a highly politicized congressional committee), and wages and prize shares competitive with those of the Royal Navy and American privateers. At the end, he offered an unusual personal insight. He was not asking for more money for himself. "I am easily provided for and am not in the least uneasy on my own account." This was not just because he had shown luck and skill at winning prizes, but because, as he said, "I have no family or dependents and probably never will."* Jones may have occasionally pined for Miss Dandridge, and he certainly compensated with serial love affairs. But he had no Lady Hamilton. He saw himself as an essentially solitary figure, fated to remain alone at sea or on land.

Jones finally got to sea on November 1. His provisions for the cruise included 600 gallons of rum, enough to keep the crew warm until Christmas. As the *Alfred* cruised down Vineyard Sound, heading east, the lookout spotted a mast in Tarpaulin Cove on Naushon Island, an old haven for pirates. The evening was mild; the wind had dropped, and the *Alfred* was coasting slowly along. Jones decided to investigate and found a privateer, the *Eagle*. Before dawn, Jones sent two boatloads of marines

---

*He meant immediate family. He tried to send money, both before and during the American Revolution, to his two surviving sisters, and he included them in a will dictated in October 1777. Jones may have felt totally alone, but from time to time apparently he remembered his surviving family back in Scotland. In later years, he corresponded with his sisters.

(some of them apparently disguised as Indians) to probe a little deeper. Using cutlasses, Jones's men pricked at bags in the hold, hoping to flush out any deserters who might be hiding there. They kicked down a false bulkhead and found what they were looking for: a pair of men who had run from their naval duty to become privateersmen. Already in a white heat about lost seamen, Jones decided to take twenty more sailors from the *Eagle*, just for good measure. The *Alfred* sailed away, leaving the *Eagle*'s enraged captain cursing about the navy's illegal "press gang"—as unjust as British tyranny!—and threatening to sue.

Jones ignored him. By mid-November the *Alfred* and *Providence* were pitching and rolling in the cold gray waters off Nova Scotia, keeping a lookout for prizes as they raced to liberate the prisoners. Off Louisburg, Jones made a great catch: the *Mellish*, a British transport carrying chests of medicine, fine silks, some important British citizens bound for Halifax, and, most critically, thousands of winter uniforms. The warm clothes were destined for General Burgoyne's army, then preparing to drive south from Canada to split the rebellious colonies in two. "The prize is, I believe, the most valuable ship that hath been taken by American arms," wrote Jones to the Marine Committee on November 12. "I found sixty women and children on board the *Mellish*, several of whom are persons of distinction. . . . The loss of the *Mellish* will distress the enemy more than can be easily imagined, as the clothing on board her is the last intended to be sent out for Canada this season. . . . The situation of Burgoyne's army must soon become insupportable." Describing his capture of some 10,000 uniforms aboard the *Mellish*, Jones wrote Robert Smith, a North Carolina merchant and fellow Mason, "This will make Burgoyne 'shake a cloth in the wind' and check his progress on the Lakes." Jones was not exaggerating the significance of his prize. Burgoyne's march down through Lake George and Lake Champlain was hobbled by the loss of uniforms. And Jones was later proud to hear that the British uniforms were used to clothe General Washington's freezing men, who recrossed the Delaware to defeat British Hessian troops quartered at Princeton and Trenton at Christmas and New Year's.

Jones did not have much time to gloat over his coup. He learned on November 16 from another captured prize that the harbors of Cape Breton were freezing, threatening to upset his plan for a dramatic shore raid to liberate the American prisoners. "Stormy and contrary winds still prevail," Jones wrote the Marine Committee, in one of his periodic reports sent home aboard a prize ship. Aboard the *Alfred* and *Providence* the pumps were working. The relentless pounding in the mountainous wintery seas had opened up the seams of both vessels. "I will however pursue the expedition while there is a possibility of success," Jones wrote.

The men aboard the *Providence* were not so keen. There arose "an unaccountable murmuring in the sloop," reported Jones. Jones rowed over from the *Alfred*, sitting grim and erect in the stern of his ship's boat as it tossed about and the sailors strained at the oars. Gathering around the crew of his old ship, he gave the men an impassioned pep talk: "I represented to them how much humanity was concerned in our endeavors to relieve our captive ill-treated brethren from the coal mines," Jones wrote. Jones had a very fluent tongue. His sailors sometimes grumbled that he used it to con them into believing that his desperate schemes were a matter of duty. But the gap between Jones's glory-seeking, theatrical zeal, and the harsh, everyday drudgery faced by his crewmen was too great. In his black, boatlike cockaded hat, his hawkish face fierce and unyielding in the streaming storm, Jones must have seemed like a madman compared with the diffident or easygoing merchant captains most sailors were accustomed to.

Jones's humanitarian rhetoric met blank stares and scowls. His urgings were "in vain," Jones recorded. "On the 18th we had a gale from the N.E. with snow—it could not be called a hard gale." Hard enough for the *Providence:* when Jones looked through the driving sleet the next morning "to my great surprise . . . I found the *Providence* had disappeared." In the dark, the sloop's men, acting in cahoots with the hapless Captain Hacker, had raised their sails and run for home. In the British Navy, such willful disobedience, not to mention cravenness, would have cost Hacker his job if not his neck. In the Continental Navy, Jones could only fume and write angry letters to Congress.

The "epidemical discontent" spread to Jones's ship. The frozen sailors were not malingering. Sailing in winter can be a brutal hardship. Climbing icy ratlines in a snowstorm to furl sails frozen stiff as a board is a heart-stopping endeavor. Ice imperiled the whole ship: the weight of ice in the rigging can unbalance a sailing vessel and make her more prone to rolling over in a storm. Still, Jones stubbornly pressed on: "The season was indeed severe and everyone was for returning immediately to port but I was determined at all hazards while my provisions lasted to perservere in my first plan."

On November 24, Jones had a scare. In "thick weather" the *Alfred* was suddenly surrounded by three ships. Jones and his officers all assumed they were in the company of enemy men-of-war. Jones had been told by local fishermen that after the attacks of the *Providence* on the British fishing fleet at Sable Island in September, the Royal Navy had dispatched three frigates to cruise for the rebel raiders.

For Jones, in his feverish state, it was do-or-die. "Resolving to sell my liberty as dear as possible" or go out in a blaze of glory, Jones steered straight at one of the three shadowy vessels. As the drummer beat to quarters, the men prepared for what they feared would be their last battle before death or consignment to a prison hulk in Halifax. Jones, sword and pistols at the ready, eagerly peered through the murk at the dark hull and perceived, to his crew's immense relief, that she was a merchantman. The enemy cruiser turned out to be a plodding collier carrying coal from the Cape Breton mines, bound for New York. Jones quickly took her as a prize, though he continued to keep a weather eye for the convoy's escort. (Indeed, the British frigate *Flora* was sailing close by in the fog.)

Seizing coal ships meant less fuel for the stoves of the British army wintering in New York, and Jones further cut the lobsterbacks' supplies by sending in armed boats to burn a British supply ship and destroy an oil warehouse in the fishing port of Canso. But from the captured collier's crew he learned some deflating news. The American prisoners in the coal pits had decided to end their suffering by capitulating. They had joined the British navy.

His rescue mission now pointless, his fleet battered by "high winds and frequent gales from the westward," Jones swung his ships and their accompanying prizes for home. On December 7, off the St. George's fishing bank, Jones again encountered the frigate that he had humiliated back in September—HMS *Milford*. In the gloom, Jones could not be sure of the identity of the looming ship, but since she was bearing down, not running, he made a good guess that she was an enemy man-of-war.

This time Jones could not bob and weave and taunt. The ice-ridden *Alfred* was slow and crank, even tippier than usual because she had almost exhausted the provisions in her hold that served as ballast. Jones needed to use his imagination. He sent for his former first officer and partner in getaways, Lieutenant Rathbun, who was at the moment commanding one of Jones's prizes, the sloop *John*. Jones obviously valued Rathbun's seamanship and resourcefulness and wanted him by his side.

The scheme they cooked up was an old dependable. The *Milford* spotted Jones's small fleet at about three in the afternoon—already dusk so close to the Arctic Circle. Jones ordered the "fastest sailors" in his little flotilla—including the *Mellish*—to make a run for it as soon as nightfall set in. Then he ordered hung from the top of his mainmast a bright light. He was hoping to lead his pursuer on another "wild goose chase" in the night while his most valuable prizes slipped away. The *Milford* took the bait. In the morning, the other ships had escaped, while Jones's nameless antagonist still hung off his quarter "at the same distance as the night before." Jones needed to find out exactly what he was up against. Viewing the pursuer from the bow on, Jones could not count her guns. He ordered his small prize brig, the *John*, to fall astern and hang to windward of the enemy, in order to take a careful look at her broadside. From the *John*, the signal came back, "Superior force." By now the wind had increased "with severe squalls to a hard gale." Jones kicked up his heels and "drove the *Alfred* thro' the water" at seven to eight knots,* a rapid clip for the old merchantman, a poor sailor in most breezes. In the night, the enemy finally broke off the chase—but she captured the unfortunate *John*, whose skipper later complained that he had been abandoned by Jones.

Jones and his crew were worn and ragged by the time they made landfall at Plymouth harbor, south of Boston, on December 14. Beating up the harbor against the wind in a violent snow squall, the *Alfred* missed stays—failed to come about from one tack to the other. She ran aground at low tide and "beat considerably" before the tide lifted her off in the morning. The ship was not damaged, but Jones's pride was wounded. He had captured the *Mellish* and escaped the *Milford* but he had not reached the prisoners in time. "My success hath indeed fallen far short of my wishes," he reported to the Marine Committee.

WHEN JONES ARRIVED in Boston just before Christmas 1776, he did not expect to be welcomed as a conquering hero. On the other hand, he did not expect to be arrested. As he walked down a street in the old port town, he was approached by an elderly lawyer, who was accompanied by the sheriff. The lawyer represented the owner of the *Eagle*, the privateer Jones had found in Tarpaulin Cove in early November. Still smarting over the impressment of his twenty hands, the owner had accused Jones of "piracy" and filed a legal complaint against him.

The sheriff approached Jones to make the arrest. Jones glared at him. He had been thrown in jail once before upon returning from a cruise, and he rankled at the memory of his days in the Tolbooth of Kirkcudbright, unjustly accused in the Mungo Maxwell affair. Jones was determined not to go behind bars again. Eyes blazing, he drew his sword and threatened to "clip" anyone who touched him. The old lawyer was flustered by

---

*A knot is the maritime measure of speed for the number of nautical miles—about one-sixth longer than a regular mile—covered in an hour. An eighteenth-century warship could make ten or twelve knots in ideal conditions, but five knots was more typical.

Jones's defiance. Forgetting that a revolution had just occurred, he stammered that the sheriff was a "King's officer" and that Jones dare not defy him. This just inflamed Jones even more. Brandishing his sword, Jones exclaimed, "Is he? By God, I have a commission then to take his head off!" The sheriff recoiled in horror. "I ain't no king's officer!" he protested. Flummoxed, the lawyer spluttered to the sheriff, "Why don't you take him?" The sheriff replied, "The Devil! Don't you see his poker!"

Jones put away his "poker" and wrote his lawyer, who countersued the owner of the *Eagle* for "inveighling away" the *Alfred's* seamen in the first place. The tangled case was eventually thrown out of the courts. Jones no doubt had a good laugh with his fellow captains as they raised their Yuletide glasses at the local tavern where Jones was staying over Christmas. Any good humor vanished with the new year, however, when he learned that his reward for two straight successful cruises was a demotion.

Incredibly, he was relieved of command of the *Alfred* and offered nothing more promising than a return to his old sloop the *Providence*. Meanwhile, captains of far lesser ability were being given command of new frigates. Jones did not know it yet, but he had been shamefully wronged by the Continental Congress. On October 10, while Jones was catching his breath in Providence between "hairbreadth scapes," the Marine Committee had promulgated a seniority list of captains. The new Continental Navy had a chance to live up to the meritocratic ideals of the Enlightenment, but instead it followed the age-encrusted custom of the Royal Navy. Seniority was crucial in the British navy; it determined the pace of promotion toward flag rank and weighed heavily in the awarding of commands. The first seniority list of the American navy had little to do with service or merit and, to Jones's everlasting chagrin, everything to do with patronage and "interest." Number one on the list was an obscure captain named James Nicholson. He had seen no action, but he had friends on the Marine Committee who rewarded him with a twenty-eight-gun frigate, the *Virginia*. Next was John Manley, who had served with George Washington's navy in 1775 but done very little since—except to travel to Philadelphia, where he stayed for months on end lobbying for position. Described by a fellow officer as "ignorant, obstinate, overbearing, and tyrannical beyond description," Manley was given the frigate *Hancock*, thirty-two guns. At number four was the haughty and incompetent Dudley Saltonstall, awarded the frigate *Trumbull*, twenty-eight guns.

Jones was near the bottom of the list at number eighteen. Even the hopeless Hoystead Hacker stood higher, ranked sixteenth. Jones was beside himself with scorn at the officers who outranked him. He described Thomas Thompson of New Hampshire (frigate *Raleigh*, thirty-two guns) as "a dull inactive genius more fit to be a ship's carpenter than a captain." Jones respected a few of his superiors, especially Hector McNeill, who became his friend and whom he regarded as "a gentleman who will do honor to the service." But in later years he liked to point out that some of his seniors on the rank list initially declined to serve in the Continental Navy out of timidity—because, as his friend Abraham Whipple often told him, "they did not wish to be hanged."

It's not clear when Jones first learned of the seniority list—possibly, no one was brave enough to tell him—but on January 12, 1777, he fulminated to Joseph Hewes: "That such despicable characters should have obtained commissions as commanders in a navy is truly astonishing and [might] pass for romance with me unless I have been convinced by my senses of the sad reality." Jones did not blame Hewes for his low rank: his patron had been away in North Carolina when the list was drawn up, and Jones had no one else in Philadelphia to plump for him. With his Scottish brogue, he was still regarded as a foreigner, and his edgy manner was not likely to win friends. Robert Morris would in time become a protector, but in October 1776, the powerful merchant-politician had been distracted. With the rout of Washington's forces in New York, Philadelphia lay open to attack. Congress was about to flee south to Baltimore.

The Marine Committee was waking up to Jones by the winter of 1777, in part because he was a singular success story on a sea of gloom, and because he demanded to be noticed by his constant flurry of reports, recommendations, and complaints. "You have herein the copy of Capt. Jones's acc[ount] of his last expedition in the *Alfred*," Robert Morris wrote John Hancock, the president of the Continental Congress on January 16. "He is a fine fellow and should be constantly kept employed." Hancock was supportive, if condescending: "I admire the spirited conduct of little Jones. Pray push him out again."

Morris encouraged Jones's outpourings, which he described as "always entertaining and in many parts useful." He saw in Jones a quality that was utterly missing from the minds of most men of the new navy: strategic vision. Jones was a dreamer and planner, not just in the cause of his own advancement, but with the hope of making America a great maritime power that could hold its own with Britain.

Even before the very first expedition to New Providence in the winter of '76, Jones had pushed a bold plan to capture the island of St. Helena off the coast of Africa. Lying in wait at St. Helena, Jones reasoned, American cruisers could intercept the British East Indiamen, laden with riches, which invariably refreshed there as they traveled around the Horn to and from India and Asia. Morris was intrigued by Jones's proposed African expedition and suggested as well a daring raid against British bases at Pensacola, Florida. The particulars mattered less than the overall concept, which can be roughly summarized as: hit 'em where they ain't. Or as Morris elaborated in a letter to Jones on February 5:

> It has long been clear to me that our infant fleet cannot protect our own coasts & that the only effectual relief it can afford us is to attack the enemies' defenseless places and thereby oblige them to station more of their ships in their own countries or to keep them employed in following ours . . . either way we are relieved.

The germ of this idea would grow in Jones's active and scheming mind. Diversionary hit-and-run raids, especially ones that sow fear and panic by striking directly at the enemy's homeland, are a powerful tool for rebels who cannot match the strength of their opponents, and thus must fight a guerrilla war. In the eighteenth century, war was an orderly, ponderous affair, set-piece battles fought between disciplined armies. Although he would not have described himself this way, Jones was a futurist. In his own intuitive way, he was able to see back to the future. The aristocratic notions of warfare of the eighteenth century sought to spare civilian populations from the horrors of siege and pillage, so common to the religious wars of the seventeenth and earlier centuries. The code broke down from time to time. As Jones was well aware, the British had brutally repressed the Scots Highlanders after the rebellion of 1745. But Jones was unusual in that he saw psychological warfare—terror, if you will—as a distinct strategy. Jones could see over the horizon, to an age when war was waged not just against professional armies, but cities and peoples, as it had been in earlier times.

Just as eighteenth-century warfare should not be overidealized, Jones's strategic genius should not be overstated. He was shrewd and prescient, but he did not write with any kind of historical sweep or espouse grand theories of war. He was simply trying to think of a way to leverage America's small force against imperial Britain. But the fact that Jones thought at all set him apart from other captains in the Continental Navy, who remained overawed by British naval power. Like the best of the Founders, who knew the risk of hanging but refused to be intimidated by British superiority, Jones dealt with long odds by pondering how he might undermine the Leviathan. While other captains essentially acted as privateers by chasing British merchantmen or—more commonly—hid safe in their harbors from prowling British cruisers, Jones increasingly turned his attention to this new kind of hit-and-run warfare.

Morris was ready to equip Jones with a small fleet to attack British bases in the Caribbean and along the southern coast of the colonies. "You should take the *Alfred, Columbus, Cabot, Ham[p]den* & Sloop *Providence*," he instructed Jones on February 5. Jones was thrilled to have such an ambitious mission. But he spent the month of February vainly trying to persuade Commodore Hopkins to give him the ships, which were in various stages of disrepair or bottled up in port by British blockaders. Jones held Hopkins responsible for the navy's "wretched condition." For months, the aging commodore had dithered aboard his new frigate, the *Warren*, in

Providence without making any discernible effort to put to sea. Jones was harsh in his judgment of Hopkins. "The navy would be far better without a head than a bad one," he wrote Morris. Unfairly blaming Hopkins for his troubles over the seized seamen from the *Eagle*, Jones refused to submit to his authority.*

Jones would have been wise to have courted Hopkins from the beginning, when he sailed under the old man in the New Providence expedition in the winter of 1776, but his pride got in the way. "You will not blame my free soul, which will never stoop where it cannot esteem," Jones wrote Morris. Hopkins finally grew tired of Jones's carping (much of it behind Hopkins's back) and turned on his too proud captain. He wrote the Marine Committee that Jones was the most unpopular captain in the navy, in part because he refused to pay his men's wages until they reenlisted. Here Hopkins was being unfair: Jones had advanced men money out of his own pocket. But Hopkins was not wrong that Jones's abrasive manner alienated subordinates. Hopkins was also sufficiently well informed to appreciate that Jones owed much of his success aboard the *Providence* to his able number one, Lieutenant Rathbun—a debt Jones himself was too self-centered or churlish to acknowledge.

As usual Jones struggled to reconcile his angry impulses with his sense of duty. On February 28, he wrote Hopkins to ask why it was taking so long to pull together the small fleet bestowed on him by the Marine Committee. Jones was unable to stop himself from dredging up an old slight. Self-conscious about his Scottish roots, Jones had accused Captain Saltonstall, the scion of an old-line Yankee family, of questioning his loyalty to the rebel cause. "I have asked Captain Saltonstall how he could in the beginning suspect me . . . of being unfriendly to America. He seemed

---

*The chain of command was blurry and fragile in the Continental Navy. In instructing Jones to put together a flotilla, Morris was apparently speaking for the Marine Committee, but Hopkins, as fleet commander, seemed to feel free to ignore or thwart his congressional masters. The slow and erratic mails were also a factor: Hopkins didn't get his authorization from Congress until February 28. Jones had already begun to badger Hopkins for leaving him "in the lurch."

astonished at the question and told me that it was yourself who had first promoted it," Jones wrote sulkily to Hopkins.

But then Jones caught himself. "The best way is to cooperate cheerfully," Jones continued. "I am earnest to do everything with good nature." If only Jones had heeded his own admonitions, much of his recurring difficulty with rebellious crews and hostile or diffident superiors might have been avoided. In any case, it was too late to make amends with Hopkins. Luckily for Jones, the aging commodore was on the way out. The Continental Congress, too, had wearied of his inertia, the fleet commander's bland resistance to their insistent prodding that he get his ships out of port and into the fight. Hopkins was soon to be suspended from his post and ultimately dismissed from the navy.

Jones decided to go in person to the Marine Committee to demand a ship—if not command of a flotilla, then any ship. Congress had slunk back to Philadelphia when Lord Howe failed to take the city during the winter (a temporary reprieve: Philadelphia would fall in September). As the heavy snows of frigid winter melted in March, Jones rode on horseback, skirting the British forces in New York, down the muddy post road to Philadelphia.

At the State House, he was effusively received by John Hancock, the president of the Continental Congress. Grand and unctuous, the wealthy Bostonian praised Jones and proceeded to double-cross him.

Jones wanted to rectify the injustice of the seniority list. Hancock promised that he would push back the date on his captain's commission from August 8 to May 10, 1776, the day Jones first took command of the *Providence.* Hancock asked Jones to leave the actual commission with him so that he could do the necessary paperwork. But when Jones returned the day before his departure, Hancock had changed the date—not to May 10 but to *October* 10 and written "18"—Jones's cursed rank on the seniority list—in the margin. "I told him that was not what I had expected and demanded my former commission," recorded Jones. "He turned over various papers on the table, and at last told me he was very sorry to have lost or mislaid it." Hancock, possibly, was overburdened or careless, but Jones naturally assumed he was malicious. Certainly, the two men were badly matched, alike only in pride. Jones regarded Hancock to be one in a long line of snobbish superiors who condescended to him. Hancock viewed "the little Jones" as a pushy Scotsman, a serving-class schemer with pretensions above his station. Though Jones was capable of flattery and ingratiation, he had difficulty hiding his testy moods.

The imposing Boston merchant may have reminded Jones of Mr. Craik, the imperious laird of Arbigland who had lorded over his father. Jones was not the first or last military man to feel under-appreciated by his civilian masters, but his resentment was sharpened by childhood experience as a pawn in the master-servant gamesmanship at Arbigland. Just as Arbigland could not be beautiful without Paul Senior's gardens, the new America could not be free without a strong navy to stand up to the British. It galled Jones to be treated shabbily, to have his contribution slighted by a stuffed shirt who had never stood on a quarterdeck under enemy fire. Describing the scene in a letter to Robert Morris written six years later, Jones stiffly wrote, "I shall here make no remark on such conduct in a President of Congress." Jones swallowed his anger and noted that Hancock had "paid me many compliments" and assured him of future commands. But the letter's tone makes clear that in 1783 Jones was still seething over long-ago slights.

Feeling aggrieved and wondering whether he would ever get another ship, Jones returned to Boston in late April of 1777. The city was as desolate as his mood. Once a bustling port, Boston had been roughed up by the British occupation. For firewood during General Washington's siege, the lobsterbacks had cut down most of the city's trees. The Liberty Tree, the rallying point for the rebels, had been reduced to a stump. When the British pulled out in March of 1776, over a thousand of the loyalist Bostonians had sailed with them for Halifax. In the spring of 1777, Jones had plenty of time to wander Boston's denuded streets, past its shuttered buildings, to the wharves, no longer smelling of imported spices—few merchantmen dared slip by the British cruisers hovering offshore—but instead reeking of dead fish and low tide.

He must have felt a twinge of bitterness to see, moored in the harbor, the brand-new frigate *Hancock*, thirty-two guns. She had been named after the perfidious president of the Continental Congress; her magnificent carved figurehead represented the great man himself, decked out in yellow breeches, a blue coat, and a cocked hat with lace. Equally galling was the *Hancock's* captain, Captain John Manley, "who keeps us at awful distance," Jones wrote sarcastically, by flying the broad pendant of the kind traditionally used by a Royal Navy commodore. Jones scoffed that Manley's brief service in the British navy had been as a "boatswain's mate."

It was a low, lonely time for a man given to solitary brooding. But Jones proved resilient. Another disappointed captain would have offered his services to the owner of a privateer—there were plenty of them about—and set sail to fatten his purse. Jones could have made his fortune, bought his farm, and retired to a life of "calm contemplation and poetic ease." But he stuck with the navy. Despite his many disappointments, he had high hopes that America would become a power on the seas and that he would be at the head of its fleet. Jones did plenty of whining, but there was an element of cussedness in him that sustained his dreams of glory. Perhaps he was not as nobly stoic as George Washington or as sure of the essential rightness of the cause as John Adams. But the effect was the same. While other summer soldiers went home, Jones was one of the men who stood fast.

Jones, though essentially a loner, enjoyed society and the company of fellow sea rovers. In Boston, he found congenial company in the captain of the frigate *Boston*, Hector McNeill. A fellow Scotsman with an edgy sense of humor, McNeill had once been captured by Indians and nearly killed with a tomahawk. With McNeill, Jones enjoyed making fun of Manley and the other political captains.

Jones also resumed his association with the Masons. He was not a carouser, but he liked to talk about poetry and politics. The St. Andrew's Lodge was a hotbed of revolutionary agitation. According to Masonic lore, the Boston Tea Party was plotted at the Masons' meeting place, the Green Dragon tavern. Paul Revere was an active member, but the lodge's greatest hero was General Joseph Warren, the Masonic Grand Master who was bayoneted to death by the redcoats as he rallied the rebel line during the Battle of Bunker Hill in June of 1775.

As always, there was time for the ladies. Jones was a lothario, but his interest in the fairer sex was not always low-minded. Sometime during his stay, he made a remarkable friendship with the black poetess Phillis Wheatley. Small-boned and frail, she was named after the slave ship she arrived on, the *Phillis*. Sold to a well-off Boston family as a household maid, she showed extraordinary precocity as a young girl, learning Latin so well that, in between making beds and mopping floors, she translated heroic couplets from Ovid. She began writing verses that sound very much like Jones's favorite, the pre-Romantic poet James Thomson.

The wealthy white men who served as the city's worthies could not believe what they heard about the girl. An investigation was launched. A committee of these stuffy wise men, including John Hancock, convened to determine whether this slip of a slave girl was capable of true literary merit. Under interrogation, she passed with flying colors. The "uncultivated Barbarian from *Africa*," as she was described in a public "Attestation," was found to be the true author of her poems. "She has been examined by some of the best Judges, and is thought qualified to write them," concluded the judges. She became a curiosity and a bit of a celebrity in Boston society. Freed by her master in 1773, she was paraded around London before the war, where she was visited by a curious Benjamin Franklin. Returning to Massachusetts, she called on General Washington at his encampment at Cambridge. She wrote a patriotic ode to Washington and other verses that likely appealed to Jones, including one called "To a Gentleman of the Navy." (These verses were penned before she met Jones, but the tone was suitably heroic.)

Jones's relationship with Wheatley was certainly cordial and may have been flirtatious or romantic. The two understood what it was like to be the object of condescension by a less clever man (in their case, the same man, John Hancock). Wheatley wrote powerfully about a subject familiar to the former slaver. "In every human breast, God has implanted a principle, which we call love of freedom. It is impatient of oppression and pants for deliverance." At some point in his dogged self-education, Jones had begun to write poetry, and he now sent her some of his own verses. As he was leaving to go to sea in the summer of 1777, he wrote his friend Hector McNeill, instructing him to put some verses "into the hands of the celebrated Phillis the African favorite of the Nine [Muses] and Apollo."

Were they love poems? The verses he enclosed with the note to McNeill have not survived, but Professor James Bradford of Texas A&M University, who collected and annotated Jones's papers, speculates that one of them was "Pity So Excellent a Face." The poem is about a black-and-white profile of a lady's head that conceals her true features: "Pity so excellent a face/Should in the *shade* preserve thy name,/Such beauty, harmony, and grace,/The painter's softest taints may claim!" Could this be an allusion, at once clumsy and delicate, to the color of Phillis's skin somehow obscuring her inner radiance? Possibly. Jones's racial attitudes were typical of his time, notwithstanding his fascination with the "African Muse" and his convert's loathing of the slave trade.*

Jones's time "on the beach" in Boston was not spent entirely on Masonic fellowship and writing poems to the gentler sex. In addition to his tireless flow of letters to the Marine Committee, he met regularly with other naval officers to discuss "useful rules & regulations." "We have had sundry meetings here for this purpose without being able to effect anything," Jones grumped to Morris. Jones decided to ignore collective wisdom and make his own suggestions: "I have determined that if I subscribe to nonsense it shall be nonsense of my own not that of others!" he wrote, jocularly, but revealing his solitary bent.

Jones did agree with his brother officers on one particular matter: that the uniforms prescribed by the Continental Congress were dowdy. In September, Congress had decreed that the ship's captains should wear a red waistcoat and blue coat and blue breeches. Not dashing enough, Jones

---

*A later verse suggests he was writing about a blue-eyed white woman: "Carnation and the blushing rose,/Should with the lily, vie./And grace, beyond all art disclose,/The mild blue lustre of thy eye." Jones sometimes sent slightly amended versions of the same poem to two different women, depending on their characteristics and circumstances.

believed. In March, he convened a committee of captains to design a
smarter uniform: blue coat, white breeches, and white waistcoat. This was
exactly the dress of a captain in the British navy. Jones was motivated by
both envy and cunning. Wearing the same uniform as a British captain
might convey some martial equivalency—and it would aid in pulling off a
ruse de guerre, making the officers play the part in a masquerade of a
British man-of-war. Jones added another, non-British touch, this borrowed from the French. On dress uniforms, all officers would be entitled
to wear one gilt epaulet. This fashion, not widely accepted by the English
until the early nineteenth century, had the effect of making short captains—like Jones and Nelson—look taller. The uniform recommendations, adopted by a committee that included Jones, Manley, McNeill, and
Saltonstall on February 27, were not adopted by Congress. No matter:
Jones was an actor on his own great stage. He needed proper costumes.
When it suited him—especially when going into battle—Jones wore a
blue coat, white breeches, and white waistcoat—the uniform of a British
naval officer.

Jones always went his own way. A fellow captain, William Grinnell,
tried to persuade Jones to settle down. "You young bachelors may think
[it] strange," Grinnell wrote Jones, but "in hard times," marriage was a
"grand step" toward softening and civilizing a man. "Therefore I have
made that leap," Grinnell wrote. He had married the woman, he wrote
Jones, that "you called the idol of my affections." Now his bride was offering to play matchmaker for Jones: "Mrs. Grinnell begs you will excuse her
boldness. She will give you letters to some ladies that she is certain will be
very agreeable to you. . . . The little angels at Salem are waiting for you."

But Jones wasn't interested in the "little angels of Salem" or anywhere
else, save for passing pleasure and amusement. He had too much to accomplish in his own cause. On he strove, seeking to be recognized as a
gentleman, unaware that that he was becoming something more native to
his new nation, a self-made man.

CHAPTER FIVE

"Delicate Notions of Honor"

*J*ONES FRETTED, he stewed, he longed for a ship. In the spring of 1777, he killed time by sitting on a court-martial of some seamen accused of mutiny. He despaired over the illiteracy of his brother officers. The captain of marines of the mutiny ship made a mark on court documents because he could not sign his own name, and the president of the court-martial, a fellow navy captain, could not administer the oath without stumbling and spelling aloud some of the words, like a child learning to read. What, Jones wondered, would sophisticated foreigners make of American sea officers who were, as he put it, "so rude"?

Jones was shaken out of his contemptuous musings by a letter from the Continental Congress, dated May 9. It was an order from the Secret Committee, set up early in the Revolution to clandestinely purchase arms and gunpowder from abroad. Jones was ordered to proceed to Portsmouth, New Hampshire, to embark on a twenty-gun French ship, the *Amphitrite*, that would carry him to France. There, the American commissioners to France—Benjamin Franklin, Silas Deane, and Arthur Lee—would procure him a "fine frigate."

A fine frigate! Jones learned that two men-of-war of thirty-two guns— 18- and 24-pounders, real smashers—were under construction in France. He could sail to glory in such a powerful cruiser. But the French captain of the *Amphitrite* refused to take him under the conditions imposed by Congress—that the two captains share command in battle and prize money—so Jones stewed some more. His joy was quickly restored when, on June 14, Congress authorized Jones to take command of a brand-new twenty-gun sloop, the *Ranger*. Jones was to proceed to New Hampshire to pick up the *Ranger*, then sail to France, where he would take command of his new frigate and cruise, with the *Ranger* as escort, against the enemy.

Jones couldn't contain his eagerness. "I ardently wish to be again on active service," he wrote the American commissioners in Paris in early June. His mind was alive with strategems. He was thinking of ways to employ what later generations would call psychological warfare or, more bluntly, terrorism. (Jones was not so bloodthirsty as the twenty-first-century variety—he intended to scare, not actually kill, civilians.) To his friend Robert Morris, he described how he would frighten the British by threatening the security of their homes. He described a scheme for putting English cities "under contribution," meaning holding them ransom with threats to burn or destroy homes and shipping. In July he wrote Morris that "even a trifling force" could wreak havoc on England's unprotected coasts. Unlike continental Europeans, Englishmen complacently believed their island nation was invulnerable. "I know them to be subject to panic under the least surprise," Jones wrote.

Jones received his orders to go to Portsmouth and take command of the *Ranger* on July 2. He was soon ordering up recruiting posters:

GREAT ENCOURAGEMENT FOR SEAMEN

ALL GENTLEMAN SEAMEN and able-bodied LANDSMEN who have a mind to distinguish themselves in the GLORIOUS CAUSE of their country, and make their Fortunes, an Opportunity now offers on board the Ship RANGER, of 20 Guns, (for France) now laying off Portsmouth, in the state of New Hampshire, commanded by JOHN PAUL JONES Esq.

Jones took some poetic license with his description of the *Ranger*, "one of the best Cruisers in America—She will always be able to Fight her

Guns under a most excellent Cover [deck]; and no Vessel yet built was ever calculated for sailing faster, and making good Weather." Possibly he was being wishful, not misleading. The ship was "scarcely half-rigged" when he first saw her.

Jones was determined to get under way as quickly as possible—"in a shorter space of time than any ship hath yet been fitted in the service," he vowed. But when he arrived in Portsmouth in mid-July, he was disappointed to discover that *Ranger*'s mast and spars were bare and that her "warlike" stores—armaments and ammunition—were still wanting. To his intense irritation, her "cordage and canvas"—ropes and sails—had been provided as "extra stores" to the frigate *Raleigh*, which rode at her anchor as "laden as deep as a merchant ship." The *Raleigh*'s precedence provoked Jones's hair-trigger envy and resentment. Her captain was Thomas Thompson, that "dull inactive genius" who, Jones had groused, was better suited to "carpentry" than the art of war. Jones was still fretting that Thompson had been placed ahead of him on the seniority list, entitling him to one of the new frigates ordered up by Congress. Jones feared that when he reached France, he would be put under Captain Thompson's orders.

"I dread such dishonor worse than death," Jones wrote his patron Joseph Hewes. In several letters to Hewes and Robert Morris, Jones worked up his indignation: "My honor must be sacred, and I am determined never to draw my sword under the command of any man who was not in the navy as early as myself, unless he hath merited a preference by his superior services and abilities." Characteristically, Jones realized that he had gone overboard, for he later wrote, a little defensively, "I am not under a childish pet. . . . I mean only to express my sentiments in decent tho' manly language."

Fitting the *Ranger* for war proved to be slow and frustrating. As usual the privateers had siphoned off the most experienced seamen, and Jones had to ask the New Hampshire state legislature to allow him to draft twenty cannoneers from the batteries defending Portsmouth harbor. Built with rakish lines, *Ranger* was a beautiful vessel—*un parfait bijou*, one

Frenchman later called her, a perfect jewel. About 110 feet long, she was a three-masted sloop-of-war or corvette, meaning that her guns were all on one deck, covered with the quarterdeck toward the stern, the gangway at the waist, and the forecastle toward the bow. But on close inspection— and few captains inspected more closely than the fastidious Jones—*Ranger* was not quite the sleek fast-sailer he had hoped for and advertised. Because of a shortage of the proper timber, she had been built with a mast and spars large enough to serve a much bigger ship. With his practiced eye, Jones could tell at once she was oversparred, with too much weight abovedeck. In a stiff breeze, she would be crank, heel too far over. Jones partly resolved this problem by removing two heavy cannon from her deck and cutting back the mast and spars. But until he had sailed her, he would not know precisely where to begin tinkering (and then he never stopped).

At the mouth of the Piscataqua River, which flows out of the New Hampshire forests, Portsmouth was the main port in New England for timber. So Jones understandably questioned why the ship's builder, John Langdon, was unable to find the proper masts for the *Ranger*. Jones suspected that Langdon favored his other interests, including several privateers. Never one to disguise his impatience, nor able to hide any feeling very well, Jones was soon quarreling with Langdon. Unfortunately, Langdon was Congress's naval agent, charged with equipping the navy's ships in Portsmouth, and he did as he pleased. When Langdon asserted his authority, Jones squawked to a friend, "he thinks himself my master—and he, who was bred in a shop and hath been about a voyage or two at sea under a nurse, had once the assurance to tell me that he knew as well as myself how to fit out, govern, and fight a ship of war!" Jones was exaggerating; Langdon had been the master of four different ships, but Jones could only see a profiteering lubber in him.

The two men squabbled over the smallest item. Langdon would not buy him a bos'un's whistle, so Jones ordered two silver ones and put them on his expense account. More seriously, Langdon could not find any decently made sails. Instead of canvas, *Ranger* had to make do with a cheaper material normally used to make gunnysacks. Jones also complained bitterly that Langdon provided his crew of 140 with only thirty gallons of rum, hardly enough to sustain them on a four- to six-week voyage across the Atlantic. Jones could not understand why Langdon had been unable to find rum, hardly a scarce commodity in Portsmouth. It later turned out that the sailors on the *Ranger*, desperate for cash, had sold their allotted rum rations back to Langdon.

Jones had manned the ship with local men from New Hampshire and Massachusetts who were, initially at least, eager for adventure. Jones had high standards for his officers, but he was given a bunch of hacks. He could not appoint his own wardroom. Langdon and William Whipple, a local congressman, controlled this bit of patronage, frequently appointing their friends and relations. The first lieutenant, Thomas Simpson, who was Langdon's brother-in-law, and the second officer, Elijah Hall, had both served in merchantmen but knew nothing about the art of war, Jones complained. Their idea of discipline was considerably more relaxed than Jones's. Both men were older than Jones, and Simpson expected to take over the *Ranger* as soon as the ship reached France. Simpson and Hall regarded Jones less as a superior officer than as a privileged passenger, a rather disagreeable foreigner to whom they had to show deference, but not real respect. Simpson, in particular, was a poor subordinate and no substitute for the able Lieutenant Rathbun. Simpson's flinty New England temperament was sure to clash with Jones's demanding and brooding nature.

Jones fared better in Portsmouth society, whose elitism rivaled that of the Virginia gentry. In Portsmouth, Jones stayed with the widow of a ship's captain, Sarah Purcell, in the best front room of her commodious white clapboard house. Mrs. Purcell was well born, the niece of Benning Wentworth, the royalist governor who had dominated New Hampshire politics before the Revolution. Increasingly well read and well mannered, Jones cut a trimly elegant figure in his captain's uniform, with its unauthorized British navy–style white waistcoat, French-style gilt epaulet, and sword.

Jones was looking for ways to embellish his own borrowed name. He had made $3,000 from his prizes, a not inconsiderable sum for a year's work. He wrote Robert Morris asking him to use half the money to purchase a "small landed estate," Fox's Ferry, on the Mattapony River in the Tidewater of Virginia. He would fight until America had won or lost her freedom, but he would be a squire yet. As a squire, he would need a suitable coat of arms. Possibly, he was thinking of his failure to successfully woo Dorothea Dandridge for a lack of a proper pedigree. Like many self-made men, he decided to make one up. He put an engraver to work fashioning a standard worthy of a lord of the manor. He borrowed the coats of arms and crest of the Jones family of Wales and the Paul family of Gloucestershire, England. Only the motto, a patriotic and idealistic *Pro Republica*, was original.

Jones had heard that Fox's Ferry was a "truly Elysian" property from a friend in Boston, Major John Gizzard Frazer of the 6th Continental Infantry (Massachusetts). Frazer appears to have been a gentlemanly soldier of fortune, a not uncommon type in that era, and also, like Jones, something of a pretender. Frazer was looking for a new chance at glory, and he had asked Jones to take him to the Continent. Major Frazer did not travel light: he asked Jones if he could bring along his "field beds," a case of "the best Jamaica spirit," two Windsor chairs, a backgammon table, and his "girl." He wanted Jones to keep quiet about the girl, whom Jones was to lodge in a "decent private house" in Portsmouth until sailing. "I wish to have as much of her company as I can," Frazer wrote. "Let none of my acquaintances there know of it." Jones was happy to accommodate in such matters. When his friend Hector McNeill, a fellow ladies' man, left for Boston, Jones was disappointed, because his departure deprived the two sea dogs of having "a frolic together."

Though he enjoyed "the ladies of Portsmouth," Jones could not stop brooding about being passed over by "illiterate" captains. "The thought distracts my very soul!" he complained to Robert Morris on October 30. He knew that he should forget about past slights, but the injustice of the seniority list continued to gnaw at him. "Why, alas, should my honor and duty seem incompatible," he wrote Morris. To Hewes he wrote, "I would lay down my life for America—but can never trifle with my delicate notions of honor."

Jones's constant obsession with honor was tiresome, but not uncharacteristic of the age. "Honor was the core of a man's identity, his sense of self, his manhood," writes historian Joanne Freeman in her book *Affairs of Honor.* Men in that age dueled with swords and pistols over mere words of disrespect, slurs like *rascal, scoundrel, liar, coward,* and *puppy.* "These were fighting words, and anyone who hurled them at an opponent was risking his life," according to Freeman. Utter them in a crowded room and "faces blanch. People go still . . . all eyes turn to the accuser and his victim." Jones's *amour propre* was easily wounded, even by eighteenth-century standards. And yet it is significant that Jones never fought in a duel—though, as we shall see, he was challenged and provoked. Jones understood that vanity and ego had to be subordinated to higher virtue. He moaned and groaned to Morris and Hewes, but in the end he placed duty over pride.

Jones's prideful pouting was aggravated by impatience. He wrote those letters to Hewes and Morris while a "heavy gale from the N.E." raged along the New England coast. "When it clears up I purpose to embrace the first wind that can carry me through the enemy's lines and off the coast." The next day the storm blew away. A dome of crystalline blue sky settled over New England; the trees, shorn of their last leaves by the gale, cast long shadows in the waning October light. At 9 A.M. on November 1, 1777, the *Ranger* swept down the Piscataqua River with the tide and out to sea, surging along the whitecaps, her gunnysack sails bellied out, past the British cruisers, bound for France. Jones's mood had improved: he was carrying dispatches with the "joyful and important news" that the Americans had scored a great victory, compelling the surrender of General Burgoyne's army at Saratoga. The news of British humiliation, he believed, was sure to help draw France closer to entering the fray against her ancient enemy.

Halfway across the Atlantic, *Ranger* nearly rolled over in the high seas of a spent gale. Her tiller rope parted, and the top-heavy ship almost broached as she slew around uncontrollably. But after a sickening moment, knocked over by a gust on her beam ends, she righted, green water spouting from her scuppers. The rest of the voyage was pleasantly uneventful—until she was almost in sight of Land's End off the English coast. The lookout spotted seventeen sail, and Jones ordered his men to give chase. *Ranger* had chanced upon a fleet of British merchantmen returning from Gibraltar under the protection of a seventy-four-gun ship of the line, *Invincible.* The mood among the crew, untested in battle, quickly went from eager expectation at the prospect of picking up prizes to panic at being blown out of the water by a man-o-war. Jones impressed the men with his coolness and cleverness. "Our captain took a very wise step," an officer later wrote home, "which was to heave to with the convoy." The fox played sheep, pretending to be a merchantman until nightfall. The British "74," *Invincible,* never noticed the intruder. "Had he suspected us to be Americans, we must have been captured," wrote the admiring junior officer, whose unsigned account was printed in the *New Hampshire Gazette.* "I expect we shall have bloody noses before we return, especially if Capt. Jones keeps the *Ranger,* for he had as lives run alongside a frigate as a merchantman . . . he is a gentleman of great COURAGE and CONDUCT, and is deserving of the best ship in America; his men greatly like him." Jones's subordinates liked the man in action all right. Their enthusiasm for Jones-the-stickler would soon wane.

Jones was frustrated not to cut a couple of prizes out of the Gibralter fleet, but "the continued alarms night and day . . . afforded me excellent opportunities of exercising the officers and men especially in the night," he wrote Congressman Whipple. To the Marine Committee he reported, "I have had agreeable proofs of the active spirit of both my officers & men . . . they pay more attention to instruction than conceited fellows who think themselves too knowing to be taught."

Jones would reverse that judgment soon enough. Still, he was in an ebullient mood when the *Ranger* anchored in the port of Nantes on December 2. Nine days later he wrote a cheery, tongue-in-cheek letter to John Wendell, a well-born Portsmouth gentleman Jones hoped to impress and whose son had joined *Ranger* as a midshipman. The letter was studded with literary allusions to Neptune and Boreus and written in the high style of a Romantic novel ("When lo! This Halcyon season was interrupted! The 'gathering Fleets o'erspread the Sea' and Wars alarms began!"). "Since I am not certain my poetry will be understood," Jones continued drily, "it may not be amiss to add . . . that after leaving Portsmouth nothing remarkable happened" until the brush with the British 74. The captain of the *Ranger* announced himself "much pleased" with the "diffidence and modesty" of young Midshipman Wendell. He made his compliments to "the fair Miss Wendell" (Wendell's daughter, whom Jones had flirted with) and "the other agreeable ladies of my acquaintance in Portsmouth."

Jones did have a few discordant notes to report. The *Ranger* was crank, as he had suspected, and slow from a foul bottom. Major Frazer turned out to be a "person different from what I thought him in America," Jones wrote Morris. "He is subject to drink even to intoxication . . . charity obliges me to think it is rather a habit acquired from disappointment than a constitutional vice." While Morris quaffed rum, Jones had stuck to wine in moderation. Drunkenness, wrote Jones, "is a weakness utterly incompatible with the characteristic of a good officer." Frazer was neither the first nor last flashy figure to fool, then let down Jones.

Jones received some disappointing news when he arrived in France. The "fine frigate" promised by Congress was not to be his after all. The *Indien*, under construction in Amsterdam, had been sold to the French. The Dutch had come under pressure from the British not to sell a warship to the Americans, and Congress, always short of cash, couldn't really afford her anyway. Still, Jones felt "unfeigned thanks" to the American commissioners in Paris for even attempting to buy for him such a grand ship, "one of the finest frigates that ever was built." Jones took the effort as a sign of respect; it eased his suffering over the inequity of the seniority list.

Jones was bursting with battle plans to try out on the commissioners. He wanted not just a ship but a squadron to sail as a stealthy pack of raiders. Jones's greater goal, beyond terrifying the English coast, was to renew his effort to free American prisoners languishing in English jails. He was angry that privateers released their prisoners instead of holding them hostage to exchange for the release of the Americans. "Were this base conduct practiced by those licensed robbers alone, 'I should have found within my soul one drop of patience,'" he wrote, "but to find individuals in our navy affected with the same foul contagion racks me with distressing passions and covers me with shame!" He blamed Captain Manley, one of his undeserving superiors on the Continental Navy's seniority list, for turning over eighty British prisoners without a fight. Meanwhile Jones ranted to Morris, "our cruel enemies are enforcing an act of parliament" that captured Americans were not to be treated as prisoners of war but rather as "Traitors & pirates & felons! Whose necks they wish to destine to the cord! And whose hearts they wish to destine to the flames!"

Jones was eager to explain the brilliance of his plan and the urgency of his mission to the American commissioners. Shortly before Christmas 1777, he climbed into a carriage bound for Paris.

THE FRENCH CAPITAL would become Jones's only real home, the city most appreciative of his martial prowess. The metropolis he saw for the first time in the grayness of December was, even to an eighteenth-century eye accustomed to extremes, extravagant beyond all imagining, a jarring mix of refinement and elegance, bawdiness and filth. If Jones arrived early in the morning, he might have bumped into one of the 7,000 barbers making their way through the streets to wash and coif the hair of gentlemen; wigs had just gone out of fashion, and men liked to have their hair curled, pomaded, and powdered. (Women, whose hair was piled high in elaborate constructions, went weeks without a shampoo.) He arrived too late in the year for the 5 P.M. parade of prostitutes, who on warmer days stood on chairs and hiked up their skirts in front of passing gentlemen in the Tuileries gardens. Snow or sun, cold or warm, the streets were always covered in *la boue de Paris*, a thick black slime of excrement, blood from animals slaughtered by butchers outside their shops, and mud so acidic it ate the hems of ladies' dresses. If Jones drank the water, he probably got sick. Pumped from the Seine and allowed to "clarify" in large bottles for a few days, Parisian water was murky and laxative. The rich bought bottled mineral water instead. Yet if Jones was brought low by the squalor, his romantic imagination was also fired by the city's grandeur, its classical domes and Gothic spires, bridges and colonnades, mighty and brooding in the gloomy short days of winter.

Jones did not stay in Paris long that December. He immediately traveled to Passy, an elegant suburb (then just outside the city, now the 16th arrondissement) of chateaux and villas. His destination was the Hôtel Valentinois, a pair of Neoclassical pavilions set amidst terraces and gardens, drab and brown in winter, but still gracefully framed by an alley of linden trees. There he found an odd household of diplomats, soldiers of fortune, war profiteers, well-born French ladies, and, though Jones did not know it, British spies. The Hôtel Valentinois served as American headquarters in Paris. It was described by one American merchant, passing through, as a "princely residence." John Adams, who arrived in Passy a few months after Jones, fretted, with characteristic Yankee frugality, about the magnificence of the estate and wondered what it was costing the badly strapped Congress.

The answer was very little, at least for the time being. The Americans' generous host was Jacques-Donatien Leray de Chaumont. He was, like Jones, a self-made man, and he would become Jones's main financier and supplier. A merchant prince who had become hugely rich in the East India trade, the middle-class Leray had bought the fifteenth-century château Chaumont, a former royal residence in the Loire valley, thereby adding the more aristocratic "de Chaumont" to his name. He also bought influence in the court of Louis XVI, using his sense of civic duty and deep pockets to win the titles of Superintendent of the Hôtel des Invalides, Overseer of the King's Forests, and Commissary of the French Army. Out of a deep grudge against the British Empire, as well as a desire to corner the emerging American market, he coveted one more title: "le grand munitionnaire des Americans." He became a sort of one-man military-industrial complex for the American cause: his East Indiamen carried saltpeter, the vital ingredient of gunpowder, and his peasants in the Loire valley sewed soldiers' uniforms.

His aid was a godsend to the Continental Army, which was so low on gunpowder that early in the war its cannons had fallen silent at Bunker Hill, unable to resist a third British charge, which broke the rebel line. Chaumont was a cog in the great power machinations of the late eighteenth century. The French were eager to help foment revolution against their global rivals the British, though discreetly at first. Merchants like Chaumont gave the French government camouflage. They acted as cutouts, funneling war supplies to the American cause without direct involvement by the King. Louis XVI hated the British, who had humiliated the French in the Seven Years War. "I tremble, I shake, I even turn purple at the very thought of England," the French King once exclaimed. But less hawkish than his father, Louis XV, he was wary of going to war. His foreign minister, the calculating Comte de Vergennes, was slowly building the French military, particularly its navy. The French had taken on the Royal Navy with a weak navy at the start of the Seven Years War in 1756. By 1778, France would have 264 ships, seventy-eight of them ships of the line. While the court of Louis XVI had little sympathy for republican revolutionaries, the King's ministers recognized a more timeless principle, that the enemy of one's enemy is one's friend. The American Revolution was a welcome diversion, sapping Britain's strength while France renewed hers.

Before the French government openly embraced America, Vergennes needed to convince the King that the rebels had staying power. The Revolution had appeared wobbly. In September 1777, the British marched into Philadelphia. But then in October, Burgoyne's drive to split the colonies from north to south came to grief at Saratoga. The news of the British surrender allowed Vergennes to argue that France needed to make a formal alliance with America before the resurgent rebels signed a separate peace with Britain.

Jones did not actually have the pleasure of delivering the good tidings. By a few days, the *Ranger* had been beaten by another American ship carrying dispatches. Still, Jones understood that such a tremendous victory over the British brought America credibility across the Continent. "It is with great pleasure that I see the political system of almost every power in Europe changing in our favor since the news of our late successes," Jones wrote a friend on December 22. The balance was certainly tipping at Versailles. In February, the ancient enemy of Great Britain and the brand-new republic would sign a formal treaty of alliance.

The three American commissioners working to seal that pact—Franklin, Deane, and Lee—formed an uneasy alliance of their own. Deane and Franklin lived at the Hôtel de Valentinois, but Lee preferred his own quarters in the city. A Virginia aristocrat educated at Eton, a bilious man with yellow skin and yellow teeth, Arthur Lee was a conniver leery of everyone. He suspected—correctly as it turned out—that his fellow commissioner Silas Deane was a war profiteer and an embezzler. Jones was quickly caught in the middle of this feud: Lee refused to sign the commissioners' orders to Jones in mid-January because he suspected that the prize agent designated by the orders was giving kickbacks to Deane. Lee was the sort of snob that Jones had suffered before; in the coming intrigues between the jealous commissioners, Lee would be no friend to Jones.

One important American official at Hôtel de Valentinois *pretended* to be Jones's friend. Edward Bancroft, the diplomatic secretary to Benjamin Franklin, was one of the most intriguing characters of the Revolutionary War. A great deceiver, he was a turncoat whose devious manueverings could have sunk the rebel cause, not to mention Jones.

Bancroft was said by colleagues to have a "gentle nature." At thirty-two, he was only a year older than Jones, and like Jones, he had used his intelligence and love of learning to achieve upward mobility. The son of a tavern owner in New England, he had been, like Jones, a restless apprentice keen on getting ahead. Running away to South America, he had used his cleverness to become the protégé of a University of Edinburgh–trained doctor, Paul Wentworth, of the same famous New Hampshire family known to Jones from his pleasant time in Portsmouth society. Moving to London, Bancroft won a reputation as a scientist in the early 1770s and became a fellow in the Royal Society. His work on inks, dyes, poisons, and electric eels caught the attention of the most famous American scientist in London at the time, Ben Franklin. The old philosopher made young Bancroft his charge. When Franklin went to Paris as one of the American commissioners in 1776, Bancroft came along as his secretary.

Bancroft pretended to be a selfless patriot. Actually, he was corrupt. He collaborated with Silas Deane to profit personally from the secret arms trade between America and France, and he used his inside information about the progress of the war to make a killing on the London stock exchange. Bancroft's coziness—he was a lively gossip—and his apparent faith in the positive role of scientific inquiry disguised a dark side. He did not really subscribe, like other scientific gentlemen of the Enlightenment, to the power of reason. Rather, as he wrote in a novel under a pseudonym, he believed that "passions governed the will." He had a creepy fascination with the science of witchcraft. In Surinam, he had watched avidly as natives experimented with a poison, curare, that caused a "slow but inevitable death."

Bancroft's double life went beyond writing novels and dabbling with native potions. He was one of Britain's most important spies. He had been recruited to spy on Ben Franklin by his earlier mentor, Paul Wentworth, who, as it turned out, was a top British agent, reporting directly to the British Foreign Office. As Franklin's secretary, Bancroft had access to all of America's secret diplomacy with France. For the payment of £400 to £500 a year (the equivalent of $70,000 today), he passed on Franklin's correspondence with Congress, the sailing dates of ships carrying contraband, the names of their captains, the invoices of their cargo. His secret communications were written in invisible ink (of his own invention) for Lord Stormont, the British ambassador to France, whom he provided with a special wash to make the ink reappear.

Spies were everywhere in Paris, and even more counterspies shadowed them. Somehow, Bancroft managed not to get caught. Every Tuesday evening before 9:30, Bancroft placed the letters in a sealed bottle, which he placed in a hole in a tree on the south terrace of the Tuileries. Then he picked up Stormont's instructions, hidden under a box tree in another part of the garden. Stormont was almost too well informed about Franco-American dealings. In a meeting with Vergennes, the British ambassador once slipped up by protesting a secret American communication to the French—before the French foreign minister had received the document himself. Armed with Bancroft's information, the British could send cruisers across the path of French ships carrying secret letters and supplies to the United States. In his first year in France, not a single one of Franklin's letters made it to the Continental Congress.

Bancroft had every reason to be lighthearted and friendly when he met Jones at the Hôtel Valentinois at Christmastime 1777. He had just profited handsomely by anticipating that the value of stocks on the London 'change would plunge on the shocking news of Burgoyne's surrender at Saratoga. It was probably Bancroft, reporting to Wentworth in London, who cost Jones that "fine frigate" he had been counting on. When the British government learned from its spies that the frigate *Indien* would be sold to the Americans at Ben Franklin's request, the British leaned on the Dutch not to make the sale.

In retrospect, it is remarkable that Jones never guessed that Bancroft was a spy. Jones's letters to Bancroft during the Revolution were more intimate and confiding than those to anyone else (male, that is). Bancroft was a less frequent correspondent, but Jones had ample opportunity to observe Bancroft and detect any subterfuge beneath the gossip and *bonhomie*. Given Jones's wary, sensitive nature, he might have sensed something amiss. But he never did.

Ben Franklin professed not to care about being spied upon. Warned by a friend to watch out for spies, he wrote back: "I have long observed one rule . . . to be concerned in no affairs that I should blush to have made public. . . . If I was sure, therefore, that my *valet de place* was a spy, as he probably is, I think I should not discharge him for that, if for other reasons, I liked him." Franklin was either being naive or, more likely, disingenuous. He had perhaps grown lackadaisical at the end of a long career. He should have been more alert: he had critical secrets to keep. He was working for not one but two clandestine organizations set up by Congress (the Secret Committee to procure arms and the Committee of Secret Correspondence to win allies). A valet who might spy on one's private life is embarrassing, but a diplomatic secretary who tips off the enemy to troop movements is lethal.

It is hard to know what Franklin really believed. He was a sly man masquerading as a simple one. Praised by Voltaire for his enlightenment, honored by the Royal Society for his many scientific discoveries, Dr. Franklin, now entering his eighth decade, was wildly popular in France. Medallions and snuff boxes with his image popped up all over Paris. His scraggly, unpowdered hair, his plain Quaker clothes, were chattered about as reverse *chic*. He often remained enigmatically silent at dinner, establishing an aura of mystery and wisdom, especially useful since he didn't speak French very well. Still, he was intuitive, patient, and cunning. He had an air of detachment, of equanimity that John Paul Jones would quickly come to revere and envy. Like Jones, Franklin was better at reciting virtues than practicing them. The man who coined the phrase "early to bed and early to rise," who extolled the rewards of hard work, temperance, and frugality, led an existence that seemed downright slothful and indolent to the censorious John Adams. But unlike Jones, who constantly wrestled with his conscience as he tried and failed to subdue his ego and vanity, Franklin appeared serene about his mild dissolution.

During his fortnight at Passy, Jones got a taste of *la vie douceur* at the Hôtel de Valentinois. As he walked through a salon called the Lantern Room, his eyes may have widened at a wall of paintings by masters including Rembrandt and Rubens. Franklin liked music, especially Scottish airs, so Jones's ears would have been pleasantly and perhaps nostalgically piqued by the light entertainment arranged in the evenings. Eager to improve his manners, he would have observed the odd French custom of kissing a lady on the neck so as not to disturb her makeup, bright circles of rouge on the cheek. A French duke once complained that dinner with Ben Franklin consisted of "only one service, and then everything all at once, without soup." But "everything" would have been a gastronomic marvel to a sea captain who had been existing on salt pork. At dinner, usually served around two o'clock in the afternoon, Franklin's guests dined on a joint of veal or beef or mutton, followed by fowl or game in season, with two side dishes, vegetable courses, pickles, radishes, pastries, two kinds of fruit in winter or four in summer, compotes, cheeses, ices, bonbons, and rivers of fine wine, brandy, and champagne.

The conversation was gay and also all at once. Jones, whose French was almost nonexistent, would have understood very little of it. But he could not have helped but notice the flirtatious banter and ribald undercurrents. The French upper classes were astonishingly frank about sex and earthy in their humor. They joked about the coincidence between the King's complaints about the pain in his foreskin, *son prépuce*, the supposed source of his sexual shyness with the Queen, and the Queen's fondness of the color puce. (When the shyness was overcome and at last an heir produced, the Queen began dressing in shades of brown dubbed *"caca dauphin"*.) Although poor and middle-class women could be whipped and driven into a convent for adultery, among the nobility, a man was expected to take a mistress and their wives did not always sit lonely. At Versailles, the Bourbon palace outside Paris, "a faithful husband cut a ridiculous figure," observed one writer of the period. Arriving four months after Jones, John Adams (who would replace Deane, recalled to account to Congress for his self-dealing), was shocked by the casual licentiousness. At dinner on his second night in Paris, he learned that both the host and hostess, a properly married couple, had brought their lovers to the table. "I was astonished that these people could live together in such apparent friendship and indeed without cutting each others throats. But I do not know the World," wrote Adams:

I soon saw and heard so much of these things in other families and almost all of the great people of the kingdom that I found it was a thing of course. It was universally understood and nobody lost any reputation by it.

The hostess at that dinner, Madame Brillon de Jouy, was a manipulative beauty who enjoyed an *amitié amoureuse*, a teasing, unconsummated flirtation with Franklin, who was four decades her elder. She sat on Franklin's lap and called him "Cher Papa" while he played with the curls in her hair. He played chess with her husband while she took a bath nearby (there was a wooden plank over the tub; still, Franklin was sufficiently aroused to later apologize).

What did Jones make of this "dissipation," as Adams called it? Upon his arrival, his fellow sea captain, Thomas Thompson of the *Raleigh*, wrote, "I hope you will enjoy much satisfaction in the pleasures which Paris affords—particularly in appearing at every public place where you can mortify the English and aggrandize the States." On later trips to Paris, Jones most certainly strutted about and found satisfaction in "the pleasures which Paris affords." He patronized prostitutes and wooed grand dames alike. Stimulated by the invitingly lewd atmosphere in Passy, he may have begun his romantic conquests right away. Some biographers have asserted that Jones plunged headlong into an affair with the wife of Chaumont. Samuel Eliot Morison writes:

> The Captain had observed, or had been told by Franklin, that the best way to get things done in France was through the ladies, and that the quickest way to learn French was to find a "sleeping dictionary." Accordingly, he made love to Madame de Chaumont.

In her lively diplomatic history of Paris during the American Revolution, *Yankees at the Court*, Susan Mary Alsop asserts that "all the world knew" of the affair between Jones and Madame de Chaumont, including her husband. It is true that Jones and Chaumont would come to have strained relations. But if the whole world knew of the affair, no one left any evidence of it. Madame de Chaumont wrote some letters to Jones that are polite, even affectionate, but there is not a hint of illicit romance. Jones was capable of a rash romance, and it was his nature to aim high. Yet it seems questionable that he would be foolish enough to sleep with the wife of his main provider. There exists a medallion of Madame de Chaumont, sculpted at about the time Jones came to Passy, by the Italian artist Jean-Baptiste Nini. To look at the plain, plump forty-five-year-old matron—some fifteen years older than Jones—is to doubt the attraction.

Jones did not have much time for romance on his initial foray to Paris. He had to get back to his ship, which had grown unhappy in his absence. The day after Christmas, his first lieutenant, Thomas Simpson, had written Jones that, while "several of the people have had colds" and others were "infested with vermin," the "men are at present in perfect peace." Simpson credited a supply of brandy, dispensed to the men in the morning at turning out and at dinner, "which gives universal content." But the peace had not lasted. The ship's log shows a steady dribble of deserters, most of them caught and thrown in irons. Brandy or no, the crew was restless and sullen, watching the ice float by on the Loire River and scratching at their lice. They resented Captain Jones, who had not yet paid them any prize money, despite the capture of two merchantmen on the Atlantic crossing. (Jones was not holding back; he had not been paid himself.) Though Jones did not yet know it, Lieutenant Simpson was encouraging their discontent. Jones was still a foreigner to the New Hampshire boys. Notions of loyalty and naval discipline were remote to Simpson and Hall, who had sailed on merchant ships with looser and more democratic customs. The *Ranger*'s officers expected that Jones would move on to another command and *Ranger* could head home, snapping up prizes on the way like the true privateer her men wished her to be.

In retrospect, Jones would have been wiser on the voyage to France to have spent more time with his officers in the wardroom. Any captain depends on his deck officers to maintain order and morale. Jones had no Lieutenant Rathbun; he had only the surly Simpson and Hall. On the voyage over, Jones had chosen as his dining companion Major Frazer, a social-climbing wastrel, and now he had no store of badly needed goodwill either belowdecks or on the quarterdeck. Coming back aboard *Ranger* in late January, Jones could hear the murmurings. "Everyone was seized with the epidemical malady of homesickness," he wrote. Simpson eventually warned the captain that the men might not obey orders. Jones was not unmindful of the need to reward his men. Before he left Paris, he raised the issue of compensation with the commissioners. Jones was planning on raids that would be more "damaging" to the enemy than "profitable" to the crew, since they involved burning enemy ships, not taking them as prizes. He had extracted a promise that, if the men showed "good and gallant behavior" and "punctual obedience to orders, so as to obtain success in the undertaking," the commissioners would recommend that Congress pay a "generous gratification proportioned to their merit." To buy off Simpson and the other officers who formed a Portsmouth cabal aboard ship, Jones resorted to a more direct bribe. He sent Captain Matthew Parke of the marines home in another frigate, in order to free up the marine captain's share of the prize money for the other officers. Jones was being expedient, but he had to be. He needed "peace and unanimity," he wrote, because "any misunderstandings among my little crew might prove fatal to my designs."

Jones's mind was active with designs or, as he called them, "scheems." On January 16, he received fairly open-ended orders from the commissioners to "proceed in the manner you judge best for distressing the enemy." The wording suggests he had proposed raiding English ports, for the orders speak of attacking the enemy "by sea or otherwise, consistent with laws of war." The commissioners clearly worried that a rampage by Jones out of French ports might embarrass their host, for they instructed: "If you make an attempt on the coast of Great Britain, we advise you not to return immediately to the ports of France."

Jones had ambitious plans not just for *Ranger* but for the French fleet. On February 10, he wrote Silas Deane that he had picked up some interesting intelligence from a merchant captain arriving in Nantes: a British fleet under Lord Howe was sitting vulnerable inside the Delaware capes. A force of no more than a dozen French ships of the line, wrote Jones, could wreak havoc on the British, who would be caught sleeping. In a "single blow" the course of the Revolution could be turned around. Jones predicted that the British sailors, "having lived long on Salt Provision" would defect in droves and that many British officers would "pull off the mask and declare in favor of Heaven and America." Sounding like Admiral Yamamoto before Pearl Harbor or General MacArthur before Inchon, Jones exhorted: "Whoever can surprise well must conquer."

Deane took Jones's brainstorm of a surprise attack on the British fleet directly to the court at Versailles—and Deane, embezzler that he was, promptly claimed it as his own idea. Jones later groused that Louis XVI had given Deane "a portrait of his majesty on a gold box set with diamonds." Inspired by the American plan, the French dispatched a fleet of warships, but they dithered and by the time the French reached the Delaware capes in July the British had withdrawn to New York. Jones's inspiration had come to naught, but his strategic vision set him apart from the other American commanders. While they concentrated on picking off British merchantmen (and lining their pockets with prize money), Jones was always looking for the main chance, the *coup de main* that would use surprise and daring to counter Britain's vast superiority in men and ships. At the end of the War of Independence, the French naval intervention first suggested by Jones would be decisive.

In mid-February, Jones began testing the new trim of his "small frigate," about which he was in "great suspense." He had ordered Simpson to rerig *Ranger* to make her less crank by cutting down the size of the masts and spars and adding more ballast into the hold. But a pair of rough shake-out cruises along the rocky and blustery Brittany coast convinced Jones that more work needed to be done. In one knock-down squall, *Ranger* nearly capsized and briefly caught fire. Ever the perfectionist, and newly flush with funds from Chaumont, Jones had the masts stepped farther back, the spars reduced some more, and new sails made (the original gunnysack ones were sold for bread bags). Jones ordered one more curious alteration: giant strips of red cloth were cut and hung over the sides to camouflage *Ranger*'s distinctive yellow-striped gun ports. Jones was getting ready to play the fox again.

He was eager to try out his schemes on the officers of the French navy. He wrote Deane in March that he had spoken "tate a tate" (*tête-à-tête;* Jones was trying out his newly acquired French) with a French captain about a "project" that involved some kind of *ruse de guerre.* Jones did not spell out the particulars, but his reference to using a "masque" (the red cloth) suggests that he planned to slip in among a fleet of British merchantmen and cut them out from under the noses of their naval escorts. Jones abandoned the plan, possibly because it leaked out. "Strange! That nothing can remain secret," he had written in early February.

The French navy encouraged the American captain's brash adventurism. Jones burbled over the French officers, the "very well bred men" who visited the *Ranger* in Quiberon Bay in March and complimented her captain on such a *bijou* of a ship. The French officer class was largely drawn from the aristocracy.* Jones was puffed up to be treated as an equal by such nobility. He chose not to hear the patronizing tone in the letters of French commanders.

Ever conscious of marks of recognition, Jones asked to return salutes with the French flagship, gun for gun. After some haughty resistance, the French condescended to fire nine guns to Jones's thirteen. Still, Jones was proud to boast that "this was the first salute received by the American flag from any sovereign power." He was exaggerating slightly; a privateer, the *General Mifflin,* flying the Grand Union flag, had earlier received a nine-gun salute. But the *Ranger* was the first warship saluted flying the Stars and Stripes, which had been adopted the same day Congress gave Jones command of the *Ranger* in June 1777. Jones was so eager to get his salute that he battled "contrary winds" and sailed by the French flagship not once but twice "to put the matter past a doubt." It is easy to picture Jones, standing on the quarterdeck as *Ranger* plunged and bucked in the chop of Quiberon Bay, intently watching and deliberately counting the puffs of

---

*About 85 percent of the officers who would sail on the French expeditionary force to America in 1780 were noblemen; roughly a third of the top officers had family titles dating back to the fifteenth century. "The newcomers who went back only as far as the 16th century were at a severe disadvantage," writes military historian Christopher Duffy.

smoke from the gun ports of a French 74. He was thinking back, perhaps, to the inspiration of his youth, Admiral Hawke's daring and unexpected pursuit of the French into this very same wind-tossed bay in the Glorious Year of 1759.

Jones was further flattered to be received on board the French warship "with every mark of respect and gladness and saluted with a *feu de joie*," a volley of musketry from the French marines, standing at rigid attention. An even more splendid reception awaited Jones in the port of Brest aboard the *Bretagne*, the 110-gun flagship of Admiral the Comte d'Orvilliers, the commander of the French fleet. In the great cabin, light and airy with its enormous stern windows, Jones encountered a nobleman ensconced in gold braid. With its paneling and parquet floors, the admiral's quarters more closely resembled the library of a manor house than any ship's cabin where Jones had ever swung his hammock or bunk. Comte d'Orvilliers received Jones "with the honors due an admiral," Jones fondly recalled. Jones's appetite for flag rank was whetted.

His ship finally squared away, Jones was impatient to get into action with a daring raid.* He had heard reports that the British were burning and sacking American towns. He could remember the brutality of British repression in Scotland after the battle of Culloden, and he was determined to deter it by teaching the British a lesson close to home. He would not attack civilians directly but rather harm their pocketbooks and give them a good fright. "I resolved," he later wrote, "to make the greatest efforts to bring to an end the barbarous ravages to which the English turned in America, bringing in their train fire to its homes." He would "put an end of burnings in America by making a good fire in England of *shipping*."

Jones did not expect much support from the feuding triumvirate of Franklin, Deane, and Lee in Paris. "The commissioners did not even promise to justify me should I fail in my bold attempt," Jones grumpily

---

*Jones was not the first American captain to operate in British waters. In 1777 and 1778, Lambert Wickes and Gustavus Conyngham took numerous prizes in and around the English channel, though no Royal Navy men-of-war.

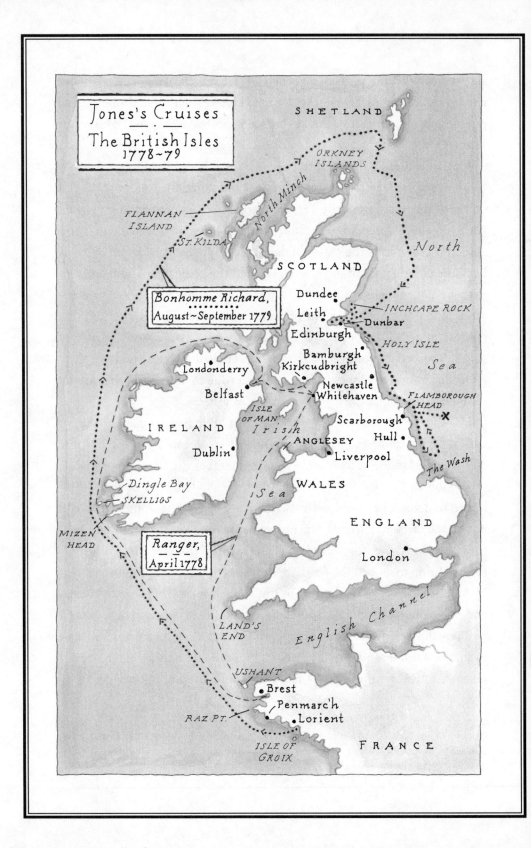

Jones's Cruises
The British Isles
1778~79

SHETLAND

ORKNEY
ISLANDS

FLANNAN
ISLAND

North Minch

St. Kilda

SCOTLAND

North

INCHCAPE ROCK

Dundee

Leith

Dunbar

Bonhomme Richard,
August ~ September 1779

Edinburgh

HOLY ISLE

Bamburgh

Sea

Londonderry

Kirkcudbright

Belfast

Newcastle

Whitehaven

FLAMBOROUGH
HEAD

ISLE
OF MAN

Irish

IRELAND

Scarborough

Hull

ANGLESEY

Dublin

Liverpool

The Wash

Sea

WALES

Dingle Bay

SKELLIGS

ENGLAND

MIZEN
HEAD

Ranger,
April 1778

London

LAND'S
END

English Channel

USHANT

Brest

Penmarc'h

RAZ PT.

Lorient

ISLE OF
GROIX

FRANCE

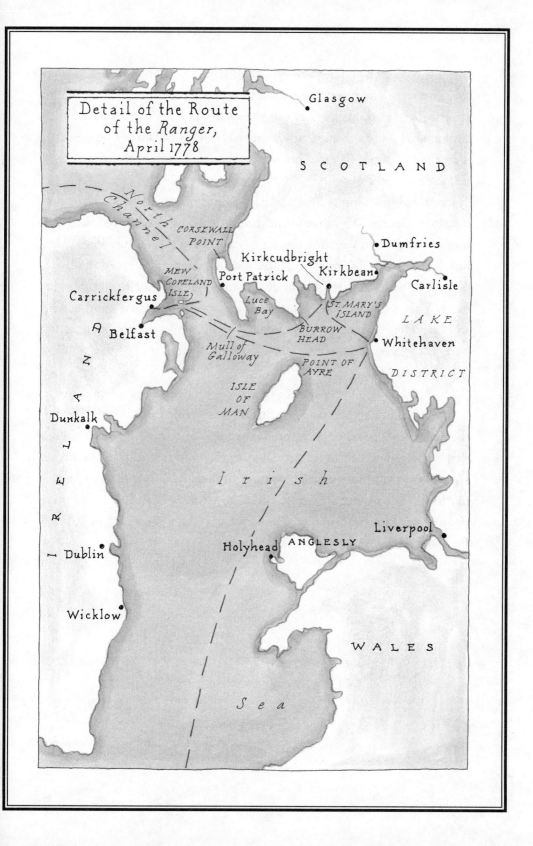

Detail of the Route
of the *Ranger*,
April 1778

Glasgow

SCOTLAND

North Channel

CORSEWALL
POINT

Dumfries

Kirkcudbright

MEW
COPELAND
ISLE)

Port Patrick

Kirkbean

Carrickfergus

Carlisle

Luce
Bay

ST MARY'S
ISLAND

LAKE

Belfast

BURROW
HEAD

Whitehaven

Mull of
Galloway

POINT OF
AYRE

DISTRICT

ISLE
OF
MAN

Dunkalk

I r i s h

Liverpool

Dublin

Holyhead

ANGLESLY

Wicklow

WALES

I R E L A N D

S e a

wrote the congressional Marine Committee. "I will not, however, under this discouragement alter my design. When an enemy thinks a design against them improbable they can always be surprised and attacked with advantage. It is true I must run great risk, but no gallant action was ever performed without danger. Therefore, though I cannot insure success, I will endeavor to deserve it."

Jones was invoking Addison's *Cato*, calling on the same stoicism that sustained George Washington and John Adams, who often repeated this meritocratic mantra against the status quo of undeserved privilege. Men may be motivated by greed or glory, and Jones certainly craved the latter, but virtue was a powerful stimulus to these children of the Enlightenment. They had a faith in the power of reason and ideas that was touching and extremely fortunate, surrounded as the Founding Fathers inevitably were by the Silas Deanes and, worse, Edward Bancrofts of a more timeless and cynical world.

On April 4, as he prepared to depart on his dangerous mission, Jones wrote the commissioners in Paris that he was setting forth, without telling them where. "You may rest assured that I will leave nothing unattempted that can be expected from the small force under my command," he wrote. He was in one of his periodic raptures of destiny. On April 8, as he was putting to sea from the port of Brest, he wrote a new friend, the prize agent John Ross, and quoted *Paradise Lost:* "As Milton said of Adam," Jones wrote, "'The world lays all before me.'"

CHAPTER SIX

"A Rash Thing"

$\mathcal{F}$RESH GALES, Close Weather" reads the log of *Ranger* for April 15, the day she entered the St. George's Channel between England and Ireland. Under lowering skies, Jones was still fussing with *Ranger*'s ballast, ordering the men to move "28 pigs of lead" farther aft, so that her bow would not dig so deeply into the waves. He wanted to coax as much speed as possible out of his "little frigate." In a few days, if all went well, she would be showing her heels to the Royal Navy. Jones was heading right into the British Lion's mouth. He planned to burn the ships in a British port and then kidnap an earl, a peer of the realm, and ransom him for the American seamen suffering in Britain's prisons.

The city Jones chose to raid, as well as the lord he wished to abduct, were familiar to him. Jones had first seen the port of Whitehaven, on the southern coast of the Firth of Solway, as a thirteen-year-old boy going to sea for the first time. The Earl of Selkirk was the lord of the largest estate near Kirkcudbright. His father had been William Craik's closest friend and a frequent visitor at Arbigland. Jones had practical reasons for choosing these targets. He knew the local waters and he could act as his own pilot to bring *Ranger* in close to shore. But he may also have been moved by a desire to gain vindication and settle old scores. Both Whitehaven the place and Selkirk the man were reminders of Jones's youthful subservience. He had submitted himself to indentured apprenticeship aboard the *Friendship* in Whitehaven because he lacked the connections to join the British navy as a midshipman or "young gentleman." Though as a youngster he had been exempt from the British press, he would have seen the navy's press gangs in the streets of Whitehaven, pulling merchant sailors out of the taverns. When the owners of the *Friendship* were forced to sell the ship, the best job he could get in Whitehaven was as third mate on a slave ship, the lowest form of maritime service. No one had bothered to know John Paul's name; but they would not forget John Paul Jones. To John Paul the gardener's son, the Earl of Selkirk symbolized the height of ruling class dominance, outranking even his father's master and the local gentry around Kirkbean and Kirkcudbright. Selkirk was one of those stuffed shirts who had believed that the well-born Mungo Maxwell was an innocent victim. Capturing his lordship, Jones believed, would bring representatives of the crown crawling with ransom money. Jones would disdain it, and demand to be paid with freedom for his fellow American seamen, proving his own nobility.

It was a daring, possibly reckless, plan from a leader possessed. Unfortunately for Jones, his men had no intention of following. They wanted to go home, not invade England. One of the crew had come down with the dreaded smallpox. They were tired of cold and drudgery, of endlessly shifting ballast and trimming yards to suit their fussy captain. Jones sensed the crew's unease in their surly looks and sluggishness. "A slow and half obedience I had observed even from the beginning," he recorded.

Within a few days of leaving France, Jones had to face down a mutiny. He was alerted by the only officer loyal to him, Jean Meijer, the lone foreigner in a wardroom dominated by New Englanders. Lieutenant Meijer had volunteered to take Matthew Parke's place (without his prospect of prize money) when the marine captain had been reluctantly purged by Jones to appease the Simpson-Hall cabal. Meijer confided to Jones that he had heard from a Swedish sailor aboard ship that the men were plotting against the captain. The mutineers planned to throw him overboard, or at least put him in irons, then make Lieutenant Simpson their captain and sail back to New England. At the appointed hour, the captain would be rushed by *Ranger*'s master, David Cullam, a burly New Hampshireman. The other officers would be nowhere to be seen; by prearrangement, reported Meijer, they were to "scat."

Alerted by his informant, Jones was ready when Cullam confronted him as he paced his familiar groove on the quarterdeck. The captain pulled out his pistol and put it to the master's head. Cullam and the rest of the Portsmouth gang backed off. They may have heard the rumors that a young Jones had run through a mutineer with a sword. An uneasy truce settled over the ship. Cullam was not clapped in irons, as he deserved to be, but rather allowed to maintain his post as sailing master. Jones knew that he would have to watch his back, especially when he went into battle with men who had little desire to fight the enemy.

The open defiance of Jones's officers and men may seem astonishing to readers more familiar with the British navy in the Age of Sail, with its tradition of taut discipline enforced by the lash. On a British man-of-war, no one could even speak to the captain on his sacred quarterdeck without first doffing his hat. Jones had to put up with insolence and downright dereliction from his men, yet the log of the *Ranger* suggests that the captain never ordered the cat-o'-nine tails taken from its red baize bag. Jones grimly appreciated that a harsh disciplinarian could find himself in shackles or swimming after the ship's wake. He was far from alone in alternately appeasing and defying unruly or craven ships' companies in the Continental Navy. The crews of the *Fly* and *Trumbull* refused to fight, and Captain Manley of the *Hancock* had to hold off a mutiny by drawing his sword. Overall, some of the officers of the fledgling navy showed so much shyness in the face of battle that congressional delegate William Ellery of Rhode Island, an exasperated member of the Marine Committee, suggested "a little Bynging." He was referring to Admiral Byng, a notably unaggressive British fleet commander executed, as Voltaire put it, *pour encourager les autres*.

Jones was hardly a soft touch. But he understood that the spirit of liberty that animated the Revolution was a double-edged sword when it came to discipline. He could see that the crew regarded their fellow New Englander, Simpson, as the defender of their rights. "As they were 'Americans fighting for liberty' 'the voice of the people' ought to overrule every measure of an arbitrary foreign captain which was not sanctified by their general approbation," wrote Jones. Jones's bitterness should have been tempered by the realization that he was himself partly to blame for the crew's truculence. Had he spent less time flattering the French and more time trying to win over his officers, he might have exercised more sway over the men. Nonetheless, he was shrewd and sophisticated enough to understand the reasons for his crew's inbred resistance to authority. Those roots ran deep: on Essex County fishing boats that supplied much of *Ranger*'s manpower, captains were regarded as no more than first among equals. Aboard privateers (and pirate ships) major command decisions were often arrived at by vote. New Englanders were accustomed to town meeting democracy, where each voice carried equally. Lord Loudoun, the British commander of colonial forces in the French and Indian Wars, was amazed at the attitude of the New England militia, who believed they were fighting under contract—subject to bargaining and work stoppages—rather than out of unquestioning duty to King and country.

How lonely and disappointed Jones must have felt as he sailed into the most critical action of his career with officers and men who could not be trusted. He would later say that he rarely slept on *Ranger*'s voyage. No wonder. With mutinies brewing belowdecks and in the wardroom, he was not safe with his eyes closed, despite the marine guard standing by his cabin door. It is an interesting question whether Jones entertained any private sense of guilt over his ship's unhappy state. Though Jones brooded, and though he appreciated the proper qualities of an officer, he rarely conceded error. His willful denial may have been useful in a way. Unwilling to look back, he was able to forge ahead. His sense of grandeur, his belief that he strode on a great stage, allowed him to appreciate the larger stakes. America's Revolutionary War hung in a state of suspended animation. The British effort to crush the rebels had been stymied at Saratoga. But Washington's army was too weak to drive the occupying army into the sea, and the Continental Navy had been inept and timid against a force that was far mightier, if over-stretched by its global reach. America needed to strike a blow that would shock the British people and sow dissension against the war.

England had not been invaded by a foreign army in more than 700 years. It had been more than a century since a Dutch raiding party burned a town on the southeastern coast of England. The last raiders to strike at the northwestern coast, by Whitehaven, had been Jones's ancient ancestors, the Vikings, in an earlier millennium. Britain was not like the continent of Europe, where populations felt vulnerable to conquest. The British slept secure in their island fortress, protected by the "wooden wall" of the Royal Navy. Jones was determined to surprise them, to show the British that the American War of Independence was not some far-off colonial dust-up but a threat to their own livelihoods and security.

Up the St. George's Channel, into the Irish Sea, *Ranger* plunged on, heading for Jones's old home waters, the wide Firth of Solway that divides the west coast between Scotland and England. On the night of April 17, Jones steered past the Isle of Man and manuevered inside of St. Bees Head, which juts out southwest of Whitehaven harbor. By cajoling and persuasion, Jones had managed to put together a raiding party of about thirty men. They were lowering away in boats at 10 P.M. when the wind shifted and came on strong. Giant rollers kicked up, breaking on the far shore. Jones realized that he risked not only losing his boats but allowing his ship to be embayed, trapped on the Solway Firth's southern coast by wind and current and driven down on the rocks. Aborting the mission, Jones tacked to the west, clawing with difficulty off the lee shore. Carrying "all possible sail to clear land," Jones withdrew from Whitehaven "to await a more favorable opportunity."

In a "fresh gale" off the Isle of Man the next day, Jones encountered the enemy. A British revenue cutter, the *Hussar*, on patrol for smugglers, sailed close by to investigate. Jones, as usual, had his ship in disguise. The commander of the *Hussar*, a Captain Gurley, later reported that "the person who appeared to be captain was dressed in white with a large hat cocked." It is not clear why, other than for reasons of sheer flamboyance, Jones was attired in white—the uniform of a French army or Russian navy officer. Atop its main masthead, *Ranger* was flying the British Union flag; atop the mizzen, a Dutch pendant. Jones had his sailing master, the mutinous Cullam, pick up a speaking trumpet and hail Captain Gurley to ask if he could spare a pilot (an old hostage-taking trick; Jones would use it again). Suspicious, Gurley called out to Jones, who was standing on the quarterdeck, "What ship are you?" Jones's reply: "*Molly* of Glasgow." Jones suddenly dropped the charade: he ordered Gurley to bring to, head the *Hussar* into the wind, or he would sink her. Gurley, a crusty salt, replied that he would do the same to *Ranger*, even though *Ranger* outgunned *Hussar* by eighteen cannons to eight. At that moment, Master Cullam dropped the speaking trumpet, grabbed a musket, and took a shot at Captain Gurley. Jones cried out, "Fire!" and the *Ranger* yawed to give *Hussar* a broadside.

But *Hussar* was too quick for *Ranger*. Gurley took Jones on a chase, just as Jones had taken larger British frigates for a merry ride in *Providence*. Though *Ranger* "far outsailed" *Hussar*, Gurley reported, he was able to lose the American ship by making short tacks and sailing into shallow shoal water. *Ranger* was able to wound the British revenue cutter, putting one 9-pound ball in her stern and two in her mainsail and peppering her with small arms fire. The *Hussar* "has received great damage in her sails, ropes and masts," Gurley reported to the Admiralty. But she escaped. The *Ranger*, the British officer reported, was last seen "skulking around under the Isle of Man," about twenty miles from Whitehaven. Jones's sullen crew blamed their captain for letting a prize "slip through our fingers," recorded the ship's surgeon, Dr. Ezra Green, in his diary.

Jones knew that his cover was blown. As soon as *Hussar* made port, an alarm would go out. He had to move quickly, to find targets of opportunity. He briefly considered striking at a merchant fleet on the coast of Scotland, but a squall deterred him. Sailing to the west toward the Irish coast, he sank a pair of smaller ships "to prevent intelligence" about his whereabouts. Then a chance for glory opened up: from a captured fishing boat, Jones learned that a British sloop-of-war, the *Drake*, twenty guns, lay unsuspecting at anchor a few leagues away at Carrickfergus harbor, outside Belfast in northern Ireland. Jones immediately wanted to enter the harbor in broad daylight and "cut her out," according to Dr. Green's diary. But *Ranger*'s "people were unwilling to undertake it," Dr. Green noted laconically. Dickering with the "voice of the people"—the reluctant Lieutenant Simpson—Jones offered a more stealthy compromise. *Ranger* would wait until nightfall, then slip into the harbor and surprise the British ship.

Jones's plan was to "overlay her cable and to fall upon her bow so as to have all her decks exposed to our musketry, etc.," he wrote in his official report to the American commissioners. Jones had armed *Ranger* with an arsenal of muskets, swivel guns, and blunderbusses that could be used in close combat. As the *Ranger* swung around the *Drake*'s bow, Jones's men would throw grappling hooks over the side of the enemy ship and sweep clear the *Drake*'s deck with a fusillade of small and large iron balls. Before the British could wake up and cut their anchor cable, they would be in the grips of the marauding Americans, clambering over the bulwarks with cutlasses, pistols, and boarding pikes.

That was the hope. The execution was botched. As a rising wind whipped through the *Ranger*'s rigging, Jones ordered a pilot seized from the fishing boat to guide his ship into the harbor in the gathering darkness. The *Drake* lay quiet at anchor, her sentries oblivious to the ship swooping down. They had not yet heard the reports of the American raider "skulking" under the Isle of Man. In the gloom, with her guns drawn in, *Ranger* looked like an ordinary merchantman. The key to Jones's attack plan was to drop anchor from the stern at precisely the right moment, swinging *Ranger*'s bow around until she was side to side with her quarry. But the crew's indiscipline showed at precisely the wrong moment. The mate in charge of the anchor detail "had drunk too much brandy," Jones recorded. He "did not drop the anchor at the instant the order was given to him, and that prevented the *Ranger* from running alongside the *Drake* as I had planned," Jones wrote. The *Ranger* was brought up a hundred feet past the *Drake*. Unable to board, Jones ordered his own anchor cable cut, and his ship drifted to leeward, before tacking out of the harbor. "We had made no warlike appearance, of course had given no alarm," Jones recorded. The sleepy *Drake* apparently suspected nothing amiss.

Jones, who must have been beside himself with anger and frustration at the drunken ineptness of the mate, was determined to try again—to "return with the same prospect of advantage which I had at the first," he wrote. But the gale was increasing, and *Ranger* barely weathered the lighthouse on the lee side of the harbor. "The weather now became so very stormy and severe and the sea ran so high that I was obliged to take shelter under the south shore of Scotland," recorded Jones in his official report.

Jones did not sulk. The next morning dawned cold and bright and brilliantly clear. Jones could see snow capping the mountains of the "three Kingdoms," Ireland, Scotland, and England, glistening white under a freakish late-spring snowfall. "I now resolved once more to attempt Whitehaven," Jones wrote.

He gathered his balky crew in the waist of the ship and addressed them from the quarterdeck. Jones's voice could be soft, almost feathery in the drawing room, but from the quarterdeck, it boomed with urgency. This very night, declared Jones, a raiding party would sneak up on the twin forts that guarded the harbor. They would take the sentinels by surprise and spike the guns. They were going to burn the fleet of merchantmen sitting in the harbor and escape before dawn. They would take two boats, the ship's cutter and jolly boat. He needed forty volunteers, including officers. Captain Jones himself would lead. He would be the first to land and the last to leave the enemy shore. Any questions?

There were, not just questions but resistance and defiance. Jones's dependably unreliable first and second lieutenants, Simpson and Hall, preferred the safety of the ship. They had not signed on to burn British cities but to take prizes, they said, or as Jones later put it, "Their object, they said, was *gain not honor*." Jones said he had no desire for profit; if there was any to be made from the raid, it was all for the crew. Jones's only interest, he said, was in honor. The two lieutenants were unpersuaded. Pathetically, they told the captain they were feeling too "fatigued" to perform their duties.

There were more principled dissents. An assault by a couple of boat-loads of sailors on a city guarded by two batteries of heavy guns was "a rash thing," opined Surgeon Green. The boats themselves would be so overloaded that they would swamp if the weather came up. The doctor made a moral argument as well: "Nothing could be got by burning poor people's property," he said. Jones acknowledged that Green was a "wise officer," but as he later wrote, the good doctor "had no turn for enterprise." Jones listened, controlling his indignation at his unresponsive crew, and continued to make impassioned arguments. By 11 P.M., he had won over, or shamed into action, some thirty volunteers.

But time and tide were working against *Ranger*. As night fell, the wind dropped, slowing the ship's progress toward the enemy shore. Jones had hoped to stealthily row into the port around midnight, as the tide was beginning to ebb. He knew from his experience at Whitehaven that at low tide, most of the merchant and fishing fleet, hundreds of ships, would be sitting high and dry on a mud bank. Jones wanted to reach port shortly after high tide, spike the guns on the forts, and then escape as the ships were settling in the mud and the tide was racing out of the harbor. But the necessity of cajoling his crew had wasted time, and by midnight the *Ranger* was drifting, nearly becalmed, several miles from shore.

Jones knew he could not wait. Finding thirty volunteers had been difficult enough. Give Lieutenants Simpson and Hall another day and the crew would be so truculent and demoralized that Captain Jones would have to row into Whitehaven alone. Seizing the moment, Jones ordered cutlasses and pistols issued to the raiding party. He had a swivel gun mounted in the stern of the launch to help cover their retreat. "Candles," incendiary devices made up of canvas and pinecones dipped in brimstone, were loaded in the boats, along with flint and steel to light them. Wrapped in his dark boat cloak, wearing his black cocked hat, Jones settled in the stern of the cutter for the long haul into Whitehaven.

It was a very long haul. Whether because of the ebbing tide, or because the men were not pulling with all their strength, the two boats did not reach the stone pier in Whitehaven until dawn was beginning to break. If the men hoped that Jones would abandon the plan with the light of day, they were mistaken. Clambering from the boats, Jones took a party of men and made for the nearest fort. The others were ordered to prepare to burn the shipping, perhaps 200 vessels resting together on the tidal mud flat.

Lacking any ladders, Jones and his men improvised, climbing up on the shoulders of the tallest and strongest men to scale the fortress wall. As he had promised, the dimunitive Jones was the first to slip through the embrasures of the parapet. Inside the fort, nothing was moving. It was a cold morning, Jones recalled, and all the sentinels were keeping warm in the guardhouse. Swords drawn, pistols out, Jones and his men kicked in the door. The dozing guards gave up without a shot. Jones and his men promptly spiked all thirty-six guns of the battery, driving heavy nails into their touchholes so the cannon could not be fired.

With the sun just beginning to rise over the hills behind town, Jones raced along the quay to the northern battery and quickly spiked the guns there. He still had the advantage of surprise. Waving, he yelled to his men to join him so they could put the torch to as many vessels as possible and hope that wood, tar, and canvas would do the rest to spread a conflagration. A group of *Ranger*'s men trudged, or in some cases, staggered over to their captain. They were drunk. While Jones was running about spiking the cannons, one of the boat's crews had broken into a tavern and found the whiskey and ale. At least the *Ranger*'s men were still on shore. They had been planning to abandon the captain on the quay and row back to the ship. Only Lieutenant Meijer had stopped them by wisely posting a guard at the boats.

Jones rallied his groggy men. Why haven't you started burning ships? he demanded. A crewman explained that they had heard "strange noises." What's more, their lanterns had gone out. They had no flame to start a fire. Jones repressed what may have been a temptation to shoot someone right there and herded the men toward a house, where they managed to get a candle lit. Jones found a large collier, a coal ship, as a flammable-looking target and hurled in the burning candle. Nothing happened. Feeling the sun on his face now, Jones ordered his men to grab a barrel of tar and pour the black, sticky goop into the smoldering hold of the collier. Finally, ignition. A blaze shot out of the collier's hatchways.

Suddenly, there was a commotion in the town. One of the seamen had slipped away and began running through the streets and banging on doors, warning the townspeople to arise and save their ships. The seaman was a traitor who went under the name David Smith. His real name was David Freeman, and he was an Irishman who had enlisted in Portsmouth for the sole purpose of returning to Europe, where he planned to desert and make his way home.

Townspeople began to run onto the quay to see what the hubbub was about. His pistol drawn, Jones turned to face them. Let Jones describe the scene, which reads as if he was writing an eighteenth-century version of *High Noon:*

The inhabitants began to appear in thousands and individuals ran hastily towards us. I stood between them and the Ship of Fire with a pistol in my hand and ordered them to retire which they did with precipitation. The flames had already caught the rigging and began to ascend the main mast. The sun was a full hour's march above the horizen, and as sleep no longer ruled the world [here Jones was paraphrasing from one of his favorite poems, Young's *Night Thoughts*], it was time to retire.

Jones's men had taken several prisoners, all but three of whom they released as they scrambled into the boats. "After all my people had embarked, I stood on the pier for a considerable space yet no person advanced," wrote Jones. He looked up at the heights above town and saw them covered "with the amazed inhabitants."

Finally, Jones jumped in the stern of the launch and ordered his men to pull hard. This time they did. As the two boats stroked out of the harbor, the Whitehaven men, furious to find their batteries spiked, struggled to mount some cannon lying on the beach. They finally succeeded in arming one or two and fired wildly after the fleeing marauders. As the cannonballs splashed harmlessly astern, *Ranger*'s men, giddy with excitement as well as whiskey and ale, laughed and fired their pistols in a mocking salute. Jones fired off a swivel gun on the stern. He was, for a moment, enjoying himself.

IT WAS NOW 6:30 A.M. Aboard the *Ranger*, the remaining crew had been "watching the night and til broad daylight in expectation of seeing the smoke of the town and shipping (ascend as the smoke of a furnace)," wrote Dr. Green. The men had begun to "fear that our people had fallen into the enemy's hands." Then, someone spotted "two small boats a great distance coming out of the river's mouth, and clouds of smoke arising from the shipping." Leaning over the rail, cheering the boats on, the *Ranger*'s crew could see a few muzzle flashes or puffs of smoke on shore as the Whitehaveners futilely shot at Jones and his men.

Jones was not welcomed aboard with a hearty handshake by Lieutenants Simpson and Hall, who were disappointed that their men had not left the captain stranded on the beach. Despite his jaunty show of defiance, Jones knew that his raid had been less than a success. The fire had been contained to only the one ship. Jones later grumbled that if he had been accompanied by his old crew aboard the *Providence*, Whitehaven's toll would have been 200 ships burned at their moorings.

But Jones could not afford to brood. He guessed that after his scrape with *Hussar*, the Royal Navy was stirring into action. Indeed, news had reached London, and officials were sending out "expresses" warning other ports and ships to beware. Whitehaven should have been more on guard. In the records of the British Admiralty, there is an envelope from Whitehaven dated April 19, 1778, and marked "haste, haste, post haste." Inside the report begins, "Mr. Gurley, the master of the revenue service here who is come in much shattered last night." It was unlikely that Jones would catch anyone sleeping a second time.

He still had the most audacious half of his plan to accomplish, the kidnapping of the Earl of Selkirk. Though he had barely rested for days, he immediately ordered the master to set a course for St. Mary's Isle, twenty miles across the Firth of Solway. From the quarterdeck, he could plainly see the snow-fringed peak of the Criffel, the mountain he had seen rising up before him every morning as he walked to the parish school in Kirkbean as a boy.

The *Ranger* entered the bay off St. Mary's Isle, which is not an island but a penisula below Kirkcudbright, around eleven that morning. The channel is a tricky one, twisting and turning between mudflats submerged at high tide, but Jones had steered it before. By noon, Jones's cutter was sliding onto the wet sand of the low wooded shore of St. Mary's. Jones jumped out with a dozen armed men, including Lieutenant Wallingford of the marines and Master Cullam. The day was brightening, the wind light. Although it had snowed in the higher elevations two days before, the coastline of St. Mary's was yellow-green with spring leafing. The air was soft, suffused with the earthy, tangy smell of mud, salt, and seawood familiar to Jones from his boyhood days. Lugging their muskets and brandishing cutlasses, Jones and his men trudged up the path toward the rambling Georgian manor house owned by the Fourth Earl of Selkirk. Jones's eyes were as always fierce and bright, if hollow from sleeplessness, but the men were unshaven, haggard, and probably none too clean, even if Jones had tried to spruce up his sailors for their audience with his lordship.

On the path, Jones encountered Lord Selkirk's gardener. Jones had a clever cover story: he told the man that his armed crew was a British press gang, come ashore to draft able-bodied men for the navy. This had the desired effect: the man was soon headed up the path to warn all the young men working on the estate. Fearful of getting pressed into a hard life at sea, the workers promptly fled—removing any potential guardians of the Earl's safety.

Jones might have exulted over this latest ruse, but for one critical piece of information: before he hurried off, the gardener had announced that his lordship was not at home. The Earl had gone to England to take the baths. This news was a severe blow to Jones. He had been thwarted by rough weather, brutish seaman, fickle officers, and now bad luck. The captain turned to head back to the boat and thence to his ship, dejected and empty-handed.

The two officers, Wallingford and Cullam, stopped him. They weren't going back, they said, not empty-handed and unsatisfied. They had come too far and endured too much to pass up such a golden opportunity. Here they were, a dozen men, armed and dangerous, standing but a short march from an undefended British lord's manor house. Inside, Wallingford and Cullam and all the others could readily guess, they would find treasure, drink, possibly other pleasures. As Jones later put it, with contempt, his men were disposed to "pillage, burn, and plunder all they could."

The captain was in a dicey spot. If he gave his men free rein, they might leave the lord's estate a burning shell, its valuables looted, its women terrorized if not raped and murdered. Jones's name and honor would be blackened for all time. If he resisted, Master Cullam and the other brigands would probably kill the captain, step over his body, and run amuck anyway. "I had only an instant to think," Jones recalled. As he had so often in the past, he nimbly temporized.

In his firmest quarterdeck voice, he gave his instructions: the two officers were to go to the manor house. While the men waited outside, the officers were to politely ask for Lord Selkirk's family silver plate. They were to accept what was given them, behave decently, and return without mischief or delay. Jones's compromise was reasonable under the circumstances. But then his vanity intruded. He did not wish to be seen as a scavenger or a mere brigand. Jones himself would not deign to go along on this tawdry mission. He would wait on the path to the boat.

This was a clear dereliction of duty. Jones was responsible for his men, and he should have accompanied them to guarantee, with sword and pistol if necessary, their good behavior. Fortunately, the Earl's formidable lady was at home when Jones's men banged on the door. The butler, an old retainer named Daniel, informed Lady Selkirk that a press gang was "on the isle" and that the "gardeners had run from their work." She peered outside, she later recalled, and saw a gang of "horrid-looking wretches" surround the house. Each was armed with a bayoneted musket, two pistols, and a cutlass. Pirates, she thought. The women and children in the household, a visiting family and Lady Selkirk's own children, fled to the third floor, fearful of the ravages about to befall them. Lady Selkirk, a brave and sturdy woman who was several months pregnant, went into the parlor. She received Lieutenant Wallingford, whom she described as "a civil young man in a green uniform, an anchor on his buttons." She observed that the other man, who was dressed in a blue coat, "had a vile blackguard look." The lieutenant, who seemed a little uncomfortable, ordered her to turn over her silver plate. "We are masters of this house and everything in it, it is needless to resist," he announced.

"I am sensible of that," she coolly replied. She summoned the butler and followed him into the pantry, where old Daniel tried to hide some of the silver in a kitchen maid's apron. Lady Selkirk told him to stop and together they carried the pieces back into the parlor. The "vile blackguard"—Master Cullam—demanded, "Then where is the teapot and the coffee pot?" These, too, were found and delivered (the teapot was still full of warm leaves from breakfast). The men requested sacks for their booty, took a glass of wine, and headed back to the boat. "Upon the whole," Lady Selkirk wrote her husband, "I must say they behaved civilly."

The men shambled back down to the shore to find their captain, who had been waiting anxiously to see if the manor house and his reputation would survive the visit. The boat pushed off for the *Ranger*, and all sail was made to run down the Firth. In the nearby village of Kirkcudbright, panic broke out. "Many of the inhabitants packed up their valuables; Mr. Murdoch, draper, pulled down his sign," according to a contemporary account. The customs collector "set off in a cart for the country, carrying along with him all the books and documents relating to his office." Among the younger men, there was much hallooing and hollering and dashing about looking for something to shoot. An ancient cannon was found and aimed out to sea. For the rest of the afternoon, it banged away at a distant rock that might have looked like a ship.

Lady Selkirk had been informed by Lieutenant Wallingford that the captain of the ship was "John Paul Jones, Esq." She wrote her husband: "It was immediately known that this Paul Jones is one John Paul, born at Arbigland, who once commanded a Kirkcudbright vessel belonging to Mr. Muir and others, a great villain as ever was born, guilty of many crimes and several murders by ill usage, was tried and condemned for one, escaped, and followed a piratical life, til he engaged with the Americans." With his name so blackened in his native land, it is little wonder that Jones never went home again.

By now, the Admiralty, alerted by letters from half a dozen ports that an American marauder was on the loose, had dispatched two warships to find and capture the *Ranger*. Yet Jones was not done. He was still thinking of HMS *Drake*, sitting dumbly at anchor at Carrickfergus while Jones's crew had fumbled around in the dark and squandered the chance to catch a valuable prize. Jones needed a victory to take back to France. If he could not burn a fleet or capture an earl, he could at the least take an enemy man-of-war. Ignoring exhaustion, he told Master Cullam, whose avarice had been momentarily sated by the Selkirk silver, to head for the coast of Northern Ireland.

As the ship rocked through the clear night across the Irish Sea, Lieutenant Simpson was once more stirring the pot with his fellow New Englanders. He held one of his town meetings on the gun deck. The captain was risking all their lives in his mad quest for glory, Simpson told the crew, who murmured mutinously in agreement. Jones stayed on the quarterdeck, wondering if he would have to shoot someone to avoid "being killed or thrown overboard," he recalled. He had not slept for two days, but the seditious rumbling from down below helped keep him awake. At dawn, *Ranger* entered the Belfast lough and drew near the harbor at Carrickfergus, where the *Drake* still rode peacefully at anchor.

While Simpson and his men agitated belowdecks, the *Ranger* drifted slowly into the harbor, until she was just a few hundred yards from the *Drake*. It was too late to turn back. "The tide and what little wind there was had imperceptibly carried us in so far that there was very little chance for an escape," wrote Dr. Green. The British warship was unfurling her sails, apparently readying to come out and challenge the intruder. But first the *Drake* sent out a boat to investigate. Eager to maintain the appearance of a merchantman, Jones kept most of the men hidden belowdecks. He ordered the helmsman to keep *Ranger*'s stern facing the British longboat. He could see a British officer peering through a spyglass, and he did not want the man to see *Ranger*'s broadside or count her gun ports. *Ranger* was flying a British flag. There was nothing to give her away as an American man-of-war.

Finally, the *Drake*'s boat came right alongside and Jones, wearing his British naval captain's uniform, welcomed the Royal Navy officer as he climbed aboard. Jones promptly informed the man that he was a prisoner of war of the United States of America. The officer was mortified to have been so easily deceived. He revealed that the *Drake* had just the evening before received an express message from the Admiralty warning of an American raider in these waters. Jones had the man and six more of his mates from the *Drake* sent below to the hold.

Suddenly the mood aboard *Ranger* was transformed. Capturing the Royal Navy men with such aplomb had an "exhilerating [sic] effect" on the crew, Jones wrote. The truculent sailors were "soothed again into good humor." Jones ordered the marines to beat to quarters. As drums rolled and the bos'un's pipes shrilly whistled, the men went dutifully, even eagerly to their battle stations.

In a freshening breeze, the *Drake* was slowly working out of the harbor, firing a signal gun repeatedly in a futile attempt to summon back her launch, which was now being towed in *Ranger*'s wake. The British sloop-of-war was accompanied by "a number of small yachts that had gentlemen and ladies on board as if for a pleasure outing," Jones recorded. But the pleasure boats sensibly backed away when *Ranger* ran out her guns. On shore, Jones observed bonfires making smoke signals to warn of danger.

Jones wanted to lure his opponent out of the harbor and into the Irish Sea, where he would have more room to manuever. He had *Ranger* play the coquette, slowing her by clewing up his main course and backing his top sails to let *Drake* draw closer, then spreading her canvas and pulling away again. On and on the two ships danced this way for most of the afternoon, until they were well off the coast. When the sun was a half hour from the horizon, Jones allowed the British warship to draw "within pistol range," about twenty-five yards. At the guns, the men rammed home powder and shot and blew on the slow matches to make them glow. In the time-honored ritual of single-ship actions, as formal as the preliminaries of a duel between gentlemen, the two combatants hailed each other. Jones had Master Cullam interject a cocksure tone into the introductions. He was instructed to inform the British ship that, as Jones later put it, "we waited for them and desired they would come on." Jones ordered the Stars and Stripes broken out; *Drake* ran up the red ensign of the Royal Navy.

No American navy ship had ever defeated a comparable British warship in one-on-one combat. The two ships were roughly evenly matched. *Ranger* carried eighteen guns, all 6-pounders. *Drake* carried twenty guns, smaller 4-pounders, but she had almost 50 percent more men aboard (roughly 150 to 110), a decided advantage in close fighting with small arms and especially if the two ships grappled and boarded. *Drake's* real advantage was ineffable: centuries of tradition. The British navy had long believed it was invincible and hence it very nearly had been in centuries of battle against the French, Spanish, and Dutch. The drilled-in discipline of British crews contrasted dramatically with the easygoing democracy on Yankee ships. The Continental Navy had no traditions, although disobedience was quickly becoming its custom. The kindest thing that could be said about *Ranger's* crew was that the men were untested. Probably none had ever fought in a real sea battle. As usual, Jones didn't have enough powder to let them practice their gunnery with real ammunition. Practice consisted of running the guns in and out, not actually firing them.

Jones needed to outsmart his opponent, to get an edge and keep it. He had maintained his ship to windward and just ahead of the enemy to give himself more room to manuever. He knew that he could not afford to let *Drake* draw too near, or the superior British forces could board *Ranger* and take her by storm. But he wanted to keep *Drake* just close enough, where *Ranger*'s greater firepower could slowly grind down the enemy. Jones filled the tops, platforms about a third of the way up each mast, with marines, sharpshooters who could keep a steady fire of musket balls raining down on the enemy quarterdeck where the officers stood.

The sun was setting, the light fading. The moment had come to strike first. "Ware ship," he ordered. The men ran to the braces and swung the yardarms around to allow *Ranger* to steer away from the wind—straight across *Drake*'s undefended bow. The helmsman put the wheel hard over. "Fire!" Jones cried, and *Ranger*'s broadside, nine guns, crashed as a volley of grapeshot tore straight down the *Drake*'s exposed deck, sending splinters flying and drawing first blood.

Now *Ranger* was vulnerable. Her broadside spent, her crews worked furiously to reload and fire again. But as she slipped past *Drake* at a right angle and the British warship surged forward, *Ranger*'s stern was vulnerable to *Drake*'s broadside. Well-aimed, British 4-pound balls or grapeshot could smash the stern windows of Jones's cabin or slice through the officers and men, including the captain, standing by the helm on the quarterdeck. Jones needed to move quickly. Before the light breeze tore away the veil of smoke that hung over *Ranger*, Jones ordered the wheel spun again, swinging the bow around so the two ships were now parallel, broadside to broadside, perhaps fifty yards apart.

A ship's quarterdeck is a very exposed place to stand when the enemy is hurling a half a hundred weight of metal from close range. By gentlemanly custom, officers did not duck or flinch. Jones stood there, stockstill, in his dress uniform and cocked hat, doing his best to ignore the iron shrieking by and the cries of the wounded and dying. A seaman grasping the steering wheel to Jones's side yelped as his finger was blown off. A midshipman standing nearby cried out as his hand was smashed to jelly. Lieutenant Wallingford of the marines, the uncomfortable man in the green coat who had been civil to Lady Selkirk, took a musket ball in the head and dropped dead. He fell out of the tops, where he had been stationed with his sharpshooters, and landed on the deck below.

The action was "warm, close, and obstinate," Jones later recorded in his official report. As the two ships banged away, Jones wanted to keep *Ranger* to leeward of the *Drake*. He was trying to take advantage of the angle of the heel: with both ships heeling over—tipping away from the direction of the wind—as they sailed along side by side, Jones's guns would be tilted upward, while the *Drake's* were canted downward. Jones wanted *Drake* as a prize. He did not want to sink her by punching holes below her water-line. He preferred to see his shot cut up the sails and rigging of the British ship, staggering and slowing her. *Drake's* 4-pound balls were probably not heavy enough to smash through *Ranger's* exposed bottom; the log of the American ship does not show that she seriously leaked after the battle or that any major holes needed to be patched.

For "two glasses"—an hour—the two ships exchanged fire, getting off ragged broadsides every couple of minutes. Through the smoke, in the last light of the long day, Jones could see that *Ranger's* shots were begin-ning to tell. *Drake's* sails were riddled with holes and no longer drawing well. On the foremast and mainmast, the topsail yards had been cut away. The topgallant yard on the foremast and the mizzen gaff hung uselessly, like broken limbs. *Drake's* jib had been shot down and dragged in the wa-ter. "Her sails and rigging [were] entirely cut to pieces and her hull also very much galled," wrote Jones. Most humiliatingly, the British ensign had been shot down and hung over the quarter gallery, the glass-enclosed protuberance from the stern used as the captain's privy.

On the *Drake's* quarterdeck, the butcher's bill was rising. Captain Bur-den had been gravely injured, shot in the head by a mustketball fired by one of *Ranger's* marines in the tops. The first officer, Lieutenant Dobbs, had been mortally wounded as well. Seeing the carnage around him, no longer able to manuever his ship, the *Drake's* sailing master cried, "Quar-ter! Quarter!" After one hour and five minutes, the battle was over. The Americans had won; Jones had at last found his measure of glory.

In the gathering dusk, Jones sent a boat of marines over to take posses-sion of his prize and shackle the prisoners. The *Ranger's* men found a pe-culiarly macabre scene. A cask of rum, brought on deck for the victory celebration the British captain had confidently predicted, had been shattered by an American cannonball. The spirits now spread along the deck, mixing with the blood of a score of men who had been wounded, some grievously. The boarding party had to step over the dead body of a British army officer who had "come to see the Yankees whipped," as one of Jones's men later wrote.

Down in the cockpit of *Ranger*, working under a swinging lantern with his saw and his crude probes, Surgeon Green was faced with a less awful, though still grim toll. He recorded the particulars in his diary: "Lt. Wallingford killed by a musket shot in the head. John W. Dangle by a double headed shot cut in two in the fore top. . . . Pierce Powers lost his right hand and his left badly wounded. James Falls [wounded] by a musket shot through the shoulder. Tho. Taylor lost his little finger by a musket shot at the wheel." Green was soon treating the British prisoners as well. Infection was routine on an eighteenth-century warship. Sponges were dipped in a bloody pail of water and used on the next man. Anesthetics amounted to opium, if Green had any, or, if not, biting on a bullet. Captain Burden and Lieutenant Dobbs survived for no more than a day or two under Surgeon Green's care. All in all the British lost four dead and nineteen wounded, the Americans three dead and five wounded. The bloodied British lay groaning in the *Ranger*'s hold, packed in with scores of other prisoners.

In London, warnings and messages were flying about between Whitehall and the Admiralty. A letter from the Secretary of State's office to the Admiralty Lords declared that "the rebel privateer which plundered Lord Selkirk's house has thrown the whole western coast into consternation." The Admiralty sent more ships to sea in search of the "rebel privateer." In addition to the two men-of-war dispatched to find *Ranger* after the Whitehaven raid, a thirty-six-gun frigate, *Thetis*, sailed forth from Glasgow and a sloop-of-war out of Liverpool ventured into the Irish Sea. A few days later, *Boston*, the thirty-two-gun frigate captured earlier from the Americans, was sent searching for the elusive Jones.

After using a calm night to patch up the *Drake*, Jones was finally ready to make his getaway. He would sail north around Ireland to take advantage of a southerly wind and elude the British cruisers. But first he indulged in a Robin Hood touch. Jones still had on board the half dozen fishermen he had seized five days earlier, the same men who had told him the *Drake* was lying in Carrickfergus harbor. The men had lost their boat in the storm that night, so Jones dipped into his own pocket for "English gold to replace their loss and recompense their services." He sent the men ashore on the coast of Ireland in one of *Ranger's* boats. He gave them, as a memento he knew they would show off, a piece of *Drake's* sail. As the men headed off, they gave the Americans three "huzzahs."

Jones congratulated his own men for putting up a "truly gallant fight" against the *Drake*. Their spirits were much improved, and they went to work fixing the rigging and mending sails. *Ranger* cruised unmolested down the west coast of Ireland and was making a last lunge for the French coast when Jones spotted a potential prize. At the time, the still wounded *Drake* was under tow, and Jones gave the order to the prize crew aboard her to cast off. The men on the *Drake* abruptly and needlessy cut the tow rope instead. That might have been a warning to Jones, who had sent Lieutenant Simpson across to the *Drake* as her prize captain. Jones had explicitly ordered Simpson, in writing, to "keep close by me" as they headed for France. Jones's fitful attempts to make peace with Simpson and his crony Hall had never lasted long. After one confrontation early in the cruise, Jones wrote, "I gave the lieutenants my hand and freely forgave the past. Yet a day or two after without any prelude or provocation Mr. Simpson came hastily onto the quarterdeck and addressed himself to me in terms and manner which amounted to an outright challenge." Now, given the chance to make his getaway, Simpson and *Drake* promptly disappeared in the mists. *Ranger* abandoned her chase of the prize, which turned out to be a Swedish merchantman, a neutral and thus hands-off, and sailed after the delinquent *Drake*. It took Jones a day to catch Simpson, during which time *Ranger* passed up several prizes entering the English Channel. He was indignant with Simpson, only now he could do something more than just splutter. Simpson had disobeyed a written order, Jones charged. Jones had him placed under arrest. With *Ranger* only a day or two from home port, he was finally free to muzzle "the voice of the people" without the people rising up in rebellion.

Ranger entered the French harbor of Brest on May 7 ahead of *Drake*, hanging an inverted British ensign beneath the Stars and Stripes. In a twenty-eight-day voyage Jones had captured several smaller prizes in addition to the British warship and 200 men. He understood the psychological impact of his raids on Great Britain. True, he had failed to burn a fleet or snatch a peer. "What was done, however, is sufficient to show that not all their boasted navy can protect their own coasts," he wrote the American commissioners in May, "and that the scenes of distress which they have occasioned in America may soon be brought home to their own doors."

If anything, Jones understated the terror he had loosed. The voyage of the *Ranger* seems so fractious and bumbling, its tangible accomplishments so far short of Jones's outsized ambitions, that it may be hard to credit its real significance. But real war, with its fogs and frictions, is often closer to the voyage of the *Ranger* than the perfectly timed, jolly-tar adventures of an Horatio Hornblower or Lucky Jack Aubrey. The real impact of Jones's daring was on the imagination of the British people, many of whom were beginning to have doubts about the cost and cruelties of repressing the American rebellion.

The British people expected their navy to keep them safe in their homes. "When such ravages are committed all along the coast, by one small privateer, what credit must it reflect on the First Lord of the Admiralty?" demanded the *London Public Advertiser*. Other newspapers made excuses: Captain Burden had been old and ill, the first lieutenant inexperienced, the *Drake*'s powder "very weak and bad." But the *Morning Chronicle and London Advertiser* of May 9 paid Jones and the *Ranger* the ultimate compliment: equating the rebels with the Royal Navy. True, the American ship had somewhat more powerful guns than the British ship. "In our engagements with the French and Spaniards, such a superiority would have been laughed at; but the case is widely different when we engage with our own countrymen; men who have the same spirit and bravery with ourselves." The British were already vexed by earlier American privateers who had cruised off Britain's coast. To have one land on British soil not once but twice in a day was too much.

Jones's daring raid played into English anxieties, both ancient and topical, about pirates and the French. The countryside in the spring of 1778 was jumpy about a French invasion; the Franco-American alliance in February had triggered rumors of war. Was the piratical Jones some kind of advance guard or diversion for a larger onslaught? Militia camps were popping up all over England. They were even becoming fashionable, with the women's dresses matching the uniform of their husbands. Mrs. Reginald De Koven, an early biographer of Jones, described the hysteria:

> Chap books depicted Paul Jones as a buccaneer, armed to the teeth, in highly colorful pictures, bloody and terrifying. Mothers frightened their children with the bare mention of his name. From this time on he was celebrated in popular song, and took his place with Captain Kidd in the histories of the Pirate Kings.

In pubs and taverns, ballads were written around Jones's name. Samuel Eliot Morison recounts one of them:

> *You have heard o' Paul Jones?*
> *Have you not? Have you not?*
> *And you've heard o' Paul Jones?*
> *Have you not?*
> *A rogue and a vagabond;*
> *Is he not? Is he not?*
> *He came to Selkirk-ha,*
> *Did he not? Did he not?*
> *And stole the rings and the jewels a',*
> *Did he not? Did he not?*
> *Robbed the plate and jewels-a',*
> *Which did his conscience gall,*
> *Did it not?*

CHAPTER SEVEN

"Officer of Fine Feelings"

TEALING THE SELKIRK silver did grate on Jones's conscience. As soon as he arrived in Brest, he wrote to Lady Selkirk, offering to give it back. Jones was determined in an almost pleading way to show his ladyship that he was really a gentleman, not a corsair. His long letter to Lady Selkirk is almost embarrassingly revealing, by turns romantic, cloying, proud, and ridiculous. Jones had great confidence in his abilities as a ladies' man, and he wrote as much as a suitor as an apologist to Lady Selkirk. This may seem preposterous, but Jones's mood must have been strangely giddy as he sat down to write. Perhaps he was over-agitated by a month without much sleep, spent plotting grand schemes while watching his back. Perhaps his ambition and pride got the better of him. Jones probably wrote the letter with an eye toward its eventual publication, and he was clearly torn between his desire to be seen as a gentleman and his more pragmatic realization that the old aristocratic rules of war were breaking down. In any case, his pen flowed with feelings that were over the top even by the standards of the age. "Madam," he began,

It cannot be too much lamented that in the profession of arms, the officer of fine feelings and of real sensibility should be under the necessity of winking at the actions of persons under his command, which his heart cannot approve—but the reflection is doubly severe when he finds himself obliged, in appearance, to countenance such action by his authority.

This hard case was mine when on the 23rd of April last I landed on St. Mary's Isle. Knowing Lord Selkirk's interest with his King, and esteeming *as I do* his private character, I wished to make him the happy instrument of alleviating the horrors of hopeless captivity, when the brave are overpowered and made prisoners of war.

It was perhaps fortunate for you, Madam, that he was far from home; for it was my intention to have taken him on board the *Ranger,* and to have detained him 'til through his means a general and fair exchange of prisoners, as well in Europe as in America had been effected.

Jones proceeded to explain how, when his men discovered that Lord Selkirk was not at home, they insisted on imitating the example of British soldiers who, on their raids on the American coast, "took away all sorts of movable property, setting fire to not only towns and houses of the rich without distinction; but not even sparing the wretched hamlets and milk cows of the poor." (Jones was overstating British atrocities. Although the British navy had bombarded one town in Maine and burned another on the Hudson, and British Loyalists were burning farms on the frontier, the redcoats had not yet launched the kind of scorched-earth campaign Jones conjured for Lady Selkirk.) Not wanting to admit that he had acceded to Wallingford and Cullam's demand for booty in part because he feared for his own skin, Jones went on to explain, rather vaguely, that since his men "had been with me, as volunteers, the same morning at Whitehaven, some complaisance was therefore their due. I had but a moment to think how I might gratify them, and at the same time do your Ladyship the least injury." Jones insisted that he had instructed the men to take only the plate and "treat you, Madam, with the utmost respect." Now that he had gratified his men, "when the plate is sold, I shall become the purchaser, and I will gratify *my own feelings* by restoring it to you."

The mere thought of such a noble gesture seemed to inspire Jones to dip his pen in the inkwell of storybook self-promotion:

> Had the Earl been on board the *Ranger* the following evening, he would have seen the awful pomp and dreadful carnage of a sea engagement, both affording ample subject for the pencil, as well as melancholy reflection for the contemplative mind.

Jones was eager to prove that he existed on a higher plane, motivated by more than parochialism or greed. He was like an ancient knight who had consecrated himself to chivalry and service. "Before this war began, I had at any earlier time of my life withdrawn from the sea service in favor of 'calm contemplation and poetic ease.' I have sacrificed not only my favorite scheme of life, but the *softer affections of the heart* and my prospects for domestic happiness. . . .

> Though I have drawn my sword in the present generous struggle for the rights of men, yet I am not in arms as an American nor am I in pursuit of riches. My fortune is liberal enough, having no wife nor family, and having lived long enough to know that riches cannot insure happiness. I profess myself a citizen of the world, totally unfettered by the little mean distinctions of climate or of country, which diminish the benevolence of the heart and set bounds to philanthropy.

Given Jones's proud, almost proprietary declarations about the American flag on earlier occasions, his protests seem hypocritical or worse. But he was just warming up. "As the feelings of your gentle bosom cannot but be congenial with mine," he gushed, Lady Selkirk should use her feminine charms—"your soft persuasive arts"—to convince her husband the Earl to use his influence to stop "this cruel and destructive war." As for Jones, "I wage no war with the fair." In a final gesture of absurdity, our Lancelot of the Oceans offered his chivalric services to her ladyship: "If I can render you any acceptable service in France or elsewhere, I hope you see into my character so far as to command me without the least grain of reserve."

Jones was very proud of his letter. He sent copies to Ben Franklin and the Marine Committee of Congress and described it as "moving" in a memoir he penned some years later for Louis XVI. He convinced himself that Lady Selkirk was so eager to make his acquaintance that she had asked Lieutenant Wallingford and Master Cullam to invite him to dinner after the raid on St. Mary's Isle.

Lady Selkirk's husband, the Earl, responded to Jones's letter with appropriate astonishment. In a long letter to Jones, Lord Selkirk pointed out that he would have made a very poor hostage, since, as an obscure Scottish peer, he had no influence with King George III. Had Jones's plan succeeded, "its only effect would have been to distress a family that never injured any person and whose wishes have certainly been very friendly to the constitutions and just liberties of America." The Earl pounced on Jones's fatuousness. He wondered how a "man of *sensibility to fine feelings*" could plot a kidnapping, and suggested that, if Captain Jones was not "under arms as an American," the "laws of war and nations" would not look kindly on a "citizen of the world" who behaved more like a pirate. He chided Jones for abandoning the "generous humanity and mildness introduced in war of late ages, through all the best civilized parts of Europe." The Earl disdained Jones's offer to return the family silver. He suggested instead that the proceeds from its sale be used to reward the seamen who had restrained themselves from rape and plunder.

The Earl's letter never reached Jones. The British postmaster, Lord Le Despencer, refused to forward it to "such a rascal and rebel as Jones." The two letters offer a painful contrast between a would-be gentleman and a real one. And yet, Jones was true to his word. Though it took him nearly seven years and much bother and expense, he finally managed to return the silver plate to Lord and Lady Selkirk. The tea leaves were still inside the teapot.

*   *   *

GIVEN THE RUCKUS stirred up by the cruise of the *Ranger*, news of which had reached Paris by the first week of May, Jones might have expected the American commissioners to be waiting on the dock to greet the hero's return with laurel wreaths. But, remarkably, for weeks Jones heard nothing from Franklin, Lee, and the newest commissioner, John Adams. Instead, Jones's draft for 24,000 livres (about $6,500), drawn on the commissioners to clothe and feed his men, was refused. Jones was outraged. "I know not where to find tomorrow's dinner for the great number of mouths which depend on me for food," he wrote the commissioners on May 27. "My officers as well as men want clothes to cover their nakedness. . . . I will ask you gentlemen if I have deserved all this?" Jones felt publicly humiliated. "That America should suffer this damned disgrace," he wrote Franklin's secretary, Dr. Bancroft, "in the presence of the French fleet, and the knowledge of every officer and person here, covers me with shame." To one of the prize agents he wrote, "I am so ashamed that I have thought of shutting myself up, except that it would appear that I deserved it."

Adept at managing large and difficult egos, Franklin tried to soothe Jones. Franklin had been too preoccupied with diplomacy, his suspicious fellow commissioners, and his own flirtations with the belles of Passy to devote his full attention to the irascible sea captain. But when he eventually turned to Jones, he was more sympathetic than the sour Arthur Lee, whose only inclination had been to scold the *Ranger*'s captain for the overdraft, or Adams, who had arrived from the States determined to rein in American profligacy abroad. At the end of May, Franklin congratulated Jones on the success of *Ranger*'s cruise. Just as meaningful to the budding courtier, he praised Jones's "gallant" letter to Lady Selkirk. Some food and clothing was procured for the ship's men, and Jones calmed down, for the time being. He wrote Franklin a long and dramatic account of the *Ranger*'s voyage, not understating his own role or the formidable obstacles.

Jones's pride was further assuaged by his warm welcome in Brest from the French fleet admiral, Comte d'Orvilliers. The old count and Jones appeared to have formed a genuine friendship. Jones was a most attentive student, and he sat rapt in d'Orvilliers's grand cabin aboard the *Bretagne* as the admiral instructed his new pupil on naval tactics and strategy. The French navy had attempted to reduce fleet movements or "evolutions" to grand theories and intricate designs. Like dancers at a ball, captains were supposed to parade and pirouette their warships, but the orderly evolutions of great fleets tended to break down in the tumult of combat at sea, where signals were often misread, winds shifted, and courage faltered. In some ways, Jones was an unlikely acolyte for the dignified if windy d'Orvilliers. True, as a gentleman of the Enlightenment, Jones nurtured an almost worshipful respect for scientific methods and inquiry. Yet in action, Jones instinctively anticipated Britain's Admiral Lord Nelson, whose approach was essentially: go get 'em. Jones on the quarterdeck and Jones in the salon were often two different men. In his constant desire for self-improvement and wish to be accepted by the *noblesse* of the French navy, Jones avidly listened to the count's ponderous lectures. At sea, fortunately, he let his better instincts take over.

Jones courted d'Orvilliers for his connections as well as his knowledge. One of d'Orvilliers's commanders was Admiral the Duc de Chartres, a witty libertine who was close to Jones in age. The Duke, as he would soon prove, had been over-promoted in the navy because of his social rank, but he was a great favorite with the ladies, and Jones studied his manners just as hard as he pored over naval tactics. The Duc de Chartres, whose given name was Louis Philippe Joseph, was Grand Master of all the Masonic lodges of France, an awe-inspiring position to Brother Jones, and he had absorbed some of the Masons' liberal idealism. During the coming French Revolution, Louis Philippe, who by then had inherited the title Duc d'Orléans, would rename himself Philippe Egalité but was nonetheless sent to the guillotine. In 1778, the Duke was a glamorous figure who could tell Jones about Voltaire while teaching him to dance a minuet.

D'Orvilliers praised Jones to the French Minister of Marine, Antoine de Sartine. The admiral's good word to Versailles was extremely useful to Jones. If the American commissioners were too strapped for funds or diverted by feuding and dalliances, then Jones would look elsewhere for support in his schemes against the British. Having signed an alliance with

America, the French were on the verge of open hostilities against their ancient foe across the Channel. Jones believed he could be a powerful
weapon for either partner in the Franco-American cause.

In the first week of June, he received the news he had been hoping for:
"I have the pleasure of informing you," Ben Franklin wrote Jones, "that it
is proposed to give you command of the great ship we have built at Amsterdam." Jones was to captain the *Indien*, the Dutch-built frigate that had
been promised him, then taken away when he first came to France in the
late fall of 1777. Mounted on a fast and big ship, *Indien*'s 32-pound guns
could deliver a murderous broadside. Franklin and Sartine had conferred
and decided to reward Jones for his exploits aboard the *Ranger*. "I was
much pleased with reading your journal," Franklin wrote. But Jones must
keep his new command a secret from the other American commissioners,
who, Franklin implied, were not his friends. Jones was to communicate
"with me alone," Franklin instructed, "it being desired that at present the
affair rest between you and me."

Jones was instructed to go to Paris to seal the deal with Sartine. His
head bursting with ideas for attacks on England and her sinews of war,
Jones immediately climbed into the Paris coach from Brest. By the end of
June, he was passing into the main courtyard at Versailles, the King's
palace fourteen miles west of Paris. He pushed through the vast, noisy,
smelly throng that came to court every day for such peculiar rituals as
watching the King and Queen eat dinner. (To enter the palace, gentlemen
were required to wear swords, which could be rented outside from ven-
dors.) He made his way to the Ministers' Wing, where the sewer smells
sometimes rose from the courtyard in the heat, and waited for his audience with the Minister of Marine. Waiting was an occupation at Versailles. Wolfgang Amadeus Mozart had come with his family in March to
meet the Queen. He would attend impatiently until September before
giving up.

Jones was ushered in to meet the busy Sartine, who was full of silky
praise and promises for the gallant American captain. Jones had written
him a letter that was encyclopedic in all the ways a few fast frigates, using

the element of surprise, could make Britain cold and hungry by winter. Jones listed the fishing towns in Scotland and Ireland that were "defenseless and might be either burned or laid under contribution [beseiged for ransom]." He suggested attacking the coal shipping off Newscastle on the east coast, "which would occasion the utmost distress for fuel in London." As usual, Jones understood the psychological impact of terrorizing the British homeland. "It is scarcely conceivable how great a panic the success of any one of these projects would occasion in England." Or, if France was uneasy about picking that kind of street fight with a neighbor, Jones suggested, the lifelines of the British Empire could be cut by "intercepting the enemy's West Indian or Baltic Fleets or their Hudson Bay ships, or to destroy their Greenland fishery."

The minister professed to be impressed by Jones's unorthodox approach to warfare. He said he would make available three fast-sailing frigates and a company of soldiers from a mercenary Irish regiment to act as raiding parties. France had sent a noble emissary, the Prince of Nassau-Siegen, to Amsterdam to bring back the *Indien* for Jones; the prince, Sartine said, would welcome the opportunity to serve under the newly famous captain of the Continentals. All this was heady for a Scottish gardener's son. Jones and Sartine began working on a plan to, as Jones put it, "astonish the world." It was all very hush-hush. Jones could not even tell the American commissioners about it.

Jones was beginning to feel quite grand. He celebrated his rising reputation by ordering a new coat of arms. The old, borrowed Jones-Paul standard was now upheld by an infant Neptune grasping a trident, with a Masonic square and compass thrown in for good measure. Flush with the prospect of prize money, he ordered "twelve silver plates with my arms" in order to more properly entertain in his cabin at sea. Jones decided he needed a secretary to handle his correspondence, not just an ordinary scrivener, "but a man of reading and letters, who understands, speaks and writes the French and English, with elegance and propriety." And not just a man of letters, but a man of the cloth. Jones himself was not particularly religious, but "for political reasons," he wrote a friend, "it would be well if he were a clergyman of the Protestant profession, whose sanctity of manners and happy natural principles would diffuse unanimity and cheerfulness throughout the ship."

Jones sought to solidify his political base back home by sending General Washington a pair of gilt epaulets. Seeking entrée into Paris society, he leveraged his friendship with the Duc de Chartres to call on the Duchess at her lavish Palais Royal. According to romantic legend, Jones promised to lay a British frigate at her feet. Beautiful, finely turned out, "the glass of fashion and the mold of form," La Duchesse seems to have been amused by the captain's flirtatious manner. Jones's capture of the *Drake* had made him a celebrity in the right circles. "The cry of Versailles and the clamor of Paris became as loud in the favor of Monsieur Jones as of Monsieur Franklin and the inclination of the ladies to embrace him almost as fashionable and as strong," wrote John Adams, with perhaps a twinge of envy.

Jones was in a rare state of contentment when he joined the Fourth of July celebration at the Hôtel de Valentinois on the second anniversary of the Declaration of Independence, July 4, 1778. A bouquet of posies had been laid beside each person's plate and the American flag and the Cap of Liberty were on vivid display. As the guests stood in the lavish gardens between the twin pavilions of M. de Chaumont's villa, on its bluff just west of Paris, they could see the City of Light twinkling nearby. The mood among the tiny American delegation was buoyant. With France entering the war against England, thanks in part to the skilled diplomacy of Franklin, the new nation's chances of survival were improving.

That July was remembered as "burning," the hottest summer France had seen for years. But for Jones it was warm and cozy after his trials at sea. He worked to master the French language (few of the French learned English) while savoring the rich life—"all elegance and magnificence," as John Adams somewhat disapprovingly described a dinner at Versailles with M. de Sartine. He befriended Franklin, whom he dubbed "my philosopher." Franklin had an interest in the sea as well as science, and the two men diverted themselves during the stifling evenings by trying to design a better ship for lightning raids against the coastline. The ship needed to be, as Jones wrote, "navigated without ballast, be ready for action at any time, draw less water, and at the same time drive little or not at all to leeward." Such a craft proved to be an impossible invention for even Franklin.

Jones remained leery of the other commissioners, Lee, whom he called "the Wasp," and Adams, whom he scorned as "Mr. Roundface." He suspected them of forming a cabal to protect the incorrigible Lieutenant Simpson. After reaching Brest, Simpson had been confined to quarters aboard the *Drake*. When Simpson continued to stir up unrest among the men, Jones had him sent to a French prison hulk. Determining that he was still a troublemaker, Admiral d'Orvilliers had put Simpson into an ordinary jail. This outraged the men of the *Ranger*, who began bombarding the commissioners with petitions. More than ninety self-described "Jovial Tars" accused Jones of "arbitrary" and "unconstitutional" actions against the "faithful, true and fatherly officer our First Lieutenant." The warrant and petty officers—led by the Master Cullam—produced a harsh indictment of Jones: "his government arbitrary, his temper and treatment insufferable, for the most trivial matters threatening to shoot the person or persons whom he in sallies of passion chooses to call ignorant or disobedient."

Adams, always on guard against conceit (a word Jones used to describe Adams himself), took a skeptical view of Jones's role: "The true source of the dispute aboard the *Ranger*, I suppose, was the same which produces most of the quarrels among Navy officers, the division of glory." Adams gave Simpson equal credit for the victory over the *Drake*, a judgment that was quite unfair to Jones. Eager to stop the bickering and get the *Ranger* back to America, both Adams and Franklin leaned on Jones to free Simpson from jail and let him go. Soothed with a strong dose of Franklin's calming philosophy, Jones surpressed his pride and anger and decided to be magnanimous—as he put it, "to relinquish the claims of justice to the softer voice of mercy and forgiveness." In July, he wrote the commissioners, "Lt. Simpson has certainly behaved amiss; yet I can forgive as well as resent, and upon his making a proper concession, I will with your appro-bation not only pardon the past, but leave him the command of the *Ranger.*"

Jones was not sorry to see the old *Ranger,* crank and slow and of "trifling force," leave with its cranky crew. Jones's cup overflowed with the promise of new commands. Sartine was offering him fast frigates, while Congress was trying to beckon the new hero home with suggestions of a squadron and the hint of higher rank. "I have reason," Jones wrote Sartine from Passy on July 17, "to expect the chief command of the first squadron des-tined for an expedition. I have in my possession several similar appoint-ments, and when Congress sees fit to appoint admirals, I have assurances that my name will not be forgot." But Jones told Sartine that he would stay in France "as I prefer a solid to a shining reputation—a useful to a splendid command." On August 6, he headed back to Brest to see which of his many schemes he would carry out, confident that a "useful" com-mand awaited "only the King's signature" to become his own.

He was severely disappointed. The *Indien* once more proved to be a mi-rage. The Prince of Nassau-Siegen reported back from Amsterdam that the ship would not be ready for sea for another three months and the Dutch, fearful of British reaction, appeared in no mood to allow her to sail under the American flag. Sartine's promise of fast frigates evaporated. Vis-iting his mentor the Comte d'Orvilliers as soon as he arrived in Brest, he was warmly welcomed—the Count "embraced me in his garden," Jones reported—but just as quickly let down. D'Orvilliers had already given away the command of a frigate he had promised Jones. The aging count was in a low mood. He had sallied forth with the fleet of twenty-seven line-of-battle ships in July and encountered a British fleet of equal strength off Ushant. The combatants had formed graceful lines, like part-ners in a quadrille, exchanged broadsides—and sailed on, not much worse off than they were before. At first, the French navy tried to proclaim vic-tory, but by the time Jones arrived in Brest, the truth was seeping out. Among the scapegoats was the Duc de Chartres, who was accused of fail-ing to read signals properly and, worse, shying from battle.

In May and June, Jones had been flattered by the attentions of French officers. Now they seemed to shun him, and he was not quite sure why. Possibly, Simpson had poisoned the well. While Jones was away in Paris, the *Ranger*'s lieutenant, freed from jail, had strutted about Brest giving his version of the battle against the *Drake* and insinuating that Jones had been dismissed from the service. Jones was embarrassed. He groaned to the Prince of Nassau-Siegen about his "shameful inactivity—such dishonor to me is worse than a thousand deaths—I have already lost that golden season of the summer which in war is far more valuable than all the rest of the year—I appear here as a person cast off and useless and when any person asks me what I propose to do, I cannot answer."

Jones was frustrated when two of his valuable prizes were sold for pittances. Shockingly, the *Drake* was plundered. Jones saw its officers' uniforms publicly sold on shore and worn by sailors. During his Paris sojourn, some of Jones's personal items from the cabin that he had been using aboard the *Drake* were thrown on the beach and left broken in the dirt. Neither the American commissioners nor the French government had tried very hard to effect a prisoner exchange by swapping Jones's hard-won 200 prisoners of war for the hundreds of Americans languishing in British prisons. Jones was "to the last degree unhappy," he wrote Nassau-Siegen on September 9.

On the same day, Jones wrote a very sympathetic letter to Franklin's secretary, Dr. Bancroft, who had been recently "indisposed." Jones had grown close to Bancroft in Paris. Franklin's secretary had been a source of intelligence, gossip, and good cheer. Bancroft had a winning smile, a "vast advantage to his features, enlightening them and dispelling the scowl that appeared upon his brow," observed Abigail Adams. Jones should have paid more attention to the scowl, less to the smile, for Bancroft was betraying his new friend. British Admiralty records show that the spy was slipping information about Jones's secret plans into the bottle he left every Tuesday night in the hollow tree in the Tuileries gardens.

The perfidy had begun even before the voyage of the *Ranger*: On March 4, as Jones was preparing to venture forth onto the Irish Sea, Lord North, the Prime Minister, and Lord Sandwich, the First Lord of the Admiralty, were apprised that "a daring enterprise is to be attempted upon the Coasts of Great Britain or Ireland by some of the rebel privateers which are now in Europe." The intelligence was not specific enough to help the British government stop Jones's raids on Whitehaven and St. Mary's Isle. But as Bancroft got to know Jones better, he began to learn more. By midsummer, he was able to detail Jones's plans with some specificity.

"J——has purchased a new ship and will sail in about ten days in company with those I before mentioned to you—that is, 3 other ships fitted out for cruising on the trade of Great Britain and harassing its coasts. They intend paying a visit to the black yard in and about Larne and Carrickfergus in the North of Ireland in case the coasts are clear," Bancroft wrote sometime in late July or early August (the message was received August 7). On August 6, the day Jones left for Brest, Bancroft wrote, "Capt. Jones . . . sets out this day to take command of the Lively frigate at Brest to proceed to St. Maloes there to join two larger frigates and wait orders to pursue one of several plans he projected. He says he does not know where exactly, but thinks his choice will be North of England." Admiralty correspondence shows the British navy preparing to send "some ships to St. Maloes to intercept them coming out."

Jones was lucky his plans collapsed and his commands never materialized. Otherwise, he would have sailed into a trap, set by Franklin's trusted secretary and Jones's own "dear friend." He could easily have been killed—Jones was not one to surrender—or, if captured, thrown into a British prison.

Unaware of his good fortune and Bancroft's treachery, Jones cast about for someone to blame for his "shameful inactivity." On September 13, he wrote Sartine, "I have been in the most tormenting suspense for more than a month since my return." He held Sartine responsible. To the Duc de Rochefoucauld, a noble *philosophe* and lover of liberty in Franklin's circle at Passy, Jones railed, "The Minister to my infinite mortification—after possessing himself of my schemes and ideas has treated me like a child five times successively by leading me on from great to little and from little to less." Sartine made no apologies to Jones. The minister was growing tired of whiny Americans and now wished to send Jones home in "*une bonne voiture*," pack him off in a coach. When this sneering remark got back to Jones he flew into a rage and came close to challenging the French Minister of the Marine to a duel. "By earth, air, and sea, Sartine must make direct satisfaction," Jones declared to a friend. Franklin stepped in, counseling patience, but Jones became so exercised that he wrote the King, complaining that he had been "chained down to a shameful inactivity for a space of near five months." It is doubtful Louis ever saw the letter.

Jones was lonely and depressed. "I need not tell you," he wrote Bancroft, "that if I had a mistress here, I have time enough on my hands to show her attention." He felt let down even by Franklin. "I have need of some of your philosophy," he wrote the old sage, but what he really needed was a ship. Franklin wearied of consoling Jones and stopped writing for a time. Jones complained to the prize agent Jonathan Williams that he had not heard from M. de Chaumont, his Passy landlord and chief provider to the American cause. "His silence has hurt me exceedingly, but this silence of Franklin has hurt me still more, as I regard him with the affection of a son to a parent." Jones was paying the price for his petulance and self-centeredness. He had become a bore, a nuisance to busy men. Jones appeared to be on the verge of a breakdown, his mind "agitated and torn to pieces." "I cannot sleep," he wrote Williams, "and I can say from my own experience,

> *Were I to curse the man I hate*
> *Attendance and dependence would be his fate.*

There was but one cure for Jones's insomnia. He needed someone to find him a ship. Chaumont, the Americans' chief provider, finally began to stir and look for a vessel that would take Jones out of his misery. Would a sloop do? Jones had not lost his pride. He wrote back, in words that have echoed down the centuries, that he wished to "have no connection with any ship that does not sail *fast*, for I intend *to go in harm's way.*"

*   *   *

THE *Duc de Duras* was not fast. In his fictional account of Jones's exploits, *Israel Potter*, Melville described the ship that Jones would make famous as "an old Indiaman, clumsy and crank, smelling strongly of the savor of tea, cloves and arrack, the cargoes of her former voyages." Well worn after sailing to China and back four times in fourteen years, the *Duras* was in "ripe middle age" for a ship of her time, wrote marine historian and artist William Gilkerson. She had been built as an armed merchantman, not as a true warship. But she was the best Jones could do.

He had learned that the old Indiaman was for sale through an American merchant named James Moylan, one of several contacts Jones had begged that fall to find him a ship. In early December, Jones went himself to examine the *Duc de Duras* as she lay at L'Orient, the port built for the French East Indies Company on the southern coast of the Brittany Peninsula. He could see that she was top-heavy, with a poop deck above her quarterdeck in the old-fashioned wedding-cake style of the treasure ships that plied the Indies trade. But she had a certain grandeur. Captains in the Companie des Indies lived like merchant princes. Jones walked into her great cabin and saw luxury worthy of Admiral d'Orvilliers. There was a drawing room and dining room, bathed in light from the broad stern windows. The decks were veneered with parquet, and the cabin opened up onto a balcony with a gold balustrade. Giltwork and carvings added small touches of maritime splendor. Jones, who still imagined a squadron under a broad commodore's pendant, could readily see himself in the great cabin, dining with his captains off those new silver plates he had ordered in Paris, engraved with his coat of arms.

The Indiaman would be sluggish in light airs, but she was intentionally over-built to withstand heavy blows. Her rotten beams and worn seams would allow in no more water than her pumps could handle. "The frame is now thought very good, and the ship bears a good character for sailing and working," Jones wrote Chaumont from L'Orient on December 11. He was praying that Chaumont would persuade Sartine to finally open the King's pursestrings. Grudgingly, eager to get Jones off his back, the French Minister of the Marine agreed in February to buy the *Duc de Duras* for Captain Jones—but only after determining that the ship was too old and weathered for duty with the French navy in India.

Jones went to Paris himself to lobby for the ship. He gave her a new name: the *Bonhomme Richard*. Jones had been reading Benjamin Franklin's *Poor Richard's Alamanack* in the French version, *Les Maximes du Bonhomme Richard*. The name Jones chose was intended to flatter Franklin, but it says more about Jones. As he was traveling from L'Orient in January, Jones recalled Poor Richard's wry admonition: "If you want your affairs to prosper, go yourself; if not, send someone." Jones loathed dependency, especially after dealing with the French Minister of Marine. He had been seduced by the charm and *politesse* of the French nobility, but the self-reliant man, Jones believed, trusts only himself.

Jones was becoming increasingly isolated. His social climbing had produced only snickering; he would have to silence it by a bold surprise stroke. "Let them place round me as many spies as they please as I have no confidantes near me, and as I do not keep my intentions by me in writing, they cannot betray my councils, and I may yet appear in a quarter of the globe which they little imagine," he wrote Franklin, still unaware that the American commissioner was served by a secretary who doubled as a British spy. One of the last few men Jones did trust was Bancroft; Jones even supplied Bancroft with a cipher, so the two men could share their secrets in code.

Jones's dignity was further offended in early March by an incident straight out of comic opera. Because of a misunderstanding, Jones let down his guard and confessed to Franklin and to Bancroft "the great misfortune" of his life, the killing of the mutinous mate in Tobago in 1773. That winter of 1779, when Jones had traveled to Paris to finally persuade Sartine to pay for the aging *Duc de Duras*, he had stayed as usual at the Hôtel de Valentinois in Passy. The day after Jones left to return to L'Orient, Franklin wrote Jones vaguely alluding to a "mystery" that concerned his friend the sea captain. Jones decided that Franklin must have gotten wind of the dark secret of his past. In a long and angst-filled letter, Jones protested that he had been meaning for a year to disclose this sad chapter to Franklin, yet had not been able to bring himself to tell a story that "must give you more pain than pleasure." Now he unburdened himself, writing of how, cornered on the quarterdeck of his ship, he had been forced to run through an unruly mate with his sword; how he had been compelled to flee "incog." to America; how he had been cheated out of his fortune and begun a new and better life in the cause of freedom.

It was all stirring reading, but a little baffling to Franklin, who couldn't recall mentioning any "mystery" to Jones. Perhaps, Franklin recollected, he had obliquely alluded to a French bedroom farce, a bagatelle in which Jones was the inadvertent fall guy. Franklin related the tale to Jones in a letter dated March 9.

On the day after Jones left Passy, the local curate, L'Abbe Rochon, had approached Franklin and Mme. de Chaumont with a *scandale*. The hôtel's gardener had come by the priory to see the priest for his guidance in a matter of grave concern: Captain Jones, it was alleged, had tried to rape his wife. "The old gardener and his wife had complained to the curate of your having attacked her in the garden about 7 o'clock the evening before your departure, and attempted to ravish her," Franklin wrote Jones. The aggrieved couple "related all the circumstances, some of which are not fit for me to write. The serious part of it was that three of her sons were determined to kill you if you had not gone off." Franklin went on:

> The rest occasioned some laughing; for the old woman being one of the grossest, coarsest, dirtiest and ugliest that we may find in a thousand. Madame Chaumont said it gave her a high idea of the strength of appetite and courage of the Americans.

If Franklin and Mme. de Chaumont had a good laugh, it's doubtful that Jones did. He wished to be seen as an officer and a gentleman, not an ignoble savage. What actually happened cannot be known; Jones's sexual appetites made him susceptible to scandal. But the story told by Franklin cleared Jones and instead suggests the ribald quality of life in Paris at the time. Franklin's investigation revealed that the old woman's assailant was a chambermaid who had stolen one of Captain Jones's uniforms and performed a little masquerade. It was the last night of Carnival, the bawdy season before Lent, when young lovers wear masques and exchange anonymous favors. As a gross practical joke, the chambermaid, meeting the old woman in the darkened garden, "took it into her head to try her chastity," Franklin wrote, "which it seems was found proof," presumably meaning that the shocked old hag pushed away the apparition in a naval uniform and fled to her menfolk, her honor to be avenged.

Franklin related all this, no doubt chuckling as he wrote, and then in a mere sentence shrugged off Jones's anguished confession about killing the Ringleader in Tobago. "As to the unhappy affair of which you give me an account, there is no doubt but the facts being as you state them, the person must have been acquitted if he had been tried, it merely being as defendendo," wrote Franklin. In other words, assuming that Jones was telling the truth about the Ringleader, he had done nothing criminal. Given Jones's tendency to find thorns in his roses, he probably dwelt on the image of Franklin and Mme. de Chaumont, whom he admired, sharing witticisms about his primitive insatiability.

It is tempting, at this deflating moment in Jones's life, to join with Franklin and Madame de Chaumont and laugh—or snicker—at Jones's thin-skinned pomposity, his unwitting hypocrisies, his unrelieved moping and self-absorption. But Jones's grievances were not imagined. He had been deceived and badly let down by the French and, with the significant exception of Franklin, foolishly neglected by his own American masters.

Jones's cruise aboard the *Ranger* had been about the only flicker of glory for the Continental Navy in 1778, or, for that matter, for the rebel forces anywhere. No less than nine American frigates had been sunk, lost, or captured by the British navy, which roamed the American coastline with impunity. After its victory at Saratoga in the fall of 1777, the Continental Army had done little more than stay alive in the north, while the British were on the move in the south, seizing Savannah in December 1778. An attempt by a French fleet, in an ambitious combined operation with American troops, to capture Newport, Rhode Island from the British had been stymied by poor weather and bad execution.

With the exception of the patient Washington, who understood the need for a professional army and knew that Minute Men or militia were a poor match for disciplined troops, no great combat leader had emerged from the American ranks. Washington had some good officers, like Alexander Hamilton, who was brave in the field and able on staff, as well as a few solid, if unspectacular commanders, like his artillery man Henry Knox and General Nathanael Greene. (It was Greene who aptly summed up the Continentals' way of war: "We fight, get beat, rise, and fight again.") Some foreign volunteers, like General Von Steuben and the Marquis de Lafayette, tried with mixed success to instill *élan* in Washington's troops. But among Continental Army officers, the closest rival to Jones for drive and resourcefulness was probably Benedict Arnold, who always led from the front and fought brilliantly in several campaigns in upstate New York, distinguishing himself at Saratoga.

Arnold, of course, became a traitor. Accused of corruption as the military commander of Philadelphia in the winter of 1779, he felt slighted and badly used by his countrymen. Sometime in the late spring of 1779, Arnold began conspiring, through secret channels, with the British headquartered in New York. He ended the war fighting as a British brigadier general. Arnold and Jones offer an interesting comparison. In addition to martial brilliance, the two men shared certain personality flaws: they could be tactless, vain, and selfish. They tended to sulk in their tents, then lash out at the boobies around them. But unlike Arnold, Jones remained steadfast to the American cause. Discouraged by official indifference and disappointed by commands offered and withdrawn, Jones, too, might have sought different employment—not from the British, who wanted to hang him, but as a privateer. With his reputation, Jones could have easily found a private backer in Paris or in Boston to finance a swift raider sanctioned with a letter of marque from Congress or Versailles. But self-consciously fighting for pride, not gold, Jones dealt with adversity by imagining new schemes for the Continental Navy and making the most of what he had.

Jones had not been entirely overlooked at home. When word of his exploits aboard the *Ranger* reached Congress in the summer of 1778, the newspapers and several congressional delegates sang his praises. James Lovell of Massachusetts saw that Jones's attack would make the British more aware of their own vulnerability. In July 1778, Lovell wrote that Jones's "conduct alone will make England keep her ships at home." But Jones had few real friends in Congress. The Marine Committee was weak, buffeted by factionalism and turnover. Joseph Hewes, his original backer, was in poor health and absent from Philadelphia for long periods. By the winter of 1779, Jones had not heard for months from his onetime patron on the Marine Committee, Robert Morris. Possibly his letters were lost, but there is no trace that Morris wrote Jones during the latter half of 1778 or the beginning of 1779. Overwhelmed with other duties, Morris was diverted from maritime affairs for a time, and he may have wearied of Jones's constant complaints. Jones had been briefly cheered in November when he received a letter from a privateer captain, Thomas Bell, reporting from the States that Hewes and Morris were "in raptures" over the cruise of the *Ranger.* "The public to the Southward thinks you the finest fellow belonging to America," Bell wrote. The privateer captain was discouraging about the navy's prospects. "Mr. Morris has left the Marine and everything is going to the devil as fast [as it] can," he wrote. Jones was troubled by Bell's report. "Your account of the situation in Philadelphia and of our poor Marine distresses much—but let us not altogether despond," Jones replied in a letter dated November 15. It was in this letter that Jones memorably imagined a shining future for his new country's capital city and its new navy:

> Tho' I am no prophet, the one will become the *first City*, and the other the *first Navy* within a much shorter space of time than is generally imagined. When the enemies' land force is once conquered and expelled from the continent, our Marine will rise as if by en-

chantment and become, within the memory of persons now living, the wonder and envy of the world.

Jones's visionary euphoria wore off and he returned to pouting over the failure of Congress to do so much as send him a note of thanks. But, in his dogged way, he soldiered on. In March, he consoled himself by trying to transform the *Bonhomme Richard* into a proper warship. "Jones enjoyed fitting out more than anything except fighting and making love," wrote Morison. He decided that the vessel could be pierced for forty guns, six 9-pounders on the quarterdeck, twenty-eight 12-pounders on the gun deck, and six 18-pounders on the lower deck, just above the powder magazine at the stern of the ship. His goal was to put together a force of some 500 marines and a small squadron, including fire ships, to attack an English port. Jones painted the *Bonhomme Richard* black, to disguise her gun ports, and added staterooms for the extra officers of the land force. Finding the cannon was difficult, however, and Jones traveled about foundries and ironworks, rejecting various aged or shoddily cast iron muzzles before settling on a battery that did not entirely satisfy him. He wanted the *Bonhomme Richard* to bristle. He laid in a supply of small swivel-mounted cannon and blunderbusses, massive shotguns, to line the rails and fortify the tops. This last preparation proved to be well taken.

Jones's spirits were boosted at the beginning of April by the arrival of an express from Paris, ordering him to appear at Versailles for consultations on a secret mission of great consequence. His comrade-in-arms, he learned upon arriving at Passy, was to be a glamorous figure whose ambition exceeded, if possible, his own.

Marie Joseph Paul Yves Roch Gilbert du Motier, Marquis de Lafayette, had become a general in the Continental Army at the age of nineteen. In search of *la gloire*, he had ventured to the new republic and been bloodied in battle and frozen with the men at Valley Forge. Titled and wealthy, Washington's "Boy General" had been laughed at in court by Queen Marie Antoinette for his clumsy dancing and weak head for wine, but his dash and courage made him beloved to his troops in the field. After

France had announced its formal alliance with the United States in February 1778, Lafayette determined to come home to press the King for an army to take back to America. But first he wanted to shock the British with a surprise attack on their own coasts.

As a warrior, Lafayette was as ruthlessly imaginative as Jones. Though very much the gentleman, the Marquis saw the strategic value of terrorizing civilians. He wanted to put under contribution or burn an English city. In conversations with Franklin and Sartine in March, Lafayette suggested Bristol, Bath, Lancaster, and Jones's old favorite, Whitehaven. Bath, with its gracious pavilions on Britain's southern coast, was particularly "tempting," Lafayette argued, because "the best of London society comes together in Bath this time of year. . . . The terror that we would spread would be felt much more intensely, and Bath would furnish some well-qualified hostages."

Franklin and Sartine knew just the man to help Lafayette in his daring endeavors. "Captain Jones, an excellent sailor, they say, knows all the coasts thoroughly," wrote Lafayette to a friend, the Comte de Maurepas, on March 23. After Jones arrived at Passy in early April, the two men spent long hours plotting and planning and taking each other's measure. Lafayette intended to embark a force of 1,500 men aboard a squadron under Jones's captaincy but at Lafayette's direction—to proceed, as Lafayette put it, "in accordance with my instructions to inflict harm on the common enemy."

The issue of command instantly became a sticking point. Jones and Lafayette had already begun to quibble over petty questions—such as whether the army and navy officers should eat at the same table aboard ship—when Ben Franklin stepped in. Franklin had recently been named Minister Plenipotentiary by Congress; the feuding trio of commissioners had been disbanded to allow Franklin greater powers. Wise as ever to the destructive potential of unbridled ego, Franklin wrote Jones a letter that shows off his talent for indirection:

It has been observed that joint expeditions of land and sea forces often miscarry through jealousies and misunderstandings between the officers of different corps. This must happen where there are little minds, actuated more by personal views of profit or honor to themselves than by the warm and sincere desire of good to their country. Knowing you both as I do and your just manner of thinking on these occasions, I am confident nothing of the kind can happen between you, and that it is unnecessary for me to recommend to either of you that condescension, mutual good will and harmony, which contributes so much to success in such operations.

Knowing you as I do . . . Franklin of course meant just the opposite of what he wrote. Jones and Lafayette got the message. They exchanged fulsome letters. "Where men of fine feeling are concerned there is very seldom any misunderstanding," Jones wrote Lafayette. "Without any apology I shall expect you to point out my errors, when we are together alone, with perfect freedom." Jones was summoning his better angels. He rolled out his favorite quote from Addison, always a sure sign that he was taming his Hobbesian id with his Lockean ego: "I cannot insure success," he wrote Lafayette on May 1, "but *we will endeavor to deserve it.*" Lafayette went right to the bottom line: "I'll be happy to divide with you whatever share of glory may expect us."

Franklin also saw the need to caution Jones, with some specificity, to show humanity when he descended upon the British coast. The near-burning of Whitehaven and near-plunder of the Earl of Selkirk's house may have given Franklin some pause about the captain's ability to control the Master Cullams of his crew. As always, Franklin couched his orders in diplomatic language, noting that British brutality might provoke, but not excuse, American treatment in kind:

As many of your officers and people have lately escaped from English prisons either in Europe or America, you are to be particularly attentive to their conduct towards the prisoners which the fortune of war may throw into your hands, lest resentment of the more than barbarous usage by the English in many places towards the Americans should occasion a retaliation and an imitation of what ought rather to be detested and avoided for the sake of humanity and for the honor of our country.

In the same view, although the English have wantonly burned many defenseless towns in America, you are not to follow up this example, unless where a reasonable ransom is refused, in which case your own generous feelings as well as this instruction will induce you to give timely notice of your intention that sick and ancient persons, women and children, may be first removed.

Jones had been duly restrained and chastened, made deferential to Franklin's ethics and Lafayette's orders. Yet he would be no ferryboat captain. The plans of attack that he and Lafayette worked over would have required tremendous seamanship and daring. Success would have insured his glory in France and America and notoriety in England. And then, with a wave of the royal wand, the whole glorious undertaking fizzled out. King Louis decided that he wanted to launch a full-scale invasion of Great Britain, not just a hit-and-run operation. Lafayette was assigned to different duties. Jones was back on his own.

HE HAD LOST a mission and a partner, but he had gained a squadron. For Lafayette's descent on the British coast, Jones had been assigned four more ships: the *Alliance*, a thirty-six-gun American frigate; the *Pallas*, a thirty-two-gun converted French merchantman; *Vengeance*, a twelve-gun French brigantine, and *Cerf*, a fast eighteen-gun French cutter. The squadron would stick with Jones, possibly, Sartine suggested, to make a diversionary attack to draw the British away from the main French thrust across the Channel. Captain Jones felt that he could call himself commodore.

A hugely ambitious war plan was in the works. At Brest, a French fleet of men-of-war and 40,000 troops were preparing for the invasion of England. In July, the fleet under Comte d'Orvilliers would combine with a Spanish fleet—sixty-four ships of the line all told—and sail north to challenge the English for control of the Channel. British soil, spared from invasion for seven centuries, would become a battleground for the great armies of ancient rivals.

Jones was given a relatively minor role in this grand undertaking, but even that would not be easy to execute. First he had to pull together a mismatched fleet captained by men of questionable loyalty. As he stood on the quay at L'Orient in May of 1778, he jealously looked out at the *Alliance*, a fast, brand-new American-built frigate whose sleek lines contrasted with those of the dumpy *Bonhomme Richard*, with her antiquated high poop deck. The *Alliance* had carried Lafayette back to France from America in February. Jones was introduced to the captain of the *Alliance*, a grave Frenchman with a Continental Navy captain's commission, named Pierre Landais. On first impression, he found Captain Landais to be a "sensible, well-informed man."

He would radically alter his opinion. Jones was not always the best judge of character, especially on first impressions. One senses that he was too busy trying to impress to be very discerning, especially if his new acquaintance had the sort of manners and style Jones envied. Landais was not the first French naval officer to snow Jones. Jones should have had an inkling of what was in store for him when he learned, upon meeting Landais, that the *Alliance*'s crew had attempted to mutiny on the voyage from America. Landais was to be cast off, in chains, in a boat without food or water. Only General Lafayette, brandishing his sword, had been able to restore order. John Adams's keen eye captured the true Landais right away. After dining with the French captain in L'Orient, where Adams had gone to await passage home to America, he wrote in his diary:

> L[andais] is jealous of everything. Jealous of everybody . . . he knows not how to treat his officers. . . . Silence, reserve and a forbidding air will never gain the hearts, neither by affection nor by veneration of

our Americans. . . . There is in this man an inactivity and an indeci-
sion that will ruin him. He is bewildered—an absent, bewildered
man—an embarrassed mind.

Adams was being eerily prescient. For just the reasons Adams outlined,
Landais would cause Jones no end of grief. He never should have been
given command of the *Alliance* in the first place. Landais had been retired
from a dead-end career in the French navy before finding an American patron in the corrupt Deane. If he was not the worst of the frigate captains
appointed by Congress, it was only because, with a few notable exceptions, so many of them were incompetent.

That spring, Adams often saw Jones and Landais together, along with
other ship's officers, in the evenings as they dined at a hotel or a tavern in
the port town on the Bay of Biscay. On one "agreeable evening" at an inn
called L'Epée Royale, Adams recalled, they "practiced the old American
custom of drinking to each other." After a glass of wine or two, they jok-
ingly discussed an old maxim that the best way to learn French was to take
a mistress or attend the Comédie Française. Adams was asked, Which
would you prefer? Both at once, he answered, to a roar of mirth. Later
that night, writing in his diary for posterity and possibly Mrs. Adams, the
chaste New Englander primly added that "the language is nowhere better
spoken than at the Comedie."

During these long and diverting evenings at L'Epée Royale, Adams had
the chance to use his close powers of observation on Jones. He noticed
that Jones was not wearing the drab red and blue naval uniform prescribed by Congress, but rather a blue coat with epaulets and a buff waistcoat, his unauthorized but carefully chosen combination of the most
dashing features of the British and French uniforms. "Eccentricities and
irregularities are to be expected of him," Adams wrote. "They are in his
character, they are visible in his eyes." Adams was fascinated that this
Thunderer of the Quarterdeck had a voice that was "soft and still and
small" and, instead of a commander's steady gaze, "his eye has keenness
and wildness and softness in it." Jones, wrote Adams, "has art and secrecy

and aspires very high." All in all, "this is the most ambitious and intriguing officer in the American navy."

When Adams used the word "intriguing" to describe Jones, he meant intrigue in the sense of scheming and conniving. Adams had been scheduled to sail back to America on the *Alliance*, but the warship had been drafted for Jones's squadron. Adams, who was pining for home and his Abigail, was stuck in France, and he fretted that he was being sacrificed as a pawn in Jones's power grab. "I am to be made the sport of Jones's ambition to be made a commodore. Is it possible I should bear this?" Adams wrote in his diary on May 12. He thought Franklin ("the old conjurer"), Chaumont, and Jones were colluding against him. "Does the old conjurer dread my voice in Congress?" Adams asked. He suspected that he was being detained so that he would not go to Philadelphia and tattle on the *vie douceur* of Franklin's circle at Passy.

Adams's sensitivity and nose for fakery had made him especially suspicious of Dr. Bancroft. He knew that the married Bancroft lived with his mistress and speculated on the stock market. Adams was shocked by Bancroft's salacious "tittle tattle" about the French court. "I had an entire distrust of him," Adams wrote. But he never guessed that Bancroft was a spy. Jones, too, remained oblivious, continuing all that year to write Bancroft about his plans. Lafayette, too, was fooled. He had even proposed that Jones bring Bancroft along on the surprise attack on the south of England.

Someone, quite possibly Bancroft, did warn of an impending raid by Jones on Liverpool early that summer of 1779. There was a flurry of defensive activity in the large port city on England's west coast—arms were stacked, beacons readied on the headlands to warn of approaching enemy raiders. There were false reports that Jones's flotilla had been sighted off the Isle of Man. But Jones did not come. Curiously, it appears that Bancroft, for at least a brief time, kept Jones and his plans out of those papers he stuck in the bottle every Tuesday night in the Tuileries. There is nothing in British government records to suggest that Bancroft sent up a warning when Jones finally did make a plunge for British waters at the end of August. Bancroft's spying was selective and dictated by self-interest. He did not, for instance, tip off the British about fleet sailings if he held a commercial interest in the cargo. Ironically, while the Americans trusted Bancroft, the British did not entirely. King George, especially, regarded him as a stock jobber and unreliable. Could it be that Bancroft had a sentimental streak as well? Had he grown too close to Jones to betray him? Bancroft could be bloodless when his own safety was at stake. He once sold out an accomplice when French counterintelligence began sniffing in his direction. But, possibly, he went soft on Jones.

In June, Jones took his squadron on a short cruise. Their duty was limited—escorting merchantmen and chasing away British raiders in the Bay of Biscay. But the shakedown sail gave Jones a chance to assess his ships and men. He did not have to wait long to be disappointed. At midnight the first night out, June 19, near disaster struck.

The *Alliance* was riding out a squall when suddenly the *Bonhomme Richard* loomed out of the darkness. The two ships were on a collision course. On the quarterdeck of the *Alliance*, Captain Landais heard shouts from the bow of the oncoming *Bonhomme Richard* and got it into his head that Jones's crew, which included some very surly British sailors, had mutinied. Rather than stay on deck and give orders that might have averted the collision, Landais went below to his cabin to pick up a brace of pistols. The long bowsprit of the *Bonhomme Richard* tore into the rigging of the *Alliance*, toppling the mizzenmast. Jones had been below in his cabin, possibly asleep, at the time. The *Bonhomme Richard*'s first lieutenant, Robert Robinson, had the con. In the aftermath, Jones sacked his first lieutenant and began to entertain some doubts about Landais's steadiness.

Jones confirmed at sea what he had suspected in port: that the *Bonhomme Richard* was a very slow ship, the pokiest in the squadron. At one point, he gave chase to a pair of British warships but could not catch them. Still, he was not cast down by the brief voyage. "I had . . . a flattering proof of the martial spirit of my crew, and I am confident that had I been able to get between the two enemies, which was my intention, we should have beaten them both together," he wrote Dr. Franklin.

His crew was a virtual foreign legion, a stew of nationalities: English, French, Irish, Scottish, Norwegian, Swiss, Italian, Bengali, and Indian. To accommodate a batch of Portuguese, Jones allowed the men to bring a statue of the Virgin Mary on board. Most of his men worshipped no God but rum and the lash. "They were generally so mean that the only expedient I could find that allowed me to command was to divide them into two parties and let one group of rogues guard the other," Jones recalled. The worst were a group of British sailors, pressed by Jones out of French jails, whose prior crimes included mutiny. The Englishmen promptly set about to be repeat offenders, though Jones broke up the plot before it could get very far. The ringleader was sentenced to 250 lashes, enough to turn a man's back to pulp and even kill him. After tolerating, through gritted teeth, the shenanigans of the New Hampshiremen aboard *Ranger,* Jones was determined to put the *Bonhomme Richard*'s crew on notice that he was in charge and would brook no nonsense.

The message got through. A seaman named John Kilby, reporting for duty, arrived at the *Bonhomme Richard* to find the quartermaster tricing up a dozen men and having them flogged, one by one, with the cat-o'-nine tails. They had offended in the worst way: by embarrassing the captain. The miscreants were all crewmen for the commodore's barge. They had rowed him to shore one morning and vanished to get drunk. When Jones returned to the beach after his business on shore, ready to return to the ship, he had found his barge but no crew. He had to persuade a fishing smack to row him back out to the *Bonhomme Richard.* Indignant, Jones ordered a dozen lashes for each man. Any British Royal Navy captain would have done the same, and Jones was generally sparing with the lash. Still, he must have felt surrounded by men he could not trust.

Jones was worn out by pushing his crew into line. In late July, he fell ill, unusual for a man who normally needed very little sleep and very rarely became sick. But he was slowly succeeding in scraping away the worst scum from the ship's roster, and as time went on, he was able to sign on more American crewmen. Some of them—like Kilby—had been American seamen seized by the British and thrown into jail. After months of wheedling and pressure, Jones had finally succeeded in forcing a prisoner exchange that liberated 100 American seamen. Kilby and others had been badly abused by their British jailers, given the "black hole" treatment. They were grateful to Jones for springing them and eager for revenge against Old Blighty.

Jones could be an articulate and persuasive leader. One of his midshipmen, Nathaniel Fanning, recalled seeing the captain spend hours on the quay using his "smooth tongue" to convince a single seaman to sign on. Jones did not always suppress his temper. Fanning also recalled Jones striking an officer with a speaking trumpet and kicking a midshipman in the rear end as he descended a ladder to go below (the midshipman was Fanning; Jones was angry with him because he dropped a chronometer). While Jones was not always popular with his crews, he was usually respected. One of his French marine captains, Captain Antoine Felix Wybert, later testified, "Commodore Paul Jones, far from commanding with haughtiness and brutality, as certain persons have endeavored to circulate, was always (though very strict and sharp in the service) affable, genteel, and very indulgent, not only towards his officers, but likewise towards the sentries and soldiers."

Wybert was one of the soldiers of fortune Jones had brought aboard to command his contingent of French marines, 140 strong, from a regiment of Irish volunteers who were only too happy to shoot Englishmen. This was an unusually large detachment of marines, perhaps three times the normal complement for a warship the size of the *Bonhomme Richard*. Jones wanted to be able to send ashore a strong landing force, and he wanted to be able to crowd the tops with marksmen in battle.

Most of the officers were Americans, and Jones was lucky in his new first lieutenant, Richard Dale, who replaced the inept Robinson after the midnight collision with the *Alliance*. Dale had served with Jones as an enlisted man aboard the *Providence* and the *Alfred*. He had risen through the ranks to master's mate and spent time in a British dungeon after being captured aboard an American privateer. He knew his captain's temperament and fighting spirit. Dale was universally liked as professional but calm, a refreshing contrast to his intense captain.

By mid-August, after nearly six months of preparation, Jones had put together his crew of 380 men. On the morning of August 14, 1779, under a light breeze in the predawn hours, Jones and his little squadron raised anchors and sailed out of the Groix Roadstead from L'Orient. They steered for Great Britain.

CHAPTER EIGHT

"Lay It in Ashes"

*T*HE MISSION THAT would guarantee Jones's fame began as a side show and was almost wrecked by a series of misadventures and displays of insubordination. The Combined French and Spanish fleet was supposed to be the main event, engaging the British in a duel for control of the Channel, then landing in force along Britain's southern coast. The battle and the invasion never happened. In the late summer of 1779, the Combined Fleet drew near—but never engaged—an outgunned Royal Navy fleet near the Scilly Islands at the Western Approaches. Then the French gave up—not because they feared the British, but because of a massive epidemic of shipborne disease. French ships were notoriously filthy belowdecks, and d'Orvilliers's fleet was wracked with typhus and smallpox. As thousands died, the Franco-Spanish fleet limped back to port in September, just as Jones's tiny squadron was sailing into harm's way in the battle that would make his name and thrill all Europe.

Jones would later write that, during the voyage of the *Bonhomme Richard*, he slept no more than three hours out of every twenty-four. He needed to keep his wits about him at all times. Even before the *Bonhomme Richard* left the anchorage at Groix, a sailor fell off the main topsail yard and plummeted sixty feet straight down. Jones was standing directly beneath him. The falling sailor knocked off the commodore's tricorned hat and landed on the quarterdeck beside him with a sickening thud. The man was dead; Jones reached down to pick up his hat.

The airs were calm, "hot and sultry" in late August, according to the *Bonhomme Richard*'s log, as Jones's small squadron slipped across the Western Approaches toward the west coast of Ireland. The *Bonhomme Richard* brought up the rear: the frigates *Alliance* and *Pallas*, brig *Vengeance*, and cutter *Cerf*, all faster vessels, had to shorten sail to wait up for the sluggish old Indiaman. They were accompanied by a pair of privateers, *Monsieur* and *Grandville*, who had joined for the prize hunt. Jones caught the captain of the *Monsieur* looting the stores of the first prize captured by the squadron, a merchantman carrying wine and brandy. The *Monsieur* promptly vanished into the night, and the *Grandville* disappeared a few days later.

Off the Irish coast, *Bonhomme Richard* was becalmed and began slowly drifting, pushed by the swell and the current, toward the rocks. Jones sent out the captain's barge with a towline to pull the *Bonhomme Richard* out of danger. The coxswain of the barge, as it happened, was one of the men who had been flogged by Jones for stranding the captain on the beach at L'Orient earlier that month. The half-dozen oarsmen aboard the barge were all homesick English and Irishmen. The night was dark; they saw their chance to escape. Cutting the tow rope, they began pulling madly for shore. Pandemonium on the quarterdeck: a 9-pounder was futilely fired in the general direction of the deserters, and the ship's longboat was lowered away and rowed after in hot pursuit. The longboat vanished in a thick fog bank. Neither returned.

That night, the next day, and the next night Jones cruised back and forth off the rugged Irish coast, firing signal cannons, but seeing nothing. Finally, he ordered the cutter *Cerf*, a smaller vessel with a shallower draft, to sail in toward the shore and take a closer look. A gale came up—and the *Cerf* disappeared as well. The storm tested the *Bonhomme Richard*'s aging frame. "She appeared to have as many joints in her backbone as a rattlesnake," wrote Midshipman Fanning, who reported that the pumps could barely keep up. Jones had been understandably vexed when he received Captain Landais on the afternoon of August 25, while he was still tacking back and forth, vainly searching for his missing boats. The captain of the *Alliance* was in a lather because Jones had forbidden him from chasing a prize into rocky waters near the coast. Landais announced that he was "the only American" among the captains of the squadron (the Frenchman had been made an honorary citizen of Massachusetts by his congressional friends). "He was determined to follow his own opinion in chasing when and where he thought proper and in every other matter," Jones recorded.

At first, Jones tried conciliation. He took Landais by the hand and led him to his cabin and told him that he was his friend, that he was the one responsible for Landais retaining his command of *Alliance* after the mutinous voyage from America. Landais scoffed at this assertion, and the conversation grew cold. Changing the subject, Jones began lamenting his lost boats. Landais offered that Jones had only himself to blame for sending them out into the fog. "That's a damn lie," Jones muttered under his breath, according to Landais. To an eighteenth-century gentleman, such an accusation—"giving the lie" was an affront to honor and enough to provoke a challenge to a duel. Few duels were actually fought; most gentlemen found ritualistic face-saving ways to back down. The way out for Jones and Landais was to invoke "the good of the service"; it would be inappropriate for ship captains, comrades-in-arms, to fight a duel aboard a warship sailing toward the enemy. But back on dry land, Jones assured Landais, he would gladly accept Landais's challenge.

If Landais is to be believed, the two men very nearly struggled then and there. In Landais's retelling of the scene, Jones reached over, grabbed a key, and began to lock the door of the great cabin, presumably to keep others out while the two men drew swords and settled their score. Landais pushed him away. Jones caught himself and calmed down. The prudent, rational side of his character reasserted itself; his voice softened and he tried to make peace. But the damage was done; the two captains were now mortal enemies.

For the rest of the cruise, Landais ignored Jones's signals and disap-

peared and reappeared whenever he felt like it. When Jones sent a delegation of officers to ask Landais to come on board the *Bonhomme Richard*,
Landais "spoke of Capt. Jones in terms highly disrespectful and insolent,
and said he would see him on shore where they must kill one or the other,
etc.," reported back the purser, Mathew Pease. Jones sent written instructions requiring Landais to appear on board and Landais wrote back, curtly
and cryptically, "I shall not go on board the Frigate B. H. Richard.... You
know the reason why."

Jones was indignant, but he knew that his authority was hobbled by a
concordat that he had very grudgingly accepted the day before leaving
L'Orient. The *concordat* was designed to sort out the division of prize
money between the different captains, but with its emphasis on "common
consent," the document was a blueprint for confusion and squabbling.
Jones had only agreed to sign it because he was impatient to get to sea.

Jones's overall orders for the voyage were similarly muddy and bound
to provoke dissension. Earlier in the summer, Jones had been told by
Chaumont, who was presumably speaking for Minister of the Marine Sartine, that the squadron should only engage in destroying commerce—in
taking prizes—and *not* stage any surprise landings on the British coast.
The French government wanted to keep the British guessing about the
movements of the "Pirate Paul Jones," as a distraction from the Franco-
Spanish invasion planned for late summer or early fall. Jones bridled at
this restriction. He had fitted out the *Bonhomme Richard* to support raids
on British ports. His ship wasn't fast enough, he complained to Franklin,
to catch other ships. Franklin had wearily responded that it was too late to
get the King's council to change Jones's orders. Jones chose instead to
reinterpret them—to insist that he was bound by an earlier set of orders,
given by Sartine back in January, that gave him carte blanche to do as he
pleased. It is possible that Franklin, who could be slippery about such
matters, signaled verbally that he wouldn't mind if Jones went his own
way. But the other captains in Jones's squadron all believed they had
signed on to seize prizes—not to take the far riskier course of invading
cities to put them under ransom.

Jones had planned to sail clockwise around the British Isles—up Ireland's west coast, around Scotland's wild shore to the north, then down England's east coast. Off of Limerick, Jones had hoped to intercept a fleet of Indiamen and was frustrated when the truant Landais wandered away to the north, compelling Jones to catch up. The reduced squadron did capture a couple of valuable prizes, carrying British military supplies, near Scotland's northern tip, but Jones's real aim was a grand *coup de main*: to hold hostage a British city or port town.

For Jones to descend on the coast of Great Britain was a dangerous undertaking. The deserters who rowed ashore in Ireland had quickly spread the alarm: Paul Jones had come armed with "combustibles" to burn a city, they warned. The country was in an "uproar," according to the newspapers; rumors flew about that Jones was preparing to sail right up the Shannon River to Limerick. Back in London, the Admiralty went on alert, dispatching two frigates to find Jones (figuring that he might come back to finish an earlier job, they looked in the waters off Whitehaven).

The British people were on edge. The American Revolution, which remained essentially stalemated, was turning nastier and threatening to widen. In the west, the British, under bloody-minded commanders like Colonel Henry Hamilton ("the Hair Buyer"), the lieutenant governor of Detroit, had organized loyalists and Indians into raiding parties. The rebels were fighting back to protect their settlements, several of which had been the scenes of Indian massacres. In Connecticut in early July, British troops had dropped their customary restraint and burned and plundered two towns, Norwalk and Fairfield, as the citizens fled. In Britain, leaders of the opposition warned in Parliament that, by violently repressing the rebels, the King's party risked bringing down violent reprisals from raiders like the Pirate Paul Jones. (Indeed, Congress was so incensed by British atrocities that the delegates debated, but did not send, an order to Franklin in Paris, directing him to hire arsonists to burn London.) The British countryside was buzzing with rumors of war. The Franco-Spanish invasion fleet had been spotted in the English Channel. Unaware of the epidemic of illness that was silently ravaging the French invasion force, English gentlemen were raising militias to resist any French landing.

Jones risked kicking over a beehive. With spies about (even if he did not suspect Bancroft), he knew that his mission might be compromised. Nonetheless, he was determined to plunge ahead. On September 14, the *Bonhomme Richard* arrived at the mouth of the Firth of Forth, the waterway that leads to Edinburgh, Scotland's capital and largest city. By interrogating seamen of captured fishing boats and merchantmen taken as prizes, Jones determined that Edinburgh's port, the city of Leith, was only lightly defended. Only a British twenty-gun ship and a couple of cutters rode at anchor, and the great guns in the fort at Edinburgh Castle could not reach the coast. The wind was right; Jones believed that he could sail right in and hold Leith ransom—extract a large "contribution" from the city or "reduce it to ashes." But first he had to persuade the reluctant captains of the *Pallas* and the *Vengeance*.

Captains Denis Cottineau and Philippe Ricot arrived aboard the *Bonhomme Richard* at eight in the evening. Jones summoned them into his lantern-lit great cabin and held a parley of war. At first, Jones recalled, he appealed to the other gentlemen's sense of honor and humanity. By laying the town under contribution, the raiding party could force the British to free American prisoners. Cottineau and Ricot made "many difficulties and objections," Jones recalled. So Jones took a more practical approach. He told them he planned to demand a ransom of £200,000. That got their attention, and the French captains consented to lend their ships to the plan of attack.

Valuable time had been lost while the captains made "pointed remarks" and engaged in "sage deliberation," Jones noted with more than a trace of sarcasm. Searching for prizes while their captains jawed aboard the *Bonhomme Richard*, the *Pallas* and the *Vengeance* had wandered off a considerable ways to the south. By the time the squadron reassembled, the wind had shifted and the three ships spent much of the next day laboriously beating up the Forth in a light breeze. Still Jones pressed on. Aboard the *Bonhomme Richard*, Jones's men prepared for a surprise attack. Posing as merchantmen, the squadron flew British colors. The marines were issued British red coats. Swivel cannons were mounted on the small boats that would take them in.

Jones planned to have the *Bonhomme Richard,* the *Vengeance,* and the *Pallas* lay along the twenty-gun Royal Navy ship and the cutters in the harbor and quickly overwhelm their crews. Then Colonel Paul Chamillard of the marines was to take 130 of his men into the port and disembark on the breakwater. He would dispatch an officer and a drum to deliver a message. It was addressed to "the Worshipful the Provost of Leith" and written by Jones, in his customary florid style. "I do not wish to distress the poor inhabitants," Jones wrote.

> My intention is only to demand your contribution towards the reimbursement which Britain owes to the much injured citizens of America. Savages would blush at the unmanly violation and rapacity that has marked the tracks of British tyranny in America from which neither virgin innocence nor helpless age has been a plea of protection or pity. Leith and its port now lays at our mercy; and did not the plea of humanity stay the hand of just retaliation I should, *without advertisement,* lay it in ashes. Before I proceed to that stern duty as an officer; my duty *as a man* induces me to propose to you by the means of a reasonable ransom to prevent such scenes of horror and distress.

Chamillard was to give the provost "exactly half an hour's reflection" to accept Jones's conditions. The colonel was to ask for half the ransom in cash, half in a note, and to take six city councilmen as hostages, releasing three with the cash payment and holding the other three "as guarantee for the note." (Jones instructed Chamillard to settle for £50,000 if he could not extract the rest.) If the city fathers of Leith refused, Chamillard was "to set fire everywhere." The colonel was given two flags. He was to wave a white flag if the provost accepted the ransom, a red one if the answer was no, and both together if fighting had broken out and he was forced to retreat.

The day was bright, and Jones, though he had not slept, was cresting on the surge of euphoria he always felt going into action. As the *Bonhomme Richard* sailed up the Forth, a cutter approached, and its captain called out. Jones and his officers, as usual, were dressed in British naval uniforms. The cutter had mistaken the *Bonhomme Richard* for a British fifty-gun ship, the *Romney*. The cutter's captain asked if the warship could spare some gunpowder. The man explained that "the rebel Paul Jones" was expected to land anyday, and that the shore defenses near Leith were weak and needed strengthening. Jones was happy to oblige. With his compliments, Jones ordered a keg of gunpowder lowered onto the cutter. Still pretending to the captain of *Romney*, Jones asked if he could borrow the cutter's pilot to help him navigate local waters. The pilot came aboard, and the cutter sailed away with the gunpowder. Standing on the quarterdeck, Jones asked the man, What news? The pilot said that the pirate Jones was off the coast and deserved to be hanged. Jones smiled. "I am Paul Jones," the captain announced. The poor pilot dropped to his knees and begged for his life. "Get up!" Jones commanded. "I won't hurt a hair on your head, but you are my prisoner."

The locals were not fooled for long. All that day, as the squadron beat back and forth, slowly working up the Forth toward the capital and its port, there was pandemonium on shore. Drums rolled, bagpipes skirled. Families packed up and began to flee. Banks closed and tried to ferry their treasure out of town. Young men scrounged around for any kind of weapon, settling for a few rusty old fowling pieces (the Scots had been disarmed after Culloden in 1746). An aging Presbyterian minister went to the shore, settled his chair in the surf, and prayed for a strong wind to blow the Americans away.

Jones planned to catch the enemy sleeping with a dawn raid on Leith. At 4 A.M., he hoisted out the ship's launch, equipped with muffled oars, and began embarking marines. It had been a very dark night, and first light brought only gloom and a rising wind. The prayers of the old minister had been answered. To Jones's immense chagrin, the wind quickly whipped up to a full-fledged gale; squalls roared down out of the Highlands, gusting rain and sweeping straight down the Forth toward the sea. The progress of the squadron, Jones recalled, halted only a "cannon shot" from Leith. An amphibious operation was out of the question. Indeed, the men of the *Bonhomme Richard* had to scramble aloft to shorten sail. As the tempest shrieked and the ship plunged and rolled, Jones told the sailing master to send the men back out on the yards to take in sails before they shredded in the gale or carried away a spar or a mast. He kept only a scrap of canvas on the mizzenmast to maintain headway. Lashed by wind and rain, Jones stood disconsolate on the quarterdeck through the day and another sleepless night, his plans blown to tatters.

Yet he was not done. There was a cocky streak of defiance in Jones that showed itself in puckish ways. Sailing in close to the isle of Lindisfarne as he eluded British warships searching the coast, Jones lobbed a cannonball into ancient Bamburgh Castle as a kind of insolent salute. He was still scheming. On the border between Scotland and England was the coal-shipping port of Newcastle-upon-Tyne. Jones summoned Ricot and Cottineau back on board and made a new proposal: they would descend on Newcastle and burn the city's colliers, its coal ships. Without Newcastle's coal, Jones argued, London would be cold that winter. Ricot and Cottineau dismissed Jones's idea as foolhardy. By now, they argued, the alarm had spread all over Great Britain. If the squadron ventured inshore, they would all be taken and cast into prison. The two captains flatly refused to sail with Jones.

Jones briefly contemplated going it alone. He was cheered that the *Bonhomme Richard*'s "young officers" were "as ardently disposed to the business as I could desire." No sullen or mutinous lieutenants, no Simpson or Hall, in this crowd. But in the end, Jones decided that odds against success were too steep. As usual, he weighed the possible consequences to his reputation, which he valued more than life. "Nothing prevented me from pursuing my design but the reproach that would have been cast upon my character as a man of prudence had the enterprise miscarried—it would have been said, was he not forewarned by Captain Cottineau and others."

The *Vengeance* and *Pallas* sailed on ahead down the English coast, in search of prizes. The *Bonhomme Richard* was moving even slower than usual, having struck her main topmast, damaged by the storm. The weather was drizzly, the winds light and variable. At 11 P.M. on Wednesday, September 22, the lookout spotted two sails through the murk. Jones gave chase. At 2 A.M., he ordered "Beat to Quarters" and the marine drummer rousted the men from the hammocks to stand by their guns and prepare for battle. As dawn crept up, Jones peered through the gray mists and slowly made out the two ships he had been stalking all night. They were his own: the *Pallas* and, remarkably enough, the *Alliance*. Jones had not seen Landais's ship in two weeks.

Jones's squadron was intact again, more or less. But Jones was running out of time. His orders were to make for the Texel, the shipping roads that served Amsterdam, by the first of October. The French ministry wanted him to escort a fleet of merchantmen that had been holed up in the Dutch port avoiding British cruisers. Jones's spirits were low indeed. After nearly six weeks at sea, he had nothing to show for his efforts but a few prizes. He might as well have been a privateersman. While he knew that the British, aroused, were on guard against his small fleet, he was unaware that he had already created a tremendous commotion in the public and press just by his presence off Britain's shores. Jones knew only that he had been thwarted by bad luck and timid and vexatious captains. It was not in him to give up. But by the morning of Thursday, September 23, 1779, he was feeling desperate.

CHAPTER NINE

"We've Got Her Now!"

*W*HILE JONES wore his customary groove on the windward side of the *Bonhomme Richard*'s quarterdeck, some twenty miles to the north another captain paced a deck that, in the British navy tradition, had been scrubbed and buffed until it gleamed in the morning light. Victory was a custom and a habit for the Royal Navy; the captain of HMS *Serapis* did not need to be a glory-seeker to motivate himself and his men. He could call on centuries of duty.

Richard Pearson was a formidable opponent for John Paul Jones. A veteran of thirty years at sea, he had been a Royal Navy captain for the last six. He had won notice as a first lieutenant for taking over from his disabled captain and guiding a ship of the line, the *Norfolk*, safely through a hurricane. He had fought in three fleet actions and been wounded by grapeshot that smashed his ribs. Despite internal bleeding, he had stood fast at his post until the action was over. He had captained two ships-of-war before being given command of the *Serapis*, a new, fast warship that carried forty-four guns on two decks. He had experienced officers and a highly disciplined crew.

On the morning of September 23, the *Serapis* and her consort, the *Countess of Scarborough*, a lightly armed sloop, were convoying forty-four merchant ships from Scandinavia to the south of England dockyards. The merchantmen were carrying naval stores—canvas, rope, timber—essential to equipping the Royal Navy. The eight-day crossing from the Baltics had been uneventful. Pearson was on the lookout for American privateers, and he was generally aware of Paul Jones from the lurid press about the marauding "pirate." But as the *Serapis* reached the English coastline, the seas looked calm and clear.

At 10 A.M., Pearson spied through the light morning haze a red flag flying over old Scarborough Castle on the Yorkshire coastline. The red flag signaled "Enemy on Our Shores." Minutes later, a fishing boat came alongside with a message from the local bailiffs: a "flying squadron" of enemy ships had been seen off the coast just the day before, slowly heading south.

Jones's squadron had actually doubled back, looking for prizes north of the mouth of the Humber River. By 1 P.M., the lookouts of the *Serapis* could see them: the masts of four ships, still hull down on the horizon. Several merchantmen sailing up ahead had already spotted Jones's squadron. They had let fly their topsail sheets, signaling "strange sail in sight." Pearson signaled his flock to run toward shore, where they would be safe under the guns of Scarborough Castle. Then he signaled his small sloop consort and manuevered to put the warships between the merchantmen and the enemy raiders.

Aboard the *Bonhomme Richard*, lookouts were calling down to a quarterdeck that was stirring with anticipation. The officers were keeping count as the lookouts cried out with each new sail sighting. Through the haze, brightening in the early afternoon, they could see at least three dozen ships scattered across the azure sea—a hunting ground rich with prizes. About three or four miles away, shimmering in the diffuse light, the chalky cliffs of Flamborough Head rose 150 feet above the Yorkshire coastline. The lookouts could see the closest merchantmen loosing their topsails to warn the others of danger. The merchant ships began to turn and run north and west, trying to get around the headland and under the guns of Scarborough Castle on the other side.

Jones was anxious to cut them off. "As soon as Jones had taken a peep or two at them with his spyglass, he expressed himself to his officers, then standing by him upon the quarterdeck," recalled Midshipman Fanning. "This is the very fleet which I have been so long cruising for." Jones realized that he had chanced upon the Baltic Fleet, with its rich cargo of naval stores. One of his early schemes, advanced to Sartine months before, was to intercept the Baltic Fleet and cut Britain's "sinews of war," its raw materials for the navy. Jones ordered the signal made, "General Chase." He needn't have. Unmindful of his signals in most events, Jones's captains could see the prizes floating ahead and made for them straightaway. Jones "appeared to be impatient," Fanning observed, probably understating his captain's intensity of feeling. Jones ordered the sailing master to crowd on all sail. Studding sails began to sprout along booms high above the deck. A cloud of canvas stretched to catch the light airs.

It was maddeningly slow going. Jones was running against the current and making no more than a mile or two an hour. But he was already imagining the battle ahead. By 4 P.M., he could distinctly make out the shape of a Royal Navy man-o-war, with her yellow topsides, as well as the smaller sloop following in her wake.

The shadows lengthened as the sun lowered in the late September sky. The golden light reflected off the gilt work on *Bonhomme Richard*'s ornately carved stern. It illuminated the gold epaulets and gold theading on Jones's blue coat. He was neatly dressed as always, his straight brown hair pulled back from a clear brow, his strong jaw shaved, his eyes bright, though red-rimmed with exhaustion. As usual, he had not slept more than an hour or two the night before. But he was fully alert, as he always was going into action. All the nagging suspicions and doubts, the highly developed sense of grievance, blew away like doldrums before a great trade wind. His pride swelled and filled and became dauntless courage.

At 5 P.M., the marine drummers "Beat to Quarters." Bare feet slapped across the decks as the men ran to their battle stations. Aloft, chains clanked as sailors braced the yards so they would not crash to the deck below if hit. In the cockpit, far belowdecks, Surgeon Brooke laid out the crude tools of his trade, the saws and knives and the tub for the sawed-off limbs.

On the quarterdeck, Jones assembled his lieutenants and gave them precise instructions for destroying the enemy. Jones's heaviest guns were the six 18-pounders, three on each side, that poked out of the gun room on the ship's lower deck. They were to send their cannonballs smashing directly into the hull of the British warship. On the gun deck, the twenty-eight 12-pounders, fourteen to a broadside, were to fire double-headed shot into the enemy's rigging, seeking to disable her. Jones wanted to be able to board the enemy, if necessary. In any case, he knew the British man-o-war could sail faster and outmanuever his old Indiaman; he wanted to slow her down. On the quarterdeck, the six 9-pounders were also to be used to cut up the enemy's sails and rigging. Jones stationed a heavy contingent of marines on the *Bonhomme Richard*'s antiquated poop deck, which enjoyed one residual advantage over the enemy's sleeker modern design: it provided a good field of fire down on the enemy's quarterdeck. Belowdecks, the ship's armory was unlocked so that, at the right moment, boarding parties could be handed cutlasses, axes, pikes, and pistols. Into the tops, Jones put no fewer than forty marines and assorted seamen. That was an unsually large force. Jones was a pioneer in using small arms marksmen high in the ship's rigging. Some captains, most famously Nelson, feared that soldiers blazing away with flintlock weapons would ignite the highly flammable rigging and sails. But Jones wanted all the extra firepower he could get, whatever the risk.

The marines and seamen were sent aloft with a small arsenal, armed with swivel guns, blunderbusses, and coehorns, a kind of small mortar to lob bombs, as well as baskets of grenades which could be tossed down to the deck below. Be ruthlessly methodical, Jones instructed the officers. First, clear the British tops of men. Then, aim down at the British decks and sweep them clean as well. The three tops were commanded by midshipmen. Fanning was in his early twenties, but neither of the others "exceeded 17 years of age," Fanning recorded. "The captains of the tops," Fanning noted, "drew up into the tops a double allowance of grog for their men."

At 6 P.M., as the sun was dipping down behind the cliffs at Flamborough

Head, Jones could see the two British ships coming about and heading west toward the shore, keeping themselves between their merchantmen and the American marauders. Jones brought around the *Bonhomme Richard* to go straight at them and signaled "Form Line of Battle." Perhaps it was the dusk and not outright disobedience that caused his other three ships to sail off on their own. (Landais, ever the contrarian, would subsequently maintain that Jones ignored *his* hail and that he never saw Jones's signal.) But, for whatever reason, Jones suddenly found himself alone.

The British ship swung open her gun ports. Jones grimly took the measure of the black iron muzzles that thrust out: among her forty-four guns, HMS *Serapis* had a battery of twenty 18-pounders, ten to a side.* At close range, a cannonball from one of these guns could smash through the thickest bulkhead of a warship and keep on going right through the other side, if it did not obliterate a man or a gun in the way. Jones had his doubts about the reliability of his own half-dozen 18-pounders, which were old. French cannon had a bad reputation for bursting.

Surveying the quarterdeck of the enemy warship with his spyglass, Jones could see his opposite, in the blue coat and black tricorned hat of a British captain, doing something peculiar. The tall staff on the stern holding up the British ensign, the white flag with the red St. George's cross, had been hauled down. The captain was bending over the long wooden pole, wielding hammer and nails, like an ordinary carpenter's mate. Actually, Captain Pearson was nailing on a new flag, an enormous, blood-red Royal Navy ensign. The message from Captain Pearson was clear to the warship's crew and equally to their foe: no one would surrender his ship by striking this flag, nailed to its staff by the captain himself.

As darkness fell, the combatants drifted across a tableau of serene beauty. The stars were beginning to show. In the east, a harvest moon was

---

*Going into battle, the *Serapis* outgunned the *Bonhomme Richard* by forty-four guns to forty. The British ship carried twenty 18-pounders, twenty-two 9-pounders, and two 6-pounders; it could fire a broadside of 285 pounds. The American ship had six 18-pounders, twenty-eight 12-pounders, and six 9-pounders; it could fire a broadside of 265 pounds.

rising, orange and huge in the low haze. Yellow light spilled from each gun port. The crews of the two ships could clearly see each other as they stood outlined by their guns, which were primed, loaded with shot, ready to fire. "The surface of the great deep," Fanning recalled, was "perfectly smooth, even as in a millpond." Captain Pearson's voice sounded across the narrowing gap of sea: "This is his majesty's ship *Serapis*. What ship is that?" (Fanning recalled that Pearson's voice was "hoarse and hardly intelligible . . . in true *bombastic English style*.")

Jones played for every advantage, trying to edge as close to the British ship as possible. Jones instructed the sailing master to reply, *"Princess Royal."* (The *Princess Royal* was a British East Indies merchantman about the same size as the *Bonhomme Richard*.) Pearson called across again, "Where from?" Jones pretended not to hear. Pearson barked, "Tell me instantly from whence you came and who you be, or I'll fire a broadside into you!"

The game was up. Jones hauled down his false British colors and broke out his Continental Navy ensign. At just that moment, a nervous marine in the *Bonhomme Richard*'s tops fired his musket. Both ships erupted, loosing their broadsides at once. The sound was appalling: the tremendous concussion of forty-two cannon and scores of small arms fired at nearly the same instant, the cracking of splintered wood, the jarring clang of a cannonball striking an iron muzzle or an anchor fluke, and, very soon thereafter, the shrieks and cries of the wounded. At the range of twenty-five yards, every gun hit home. For the officers standing exposed on the quarterdeck, it must have taken extraordinary willpower not to flinch or cringe, much less dive for cover.

"The battle thus begun was continued with unremitting fury," wrote Jones. The second broadside was more cataclysmic than the first. In the gun room, one, possibly two of the *Bonhomme Richard*'s aging 18-pounders burst in a blinding flash. The force of the explosion was so great that it ripped a chunk out of the ship's starboard side right above the waterline. Inside the gun room there was utter devastation. Men lay dead, dismembered, and horribly burned. Jones knew right away what had gone wrong, and he ordered the gun room abandoned. The remaining 18-pounders were useless, made unreliable by age and poor casting. The ten 18-pounders on the port side of the *Serapis* were in perfect working order, however, and they were manned by crews who had relentlessly practiced loading and firing. Jones had rarely (if ever) exercised his great guns with live ammunition; he lacked sufficient gunpowder.

As the two ships glided along, blasting away in a pall of smoke, Pearson outfoxed Jones. The American commander had wanted the *Bonhomme Richard* to sail to windward of the *Serapis*. Normally, the ship to windward has more manueverability, and hence more ability to dictate the course of the battle, because a square-rigged sailing ship has a much easier time bearing down, sailing away from the wind, than trying to head up into it. The more aggressive British generally tried to get to windward against the French, who stereotypically hung to leeward because it was easier to escape. By sailing to windward, Jones thought he had seized the role of the aggressor and put the *Serapis* on the defensive. As the *Bonhomme Richard* blanketed the *Serapis*, stealing the light and eddying breeze from her sails, Jones's ship drew ahead. Then Pearson made his play. As soon as the stern of the *Bonhomme Richard* cleared the bow of the *Serapis*, Pearson veered up a few points, cutting to windward and behind the *Bonhomme Richard*. The British ship gained momentum and briefly blanketed the American ship. Then, at just the right moment, Pearson ordered, "Ware ship!" The helmsman spun the wheel, and the *Serapis* slipped down at right angles to the *Bonhomme Richard*'s stern. Those beautiful stern windows that lit up Jones's great cabin, all the carving and gilt work, presented a fat target to the port battery of the *Serapis*. A basic tactic of single-ship battles is to rake the enemy, to cross his undefended bow or stern and send cannon-balls or grapeshot sweeping down the length of the enemy ship. One by one, the guns of the British ship crashed out, smashing through the stern of the *Bonhomme Richard*, shattering glass and wood and ripping through anyone standing in the way. With the wind dying, Pearson backed his sails and got off another broadside. Then another.

The carnage aboard the *Bonhomme Richard* was unspeakable. On the

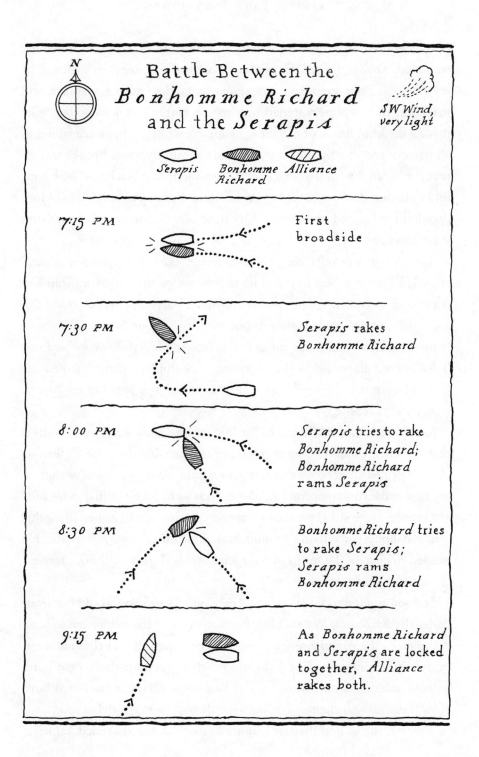

Battle Between the
Bonhomme Richard
and the *Serapis*

SW Wind, very light

Serapis *Bonhomme Richard* *Alliance*

7:15 PM	First broadside
7:30 PM	*Serapis* rakes *Bonhomme Richard*
8:00 PM	*Serapis* tries to rake *Bonhomme Richard*; *Bonhomme Richard* rams *Serapis*
8:30 PM	*Bonhomme Richard* tries to rake *Serapis*; *Serapis* rams *Bonhomme Richard*
9:15 PM	As *Bonhomme Richard* and *Serapis* are locked together, *Alliance* rakes both.

poop deck, twenty-two of twenty-five marines had been killed or wounded. Down the length of the ship, guns had been overturned or knocked off their carriages. The superior tactics, manueverability, and firepower of *Serapis* threatened to turn the battle into a slaughter. "She made a dreadful havoc of our crew," Fanning wrote. "Men were falling in all parts of the ship by the *scores.*" In the cockpit, Surgeon Brooke was already splattered with blood; a clutch of seamen, skin blackened by burns, limbs shattered or missing, lay groaning and crying around him. More dreadfully wounded men, carried by their shocked mates, were arriving every moment.

The *Serapis* was outsailing the *Bonhomme Richard* "by *two feet to one,*" recorded Fanning. She rounded up to leeward of the American ship and continued to pour in grape- and roundshot as fast as her crews could fire and load—a rippling broadside about every two minutes or less. Stabs of flame flared across the narrow gap of water. The *Bonhomme Richard* was holed several places below the waterline. The ship's carpenter dashed below with canvas and large wooden plugs to stanch the flow, but the pumps were barely keeping up.

Jones was losing the battle of his life, and he knew it. "I must confess that the enemy's ship being much more manageable than the *Bonhomme Richard* gained thereby several times an advantageous situation in spite of my best endeavors to prevent it," Jones later wrote, a bit stiffly, in his official report. As he stood on the quarterdeck, trying not to notice the splinters and body parts flying around him, Jones tried to concentrate. He needed to change the terms of engagement; his ships would not survive a cannon duel much longer.

Pearson wanted to finish off the American. As the *Serapis* slid out from under the *Bonhomme Richard*'s lee, Pearson ordered the helmsman to head up, to cross the American's bow and rake her again. But at that moment, Pearson's luck ran out. The light wind died altogether; the *Serapis* hung without steerage way, just off of the *Bonhomme Richard*'s starboard bow. Now Jones saw his chance. Feeling a gentle puff from the dying southerly, he ordered the sailing master, Samuel Stacey ("A true-blooded Yankee," according to Fanning), to "lay the enemy's ship on board." In the next breath, he ordered the officers to muster the boarding party. Seamen and marines were handed cutlasses, pikes, and pistols and assembled in the ship's waist and on the forecastle. The helmsman was barely able to steer the sluggish ship in the feeble breeze, but the *Bonhomme Richard* drifted toward the stern of the *Serapis*. The bowsprit of the American ship gently nudged into the rigging of the British ship's mizzenmast. "Well done my lads, we've got her now!" cried Jones, full of the savage joy that seized him at moments of maximum peril. The sailors hurled grappling hooks across to the *Serapis*, catching them in the rigging and hooking on to the bulwarks. British seamen and redcoats, armed with axes, just as quickly began cutting them away while Royal Marines peppered musket fire at the small knot of Americans trying to climb out onto the bowsprit.

It was no use. A bowsprit is a precarious bridge; the boarding party was on a virtual suicide mission. Jones called it off, and the men drew back; the lines to the grappling hooks were hacked off. The *Bonhomme Richard* backed its sails and the two ships drew apart. Pearson wanted to resume hammering his foe, so he ordered his topsails backed to check the *Serapis* and bring the two ships parallel again. The heavy guns of the *Serapis* flashed out and another several hundredweight of iron ripped through the *Bonhomme Richard*'s aged planks. At some badly mauled gun stations, the decks were wet with blood. Jones was truly up against it now. The *Bonhomme Richard* was barely sailing. Jones needed to make a last attempt to gain the upper hand.

He did have one small advantage. Because the *Bonhomme Richard* was to windward of the *Serapis*, Jones was able to blanket his opponent and steal her wind, catching what little zephyrs still rippled the water in the settling darkness. A slight puff nudged the American warship ahead, and Jones made his move. "It was my intention to lay the *Bonhomme Richard* athwart the enemy's bow," Jones wrote. He wanted to cross the T, putting his ship at a right angle to the *Serapis* in order to rake the enemy ship with cannon and musket fire from stem to stern.

The sailing master ordered the helmsman to spin the wheel, and the old Indiaman made the last course change of her life. The *Bonhomme Richard*'s bow began to swing ponderously around, but the manuever didn't quite work. Some of the braces, the blocks and tackles used to swing the yardarms to trim the sails, had been shot away. The *Bonhomme Richard* stalled in front of the *Serapis*. Pearson ordered his helmsman to steer around the smoldering hulk, but too late: the bowsprit of the British ship drove into the *Bonhomme Richard*'s mizzen rigging.

Jones decided to make a virtue of necessity. A forestay from the *Serapis* had parted and lay across the *Bonhomme Richard*'s poop deck. Jones scrambled up the ladder to the poop deck and made fast the line to the mizzenmast. He called for Sailing Master Stacey to find a heavier rope and help him lash it around the *Serapis*'s jib boom and *Bonhomme Richard*'s mizzenmast, binding the two ships together. Stacey, a salty sea dog, was swearing a blue streak. "Mr. Stacey, it's no time to be swearing now," teased Jones, almost lighthearted in the gloom and chaos. "You may by the next moment be in eternity, but let us do our duty."

The wind had now died altogether. The sea was "smooth as glass," recalled Fanning. A strong tide was running. Pearson was anxious not to be caught in a fatal embrace with the dying *Bonhomme Richard*, which, he feared, could blow up at any minute. The British captain ordered an anchor dropped. He figured that as the anchor bit into the bottom and held the *Serapis*, the *Bonhomme Richard* would pull away and drift off on the tide. Once the two ships were apart, the British guns could deliver the final blows.

But the *Serapis* could not break free. As the two ships swung around in the tide, the *Serapis*'s jib boom bent and snapped off, but Jones's men were able to throw grappling hooks—"at least 50 of them," according to one witness—onto the rigging and bulkheads of the British ship. The sailors of the *Serapis* tried to cut away the lines, but the marines in the tops of the *Bonhomme Richard* picked the sailors off as they were swinging their axes. The fluke of Pearson's spare anchor caught in the mizzen chains of the *Bonhomme Richard*. The two ships ground together, facing in opposite directions but hopelessly entangled. They were literally muzzle-to-muzzle now.

It was about 8:30 P.M. The battle was more than an hour old. A few miles away, atop the cliffs of Flamborough Head, large crowds were gathering. About a thousand people had walked or ridden from the surrounding villages, lured by the news that a British man-o-war had trapped the Pirate Jones. Under the silvery moon, across the glistening water, they witnessed a fantastic sight. The two warships were locked inside a yellowish cloud that pulsated with flashes of orange and white light. In the dead calm, the smoke from the cannon and numerous small blazes created a thick blanket of sulfurish smoke, eerie and ghostly to the onlookers on the cliff, choking and toxic to the men trapped within.

The death struggle had become two battles, a race to extinction on two fronts, one abovedeck, one below. Jones's sharpshooters had cleared the British tops and now they were sweeping the decks of *Serapis* with musketry and shot from the blunderbusses and swivel guns. Captain Pearson, though stoic, was finally forced to move out of this dangerous hailstorm and take refuge beneath the quarterdeck. He still controlled the battle belowdecks, however. The *Serapis*'s 12- and 18-pounders continued to blast away. The cannonballs went in one side of the *Bonhomme Richard* and out the other, creating ever larger holes at and below the waterline. The gun deck of the American ship was a wasteland, strewn with bodies and shattered cannon. One by one, the last of Jones's 12-pounders were silenced. By 9 P.M. or so, the American captain was left with only his three 9-pounders on the quarterdeck. When one of them was smashed, its gun captain badly wounded, Jones himself helped haul a 9-pounder across the deck from the other side and aim at the *Serapis*. Jones's target was the three-foot-wide mainmast of the *Serapis*, painted yellow and easy to pick out in the swirling smoke.

The smoke was getting thicker. Both ships were on fire. The stabs of flame from the cannons had ignited scraps of wood and canvas hanging down from the cut-up rigging and mast of the *Serapis*. Burning cartridge wads from the British guns were smoldering in the shattered timbers of the *Bonhomme Richard*. On a wooden ship laced with highly flammable tar and resin, fire was dreaded more than enemy cannonballs. Flames were creeping up the sails and the rigging; down below, hot coals were erupting in little blazes that threatened to create a conflagration that would reach the powder magazine. For a brief time, the shooting and cannonading died down; as if by mutual agreement, the men left their guns to fight the fire, cutting away burning cordage and dousing flames with buckets of water hauled from the sea.

Jones had a moment to catch a breather. He sat on a hen coop on the quarterdeck and looked out into the darkness, wondering what had happened to his disloyal squadron. He was glad to see that not all the captains were timid. He could pick out the *Pallas* about a mile off in the night. She was bashing the outgunned *Countess of Scarborough*. Captain Cottineau was too cautious for Jones's taste, but at least he had not shied from taking on the smaller British sloop. The *Countess of Scarborough* was beaten and would soon strike. Somewhere out there, Jones guessed, the *Vengeance* was biding its time, waiting to see if the British escorts would be defeated by braver men, thus leaving the merchantmen easy prey for scavengers. But where was the *Alliance* and its erratic Captain Landais?

Jones found out soon enough. At about 9:15 P.M., a broadside of grapeshot ripped through the bow of the *Serapis* and the stern of the *Bonhomme Richard*, wounding and killing men on both ships. It was the *Alliance*, apparently firing wildly into the inferno. Aboard the *Bonhomme Richard*, men cried out, yelling, "For Gods sake! Wrong ship! Stop firing!" But the *Alliance*, sailing along serenely only a musket shot away, rounded the *Bonhomme Richard*'s bow and loosed another broadside of grapeshot. Among the mortally wounded on the *Bonhomme Richard*'s forecastle was a young midshipman, Jonas Coram. "*Alliance* has wounded me," he said with his dying breath. Then, just as he had suddenly appeared, Landais vanished again into the blackness. Jones was "astonished." He ordered his men to hang lanterns fifteen feet high in the shrouds of each mast and the commodore's private signal, two lanterns at the peak of the mizzenmast, so there would be no mistake if the *Alliance* deigned to rejoin the fray.

Holed several times below the waterline, the *Bonhomme Richard* was slowly settling. The carpenter, John Gunnison, descended into the hold and sank to his chin in water. He could hear the screams of a hundred British prisoners, taken off the *Bonhomme Richard*'s prizes, and locked in the hold. Sure that they were going to drown, they begged to be set free. Gunnison climbed back up on deck looking for an officer. He found the gunner's mate, Henry Gardner. "We're sinking," he told Gardner. The two men made their way aft and climbed the ladder to the quarterdeck on the port side, away from the fighting. They saw that the *Bonhomme Richard*'s ensign staff on the taffrail was gone. Dazed, frightened, unable to identify Captain Jones (he was on the starboard side, bent over a 9-pounder), the two men assumed that the captain was dead. First Lieutenant Dale was nowhere to be seen. Gardner, an Englishman, determined that he was the senior surviving officer. He decided to end the slaughter before the ship sank or blew up. Raising his voice to be heard amidst the din, he cried the word for surrender: "Quarters! Quarters!" The two master's mates turned and started for the mainmast, where they intended to lower the broad pendant flying at the peak, thus striking the last American flag.

Jones was concentrating on slowly cutting down the enemy's mainmast with barshot from his 9-pounder when he heard someone on the quarterdeck cry "Quarters!" In a rage, he wheeled, shouting, "Who are those rascals? Shoot them! Kill them!" He lunged across the deck at Gardner and Gunnison. The two men took one look at the gleaming eyes of their captain and the pistol he was drawing from his belt and made a dash for it. Jones tried to shoot Gunnison, but when he pulled the trigger, he heard only a click. He had forgotten that he had already discharged the weapon at the *Serapis*'s quarterdeck, hoping to wing an officer, earlier in the battle. In a fury, Jones gripped the pistol by the muzzle and hurled it at Gardner's head, just as the gunner tried to scramble down the ladder. Knocked cold, the man collapsed into the ship's waist.

Aboard the *Serapis*, Pearson, too, had heard the cries for "Quarters!" aboard the *Bonhomme Richard*. Were the stubborn Americans at least relenting? The British captain came to the quarterdeck rail and yelled across, "Have you struck? Do you call for Quarters?"

*   *   *

JONES'S RESPONSE, delivered as his ship was sinking beneath him, has become his most enduring legacy. In his official report, Jones wrote that he answered Captain Pearson "in the most determined negative." Some forty-five years later, an aging Lieutenant Dale (Captain Richard Dale, USN Ret.) told an early Jones biographer that the captain had shouted defiantly, "I have not yet begun to fight!" Those words became immortal, but they are probably not the exact ones he used. In a memoir Jones wrote to Louis XVI, Jones reported replying, "Je ne songe point a me rendre, mais je suis determine a vous faire demander quartier"—literally translated, "I haven't as yet thought of surrendering, but I am determined to make you ask for quarter." Even by eighteenth-century standards, that is a mouthful for a man standing at the brink of doom. One contemporary account suggested a pithier exclamation: "I may sink, but I'll be damned if I strike."

Jones was beset on all sides. The master-at-arms, John Burbank, took pity on the crying prisoners, trapped in the hold while the water rose around them. He set them free, and a hundred Englishmen clambered up onto the deck. Jones was suddenly faced with a potential prisoner revolt. That many men, if determined enough, might have overwhelmed Jones's bloodied and dwindling crew. Fortunately for Jones, the freed prisoners were so terrified, and so grateful to be gasping fresh air, that they proved docile. Jones and Dale were able, with a wave of their pistols, to convince the Englishmen to man the pumps, lest they all drown together.

Through the crack of musket fire and the continued pounding of the *Serapis*'s heavy guns, Jones heard a cry go up and saw a commotion toward the bow. The British were boarding. A gang of twenty or thirty seamen and Royal Marines scrambled over the bulwark and, armed with cutlasses and pistols, ran down the *Bonhomme Richard*'s gangway along the waist to the quarterdeck ladder. There they were met by Jones, wielding a boarding pike, supported by his seamen, some of whom remembered their recent confinement in a British jail. Steel met steel, clanging and jarring;

men grunted and yelled; pistols popped. The fight was vicious but brief. Rather than die where they stood, the outnumbered and exhausted redcoats and tars scrambled and slipped back to their ship.

The last assault came from Jones's dubious ally, Captain Landais, a little after 10 P.M. Once more, the *Alliance* glided by the two ships in their desperate clinch and unloaded an indiscriminate blast of grapeshot. The moon was bright, and Jones's signals, hung after the last assault, were hard to miss. The topsides of the *Serapis* were yellow; those of the *Bonhomme Richard*, with its high poop deck, were black. But the men of the *Bonhomme Richard* could only scream and wave their fists as Landais sailed off again, to sit out the battle's climax.

The end came with surprising suddenness. In the maintop, a roughly fifteen-foot-by-fifteen-foot platform some forty feet above the deck, Midshipman Fanning, fifteen marines, and four sailors had been plinking away at the British marines, dropping them one by one from their platforms high in the rigging above the *Serapis*, then shooting at anything that moved on the deck below. Fanning's position was precarious. The *Bonhomme Richard*'s mainmast had been shot through by an 18-pound ball at its base; the mast was held up largely by the rigging. The sails and tarry ropes around the maintop kept catching on fire. Having exhausted a large tub of water, Fanning's men were using their clothes to snuff the flames. "The coat on my back was partly burned . . . together with the blackness of my face with powder, I had more the appearance of a runaway negro that that of an American officer," Fanning recalled. Still, the *Bonhomme Richard* had won the battle of the tops. Indeed, a nimble sailor was able to crawl out onto the mainsail yard, which extended out over the deck of the *Serapis:* a perfect bombing platform.

The sailor was a Scotsman named William Hamilton. As the battle entered its fourth hour, around 10:15 P.M., Hamilton edged out along the footropes of the mainyard carrying a lighted slow-match and a leather bucket of grenades. These were small bombs, about the size of baseballs. When lit, their fuses burned for about twenty seconds before detonating. Hamilton saw a half-open hatch on the deck below and began lobbing grenades, hoping one would drop through to the gun deck below. On the second or third try, he succeeded. The grenade glanced off the coaming around the hatch and tumbled below. Hamilton waited and listened. He heard a loud bang—then, in rapid succession, a series of thunderous explosions.

He had caught the British navy in an uncharacteristic moment of carelessness. It is a time-honored rule of the gun deck never to leave powder cartridges lying around, for the obvious reason that they are flammable and explosive. But during the course of the long and wearying struggle, the powder monkeys, the small boys used to ferry the cartridges from the magazine in the bowels of the ship to the gun deck, had gotten ahead of the exhausted gun crews. Cartridges haphazardly lined the deck behind the great guns.

Hamilton's grenade came bouncing down the hatchway ladder, its fuse sizzling. The explosion set off a chain reaction among the loose powder cartridges with devastating effect. Two-ton guns were blown from their carriages, men were ripped apart and scorched. A flash fire raced the length of the gun deck, which was packed with sweltering men. Some, their lungs seared, their hair on fire, leapt through open gun ports into the sea.

Pearson had lost five guns from his battery. He could see the mainmast begin to sway and lean to port, held up only by the web of rigging. Jones's 9-pounder had done its work, virtually chopping the 150-foot mast off at its base. The British captain had lost half his men; his ship was on fire in a dozen places. It was now 10:30 P.M.; he had fought gallantly. His duty was done.

Pearson climbed up the ladder to the quarterdeck and walked to the rail. Spotting his nemesis still hunched over the 9-pounder twenty yards away, he called, "Sir, I have struck! I ask for quarter!" Jones looked up at this apparition in a blue coat. The commodore wondered: could he really be hearing a plea for surrender? He demanded: "If you have struck, haul down your ensign!" Pearson walked, stiff-backed, to the taffrail and began ripping down the giant red ensign, now shredded by musket balls and grape, nail by nail from its staff.

"Cease firing!" Jones yelled. He ordered Lieutenant Dale to take a boarding crew across to secure the enemy ship. Grabbing a stray line hanging from a yardarm, the lieutenant swung himself across to the quarterdeck of the *Serapis*. Midshipman John Mayrant followed with a party of men and was immediately run through the thigh with a pike; some of the British sailors had not gotten the word. Pearson's first officer, Lieutenant John Wright, was also caught by surprise. Dale was just informing Pearson, "I have orders to send you on board the ship along side," when Wright, breathless from running up the ladder, appeared and asked his captain whether the Americans had struck. Dale interjected, "No sir, the contrary, he has struck to us." Wright was taken aback. He turned to Pearson. "Have you struck, sir?" Pearson quietly replied that he had. Wright could not hide his shame. "I have nothing more to say, sir," the first lieutenant stammered. Collecting himself, he asked Pearson's permission to go below and silence the remaining guns.

With a grinding, wrenching crash, the mainmast of the *Serapis* toppled over the side, ripping with it the mizzen topmast. After Pearson had crossed over, Jones ordered his men to cut away the grappling hooks and tangled rigging and let the *Serapis* float free. If the *Bonhomme Richard* was going to sink or burn, Jones wished at least to save his prize. Aboard the *Serapis*, Dale backed the remaining sails and was puzzled when the British ship did not respond. He did not realize that the *Serapis* was anchored. Deciding to investigate, Dale jumped off the binnacle, where he had been sitting in a state of semishock, and promptly fell to the deck as his leg collapsed under him. His calf had been badly cut by an iron splinter. In the heat of the battle, he had not realized that he had been wounded.

Captain Jones may have been lightly wounded, grazed by a piece of shrapnel, perhaps; in later years, Jones would refer vaguely to the blood he shed, but no record exists of any kind of serious injury. It is doubtful that he felt any sensation beside pure exultation as he stood, begrimed and haggard but erect, to greet Captain Pearson on the quarterdeck of the *Bonhomme Richard*. Against the *Drake*, he had been cheated out of the surrender ceremony by his opponent's demise: mortally wounded in the battle, Captain

Burden had been unable to hand over his sword in the ancient ritual of submission. Now Jones's moment of triumph, of sweet vindication, had arrived. Pearson, the symbol of Britannic rule, his soot-stained face struggling to remain impassive, stood before Jones, holding out his sword. Jones took it. "Sir," Jones said to Pearson, "you have fought like a hero, and I make no doubt that your sovereign will reward you in a most ample manner for it." Fanning and gunner's mate John Kilby both recalled hearing Pearson ask Jones the nationality of his crew. Mostly Americans, replied Jones.* "Then it was diamond cut diamond," Pearson responded. The British captain did not want to hear that he had succumbed to Frenchmen or Spaniards; Americans were at least cousins, endowed with English virtues. Fanning reported that Pearson also said that it "pained" him to hand his sword to a man who "has a halter around his neck," i.e., a pirate who would hang if caught. This blatant snub seems unlikely, though Pearson would be surly and haughty to Jones as a prisoner in port. Jones, for his part, tried to play the gentleman. According to Fanning, he asked Pearson to join him in his cabin for a glass of wine.

When he opened the cabin door, Jones must have had difficulty finding anything not blown to smithereens, much less a pair of wineglasses and a bottle of claret. His once elegant great cabin had taken a broadside from the *Serapis* in the first minutes of battle. Captain Pearson was stunned at the condition of the *Bonhomme Richard* belowdecks. "I found her in the greatest distress," he wrote in his official report to the Admiralty. Jones was also taken aback by what he saw. "A person must have been an eye witness to form a just idea of the tremendous scenes of carnage, wreck, and ruin which everywhere appeared," he recorded. The timbers on the lower deck were "mangled beyond my powers of description," wrote Jones after surveying the impact of the 18-pound balls that had smashed, by the dozens, through the ship during three hours of combat. "Only an old timber here and there kept the poop from crashing down on the gundeck."

---

*He was telling Pearson what he wanted to hear. In fact, Americans accounted for perhaps a third of the *Bonhomme Richard*'s crew, though seventeen of twenty officers were Yankees.

Gaping holes had been knocked in the topsides of the *Bonhomme Richard*. One breach was so wide, Fanning wrote, "One might have drove in with a coach and six."

The human toll was ghastly. Fanning wrote of his horror at seeing "the dead lying in heaps." The surgeons on both ships were overwhelmed. The burns were particularly gruesome aboard the *Serapis*. On the gun deck, Dale found men wearing "only the collars of their shirts." Their clothes, their hair, and their skin had been singed off. "The flesh of several of them dropped off from their bones and they died in great pain," wrote Fanning. The number of dead and wounded for the two crews (the *Serapis* had about 270 men aboard, the *Bonhomme Richard* roughly 320) has never been worked out with precision, but the casualty rate on both ships was close to 50 percent, extraordinarily high for a single-ship action in the Age of Sail.

The death toll was very nearly higher. The fires aboard the *Bonhomme Richard* threatened to blow up the ship. The flames came "within a few inches of the powder," reported Jones, who hastily ordered that the kegs of gunpowder be moved from the magazine to the upper decks. A human chain was formed to pass the volatile barrels up the smoky companion-ways. The fact that British officers volunteered to stand shoulder to shoulder with American sailors suggests the sense of urgency.

Jones tried to lighten his sinking ship by ordering the useless old 18-pounders thrown over the side. At daybreak, the ship's log cryptically reported, "The leak still gaining on us. We were supplied with men from the other ships who assisted in heaving the lower deck guns overboard & the dead, etc." Once their captains could see the American ensign flying from both the *Bonhomme Richard* and the *Serapis*, the *Alliance*, *Vengeance*, and *Pallas* (with her prize the *Countess of Scarborough*) all came skulking back to Jones. There is no record of the words exchanged between the various captains and Jones, but the congratulations must have been strained, particularly in the case of Captain Landais. Jones had already formed the opinion that Landais had intentionally fired on him.

Dawn of September 24 came with a mercifully thick blanket of fog and still calm seas. Jones needed time to jury-rig a mainmast and a mizzen topmast for the *Serapis* before he could make a run for it. British cruisers could not be far off. Jones was determined to save the *Bonhomme Richard*. He wanted to sail her into port leading his prize. But the old Indiaman's wounds were mortal. Slowly, the pumps lost the battle. By nightfall on the 24th, Jones had given the order to abandon ship. The wounded were carried over to the *Serapis* and the other ships. At the last minute, Jones sent Fanning back to recover his papers and personal effects, but the midshipman never made it on board the *Bonhomme Richard*. He could see the water pouring through her lower gun ports. With a great heave, the battered warship plunged quickly, bow first, with her colors flying. Jones watched, he wrote, "with inexpressible grief." He was not really mourning his ship, which he had regarded as an old clunker. More likely, he was feeling the letdown that always followed the exhilaration of battle.

CHAPTER TEN

"No Sooner Seen Than Lost"

*J*ONES HAD NO TIME to brood. At least eight Royal Navy warships, dispatched by a frantic Admiralty, were converging on Flamborough Head. The sea and wind were rising, the sky lowering. Jones and his squadron slipped over the horizen as the first of the British cruisers arrived on the scene. They split up and searched for Jones to the northeast, toward Scandinavia, to the southeast, toward Holland and France, and all around the British Isles. They never found him. Jones zigzagged in the North Sea for ten days and finally made a dash for the Texel island, the deep-water anchorage off Amsterdam, and the safety of a neutral port.

Jones's legend was made. "Paul Jones resembles a Jack o' Lantern, to mislead our mariners and terrify our coasts," wrote the *London Morning Post*. "He is no sooner seen than lost." As the reports of the battle began to filter back to London, the British press responded with lurid stories and illustrations. In the confused aftermath of the battle, a half-dozen British sailors who been set free from the hold of the *Bonhomme Richard* had stolen a small boat and rowed ashore near Flamborough Head. They described the incident of Jones throwing his pistol at the *Bonhomme Richard*'s carpenter, as the frightened man was trying to strike the American flag. The tale was quickly and colorfully embellished by the newspapers:

During the engagement, Paul Jones (who was dressed in a short jacket and long trousers with about twelve charged pistols slung in a belt around his middle and a cutlass in his hand) shot seven of his men for deserting from their quarters, and to his nephew, whom he thought a little dastardly, he said that damn his eyes he would not blow his brains out, but he would pepper his shins, and actually had the barbarity to shoot at the lad's legs, who is a lieutenant in his ship.

It was important for the British establishment to depict Jones as a lowlife, a brigand who wore short jackets and trousers, not a gentleman in breeches and coat. The navy had been embarrassed and wanted to belittle its adversary. "Jones flings us all into consternation and terror, and will hinder Lady Carlisle's sea bathing," the Earl of Carlisle wrote, a little flippantly. A London paper sent a correspondent to Kirkbean to learn more about the devil's incarnation; he reported back that Jones as a schoolboy had been a "blockhead" who lay in wait for his teacher and beat him almost to death. But the poems and ballads in the cheap penny chapbooks also made Jones out to be a Robin Hood figure, outfoxing the clumsy sheriff's men.

The more abuse the press heaped on Jones—he was a "desperado," "a good seaman but a bad man," "a vile fellow," "a daring pirate who has for some time past done so much mischief on the coast of Great Britain"— the greater the victory he could claim. His achievement was not simply to defeat a superior warship, but to spread fear all through Britain. He was teaching the British a lesson: that the price of keeping America as a colony was too high. By taking the war to the British homeland, Jones helped fuel an already vigorous anti-war movement amongst the loyal opposition, which questioned His Majesty's government's labored prosecution of a costly war that might not be lost, but which could not be won either. Jones was raising the stakes in uncomfortable ways. Intelligence reports seeping into the London papers hinted at dreadful escalations: "A gentleman in the city, well known at the 'Change for his early American intelligence," reportedly learned that Ben Franklin was pressing Congress to put the

British on notice: if Jones was captured and hanged, "the Congress would immediately retaliate, by treating a British prisoner of equal rank exactly in the same manner."

The British might still hang the pirate, but first they had to catch him.

JONES AND HIS PRIZES safely reached the Dutch coast on October 3. The sight of the Stars and Stripes flying over a British warship thrilled the American agent dispatched by Benjamin Franklin to await Jones's squadron. "My telescope, if not my imagination, gives me red & white lines, & a blue square in the head quarter," wrote the agent, Charles-Guillaume-Frederic Dumas, as Jones's ships anchored off the island of Texel, Amsterdam's roads, seventy-five miles away down a winding channel through the Zuider Zee.

In a small cabin aboard the *Serapis* (Captain Pearson had been allowed to keep his quarters), Jones drafted, in his clear, precise handwriting, a long and vivid report of his voyage to Benjamin Franklin. Always keen to burnish his reputation, Jones would make sure in the days ahead that the report received wide distribution. Copies were sent to Congress and variations on it began appearing in the newspapers. It was a detailed and reasonably accurate accounting, in which Jones took pains to make Captain Landais the villain. As historian Thomas Schaeper has documented, Landais was probably more bewildered than malign that night off Flamborough Head. He had recklessly fired grapeshot intending to hit the *Serapis* but spraying the *Bonhomme Richard* as well. Nonetheless, Jones could hardly be blamed for nurturing a sense of grievance and resentment against Landais, who had been nothing but an aggravation from the beginning, and he had every reason to be appalled that Landais had fired on his ship.

Jones was rightfully annoyed with Captain Pearson as well. Jones had been magnanimous in victory. He had returned Pearson's sword a few days after accepting it on the quarterdeck, and once the vanquished captain was installed in perfectly comfortable quarters on shore, Jones made sure that he was provided with his furnishings and silver service from his cabin. But Pearson announced that he would not deign to receive his possessions from a "rebel." So Jones, showing unusual forbearance, used Captain Cottineau, who held a more respectable French commission, to deliver the items. Pearson never offered any thanks.

Pearson was at least a useful hostage. Jones wanted to swap his 500-odd prisoners for a like number of Americans stranded in British jails. The American captain was worried, however, that his long-held dream of using hostages to force Britain to release American prisoners would become caught in diplomatic snares. Three days after arriving at the Texel, Jones set off for Amsterdam to try to push the idea of setting up a prisoner exchange.

As he was rowed away from the *Serapis,* the men of the late *Bonhomme Richard* gave their captain a hearty three cheers. The reception he received in Amsterdam was overwhelming. Jones was a curiosity, a celebrity. He was mobbed by crowds, craning to get a glimpse of the lion-killer. "We have almost been smothered at the Exchange and in the streets," wrote the agent Dumas to Ben Franklin. "Captain Paul Jones arrived here yesterday," a correspondent wrote to the *London Evening Post* on October 8. "At two o'clock he appeared at 'Change; the crowd of persons assembled together to see him was astonishing and it was with the utmost difficulty he could afterwards pass to the house of the gentleman with whom he was to dine." Jones, "dressed in a blue frock coat, metal buttons, white cloth waistcoat and breaches, with a broadsword under his arm," was "huzzaed all the way home," according to another paper.

Picture the scene in the streets outside the Amsterdam Exchange, a prosperous neighborhood of mercantile mansions in the Dutch style, where a throng of moneychangers, stock jobbers, sea captains, merchant princes, soldiers of fortune, and the common rabble jostle about a small, proud man, dressed in the irregular uniform of a British naval officer. They are "overjoyed and mad to see the vanquisher of the English. They applaud him and bowed down to his feets, ready to kiss them," wrote Dumas, who was caught in the crowd with his new friend. Jones, accustomed to the solitude of the quarterdeck, kept his dignity. While one English gentleman demanded to know how "this desperado" could be allowed to "parade the streets," another correspondent observed, "he is a very different man from what he is generally represented; good sense, a genteel address, and a very good, though small person. Great Britain will find him a man capable of giving her a great deal of trouble."

The news of Jones's triumph caused a sensation from Paris to Philadelphia. It had been a grimly disappointing summer at sea for the Franco-American alliance. The French invasion fleet had returned to Brest with no glory to show and thousands of mortally ill men aboard. In Penobscot Bay, Maine, an American naval expedition against the British—commanded by Jones's detested first captain, the snobbish Dudley Saltonstall—had been a fiasco. "A great hue and cry raised by John Paul Jones," Abigail Adams wrote a friend from Braintree, Massachusetts. "Unhappy for us that we had not such a commander at the Penobscot expedition." Ben Franklin was gratified that Jones had given the British people a "little taste" of what their soldiers were dishing out in America. He praised Jones for occasioning "terror and bustle" along the coasts of the British Isles.*

Colonel Chamillard of the marines, who had traveled overland to Paris from Amsterdam in early October, found himself in the bard's role, recounting Jones's exploits under fire. The victory at Flamborough Head "immortalizes you," Chamillard wrote Jones, after regaling a rapt table at Passy. Chamillard's tale of the pitched battle—the fires in the night, the flames creeping ever closer to the magazine, "made our hair stand on end," wrote Jones's financier and patron, Jacques Leray de Chaumont. Dumas, the American agent who first greeted Jones at the Texel and quickly became his companion, was amused to pass on this bawdy felicitation from a "friend": "Congratulations for the commander, the same one who screwed the lady who works in the garden at Passy, and who is now screwing the English so nicely."

---

*Typical was this letter to the London papers from a lady in Limerick, Ireland, after Jones appeared off the Kerry coast: "We already smelt the fire of the burning city and felt the wicked embrace of Paul Jones and his merciless crew. Those that had money hid it; those that had none had less trouble."

Jones naturally hoped to convert some of his glory from martial into romantic conquest. He courted the ladies in Amsterdam and at The Hague. His most interesting flirtation was probably not innocent, but it was at least chaste. He wrote verses ("un petit badinage") to Dumas's beautiful thirteen-year-old daughter, Anna Jacoba Dumas, whom he dubbed "the Virgin Muse":

Were I dear Maid "the King of Sea"
Such merit has thy Virgin song
A coral crown I'd give to thee
Thy throne on Azure waves should smoothly glide along;
The Nereides all around thy car should wait
And gladly sing in triumph of thy state
Vivat, vivat the happy Virgin Muse
Of Liberty the Plume! What Tyrant power pursues!

Or happier Lot! Were fair Columbia Free
From British Tyranny and youth still mine
I'd tell a tender Tale to one like thee
With looks as artless as her own or even as thine
If she approved my Flame, distrust apart
Like faithful Turtles we'd have but one heart
Together would we tune the silver sounding Lyre
And Love of sacred Freedom should our lays inspire.

But since alas! the rage of war prevails
And cruel Britons desolate our Land
For Freedom still I spread my willing Sails,
     My sword unsheath'd my injured country shall Command;
Go on bright Maid, the Muses all attend
Genius likes thine and wish to be its friend
Trust me altho' convey'd thru this poor shift
My New years thoughts are grateful for thy Virgin gift.

Jones kept a copy so he could recycle it to future muses, virgin and otherwise. But Dumas reported to Jones that "the Virgin Muse has snatched from me your agreeable couplets." She charmed Jones by making up and singing a song about his exploits. "The Virgin Muse had my Virgin Thanks for her Virgin Song," trilled Jones.

JONES'S PLEASANT SOJOURN was interrupted by a tense standoff with Landais. The two men encountered each other in an Amsterdam tavern, and Landais reminded Jones that he had agreed to duel once they were away from their ships and on dry land. Landais wanted to fight with small swords, at which he was expert. Aware that he had gone without fencing lessons while growing up in a gardener's cottage, Jones wisely found a way to duck Landais's challenge. Their differences, he said, would be resolved by a court-martial back in the United States. Landais, unstable at the best of times, was a dangerous man to cross. According to Fanning, at about that time Landais and Captain Cottineau dueled over some unknown slur or slight and Cottineau was badly wounded.

Despite his high profile in Amsterdam, Jones struggled, with mixed success, to appear humble. "Paul Jones frequents the coffee house and the Exchange, and seems not very fond of courting the attention of the crowds that daily surround him," reported a London correspondent. He "seems perfectly indifferent as to the popularity he has gained by his desperate courage and unprincipled practices." Maybe so, but he was surely aware of the figure he cut in his gold-laced roqueleau, a fur-lined cloak with a cape that he wore against the autumn chill.

Jones was always on the alert for put-downs as well as praise, and he began to hear whispers that he was overstaying his time in Amsterdam while neglecting the needs of his men back at the Texel. On October 18, he received a disturbing letter from Dumas. The American agent, who was a bit of a busybody as well as a *philosophe*, had been talking to "important people" who were "great friends of America."

Their feeling is that you have not done wrong, sir, to come and show yourself over here; but on the other hand they feel that it would not be right to repeat this visit, because it would amount to too much parading, and that would look bad even among the friends of America to see you visit especially public places.

By embarrassing the British with his visible presence, Jones was putting the neutral Dutch into an awkward position and making it harder for them to accommodate Jones's needs, especially his pressing need to get medical treatment for his numerous wounded. On this last score, Dumas reported some distressing gossip of grotesque conditions aboard the *Serapis:*

I must warn you also, my dear sir, that these same friends have told me something which, whether it is true or not, hurts me as much as it does them: It has been said that a high degree of dirtiness and infection reigns aboard the *Serapis*. Pieces of corpses from combat have been seen there, from which people conclude that the ship has not been cleaned since the battle. This is quite shocking here at the moment, and raises fears as to the consequence of such negligence. In the name of God, my dear sir, put some order in all this. Do not leave your ship any more; have it cleaned and purged from this filth.

Jones had just arrived back aboard the *Serapis* when he received this letter. Jones abhorred a dirty ship, so it is puzzling to think that he would leave his prize stinking of rotting flesh. Where, in Jones's absence, were his officers, including the normally reliable Lieutenant Dale? In any event, on October 19, the day after Jones returned from Amsterdam, the log of the *Serapis* notes—for the first time since the battle—"People employed cleaning the ships decks" and again three days later, "People employed cleaning the upper and lower gun decks."

Jones's own people were unhappy, and the British prisoners angrier still. Jones's efforts to arrange a prisoner exchange had gone nowhere.

The prisoners schemed to kill Jones within a few days of his return. "Last night I very fortunately discovered a plot that had been formed by the prisoners on board here to play a game at throat cut. They will not find opportunity a second time," Jones wrote John de Neufville, a local agent who was (neither expeditiously nor well) refitting the *Serapis*. Word spread on the ship that Jones had been galavanting around Amsterdam while the officers and men, many of them nursing terrible wounds, suffered on board ship. Many of the hands from the *Bonhomme Richard* had only the tattered shirts on their backs; they grew cold and miserable as the days shortened and the temperatures dropped. The log shows entry after entry of "dark foggy weather" and winds sweeping in off the North Sea. While Jones was in Amsterdam, a score of sailors made a run for it in a stolen boat, and five of them drowned before they could be recaptured. The log lists a steady trickle of desertions thereafter, including the name of the hero of the battle off Flamborough Head, William Hamilton, the brave seaman who climbed out on the mainyard and dropped the grenade through the hatchway on the *Serapis*.

Jones at last tried to provide for his men, petitioning the Duc de la Vauguyon, the French ambassador to The Hague, to pay, clothe, and feed his crew. "The bread that has been twice a week sent down from Amsterdam to feed my people has been literally speaking *rotten*," Jones angrily wrote on November 4. But he was caught in a diplomatic tangle. The British ambassador, Sir Joseph Yorke, had begun pressuring the Dutch government as soon as Jones's squadron hove into view at the Texel. Sir Joseph demanded that "the Pirate Paul Jones" be arrested as a criminal in the street by Dutch authorities, his prisoners released, and his prizes turned over to the British government. The Dutch temporized, and at Jones's prodding, allowed the American commander to jail his prisoners in an old fort on the Texel. The French played a shadowy, ambiguous role. France did not want to see an open breach between Holland and Britain; Paris wanted the Dutch to remain neutral, so they could continue to ship goods to blockaded France without interference by the British navy. France's Ambassador Vauguyon was not eager to see Jones stir up trouble between

Holland and England. In mid-November, Jones was informed that the *Serapis*, *Pallas*, and *Vengeance*, along with the prizes captured on the cruise, were all being put under the French flag. Jones was a captain again, not a commodore. He was ordered to transfer with his men to the *Alliance*, now the only ship still under the Stars and Stripes. The switch was made quietly, in the dead of night. Enraged, feeling poorly used, Jones looted the prize he had fought so hard to capture, moving everything that could not be nailed down, including twelve casks of rum, sixty cutlasses, four hen coops, and 100 pair of leg irons (for his increasingly mutinous crew). In their private correspondence, Dumas and Jones sarcastically referred to Vauguyon as "the great man."

Under pressure from Sir Joseph, the Dutch waffled and finally turned against Jones. A squadron of Dutch warships, led by a seventy-four-gun ship of the line, sailed into the anchorage at the Texel in mid-December to intimidate Jones into leaving. Jones received a Dutch captain, who told him the Americans were no longer welcome in Dutch waters and must put to sea immediately. Jones politely dismissed him, saying that he would sail when the wind was right. The Dutch admiral sent Jones a series of insolent messages, which the American captain ignored. Jones knew what was waiting for him just beyond the Texel Roads: a squadron of British men-of-war, which had been patrolling there on and off for days. "They have done me the honor to place four line ships at each entry to this Road, to give me a Royal Salute when I set sail," Jones wrote a friend. The British burned to capture the Pirate Jones. "For God's sake," the First Lord of the Admiralty urged one of his captains at the end of November, "get to sea instantly in consequence of the orders you have received. If you can take Paul Jones you will be as high in the estimation of the public as if you had beat the combined [Franco-Spanish] fleet."

The French ambassador stepped in to offer Jones a fig leaf: a letter of marque, designating the *Alliance* as a privateer ship temporarily under French protection. The Dutch might not respect the Stars and Stripes, but they would have to honor the French flag. Jones's pride flared. Disdainful of privateers who fought for profit, not honor, he would not touch this "dirty piece of parchment," he informed Ben Franklin. He would leave on his own time, when the weather was right. "I do not much fear the enemy in the long and dark nights of this season," Jones wrote defiantly.

On Christmas Eve, Jones received a gift. The wind backed around to the east and blew a frozen gale, driving the British blockaders off their station. Jones decided to make his getaway. The day after Christmas, after a temporary delay (a drunken pilot had run the *Alliance* afoul of a merchantman), Jones was at last ready, he wrote Dumas, to "escape this Purgatory." The captain was in an ebullient mood as the *Alliance* sailed out of the Texel Roads and went tearing down the Flemish coast. "I am here, my Philosopher, with a good wind at East and under my best American colors," Jones wrote Dumas on December 27 from "Alliance at Sea."

Jones's plan was to catch the British off guard by taking the most direct route. Rather than head out into the wide expanse of the North Sea and sneak around the Scottish coast, Jones made directly for the straits of Dover. He would drive straight down the English Channel, right past the guardians at the British gate. No false colors or *ruses de guerre*; his gambit would be sheer brazenness. The *Alliance* was a fast ship, and her log shows Jones cracking on sail, pushing the limits, running the risk of carrying away a spar as he flew westward at nine and ten knots. A split main topsail checked him for a moment, but still he pressed on through a cold winter's night, exhilarated to be back on the quarterdeck taunting the enemy.

At 9 A.M. on the morning of December 27, while British seamen were still recovering from their Yuletide carousing, the *Alliance* raced past the British fleet lying at anchor at the Downs. "Our thirteen stripes now floated over our stern, and we had a long streaming pendant aloft, and an American jack set forward," wrote Midshipman Fanning. "I believe those John Englishman who now saw us thought we were pretty saucy fellows." Master's Mate Kilby recalled the scene on the quarterdeck, where the officers and men stood wide-eyed at their captain's audacity as the *Alliance* cruised in plain sight of dozens of British men-of-war.

The morning was very clear, though the wind blew fresh. We were then under close reef topsails. Jones ordered out a reef. It was done quickly. He ordered out the second and it was not long before it was done. He ordered out the third, and also that the topsail yards should be hoisted up taut. It was done. One of the Lieutenants observed to Jones that he was fearful lest we should carry away the mast. Jones answered, "She shall either carry this sail or drag it."

On she drove down the Channel. At 9 A.M. the next morning, *Alliance* slipped past another British fleet, at Spithead on the Isle of Wight. By now the breeze had moderated but "thick weather" helped disguise the *Alliance* from enemy cruisers. In the Western Approaches, Jones was even emboldened to catch a prize, though she turned out to be a neutral ship, a Swedish merchantman that was off limits.

On January 16, Jones happily wrote Dumas from the port of La Coruña, Spain, "We have made our way through the Channel in spite of the utmost efforts of the British to prevent it. I had the pleasure of laughing at their expense as we passed the Downs in sight of their ships of war and along the coast in full view also of the Isle of Wight." He wrote Franklin, "I made my passage safe through the Channel notwithstanding all the watchfulness of the many ships." In the margin, Jones penned in, "The enemy employed 42 ships of the line and frigates."

But Jones's joy was tempered by dissatisfaction with the sailing qualities of his ship and the growing surliness of his crew. He had wanted to cruise in the Bay of Biscay, where British warships often patrolled. "Had the ship been in a condition to sustain stormy weather I should have given our enemies fresh alarms and would I think before this time have made some good prizes and taken a number of prisoners," Jones wrote Franklin. "But to my great disappointment both sails and rigging are in so bad a condition thro' want of former care that it would have been impossible to sustain such gales as I might have expected on that rude coast at this season." The *Alliance*, though speedy, was crank and oversparred, and Landais had allowed her to become a filthy ship. Jones had such difficulty exterminating the vermin aboard that he had to close all the hatches and try to smoke out the rats by burning brimstone belowdecks.

Jones wished to come back to France with a string of prizes—perhaps even a British frigate. His crew was less enthusiastic. His men were still poorly clothed for the winter and still unpaid for their heroic work. In the fall, the sailors in Jones's squadron had been paid a single ducat, worth a few pennies. Many of the sailors flung theirs overboard in disgust. Now, as the *Alliance* rode at anchor at a Spanish port, there was no money for drink or women. Jones wanted the crew to look sharp for visiting dignitaries (Fanning remarked on the length and cleanliness of the fingernails of the local nobility), and he harshly berated a crewman who was slow to dip the Spanish colors on demand. Jones apparently thought the bos'un meant to embarrass him; in a rage, the captain drew his sword and turned on the cringing mate, as if to run him through.

That was the last straw. On January 19, the log of the *Alliance* reported, "All the people refused doing duty, until they got some part of the money due them." The officers had to go below with swords and drive the men on deck. From the quarterdeck, Jones, by now accustomed to mutinous crews, promised to get their prize money once they returned to L'Orient. He could truthfully say that he had not been paid either. In the meantime, Jones ordered up a soothing double round of grog. "The people were satisfied by the captain so as to appear cheerfully to duty," the log reported the next day.

Jones's wardroom was fractious. Jones liked his junior officers, who were loyal and had been very brave in the action off Flamborough Head. Fanning wrote that Jones made a practice of dining with two midshipmen (there were six on board) every day, requiring the "young gentlemen" to show up in their best togs and make intelligent conversation. But the *Alliance*'s first officer, whom he had inherited from Landais, was a drunk, and the rest of Landais's old officers bitterly feuded with the *Bonhomme Richard*'s men, refighting the night when the *Alliance* had mistakenly opened fire on Jones's ship. None of the officers was keen to take another dangerous cruise. A delegation confronted Jones in his cabin, demanding to go home. He angrily told them to do their duty, that they still had a chance to fall in with a British frigate and carry her. The officers warned that the men were on the verge of another rebellion. Jones "stamped his foot," wrote Fanning, and told them to get out.

Jones cruised for another seventeen days but found no prizes. When the *Alliance* finally dropped anchor off the Island of Groix near L'Orient on February 10, 1780, Jones himself was in poor shape. He was exhausted and his eyes had become infected. "I am almost blind with sore eyes, which prevents me at present from paying a visit to my friends on shore," he wrote his maritime agents at L'Orient, Gourlade and Moylan. Jones "appeared much agitated," observed Fanning, "and bit his lips often, and walked the quarterdeck muttering something to himself."

Jones's behavior began to fit into a pattern recognizable in isolated sea captains before and since. He was becoming Queeg-like, suspicious, jumpy, slightly dotty. He badly needed a respite from the burdens of command and his own unceasing ambition. From time to time as he brooded at the Texel in the late autumn, he had wondered if his warrior days were coming to an end. He had been in the naval service for four years. He moaned to a friend that he was an "old man" (he was thirty-three). He still entertained notions of becoming a gentleman farmer and settling down in Virginia. "It is very probable that I may retire from the naval service when I return to the continent, for I neither love the profession of arms or the Sea Service," he wrote a friend, Thomas Scott, whom he had befriended while living in London in the early 1770s. Or perhaps he could find a place in genteel Dutch society by finding a proper wife. Writing in a somewhat stilted third-person voice on November 26, he had declared to John de Neufville, his Amsterdam agent, "So great is the respect of your humble servant for the friendship of Amsterdam that, if he [Jones] should be so fortunate as to escape the dangers that now surround him, he would esteem it an honor to become a member of that society by giving his hand to the fair daughter or sister of some patriotic citizen whose breast is all alive to the noble feeling of philanthropy, and who has influence to save his country." Jones apparently had a particular matchmaker in mind, a woman of some influence, for he went on: "You can communicate this hint to the fair and *sentimental lady* with what delicate turn of expression you please, assuring her of my respect and asking her advice etc., etc., etc. If that amiable lady should undertake to stand my friend you may expect another visit from me very soon."

But Jones never did go back to Amsterdam, either because the "sentimental lady" failed to find a father or brother with sufficient "philanthropy" to further Jones's romantic ambitions, or because his duties carried him away. Jones was half-hoping to return to the United States soon after he landed in L'Orient in February. But once again, he was caught up in time-consuming intrigues of his own and others' making.

Benjamin Franklin was eager to send Jones and the *Alliance* quickly back to America with badly needed supplies for the Continental Army, 16,000 stands of arms procured by Lafayette and 120 bales of uniform cloth. Jones was also asked to carry a prominent passenger, Arthur Lee, the meddlesome former American commissioner who had been traveling about the courts of Europe, vainly trying to drum up support for the American cause. Lee did not travel light. Along with various servants and a great mound of baggage, he asked Jones to transport his traveling coach. Jones diplomatically replied that he would if he could find room.

Before he left for America, Jones needed to live up to his promise to get his men paid and rewarded with their prize earnings. This seemingly straightforward task would require literally decades to accomplish. By the time the U.S. Congress finally voted to compensate the crew of the *Bonhomme Richard* for the prizes taken on their famous cruise of September 1779, the year would be 1848. The men and officers of the *Bonhomme Richard* were all dead by then. The money—$165,598.37—was ultimately paid to their descendants. There were murky and tangled reasons for the delay; Congress's indifference to promoting a professional navy was an underlying cause. But Jones had no difficulty identifying an immediate villain: Chaumont, the French merchant prince, who had faithfully served as all-purpose provider and paymaster for the American cause in France. Chaumont was overextended and strapped for cash (he would ultimately go bankrupt). Jones, in his paranoid way, believed that Chaumont and his "cabal" in the French government were conspiring against him, trying to humiliate him in the eyes of his crew. "My mind is torn to pieces and can no longer bear the shameful wrongs that are practiced against the poor, the gallant seamen that fought so faithfully by my side and have followed their captain through so many dangers," he wrote his "dear friend," the spy Edward Bancroft on April 10. A few days later, Jones set out for Paris to confront the "cabal" and demand pay for his men. Jones had another motive as well: to find out just how much fame he had garnered since he last strolled in the Tuileries or the great *places* of the French capital.

CHAPTER ELEVEN

"Caressed by All the World"

*J*ONES ARRIVED AT Passy at four o'clock in the morning of April 17, 1780. "Capt. Jones not having stopped since he left L'Orient is lain down for a little sleep," Bancroft wrote his nominal boss, Benjamin Franklin, later that morning. "I shall call him in about half an hour and as soon after as he can dress I suppose he will wait on you." Jones was in a hurry to see Franklin to enlist his help. The French crew that had sailed the *Serapis* back from Holland to L'Orient was dismantling the British warship in order to sell off its spars, cordage, and guns. The *Alliance* lay moored only a few hundred yards away. Jones's men, still wretchedly clothed and unpaid, watched in disbelief. They were sure that the hulk would be sold for a pittance, robbing them of their prize money. Jones was eager to enlist Franklin's help in stopping this latest outrage.

Jones intended to deal with such matters, secure his prize money and sailing orders, and return to L'Orient. He ended up staying in Paris for six weeks and having the time of his life. He was "feasted and caressed by all the world," he later wrote his friend Dumas, not exaggerating by much. The city, green and blooming in springtime, was gay with pre-revolutionary excess and innocence, and Jones was the magnificent man of the hour. He was applauded at the opera, painted, sculpted, titled, and (almost) crowned with laurels. With varying shows of modesty, Jones lapped it up: the honors, the flattery, the attentions of the ladies, all the glory that the most glorious city in the world could bestow.

Jones had expected to stay in Paris for only a few days. At Versailles, Minister of the Marine Sartine "received me coldly and did not even ask me if I felt any ill effects from the wounds I have received," Jones recalled. But the next day, Jones was presented to the King by the Prince de Beau-veau, captain of the guards. Louis XVI smiled blandly at the slender American naval officer in the well-worn blue coat, but his wife, Queen Marie Antoinette, was more curious. Attended by her ladies-in-waiting, peering through a glass partition, she had come to the King's *levée* to get a peek at the Hero Jones. His victory over the *Serapis*, coming after the hu-miliating anticlimax of the French fleet's failure to invade England in Sep-tember, had caught the imagination of Paris society. That fall, a ballet had been staged with a dancer dressed as the brave *Le Capitaine Paul-Jones*. *Tout* Paris was eager to see the real man. The Queen herself would be honored to receive him at her box at the opera. It would be too sad if he hurried back to his duty. . . .

He did not disappoint. He went to the theater, to the Comédie Itali-enne, to the ballet, to the opera; he paraded down the boulevards and av-enues; everywhere, people stopped and stared, stood and applauded. At the opera, he upstaged the stars. "Since the public knew about his visit," wrote one diarist, "a huge crowd was present." The proprietor had built an elaborate contraption that would allow a laurel wreath to slowly de-scend from the ceiling until it adorned the hero's head. "Forewarned of this silly project, Paul Jones humbly begged not to go forward with it," recorded M. de Bachaumont in his *Mémoires Secrets*. He did, however, per-mit himself to be escorted to his carriage by the lead singer, who was dressed in the costume of his role, Admiral Comte d'Estaing, in the *Siege of Granada*.

Jones's old leg-up in social climbing—Freemasonry—vaulted him onto a stage he could scarcely have imagined a decade earlier when he joined the Kirkcudbright Lodge. On May 1, 1780, he was inducted into the lodge of the Nine Sisters, the most significant Masonic lodge in Europe.

Named after the nine muses, populated by *philosophes* and the progressive fringe of the nobility, the lodge was a temple to Enlightenment thought. Its members included Voltaire and Ben Franklin. Meeting in semisecrecy in the Jesuit novitiate on Rue de Pot de Fer Saint-Sulpice, the brethren of the Nine Sisters gathered to praise Jones in the most fulsome fashion. Jones was extolled as a poet and a warrior, a man of learning as well as martial brilliance, who had "courted Apollo before enrolling under the flag of Mars." The evening's orator, Brother Dixmarie, compared him to the "poet Tirthee who inspired the Spartans with the courage they thought they had lost" and to Alexander, who "possessed all the learning of Aristotle and carried the *Iliad* constantly with him." The "Order of Muses draws its origin from Ancient Chivalry, which in turn draws its own from ancient initiates since Hercules," the orator intoned. How heady for Jones! He was no mere gardener's son; he was descended from the gods.

Jones's intention to return to his ship was buried in invitations and calling cards. He was entertained by the Duchesse de Chartres at the Palais Royal. He was informed by the Prince de Nassau-Siegen that Mlle. Guimard, the premier ballerina of the opera, would be pleased to receive him. Madame d'Ormoy, the widow of a presiding magistrate of justice known in society as Madame la Présidente, welcomed the famous captain to her salon. D'Ormoy was a collector of celebrities. At her dinner parties, women in white diaphanous gowns sang verses to honored guests. Madame la Présidente sought to tempt Jones by promising him that "the ladies are practicing some new couplets to sing."

Jones was formally honored by the King, presented with a gold-hilted sword, engraved, Jones happily recorded, "with these extremely flattering words: *Vindicati Maris Ludovicus XVI remunerator Strenua Vindici* (reward from Louis XVI to the valiant avenger of the rights of the sea)." Jones worshipped the finely wrought blade, adorned with medallions of Mars, Hercules, Neptune, and Minerva. "A superb sword," Jones wrote his friend Dumas, "much more elegant than that presented to the Marquis de Lafayette." (Benjamin Franklin had awarded Lafayette a ceremonial sword for his services to the American cause.) The King also wished, with the necessary approval of the U.S. Congress, to make Jones a member of the Ordre du Mérite Militaire. Captain Jones would become Chevalier Jones, the French equivalent of a Knighthood.

Such recognition was occasion for Jones to order up yet another coat of arms, this time with the Jones and Paul quarterings surmounted by a coronet, indicating his new rank. The coronet was topped by a screaming eagle. The brethren of the Nine Sisters commissioned a bust of Jones by Houdon, the greatest sculptor of the age, whose subjects included Franklin, Washington, Jefferson, and Voltaire. Houdon captured Jones's strong jaw, high brow, and determined mouth and some of the mystery of his lidded eyes. A drawing done at the same time by J. M. Moreau, one of the best engravers of the age, reveals an undercurrent of anxiety behind Jones's visage. His eyes are averted and seem to be looking for something they cannot have.

Jones surprised his hosts. They expected a corsair and got a courtier. Jones did not boast or strut; he was not loud or coarse. "I have never met so modest a man," wrote the artist Vigée-Lebrun. "It was impossible to get him to talk about his great deeds, but on all other subjects, he willingly talked with a great amount of sense and wit." Though Jones's French was at best halting, he could be droll. Had he seen the French Guard Regiment parade on review? "I would rather see them manuevering in St. James Park," he replied—fighting in London rather than marching in Paris. The Marshal Duc de Biron invited Jones to dinner, and conversation turned to Jones's adversary off Flamborough Head, Captain Richard Pearson. The British captain had not suffered any disgrace for his defeat; far from it, he was deemed a hero for bravely putting his ship between Jones's squadron and the Baltic convoy, which had escaped during the battle. The Russia Company, owners of the merchant fleet sailing from Scandinavia to London, presented Pearson with a silver service, and the King made him a Knight of the Bath. Told that Pearson was now Sir Richard, Jones remarked, offhand, "Were I only able to make him a Lord someday."

Jones was emboldened to spout his own verses, including this one, "addressed to the ladies who have done me the honor of their polite attention:"

> *Insulted freedom bled—I felt her cause*
> *And drew my sword to vindicate her laws*
> *From principle, and not from vain applause*
> *I've done my best; self-interest far apart*
> *And self-reproach a stranger to my heart;*
> *My zeal still prompts, ambitious to pursue*
> *The foe, ye fair, of liberty and you*
> *Grateful for praise, spontaneous and unbought,*
> *A generous people's love not meanly sought;*
> *To merit this, and bend the knee to beauty,*
> *Shall be my earliest and latest duty.*

Jones's flowery attempts to present himself as a paragon of distinterested virtue may have made some sophisticates roll their eyes. But, thrilled by Jones's novelty—the rebel pirate as poet—court society, habitually bored and seeking new entertainments, was willing to see him as he wished to be seen, as a Galahad in gold braid. Baron Grimm, the Swiss diplomat who knew *tout le monde* and reported on it for Russia's Catherine the Great, was fascinated by Jones. He wrote in his diary:

This brave corsair who has given so many proofs of the strongest heart and the most distinguished courage is none the less a man of the world, of great intelligence and sweetness. It is a curious thing that he makes many verses characterized by delicate sensibility and grace.

The ladies queued up to make his more personal acquaintance. Parisian women were not shy. John Adams reported that he was intimidated by the "learned ladies" of the Parisian salons. "I have such a consciousness of inferiority to them," Adams wrote. "The manners of the nation allow them to visit, alone, all persons in office," Adams explained to George Washington. He thought that French women were dangerous schemers (to match them against American women, he wrote, was a "comparison of Amazons and Angels"). Jones, on the other hand, was quite willing to use and be used, although he, too, would learn that he was outmatched.

Jones's correspondence during this period is so full of discreet longings and tiny pouts that the smell of perfume almost emanates from the page. On May 17, Madame de St. Julien, an intelligent woman who cared for Voltaire in his dotage, wrote that she "regrets very much that she was not at home yesterday to welcome her dear and brave Mr. Paul Jones. . . . She kisses him with all her heart." But on May 28, she is cross with her hero. "It is quite a pity, my dear captain, that you cannot keep your word as well as you do your bravery, and that you do not know how to [illegible] as well as you vanquish your enemies. . . . So love better those who love you." Jones pursued, and was pursued by, women of all classes. He was always *sympathique* to a damsel in distress. From Angelique, a lady's maid: "The good Madam de Bonneuil will forgive me for telling you of my misfortunes. You have had the kindness to promise me your portrait, and I am quite certain it will make me very happy."

Jones's most ardent attempt at conquest came with a high-born beauty who was willful, manipulative, and proud. Charlotte-Marguerite de Bourbon, Madame La Comtesse de Lowendahl, twenty-six years old, possessed royal blood, a sweet singing voice, artistic ability, and ambitions for her husband, a brigadier general who was looking for work. It was not uncommon for French women to seek favors from their lovers for friends, brothers, and even husbands. Mme. de Lowendahl commenced a flirtation that dizzied Jones. The two encountered each other at the salon of the Genets, a politically influential family adopted by Jones as his home-away-from home in Paris (the Hôtel de Valentinois had grown less congenial; Jones and the landlord, Chaumont, were on the outs over money). An English-woman named Caroline Edes was another frequent guest at the Genets'.

She observed Jones as he circled the comtesse, identified in this letter to a London friend as "Lady ——":

> The famous Paul Jones dines and sups here often. He is a smart man of 36 [sic], speaks but little French, appears to be an extraordinary genius as a poet as well as a hero. A few days ago he wrote some verses extempore of which I send you a copy. He is greatly admired here especially by the ladies, who are wild with love for him, but he adores Lady —— who has honored him with every mark of politeness and attention.

The Countess flattered Jones greatly by painting his portrait in miniature and bestowing him with a ribbon as a keepsake. As Jones sat for his portrait, studied intently by a great beauty sitting in an elegant drawing room in Paris, cooled by gentle May breezes, intoxicated by sweet scents, he was far removed from the quarterdeck of the *Alliance* and the demands of its surly crew. Only two months before he had been half-blind from "sore eyes" and half-mad from thwarted ambition.

Jones was just beginning his campaign for the Countess's heart when reality intruded and duty called. On June 1, the captain was ordered by Franklin, whom Jones had rarely seen while he gadded about town, to get back to his ship at once. The arms and supplies stacked in *Alliance*'s hold were badly needed by the Continental Army; it was imperative for Jones to set sail for America as soon as possible.

Jones was not indifferent to duty. He had not spent all of his time over the prior six weeks taking bows at the opera and reciting verses to the ladies. He had pressed Sartine to pay his men and tried to interest the French government in a new and more spectacular raid on Great Britain, this time with a squadron of a dozen ships, including a ship of the line commanded by Jones. But Jones was dilatory about returning to the *Alliance*, in part because he was not bringing back a bag of prize money to satisfy his disgruntled crew. Jones made a somewhat meandering passage to L'Orient through Nantes, where he was inevitably feted by the local Masons. On June 7, still in Nantes, he paused to write the Countess:

Nothing short of my duty to the glorious cause of freedom in which I have the honor to be engaged could have induced me to leave Versailles a little hour after I parted from you, while *my heart* urged me to stay that I might have the happiness to see you the next morning. . . . You have made me in love with my own picture because you have condescended to draw it. . . .

I beseech you to accept the within lock [of hair]. I am sorry that it is now 18 inches shorter than it was three months ago. If I could send you my heart itself or anything else that could afford you pleasure it would be my happiness to do it.

Along with his hair, Jones enclosed his private cipher "so you will be able to write me very freely and without risk." Jones slyly suggested that perhaps the Countess was unhappy in her marriage: "I . . . am much affected at some words that fell *in private conversation* from Miss Edes the evening before I left Versailles. I am afraid that you are less happy than I wish and am sure you deserve to be." Jones did not make clear what tale of marital distress Miss Edes let slip. Jones had been cozy with Miss Edes—she was in France with her husband, a diplomat working on a cause dear to Jones, prisoner exchange. But the English gentlewoman was also a gossip—on a grand scale. Miss Edes's letters home were reprinted in the London newspapers. She wrote for all the world to see:

Since my last, Paul Jones drank tea and supped here. If I am in love with him, for love I may die; I have as many rivals as there are ladies, but the most formidable is still Lady ——, who possesses all his heart. This lady is of high rank and virtue, very sensible, good natured and affable. Besides this, she is possessed of youth, beauty, and wit, and every other female accomplishment. He is gone, I suppose, for America. They correspond and his letters are replete with elegance, sentiment, and delicacy. She drew his picture (a striking likeness) and wrote some lines under it, which are much admired, and presented it to him, who, since he received it, is, he says, like a second

Narcissus, in love with his own resemblance; to be sure, he is the most agreeable sea wolf one could wish to meet with.

Miss Edes had, inadvertently or not, pushed "the agreeable sea wolf" and the countess out into forbidden territory. Private assignations were routine, even expected in upper-class society, but publicity was to be abhorred. No married lady was ever to be shamed in the public prints. By describing the circumstances and details of Jones's courtship, the painting and the poetry, Miss Edes effectively identified "Lady ——" as the Countess de Lowendahl. This was more than the virtuous Countess could countenance. She was not really in love with Jones anyway, but rather trying to use his fame and standing in court to advance her husband's stalled military career. She had already been fending off Jones's advances, writing him before he left Paris:

I am touched by the feelings you have for me, and I would have liked to be able to answer them, but I could not do so without deceiving a gentleman with whom I live, and I am incapable of doing that. Now you should be able to understand my way of thinking, and to know that what I told you yesterday was only in jest.

Jones, it seems, had mistaken her playful badinage as an invitation to seduction. By sending her a packet containing a lock of his hair and a codebook for secret communication, Jones was behaving presumptuously —especially now that their *amitié amoureuse* had become the squalid fare of gossip columnists. The Countess decided to put Jones in his place by pretending, preposterously, that the intimate packet from Jones was not really intended for her, but sent to the wrong address. At the same time, she pointedly begged to introduce him to her husband, who would be shortly passing through L'Orient, and was eager to follow in the footsteps of Lafayette.

Jones responded to this dismissive letter with dumbly wounded pride. "I have carefully examined the copy of my letter from Nantes [dated June 7, above], but am still at a loss, and cannot conceive what part of the letter itself could have occasioned your imagining I had mistaken the address? As for the little packet it contained perhaps it might have been better omitted. . . . if my letter has given you even a moment's uneasiness, I can assure you that to think so would be as severe a punishment as could be inflicted upon me." Jones went on to say how "honored" he was by the visit of her husband, the Count, and that he was "so well convinced of his superior understanding that I am glad to believe Miss Edes was mistaken [by hinting that the Countess was lonely in love]." Yet Jones was not one to give up the fight. He blundered on like Don Quixote toward the windmill, asking her to accept his treasured gold sword from the King for safekeeping. He wished, he wrote, "to prove myself worthy of the title of your Knight." And he still wanted to have the miniature she painted to wear around his neck. "As you are a philosopher, and as friendship has nothing to do with sex, pray what harm is there in wishing to have the picture of a friend?" The Countess was done with this little charade. She wrote him a final brush-off, refusing to accept his sword. But by then, Jones had moved on to more reliably submissive mistresses.

THE CLUMSY WOOING of Countess Lowendahl was characteristic of Jones on dry land. Having been a genuine hero on the burning deck, he became a self-absorbed and overly ardent figure in the salon. The summer of 1780 was for Jones part romance, part tragedy, and part farce. He lost and gained a ship, gained and lost a mistress (or several), and thrashed about—before sailing into a tempest that nearly sank him.

Jones was plagued once again by Captain Landais. The half-mad Frenchman had showed up in L'Orient in March, hoping to secure passage to America—and to kill Captain Jones in a duel. The Chevalier de Pontgibaud, one of a number of young nobleman seeking to follow Lafayette to America, had encountered Jones in April at the French port city, shortly before Jones left for Paris for his encounters with laurels and ladies. Now, six weeks later, the Chevalier was still awaiting passage to

America when a man in uniform burst into his room. "It was no other than our brave—indeed more than brave—commodore, the famous Paul Jones," wrote Pontgibaud.

"Shut the door!" cried Jones. "That scoundrel Capt. Landais met me in the town and wants to fight me. He is pursuing me from street to street, sword in hand. I do not know how to fence and I do not want to be killed by that rascal." Pontgibaud was taken aback, but he locked the door. "Certainly, Paul Jones acted very sensibly, for the match was not equal," wrote Pontgibaud in his memoir. "Captain Landais with his drawn sword would have made short work of him, and Paul Jones had nothing to gain but blows from the encounter."

Jones escaped Landais's sword, but not his scheming. While Jones was enjoying the opera in Paris, Landais had been plotting to subvert him with the unhappy crew of the *Alliance*. Landais made an unholy alliance with Arthur Lee, the inveterate troublemaker who saw an opportunity to embarrass Franklin and Jones. Lee—along with his traveling carriage, trunks, and servants—was growing impatient waiting for Jones, who was to sail him home. As they bided their time in L'Orient through April and May, Lee convinced Landais that he was the rightful captain of the *Alliance*, the holder of a congressional commission that neither Jones nor Franklin could take away. This sea-lawyer's argument found a willing audience in the men of the *Alliance*, who were grousing that Jones was galavanting about Paris while they shivered, penniless.

On May 31, seventeen officers and mates of the *Alliance* petitioned Franklin to reinstate Landais as captain and let them sail home. Franklin wrote back on June 7 ordering the officers to do their duty and obey Captain Jones. Franklin tried to shame the men of the *Alliance*. It would not go unnoticed, he observed, "that Captain Jones loved close fighting," while "Captain Landais was skillful at keeping out of harm's way, and that therefore you thought yourselves safer with the latter." At the same time Franklin wrote Jones, warning him about the restless officers and crew and the machinations of Landais. "I see you are likely to have a great deal of trouble. It requires prudence. I wish you well through it. You have shown your abilities in fighting. You now have the opportunity of showing the other necessary part of the character of a great chief, your abilities in governing."

Like so many of Franklin's encouraging little homilies, this one cloaked a sharper point: that Franklin entertained some doubts about Jones's "prudence" and "governing abilities." Jones, who worshipped his "philosopher" Franklin, might have gotten the point, but it was already too late. By the time Jones received Franklin's letter in mid-June, Landais had already staged a coup.

When Jones finally arrived in L'Orient after his leisurely victory tour from Paris via Nantes, probably about June 9, he discovered that the *Alliance* did not have room in its hold to carry all the uniforms and arms destined for the American army, in part because Arthur Lee's carriage and luggage had taken up so much space. On the morning of June 12, Jones was ashore, trying to arrange for another ship to help carry the badly needed supplies, when Landais stepped aboard the *Alliance*. "I now command this ship. Call the master at arms to me," Landais announced. ("Capt. Landy came aboard," the *Alliance*'s log noted, "and took command, he said, by the orders of Congress, his orders were read to the Officers & People.") Landais quickly culled out from the *Alliance*'s crew several dozen old hands of the *Bonhomme Richard* who were still loyal to Jones. Some officers were sent ashore, but the seamen were sent below and put in irons.

Jones was appalled. "Open your eyes, I beseech you," he wrote Captain Matthew Parke of the marines, who had chosen to side with Landais. "You know me. I scorn to mislead any man." Jones promised—yet again— that he would get the men their pay and prize money. But he did not want a direct confrontation with Landais, perhaps because he feared that the men would choose sides against him—or that Landais would draw his sword and provoke a duel then and there. Instead Jones headed back to Paris to appeal to higher authority. Reaching the capital in fifty-seven hours, Jones did not tarry, but returned to L'Orient by June 20 with orders from the King to place the *Alliance* back under his command.

Ordered to stop the *Alliance* from sailing under Landais, French naval officers at L'Orient arranged a formidable series of obstacles. A boom was drawn across the channel; the guns of the fort were loaded and aimed at the *Alliance;* launches were filled with soldiers prepared to board and carry her; no fewer than three warships were "poised to hold the ship back with their fire, and ready to ram it," according to the official orders. Given Landais's aversion to battle, Jones could have easily stepped aboard and retaken his ship.

But he did not. Instead, he chose to let her go. *Alliance*, with Landais in command and most of its crucial cargo still sitting on the dock, sailed for America during the first week of July. Why did Jones so meekly step aside? He pompously explained to his old congressional patron, Robert Morris, "My humanity would not suffer me to remain a silent witness of bloodshed between the allied subjects of France and America." This was mostly nonsense. Knowing his rival's aversion to ship-to-ship combat (as opposed to dueling), Jones could have reasonably guessed that Landais, faced with cannons all around him, would have given up the *Alliance* without firing a shot. The real explanation has to be that Jones was glad to see Landais and his sorry crew sail out of his life, he hoped, forever.

America's French benefactors were deeply disappointed at Jones's failure to get his ship in order and transport the arms and uniforms to Washington's men. A French admiral leaving with a fleet for America wrote Lafayette, "I sent word surreptitiously and secretly four times to Paul Jones to come and place himself in our convoy. I have heard nothing of it." Lafayette in turn wrote Washington, "I . . . confess it is impossible not to be very angry at Capt. Jones's delay and much disappointed in our expectations." The Continentals needed all the aid they could get: in May, British forces had seized Charleston, South Carolina, after another disastrous failure by the Continental Navy. The British hoped to consolidate control of the southern colonies and work north to squeeze Washington's army. At their starved camp in New Jersey late that spring, some of Washington's men had mutinied over lost pay and cut rations.

Franklin finally lost his legendary patience with Jones. He heard from Bancroft that Jones had been whining about a lack of support from the French officials in L'Orient, who, according to Jones, had "acted rather like women than men." Franklin sent Jones a sharply worded and telling reproach:

> If you had stayed aboard where your duty lay, instead of coming to Paris, you would not have lost your ship. Now you blame them [the French officials] as having deserted you in recovering her. . . . Here-after, if you should observe on occasion to give your officers and friends a little more praise than is their due, and confess more fault than you can justly be charged with, you will only become the sooner for it, a great captain. Criticizing and censuring almost everyone you have to do with, will diminish friends, increase enemies, and thereby hurt your affairs.

No superior had ever been so perceptive and direct with Jones, at least in writing. Coming from an elder he worshipped, Franklin's blunt words struck home. Jones himself had preached the need to show respect to sub-ordinates when he complained to Joseph Hewes about his shabby treat-ment by Captain Saltonstall aboard the old *Alfred*. Jones could not have been completely surprised by Franklin's letter, and as time went on he tried harder to be gracious and patient with his comrades-in-arms. But his pride was too great to be sublimated for long.

Franklin and the French arranged for a new frigate for Jones, the *Ariel*, to sail home with the war supplies in her hold. Franklin was tired of Jones's shilly-shallying. "I am perfectly bewildered," he wrote, "by the dif-ferent schemes to get the goods across. Now you have *Ariel*; for heaven's sake, load her as heavily as she can bear, and sail! I will see to moving the rest."

*   *   *

BUT JONES DID NOT SAIL. Though the ship's log showed day after day of "fine weather" through July and August, the *Ariel* sat at her mooring or tied to the wharf. Some of the delay was unavoidable. *Ariel*, a small French frigate, had to be stripped of most of her guns and refitted to accommodate the cargo of arms and uniforms. Jones was busy as well promoting his ambitions and "schemes." Jones was hoping that the Continental Congress would reward him with command of a ship of the line under construction in New Hampshire, the *America*, and send him back to Europe as commodore of a squadron of frigates, some American, some French. He did not wish to return to the United States without a clear plan and a firm commitment from the French government for raiding England on his return. At the end of July, he was still writing Sartine, proposing "a plan for future expeditions" to "make England tremble." In August, he lobbied the French Foreign Minister, the Comte de Vergennes, angling for another crack at the Baltic Fleet and the chance to "alarm England's coasts."

Jones was distracted by sex as well as strategy. At the end of May, Count Murray-Nicolson, a wealthy Scottish émigré, invited the intrepid naval hero to stay with him and his wife at their château outside Paris. Jones promptly plunged into a torrid affair with la Comtesse de Nicolson. Jones called the Countess "Delia" after a popular song which began, "Return, enraptured hours/When Delia's heart was mine."

Delia arrived in L'Orient with her brother at the end of June or in early July. She was hoping to persuade Jones to give her brother an officer's commission. Jones repaired with the Countess to an inn in the village of Hennebont, a few miles down the river from L'Orient, for five days. Delia's letters to Jones after he returned to his ship are wild with desire and longing:

Dear Jones, I am useless when you are far from me. What will become of me! My God, how unhappy I am! My angel, my adorable Jones, when will we be reunited never to be separated again? . . . If I must be deprived of you, I feel that I may not go on living, Jones! My dear lover! . . . I think that in all my life I never really existed except for those five days that, alas, have passed like a dream.

These outpourings and pages more like them apparently evoked no response from her lover, so Delia tried some different approaches: First flattery:

Everything about you is enchanting. Those charming verses that describe so well your soul and your noble mind, Dear Jones you make me cry a river of tears. You are unequalled in your perfections and never has a man been adored as much as my heart loves you!

Then bribery:

I have been told that neither you nor your crew have been paid. In the name of all the love that consumes me, tell me if I can help you. I have diamonds and all sorts of jewelry; I will easily find money. To give an order to your mistress is to make her happy and her heart will fly to your support. Twenty times when I was in your arms, I wanted to talk to you about this, but I was afraid to displease you.

Still no response. "My god, my servant has just returned from the post office and there is no letter! Good heavens! . . . Alas, could you be so cruel as to depart without telling me goodbye? . . . I cannot go on." Two more letters filled with cries of "Alas!" and "God!" then finally, momentary relief: "The two letters I have just received make me live again. . . . I almost died upon seeing the tracks of your tears! I have pressed the tracks of your tears to my lips and heart. Oh god, how miserable I am!"

Jones's letters do not survive, and it is hard to know if he was crying on the page or sprinkling salt water for effect. His sincerity may be measured by a poem he wrote her—those "charming verses" that she found evidence of a "noble mind." In the poem, Jones compares himself to Jove ("When Jove from high Olympus goes . . .") and Delia to Juno ("All Heav'n laments—but Juno shews/A jealous and superior woe . . ."). But in a draft of the last verse, Jones put brackets around certain words, thus creating alternate versions—one for a poem intended for a lady living in France, the other for a lady living in America ("fair Columbia").*

Jones did not pine long for any one woman, with the possible exception of Dorothea Dandridge, the Virginia gentlewoman who spurned him for Patrick Henry. According to Fanning, he patronized a prostitute at L'Orient that summer and slept with the wife of his agent, James Moylan. An aging Irish gentleman, Moylan had recently acquired a frisky seventeen-year-old wife. Moylan surprised Jones and his wife "in a very loving position," wrote Fanning. Hoping for some privacy, Jones arranged for Moylan to be kept on board the *Ariel* and rendered senseless with drink while he spent the night ashore with Mrs. Moylan. On another occasion, Jones left his gold watch in a room he had visited with a "lady of pleasure." An officer of the *Ariel* found the watch when he used the same room, perhaps with the same lady. The officer and Fanning decided to have some sport with Jones by pawning the watch. Jones had to pay for a case of good wine to get the timepiece back.

With his geographically adaptable poetry and willingness to seduce the teenage wives of his friends, Jones appears to be a callous lover, even measured by the mores of his time. Jones was a peacock who preened, espe-

---

*Thus when the Warrior, though no God,
   Brings Freedom's standard [from] o're the Main,
   Long absent from thy blest abode
   [In fair Columbia Moors again]
   Casts anchor in dear France again;
   O! Thou more heavenly! Far more kind
   Than Juno, as thy Swain then Jove,
   With what hearts—transport; raptur'd-mind!
   Shall we approach on wings of Love!

cially once he had a chevalier's ribbon in his lapel. But it is also likely that he was lonely and desperate for intimacy. Like many sailors, Jones was sexually starved during long voyages. A few scraps of paper have survived that suggest Jones's sexual longings. Undated, written in Latin, the first of these appears to be homoerotic:

> *Give [show] your rear to men, your arrow to sweet women. Those who are worthy shall have access to your behind.*
> *Erect it . . . do feel like a male*
> *And why do you show your behind to the girls of Venus? Well, if they want to, I could show them my front.*

If Jones did have male as well as female lovers, no evidence has emerged. He writes in letters of "loving" other men, but that was the florid style of the time. Sodomy in the navy was punishable by death or a thousand lashes, the same thing. Despite the stereotype ("rum, sodomy, and the lash"), the disciplinary records of the British and American navies show that few men were caught and executed. A conspiracy of silence may have reigned.

Jones's fantasies and frolics diverted him for a time, but the burdens of command were never shrugged off for long. Money woes continued to nag. The awarding of prize money was entangled in complicated jurisdictional issues between the French and Americans. By now Jones was properly skeptical of the promises of French officials to produce his long overdue share. "Though the *Ariel* is nearly ready it will be impossible for me to sail until the prize money etc. for the last expedition is at least so far settled that I know with certainty in *what bankers' hands in Paris* the money will be lodged, and that I may draw on my arrival in America the balance due to the crews of the *Bonhomme Richard* and *Alliance*," he wrote his friend Edmé Genet, a high-ranking official in the Ministry of Foreign Affairs, in Paris on August 9. King Louis's ministers were vague and dodgy in their promises of support for Jones's future expeditions. "At the moment it is impossible to know the number of frigates that could be available . . .

the plans for the forthcoming campaign are not clear enough," wrote Count Maurepas, the King's Prime Minister, on August 15.

Though Jones constantly complained about money, he managed to find the resources to entertain lavishly. Before sailing, Jones staged a spectacle for local worthies—several admirals, a prince, and their ladies—aboard the *Ariel*. On September 2, the log reads, "Had a grand entertainment on board. Expended 2 cases [of ammunition] no. 7 & 20, fired salutes, exercised great guns and small arms." From dinner on deck at 3 P.M. until midnight, Jones hosted his guests with wine, fireworks, music, and a reenactment of his famous battle against the *Serapis*, complete with seamen and marines in the tops flinging grenades onto an imaginary deck below. Fanning recounted:

> Neither cash nor pains were spared in order that the scene every way should appear magnificent. In a short time, our quarterdeck had the appearance of a ladies' quality drawing room. Overhead was suspended an elegant awning . . . decorated with a variety of silk roses, tassels. . . . French cooks and waiters or servants were brought from the shore. . . . We were almost suffocated with garlic and onions, besides a great many other stinking vegetables.

The *pièce de résistance* was the mock sea battle. Jones lit up the night sky with cannon and musket fire; bombs exploded and men waved their swords and shouted oaths. "Some of the ladies," Fanning reported, "were much frightened and the sham fight would have continued longer had it not been that some of them entreated Captain Jones to command the firing to cease."

Jones bellowed "Cease fire!" just as he had that night aboard the *Bonhomme Richard*. He struck up the band, the waiters continued to pass the bottle, and all was "glee and harmony." In his journal, Fanning chided Jones for his overindulgence, claiming that inside the brocaded tent on the quarterdeck, the captain hung "indecent pictures." The midshipman may have just been smarting over his own embarrassment. After describing the "grand entertainment," the log entry for September 2 also noted: "The Capt. kicked Mr. Fanning, Midshipman, and ordered him below."

The voyage to America was delayed, then delayed again. Two days after the great spectacle, on September 4, the *Ariel* cast off its mooring at L'Orient and sailed to the anchorage at the island of Groix, the jumping-off point for a sea voyage. But the wind and the weather turned unfavorable. "I have been detained here and in the port of L'Orient by contrary and stormy winds for a whole month," Jones wrote Edmé Genet on September 21.

Sitting in his cabin, watching the westerly gales lash rain across the crowded anchorage, Jones had time to reflect, always a dangerous invitation for him to brood. He began writing sullen letters castigating various foes, real and imagined, including John Adams ("that wicked and conceited upstart") and Chaumont ("that hairbrained [sic] man"), whom he blamed, probably unfairly, for spilling his secret plans and sitting on the *Bonhomme Richard*'s prize money. With Silas Deane, Jones struggled to be "philosophical." He wrote Deane, "As human nature is imperfect, some opposition is perhaps necessary to excite my perserverence, to keep my patriotism constant and unwarped." True enough at sea. On land, opposition of any kind seems to have warped Jones's judgment. While he looked down on John Adams, he continued to confide in the duplicitous Edward Bancroft, "my dearest friend. . . . No man loves and esteems you with a more tender and heartfelt affection," he gushed.

Clearly, Jones needed to get back to sea. In early October, the gales calmed and the log showed the *Ariel* preparing to get under way. Jones by now was impatient. He had heard that he would be greeted in Philadelphia as a hero, and he was eager to get there.

CHAPTER TWELVE

"The Gale Still Increasing"

*A*T 2 P.M., on October 7, Jones's heavily laden frigate weighed anchor at the Isle of Groix and sailed into the Bay of Biscay. Extending from the southern coast of the Brittany Peninsula to the north coast of Spain, the bay is a mixing bowl for weather systems, a cold, turbulent body of water where storms sweeping off the Atlantic or the Continent collide and become tempests. Waves in the bay can rise to enormous heights and become riotous and confused by rapidly shoaling water and strong crosscurrents. To be trapped on the lee shore of the bay, pushed against the rocky coast by westerly gales, was for centuries a sailor's nightmare. Hidden reefs south of the Brittany Peninsula wrecked ships by the score. Indeed, the waters were deemed to be so dangerous that in Paul Jones's day, ship owners operating in the Bay of Biscay were required to pay premium insurance rates.

"Begins with fine pleasant weather," is the first log entry for the *Ariel* at noon on October 7. Reaching along on a gentle northwesterly breeze, all sails set, Jones plotted a course south and west, to cruise down past the Azores and pick up the easterly trades for the Atlantic crossing. Standing on the quarterdeck of his trim new frigate, 130 feet long, thirty feet wide, Jones had no reason to fear anything but a passing British squadron.

As darkness fell, the wind nearly died. The night was "serene," reported Jones's faithful first lieutenant, Richard Dale. But the stars, obscured by high thin clouds, began to vanish by midnight. Sea and sky became an inky void. At about 2 A.M., the breeze began freshening and swinging more westerly, then southwesterly, right on the *Ariel*'s nose. Small puffs made the canvas sails shudder. Unable to sail directly into the wind, the *Ariel* fell off on port tack and began to steer northwest on a course which, if held, would clear the western tip of the Brittany Peninsula.

In 1780, weather forecasting was more art than science. Captains could sometimes spot a storm coming from a long swell in the ocean, or by flights of birds and the changing light and look of the sky, or by just their gut instinct, born of experience. An eighteenth-century mariner's only forecasting device was a barometer, which could provide a few hours warning. An approaching low pressure system in the atmosphere would make the "glass fall," i.e, the barometric pressure gauge (a column of mercury in a thin glass tube) dip to a low level, appropriately marked on the barometer's face as "stormy weather."

Aboard the *Ariel* during the midnight-to-4-A.M. watch in the early morning of October 8, the glass was plummeting. Before dawn, Captain Jones was awakened and summoned to the quarterdeck. His first act was to shorten sail: to take down the uppermost spread of canvas, the gallants and royals, and to reef the topsails. He did not alter course. If the wind continued to veer south, *Ariel* would be able to safely weather the Brittany coast. In the dim light of a gray morning, Jones could see the island of Groix, vanishing far astern.

Squalls began to sweep in from the west. The rain, slanting horizontally, was cold in early October. Jones and his officers donned oilskins and closely watched the sails, to see how much they could bear without tearing or carrying away a spar. All morning, the wind rose, until by late morning the officer of the deck wrote in the log, "heavy gales." The wind was now exceeding forty miles an hour in gusts. It tore the foam off the tops of the whitecaps and blinded the men on deck with salt spray.

Every captain comes to know his ship, but Jones had never sailed this one. He could not know for sure *Ariel*'s strengths and weaknesses, her tolerances and tendencies. Was she crank? Did she "gripe", i.e., side-slip to

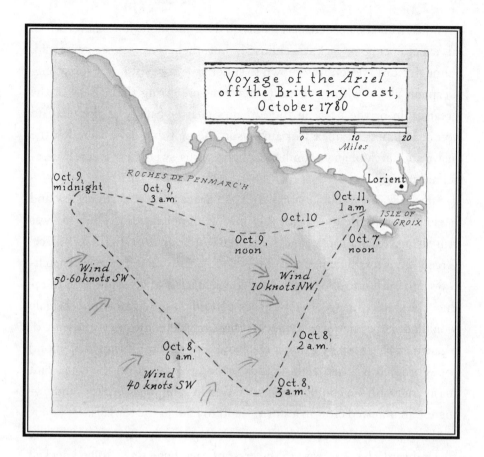

Voyage of the *Ariel*
off the Brittany Coast,
October 1780

leeward? Jones needed to know to be able to judge whether *Ariel* could hold her course and clear the reefs along the lee shore. He needed to know, as well, whether he could count on his men. The ship's crew consisted of about forty-five veterans from *Bonhomme Richard*, for the most part reliable sailors, and an equal number of less certain hands, Englishmen dumped out of French jails and some French soldiers, landlubbers drafted to serve as marines.

On the stormy morning of October 8, many of the men were haggard, greenish, and bent over the rail. Seasickness strikes all but the saltiest old hands in the first day or two. A storm on the second day out before the crew had a chance to get its sea legs was especially debilitating. The extreme nausea and lassitude of seasickness meant that Jones had a stricken crew just when he needed alert hands on deck and aloft. Jones never wrote of experiencing seasickness himself, but then, few sea captains did. Though Lord Nelson was known to suffer, *mal de mer* was not something a captain would wish to reveal to his crew, preferring the privacy of the great cabin or the privy in the captain's quarter gallery as the place to vomit. If Jones felt queasy or anxious in the morning gale, as he felt the heave and lurch of an unfamiliar deck in a rising swell, he was surely careful not to show it.

Stuffed with cargo and stores for the voyage, *Ariel* was riding low and heeling over a little too far for the comfort of her captain. The wind was still rising, reaching fifty and sixty miles an hour, near hurricane-force. Green water was sluicing in over the lee rail, threatening to smash hatchways and gush into the hold below. Jones needed to do something to reduce the ship's windage, to lower the sails and mast so the blast of the gale would not knock her over so much. (One can get a sense of the pressure of a gale on a ship's sail by extending a hand out of a car moving at 50 mph.) Jones ordered his men aloft, seasick or not, to take down the topgallant masts and yards—a cumbersome operation in calm weather, risky and trying for an untested crew in a storm—and to haul in the topsails.

"Heavy gales and a great sea," reads the log shortly after noon. Clawing to windward, the *Ariel* rose to the crest of each huge wave, to be knocked over by a torrent of wind. Down the foamy face she surfed, into the valley between the waves. Sheltered for a moment by the trough, she righted, her sails slackening in the lull. Then, back into the maelstrom: up the watery wall, climbing, climbing, into a fresh blast that punched at the sails and made each spar creak and groan under the pressure.

In the gloom of autumnal dusk, darkened by storm, Jones made some mental calculations. He could feel the ship working and straining and deeply complaining. Her seams were opening under the assault of wind and wave. The carpenter was reporting water in the hold. Would the *Ariel* clear the western point? Or be driven down on the rocks of the lee shore?

Visibility was near zero. Peering into a wet gray veil, the only way Jones could tell whether *Ariel* was being pushed to leeward was to test the depth of the water, to see if the ocean bottom was shoaling upward toward the shallows—and the reefs and rocks that waited to tear out the bottoms of ships. Jones ordered the crew to begin sounding the depths with the deep-sea lead line, a long rope with a very heavy weight on the end. A seaman climbed into the chains, where the mast's rigging was secured to the sides of the ship's hull, and heaved out the line of lead. The rope ran out until the lead weight hit bottom. Markers along the rope indicated the depth, six feet to a fathom. Aboard *Ariel,* the line stopped reeling out at fifty fathoms, indicating 300 feet of ocean depth. Then forty-five fathoms. Then forty fathoms. Still plenty of water for a ship that drew twenty-five feet, but the sea bottom was beginning to shoal. *Ariel* was not holding course but drifting to leeward, toward the shore. There was a strong possibility, Jones knew, that the *Ariel* would run out of sea room before she cleared the western point.

Jones decided that he could not take the risk. "Ware ship," he ordered. He planned to head off, before the wind, and come around on the opposite tack—heading southeast instead of northwest. He was hoping to make it back to the Isle of Groix and its safe anchorage. But he would still be hemmed in along a lee shore. He worried, too, about the Penmarchs, a long ledge of submerged rocks well known to captains as a mariner's graveyard. It was essential that the *Ariel* hold her new course and keep on making headway in the storm.

Every sailing ship captain listens to wind, the rising register of sound that records the ferocity of the gale as it whips through the sails and rigging. The pitch grows sharper: a roar becomes a howl becomes a shriek. Like a patient crying out in pain, a ship will groan and moan until, with a loud crack, some vital limb gives way. Jones needed to keep some forward progress to stay off the lee shore; he could not run or "scud" before the wind without surging straight onto a reef. He needed to keep *Ariel* creeping or scuttling sideways. But even the few scraps of sail aloft were too much. "At 10 handed the main sail," reads the log. The men, clinging precariously to the rigging, took in the mainsail, or "course." "The gale still increasing, set the chain pumps to work," the log continued. "The lee gangway was laid entirely under the water and the lee side of the waist was full. The water in the hold flowed into the cockpit notwithstanding the great efforts of the chain pumps," wrote Lieutenant Dale. The men heaved on the bars of the pumps, struggling to stay ahead of the water coming in over the side.

The landsmen, the lubbers who had never seen the fierceness of a storm at sea, began to lose hope. "Some French soldiers which we had on board, and who were stationed at the cranks of the pumps, let go of them, crossed themselves, and went to prayers," wrote Midshipman Fanning. With drawn swords, the officers had to drive them back to their duty.

There was good reason for even the hardiest sea dogs to be afraid. The sea was running "mountains high," Fanning recorded in his journal (with an asterisk: "This was the Bay of Biscay," he wrote in the footnote). *Ariel* was losing a fight to stay afloat. Sailors dread broaching, turning sideways to wave and wind and rolling over on a ship's beam ends. If the cargo and ballast shift from a violent lurch, if the hatches tear open, or a cannon gets loose and rips a hole in the bulkhead to let in the sea, a sailor might as well pray. If anything occurs to upset a ship's fundamental equilibrium, sinking is only a matter of time, and sometimes a very short time.

Jones's ship was reaching the tipping point. As she came off large waves after a knockdown blow, *Ariel* was no longer righting herself. Even in the trough, she lay over so far on her side that the leeward yardarms were dipping in the water. The giant rollers were cresting and breaking over the ship, threatening to engulf and overwhelm her. *Ariel* needed to purge the water filling her hold and threatening to capsize her.

One of the ship's two main pumps choked. As the carpenter's mates worked desperately to clear it of debris, the French soldiers were freed up from the labors. They had time to cross themselves and say their final prayers. The situation was now truly grave, and Jones no longer pretended otherwise. He had personally climbed into the chains and "with his own hands," wrote Fanning, sounded the lead. The bottom was shoaling fast: thirty-five fathoms. The Penmarchs, with their rocky teeth, beckoned only two or three miles to leeward. The *Ariel* would slowly drift down and break apart on the reef—if she did not roll over and sink first. Either way, everyone aboard was in mortal peril.

The time was about 2 A.M. The ship was writhing in utter blackness. The sound of the storm—"the Gale increasing" noted the log—was deafening; rain and sea had been melded by wind into a torrent that made breathing difficult. Time was stopping for those on deck and huddled below, standing in seawater sloshing everywhere. They were helpless to do anything but wait to die.

On board were a number of civilian passengers, including the wealthy Philadelphia merchant Samuel Wharton, who had been in France procuring supplies for the revolutionary cause. "We were all summoned on deck to meet our fate, and had taken a solemn farewell of each other," Wharton wrote. "We momentarily expected to founder." One pictures a sodden gaggle of gentlemen, struggling to stand upright in the cataclysm, gravely shaking hands and trying to disguise their terror.

But Jones was still fighting. Inspired by what Wharton described as a "fortunate celerity of thought," the captain summoned the officers and proposed a plan. Their last hope was to bring around the head of the ship, to force *Ariel*'s bow to face into the wind and waves before she capsized. At the same time, they needed to halt their drift to leeward toward the Penmarch rocks.

Shouting above the shriek of the tempest (no dulcet drawing room tones now), Jones gave his orders. They would throw over the best bower anchor with as much line as possible, then, if necessary, cut the windward shrouds on the foremast. The mast would instantly break off, relieving some of the pressure that was keeping the *Ariel* on her beam ends. Sacrificing a mast was a draconian step, but far from unheard of. In the Great Storm of 1703, a hurricane that devastated England, an admiral had saved his ship of the line and 600 men by cutting away all three masts.

Over went the anchor. The cable was played out to the bitter end—and the anchor did not bite. A second cable was spliced on and paid out. Still, no relief. The *Ariel* wallowed in her final throes. Jones ordered the foremast cut away. As the tall timber toppled over the side, the anchor at last grabbed the ocean bottom, and the *Ariel* brought to—the bow swung into the wind, and the laboring ship slowly righted.

There was little time to cheer. One mortal peril was soon replaced by another. In the giant rollers, the bow would dip down into the trough, then at the peak give a sudden jerk as the anchor cable snapped taut. The motion was so violent that it threatened to shake apart the ship. The mainmast began to "reel about like a man drunk," according to Dale's report. Amidst the awful sounds of the storm, the howling and groaning, Jones, with his practiced ear, heard another, more sickening noise. From deep in the bowels of the ship came a sharp boring and grinding. The mainmast had kicked out of its step. Loosely bound by the rigging, tortured by the bucking of the vessel, the thick oak trunk had been transformed into half–battering ram, half-drill. If the mast did not first break in half, its wildly rotating butt would drive a hole through the bottom of the ship.

Jones had one last chance to save the ship. He ordered the men to cut away the windward shrouds of the mainmast. But before the crew, stumbling and slipping across the wildly heaving deck, could swing their axes, a sharp popping and cracking stopped everyone. The mainmast's chain plates were ripping right out of the ship's sides. With a tremendous crash, the mainmast, suddenly unmoored, went over the side, taking the mizzenmast with it. The *Ariel* had been reduced to a hulk.

But she was still afloat. No one had died. A glimmer of hope returned "that our lives might be spared," Fanning wrote. In the morning, the storm abated, if only slightly. By noon, the sun had broken through the racing clouds. When the *Ariel* mounted the crest of a wave, Jones could see a fantastic display, vast green-blue mountains, flecked and streaked with white foam, marching for miles. He could also see the French coast and the vast rollers crashing with murderous power on the Penmarchs a few miles away.

The *Ariel* was still in danger. Jones could not count on the single anchor holding his wildly careering ship (the ship's other two anchors had been torn away when the foremast went over the side). Although it was impossible to stand on deck without holding on to a rope or rail for support, Jones

1

John Adams once described John Paul Jones as "leprous with vanity." Jones was, in a way, sickened by his own pride, driven by an unquenchable thirst for glory that was off-putting to others. But he was also a true-blue patriot, and he was unusual in the rag-tag Continental Navy for his ability to fight. In battle, Jones was exuberant, re-sourceful, relentless, and brave. "Eccentricities and Irregularities are to be expected from him—they are in his character, they are visible in his Eyes," John Adams wrote about Jones. "His voice is soft and small, his eye has a keenness and Wildness and softness in it." This portrait by J. M. Moreau, one of the best engravers of the age, reveals an undercurrent of anxiety behind Jones's strong visage.

He was born John Paul, Jr., in a small white-washed cottage (*above*) at Arbigland (*below*), a great estate on the southwest coast of Scotland, where his father was the head gardener. Young John Paul went to sea at the age of thirteen. Fleeing to America after killing a man, he changed his name to Jones.

4

John Paul was rumored to be the bastard son of the "laird," or landlord, of Arbigland, William Craik (*above*). Young John Paul was packed off to Whitehaven (*below*), an English city across the Firth of Solway from Scotland, to obtain an apprentice's berth on a merchant ship. As an American navy captain, Jones returned to Whitehaven eighteen years later to try to burn the ships in the port.

5

6

Joseph Hewes (*above*) of North Carolina and Robert Morris (*right*) of Philadelphia were Jones's patrons in the Continental Congress. They recognized and promoted his talents but had to put up with his constant complaints that less able captains were getting better ships. Jones lobbied for a "fast ship...for I intend to sail in harm's way." He had to sail into his greatest battle in an old, slow tub.

7

IN CONGRESS.

The DELEGATES of the UNITED STATES of *New-Hampshire, Massachusetts-Bay, Rhode-Island, Connecticut, New-York, New-Jersey, Pennsylvania, Delaware, Maryland, Virginia, North-Carolina, South-Carolina, and Georgia,* TO

John Paul Jones, Esquire,

WE, reposing especial Trust and Confidence in your Patriotism, Valour, Conduct, and Fidelity, DO, by these Presents, constitute and appoint you to be *Captain* ———————————————————————— in the ———— of the United States of North-America, fitted out for the Defence of American Liberty, and for repelling every hostile invasion thereof. You are therefore carefully and diligently to discharge the Duty of *Captain* ———— by doing and performing all manner of Things thereunto belonging. And we do strictly charge and require all Officers, Marines and Seamen under your Command, to be obedient to your Orders as *Captain.* And you are to observe and follow such Orders and Directions from Time to Time, as you shall receive from this or a future Congress of the United States, or Committee of Congress for that Purpose appointed, or Commander in Chief for the Time being of the Navy of the United States, or any other your superior Officer, according to the Rules and Discipline of War, the Usage of the Sea, and the Instructions herewith given you, in Pursuance of the Trust reposed in you. This Commission to continue in Force until revoked by this or a future Congress.

DATE at *Philadelphia, October 10th 1776.*

By Order of the CONGRESS,

John Hancock PRESIDENT.

ATTEST.

8

John Hancock, the president of the Continental Congress, signed Jones's captain's commission, but he condescended to him. "I admire the spirited conduct of little Jones," Hancock wrote about Jones (who was 5´6˝) after hearing of Jones's daring attacks against British shipping. Jones quarreled with Hancock over his rank on the seniority list. "You will not blame my free soul, which will never stoop where it cannot esteem," Jones wrote his congressional ally, Robert Morris. Jones tried to swallow his pride: "The best way is to cooperate cheerfully. I am earnest to do everything with good nature," he wrote. But then he returned to brooding.

9

"Our 'hair's breadth scape' and the saucy manner of making it must have mortified him not a little," gloated Jones after outfoxing a British frigate aboard *Providence* (*above*). Aboard *Ranger* (*below*), Jones was saluted by French warships before staging raids on the English coast.

10

11

The British press caricatured the fearsome "Pirate Paul Jones." In 1770, as the master of a merchant ship, Jones had been unjustly imprisoned in Kirkcudbright (*below*) for flogging the son of an influential local. In 1778, as an American Navy captain, Jones returned to Kirkcudbright to kidnap the Earl of Selkirk. The Earl was gone, so Jones settled for stealing his lordship's silver. Wishing to be seen as a gentleman, Jones later returned the silver.

12

13

The sea battle off Flamborough Head on the east coast of England on the evening of September 23, 1779, was one of the bloodiest ship-to-ship duels of the Age of Sail. When Jones's Continental Navy ship *Bonhomme Richard* encountered His Britannic Majesty's ship *Serapis*, the Americans were outgunned and faced a newer, faster vessel—not to mention a centuries-old tradition of superiority in the Royal Navy. But Jones succeeded in locking the British ship into a death struggle and simply refused to surrender. Jones himself lashed the jib boom of the *Serapis* to the *Bonhomme Richard*'s mizzenmast, enlisting the sailing master, a man named Stacey, to help him make fast the rope. With Stacey swearing a blue streak, Jones, who could be almost giddy in battle, teasingly admonished, "Mr. Stacey, it's no time to be swearing now. You may be the

14

next moment in eternity, but let us do our duty." Cannon balls went in one side of the *Bonhomme Richard* and out the other. When one of his mates tried to haul down the American flag and surrender, Jones threw his pistol at the man and knocked him out. "Have you struck?" the British demanded. According to legend, Jones replied, "I have not yet begun to fight." (He probably said something more like, I may sink, but I'll be damned if I surrender.) During the height of the battle, Jones took over aiming and firing a nine-pound cannon at the main mast of the *Serapis*. After more than three hours, with half the men on both ships dead or wounded, the British finally surrendered. And a day later, the nearly gutted *Bonhomme Richard* did sink.

15

None of these romantic paintings of the engagement is entirely accurate. Jones and his flotilla, which included the American frigate *Alliance* under the mad Captain Landais and the French frigate *Pallas*, spotted the British Baltic fleet carrying ship-building supplies to England and convoyed by the *Serapis* and the smaller sloop *Countess of Scarborough*, on the morning of September 23. When Jones made the signal to "Form Line of Battle," the other captains in his flotilla ignored him. The *Pallas* eventually engaged and defeated the *Countess of Scarborough*; their battle is pictured in the background of most of the paintings. The duel between the *Bonhomme Richard* and the *Serapis* began at dusk, on a flat calm sea under a rising harvest moon, and con-

16

tinued into darkness. Both ships caught fire from flying sparks and flame; during a lull in the battle, the crews of both ships scrambled to extinguish the flames lest the ships blow up. To spectators gathered on the bluff at Flamborough Head several miles away, the scene was eerie and ghostly: two warships locked inside a yellowish cloud that pulsated with flashes of orange and white light. The main mast of the *Serapis* did not topple until after the engagement was over. The two ships were side-by-side, not at angles, when the *Alliance* opened fire, striking the *Bonhomme Richard* as well as the *Serapis*. "For God's sake," the men of the *Bonhomme Richard* called out, "Wrong ship! Stop firing!" Jones believed that Landais intentionally had tried to sink his ship.

17

In this nineteenth-century engraving of the battle with the *Serapis*, Jones is shown cradling his telescope and waving a pistol, directing his men to repel boarders. In the last stages of the battle, about twenty to thirty British seamen and Marines did try to rush the *Bonhomme Richard*'s quarterdeck. Armed with a pike, Jones met them at the gangway and, together with his sailors, drove them off.

"Sir," said Jones to the captain of the *Serapis*, Richard Pearson (*left*), as Pearson surrendered, "you have fought like a hero, and I make no doubt that your sovereign will reward you...." Indeed, Pearson was bestowed a knighthood. Learning that his vanquished foe was now Sir Richard, Jones (*below*) dryly joked: "Were I only able to make him a Lord someday."

18

19

20

Jones venerated Ben Franklin (*above*), the American Minister in Paris who essentially acted as his boss. Franklin valued Jones's fighting qualities but warned Jones to control his ego and share credit with others. Jones was ordered by Franklin to join forces with the Marquis de Lafayette (*right*) to attack the British coast.

21

Desperate for action, Jones joined the Russian Navy of Catherine the Great (*left*) in 1788. He fought well in several battles and clashed with Catherine's favorite lover and generalissimo, Prince Potemkin (*below*). In St. Petersburg, Jones was disgraced in a sex scandal, accused of raping a ten-year-old girl. His enemies probably set him up.

22

23

24

Buried in a forgotten grave in Paris in 1792, Jones was finally laid to rest in this tomb more than a century after he died. Jones's crypt, modeled on Napoleon's tomb, lies beneath the transept of the Naval Academy Chapel. "He gave our navy," an inscription reads, "its earliest traditions of heroism and victory."

got his steadier hands to work, attempting to jury-rig a mast from some un-used spars. It was slow going. "Squally weather and rain with heavy seas," reads the log on October 10. Not until 1 A.M. on the morning of October 11 were the men able to cross a yard and raise a jib and staysail. At last the anchor cable was cut, and the *Ariel* ponderously plowed through the swells toward Groix.

Jones's ship was shattered, her provisions wet and partly ruined. But her survival was considered something just short of a miracle. All up and down the Bay of Biscay, the wrecks of less fortunate ships dotted the coast. Jones was once more a hero. "The crew and passengers all credit him with saving the ship," wrote the L'Orient port captain. "A delivery from death," wrote Samuel Wharton to Benjamin Franklin: "Through the matchless skill, and cool, and unshaken intrepidity of our captain—'Who truly rode in the whirlwind and directed the storm'—we were saved."

Jones made his usual stab at modesty. In a brief letter to Edmé Genet on October 13, the day after returning to L'Orient, Jones wrote, as almost an afterthought, "I will only add that the tempest we rode out at the same lat-itude as the Penmarch rocks exceeded all my former ideas of storms or ship wreck and I believe no other ship has ever escaped from an equal dan-ger of those rocks." To Madame La Présidente d'Ormoy, he was a bit more dramatic: "I can give you no just idea of the scene that nature just presented; which surpassed the reach of even poetic fancy and pencil." Yet Jones quickly moved on to a subject he never tired of explicating or de-fending: his honor. Apparently, he had heard that an Englishwoman, pos-sibly the gossipy Miss Edes, was saying unflattering things about him in the salons of Paris. "I am extremely sorry that the young English lady you mention should have imbibed the English hatred against me," he wrote Madame La Présidente. "I cannot imagine why any fair lady should be my enemy, since upon the large scale of universal philosophy, I *feel*, acknowl-edge and bend before the sovereign power of beauty. The English nation may hate me; but *I will force them to esteem me, too.*" His pride was intact. There is the tiniest hint in the letter that Jones had felt his mortality off the Penmarch rocks and required comforting. "Pray, have you seen my fair friend the Comtesse de N.?" Jones inquired. "I am very anxious to hear from her."

On the other hand, he may have just been trying to use Delia to further his career. Jones had taken on Delia's brother, William Nicolson, as captain of marines aboard the *Ariel*. With the *Ariel* still a wreck, Jones was, as usual, manuevering for a better ship, the frigate *Terpsicore*. In November, Nicolson wrote Jones that his adoring Countess was at Versailles, lobbying in court on his behalf. The pro-Jones faction wasn't having much luck. Franklin, afflicted with the gout, had grown tired of hearing Jones complain and French officials were indifferent. Nicolson wrote Jones that he would have to come himself to get results: "Everyone here thinks your presence Sir, absolutely necessary at Paris." Jones had learned by now not to run off from his ship to Paris, even if the reward was a tumble with Delia. He stayed with the *Ariel*, which was getting fitted with new masts at L'Orient.

Jones needed to get back to sea and return to America.* "My friends tell me the new 74-gun ship, called the *America* at Portsmouth, will be reserved for me," Jones wrote Robert Morris in Philadelphia on November 8. Jones wanted to be more than a sea captain. He wished to be a naval reformer as well (and if that meant flag rank, so much the better). "Our navy has not only been put in bad hands, it has been unwisely employed," Jones wrote Morris. "It has served to enrich a few ignorant individuals and has done almost nothing for our cause. If my feeble voice is heard when I return to Philadelphia our navy matters will assume a better face."

The refitted *Ariel* sailed from L'Orient on December 18. Because he was carrying secret dispatches to Congress as well as tons of gunpowder in *Ariel*'s hold, Jones wanted to avoid British warships. *Ariel* sailed south along a less-well-traveled route to the continent, picking up the northeast

---

*Jones's temper got the better of him again as he waited to sail in L'Orient. He threatened to "run through" a junior lieutenant, a general's nephew whom he found to be insubordinate, and had the young man thrown in irons. Aggrieved, the lieutenant challenged Jones to a duel on land, and when Jones refused, beat Jones bloody with a cane. The lieutenant escaped, protected by French officers unsympathetic to Jones.

trades, warm in that winter season, and skirting south of Bermuda. He slipped along unnoticed until, in January, he neared the West Indies and fell in with a British privateer, the *Triumph*.

Sailed by American Tories loyal to the British crown, the *Triumph* cruised under the British ensign out of New York. With twenty guns, four more than *Ariel*, the *Triumph* was better armed and faster. Jones tried to run for it and lose the privateer in the night, but by dawn, *Ariel's* pursuer had drawn closer. Jones was unable to shake the enemy, so, in classic fashion, he aimed to trick her.

Jones ordered his marines hidden below. The ship was cleared for action, but the guns were not run out. As part of his standard *ruse de guerre*, Jones was flying British colors. Jones, wearing his usual British uniform, allowed the *Triumph* to range up on *Ariel's* quarter. Assuming the confident manner of a Royal Navy officer, he proceeded to engage the *Triumph's* captain in a lengthy conversation as the two ships glided along, not thirty feet apart. Jones inquired of his opposite, who introduced himself as Captain John Pindar, What news? Pindar had just come from the continent, and he was able to fill in Jones on the war news. Jones continued to bluff. He pretended to believe that *Triumph* was not really a British privateer. Remembering how he conned the British pilot to come aboard at Leith, Jones insisted that Pindar row over to show him his letter of marque, proof that he was sailing under British orders.

Pindar was not a fool. He excused himself, saying that his boats were leaky. He accosted Jones for revealing neither his name nor the name of his ship. Jones blustered that he did not have to account to Pindar—and gave him five minutes to decide if he was coming across with the necessary papers.

Time to spring the trap. Shouting commands, Jones ordered the helm put over, the American flag run up the mast. The port lids to the cannons swung open and Jones's small battery of 9-pounders was run out. *Ariel* swerved across *Triumph's* stern and opened fire, raking the British privateer. For ten more minutes, the guns of the *Ariel* pummeled the enemy. Putting up only "feeble" resistance, according to Jones, Captain Pindar hauled down his flag and asked for quarter, saying that half his men were dead. "In earlier combats I had never felt so satisfied as I did during this one with the regular and vigorous firing from the rigging and the batteries of the *Ariel*," Jones wrote. He was proud of the veterans of the *Bonhomme Richard*, especially her officers. The rest of the crew he did not trust for a moment. He had enlisted the officers and even the passengers "to stop men from abandoning their posts and to encourage everyone to do his duty."

The men of the *Ariel* were still cheering when Pindar pulled a fast one of his own. Slipping up to windward, he suddenly ordered all sail set and drew away. The laden *Ariel* was too slow to catch her. Jones was indignant at this "base" act by a vanquished foe. Like other naval officers of his time, he believed that it was one thing to use deception to lure an opponent into battle, while it was quite another to play tricks after the battle had been decided, fair and square. In his retelling, Jones huffed that "if the English government had possessed the sentiments of honor and justice that become a great nation, they would have delivered this frigate to the United States as their property and punished the captain in an exemplary manner for having violated that laws of war and the practices of civilized nations."

Jones was not quite home free. The Englishmen in Jones's crew, riffraff from the French jails, were a mutinous lot. Jones's officers nipped a plot and put twenty of the blackguards in irons. A pair of British frigates had been ordered to lie in wait for Jones at the Delaware capes, but *Ariel* slipped by in the winter weather and cruised up the river to Philadelphia. Jones dropped anchor a short row and walk from the State House on February 18, 1781. He had been away from his adopted country for more than three years.

PHILADELPHIA HAD BEEN TRANSFORMED by war. The once elegant city was shabby and worn. Public buildings, where British troops and horses had been quartered, still stank from the British occupation of 1777–78. Jones could not have missed the peeling paint and crumbling brickwork as he walked the muddy streets. The city was much battered since he first saw it in the late summer of 1775; his own situation, however, had vastly improved. He was able to hire a French manservant and call himself "Chevalier Paul Jones," and his victories at sea were celebrated, in part for their rarity. The French ambassador, the Chevalier de la Luzerne, pinned the cross of the Ordre du Mérite Militaire on Jones's breast at a reception "for all the members of Congress and all the leading citizens of Philadelphia," Jones proudly recalled. Jones always loved a celebration, so when the Continental Congress passed the Articles of Confederation at the end of February, he dressed the *Ariel* with flags and had his marines (under the command of Delia's brother, Captain Nicolson) fire a salute, a *feu de joie* in the French manner.

The *Ariel* delivered to the rebel cause 437 barrels of gunpowder and 146 chests of arms. As it turned out, the supplies proved useful to General Washington, who would march south against the British in August. Still, even Jones's friends were grumbling about the long delay in the arrival of arms, ammunition, and uniforms from France. Almost a year earlier, America's ally had promised 15,000 arms and 100,000 pounds of powder. When the *Alliance* had straggled into Boston in late August, she carried only 2,000 arms and little powder. In a letter to Ambassador Luzerne, Lafayette had bitterly complained, "All Paris runs after Paul Jones. Meanwhile, our uniforms remain on the beach." Lafayette was still miffed after Jones arrived in February. "How disappointed I have been in hearing that the *Ariel* brought no clothing," the Marquis wrote Washington. In Congress, there were calls for a formal inquiry into the reasons for the long delays.

Jones might have been embarrassed by close scrutiny. Fortunately, his arrival had been preceded by that of Captain Landais. Jones's rival had gone mad on the return voyage. He had put his first mate into shackles and challenged his political ally, Arthur Lee, to a duel. He had sailed erratically and provoked a near mutiny. Landais was blithering by the time he reached port; he had to be carried, kicking and screaming, off his own ship. He was later broken and dismissed from the service.

Landais gave Jones the perfect smoke screen. On February 20, when Congress presented Jones with a list of forty-seven questions examining "the causes which prevented the clothing and military stores coming out last spring and summer; and who was delinquent," Jones was able to answer, in essence: it was all Landais's fault. Jones skillfully finessed the tricky questions, such as: Why had the *Alliance* failed to join an armed French convoy leaving in early June? The real answer was that he had been distracted by his social life in Paris, but Jones blandly answered, "the reasons already assigned." Jones was able to portray Landais as a wretched captain. When he had taken over the *Alliance* from Landais at the Texel, Jones wrote, "I never found a frigate in so bad a condition. Epidemical disorders raged among the crew; the officers were always drinking grog, and there was a total want of subordination, and negligence." At the same time, Jones, always a vivid writer, used the questions to lay out a stirring narrative of his own exploits and noble motives (" . . . to put a stop to the savage burnings and wanton cruelties of the enemy on this continent . . .").

Like a seaborne *ruse de guerre*, Jones's blandishments and equivocations threw off his congressional pursuers. In Congress's final report in April, Jones was not only cleared, he was praised for "making the flag of America respectable among the flags of other nations." American troops were beginning to hold their own on the southern front against the British, and Congress wanted heroes, not scapegoats. Jones fished for, and received, a letter of exoneration from General Washington. The general praised him for the decorations and honors from the French government "so justly acquired." Only one ambition lay beyond the Chevalier's reach: the rank of admiral.

Jones was denied his flag by the machinations of jealous fellow captains. Leading the opposition was Captain James Nicholson, who had done nothing to deserve his place at the top of the seniority list in October 1776 and nothing since to vindicate it. Nicholson was enjoying tavern life while his frigate sat at anchor on the Delaware River, when he heard whispers from a congressman's wife that Jones was lobbying to be made admiral, a rank never before awarded by the Continental Congress. Swinging into action, Nicholson wrote a fellow captain:

> The Chevalier ever since his arrival in this city has devoted his time, privately, by making personal application to the individual members of congress to give him rank at the head of our navy, and after interesting (by being an accomplished courtier) every member who was weak, or of his own stamp, in his favor . . . congress was upon the point of [making Jones an admiral] had we not by the greatest accident discovered it.

Nicholson described how "with very little ceremony" he went hat in hand to congressional leaders. He was not surprised to find Jones himself loitering outside the committee room of the Admiralty Board (the old Marine Committee, renamed). Demanding to be heard behind closed doors, Nicholson savaged his upstart rival. "I said many things pretty severe of the Chevalier's private as well as public character too odious to mention and yet unnoticed," Nicholson wrote his brother captain. That seemed to do the trick. Congress decided to stay out of the thicket of favoring one captain over another. Jones was denied flag rank.

His consolation prize was one that he had been told to expect: command of his country's first line of battle ship, the seventy-four-gun *America*. Still under construction in Portsmouth, she was not just the navy's grandest vessel, she was virtually the only one. All but two of the Continental Navy's dozen frigates had been burned, taken, or sunk, often through the blunders of their captains.

Jones was eager to take command of the *America*, collect the remnants of the Continental Navy under his commodore's pendant, and sail for Europe, to terrorize once more the British coasts. In August he rented a phaeton, a carriage and three horses, and set out for Portsmouth. He stopped at Washington's headquarters in White Plains, New York, to pay his respects, and was discreetly informed by officers there that his chevalier's ribbon and cross would grate in egalitarian New England. Jones knew, however, that it would smooth his way in elitist Portsmouth. Putting away his medal for the journey, he pinned it right back on for Portsmouth society. He rented the best front room of the best boarding-house, carving his initials in the windowpane.

Jones hurried out to Hackett's boatyard on Rising Castle Island in the Piscataqua River. His magnificent ship stood on the stocks—only half-finished. Over 220 feet long, fifty feet beam, she had the Goddess of Liberty as her figurehead and the figures of Tyranny and Oppression, chained under a Liberty Cap, on her stern. But she was still missing her upper decks. On his first inspection, Jones was pleased with the work done so far. "I have had her bottom opened up in several places and find it per-fectly sound, the timber seasoned, and the work everywhere a master-piece," he wrote John Barry, a fellow captain, in early September.* But "there was neither wood, nor iron, nor other material prepared to finish the job," he recorded in his memoir. More discouraging was the identity of the man in charge of building *America:* John Langdon, the wealthy merchant and Congress's naval agent in Portsmouth. Neither man had forgotten their wrangling over outfitting *Ranger* in the fall of 1777. Jones immediately suspected Langdon of double-dealing, of diverting the best shipbuilding materials to his own merchant ships. Work on *America* went slowly; there were not enough carpenters, and they did not work to Jones's always demanding specifications. "What has been done is not to my satisfaction," Jones wrote John Brown, a friend from Philadelphia and secretary to the Admiralty Board, in December.

Jones and Langdon each complained about the other to Robert Morris. The Philadelphia merchant, who, aside from almost singlehandedly buck-ing up the shaky finances of the Continental Congress, had now also been

---

*An important exception to the otherwise sorry record of the Continental Navy captains, Barry took command of the *Alliance* after Captain Landais and cruised successfully against the British until the end of the war, battering a frigate and capturing several privateers and two smaller Royal Navy warships. For years, naval scholars have argued over who deserves the title of father of the American navy, Jones or Barry. Jones was the flashier of the two and a greater visionary, while Barry may have been a better commander. Partly because Jones was an able self-promoter, he became the more mythic figure.

named Agent of the Marine, roughly equivalent to Britain's First Sea Lord. Morris scolded Jones: "Coldness begets difference, and difference seldom proceeds to any length without producing faults on both sides." Jones, who venerated Morris almost as much as he did Franklin, wrote back like a chastened schoolboy. Morris's letter gave him "pain," he replied. He understood that "bickering and uneasiness between persons employed in the same service always do mischief." For a moment, Jones's eyes flickered open to his own faults. But, once more, he struggled without success to find the "cheerful ardor" he had described as an essential attribute in a naval officer.

Jones was touchy in part because the war was passing him by. While he was pacing about a shipyard waiting for the carpenters to show up for work in the autumn of 1781, America was scoring a glorious victory hundreds of miles to the south. In October, trapped and besieged at Yorktown, Virginia, by General Washington and his troops, General Cornwallis surrendered an entire British army. The French navy had provided a vital hand by controlling the Chesapeake and heading off British reinforcements. Jones had toyed with the idea of rushing south to join with his French comrade the Marquis de Lafayette, but it was too late. "I should have been with the fleet or army, had I known the exact situation of the *America* before I left Philadelphia last August," Jones fretted in a letter to his "philosopher," Ben Franklin, on December 13. Lafayette tried to cheer Jones up, reminding him that the war was not over, that they could still be brothers-in-arms. "Your coming to the army I had the honor to command would have been considered as a very flattering compliment to me, who loves you and knows your worth. I am impatient to hear you are ready to sail; and I am of the opinion we ought to unite under you every continental ship we can muster; with such a body of well-appointed marines as might cut a good figure ashore and then give you plenty of provision and *carte blanche*."

What Jones would have done for "plenty of provision and *carte blanche*." He was forced instead to console himself by assuaging his "finer feelings." Jones was not a complete cad. On Christmas Day, he wrote a tender note to "my most lovely Delia." He complained that his desire to return to France had been thwarted by the slow progress on his ship. "The situation is doubly irksome to me my lovely friend, as it stops pursuit of honor, as well of love!" Jones's memories of his affair were more genteel than tawdry, at least as he sat at his writing desk, looking out over the snowy streets of Portsmouth with some Christmas cheer and plum pudding in his belly. "I rest . . . sure that absence will not diminish but *refine* the pure and spotless friendship that binds our souls together," he purred.

Jones had plenty of time, between squabbles with Langdon at the shipyard, to pursue the ladies of Portsmouth. He wished to cut a fine figure. A visiting Swedish officer found Jones to be "of medium height and square built." No longer the lithe young rake, Jones was beginning to fill out his uniforms (now half–Royal, half–Continental Navy: in a portrait by Charles Willson Peale, painted in Philadelphia, he is wearing a buff waistcoat but a blue jacket with regulation red facings). He was always careful about his dress and cleanliness. He asked John Brown to send him from Philadelphia "a good piece of linen for shirts, and a piece of cambric for stock [the high collar worn by gentlemen]. I have muslin for ruffles, but thread and buttons are wanting." His coiffeur demanded attention. Shorn of his long ponytail, his brown hair was just beginning to slightly gray, judging by the Peale portait. From his old friend Captain McNeill in Boston, Jones asked for "good hair powder. . . . Entre nous, there is none of that luxury to be had here, except such as is impregnated with luxurious mites."

Portsmouth may have had lousy hair powder, but its social life was genteel. A few days after making his plea for superior powder, Jones wrote John Brown, "I reached Portsmouth, just when they began to light the candles after tea, and the dancing did not end till after two in the morning." Just as he had aboard *Ariel*, Jones staged elaborate entertainments for the local gentry, with cannon salutes to celebrate the birth of a male heir, a dauphin, to Louis XVI and fireworks on the Fourth of July. Loving dress-up and show, Jones at least found the *America* to be a magnificent stage set. If Jones made any conquests among the ladyfolk, his letters do not reveal them. He had apparently enjoyed a serious flirtation in Philadelphia, for he wrote John Brown about "an affair of the heart" and asked if Brown, who was still in Philadelphia, had any news to report about the lady in question. "I wait patiently to hear *much* on that subject from you," Jones pressed. When Brown did not reply for a time, Jones wrote, "Your silence, I fear carries with it a disagreeable meaning." The lady, it appears, had married: "It is all over . . . think no more of it," replied Brown.

Greater disappointments awaited. He tried to remain civil toward Langdon, but patience was as ever a struggle for Jones. "Will *America* ever be finished?" he despaired to Brown in April. Rumors reached him that a raiding party off a British frigate, known to be sailing in the Gulf of Maine, would swoop in to burn the *America* as she stood on the stocks. Jones arranged to have a guard posted and even stood watch himself every third night. There were reports of shadowy boats with muffled oars in the dark, but the attack never came. He lost his line-of-battle ship to penury and diplomacy instead.

In August, a French ship of the line, the *Magnifique*, struck a hidden ledge entering Boston harbor and was wrecked. Bankrupt Congress, unable to pay for the completion of *America*, seized on a face-saving way out of finishing the project.* In gracious thanks to America's ally, Congress voted to give *America*, minus most of its guns, rigging, masts, sails, and cordage—an "empty shell," scoffed Jones—to the French. Jones was downcast, but he did not carry on about having been cheated out of his just rewards. "It is a sacrifice I shall make with pleasure," Jones wrote stoically to Robert Morris, "to show my gratitude to France." The Chevalier was pleased to demonstrate Addisonian selflessness to Morris. "I have felt,

---

*Desperate to raise money for *America*, Jones had paid workmen out of his own pocket and suggested to a friend in Philadelphia, Gouverneur Morris (no relation to Robert), a "voluntary contribution of the public spirited ladies of Philadelphia, especially under the patronage of Mrs. Morris. . . . I should hope also to be able to give the ladies a ball on board soon afterwards at Philadelphia."

and do feel myself particularly happy, by such severe trials, to show the world, that my patriotism has been superior to ambition, and a stranger to self-interest," he wrote his congressional patron.

Jones cared deeply about the opinions of the good and great. Although he had disdained John Adams as "Mr. Roundface" in a moment of pique, Jones had been gratified to get a letter from Adams in August, before *America* was given away to the French. "The command of the America could not have been more judiciously bestowed, and it is with impatience that I wish her at sea," wrote Adams. "Nothing gives me so much surprise, or so much regret, as the inattention of our countrymen to their navy. It is to us a bulwark as essential as it is to Great Britain."

It is impossible to read Adams's letter without a twinge of regret for what might have been if the two had not chafed against each other. If only Jones had not pushed away Adams in France by regarding him as another persecutor. And if only Adams, who could be as thin-skinned as Jones, had not suspected Jones of plotting with Adams's political rivals. The two men were rare visionaries about the navy. They should have been solid allies from the early days of the Revolution, not wary acquaintances.

Still, maybe it was not too late. Though Britain had put out peace feelers after Cornwallis's defeat at Yorktown, Adams worried that the war was not over. In April, a British fleet under Admiral Rodney had defeated a French fleet off the Saintes in the West Indies. "Rodney's victory has intoxicated Britain again," Adams wrote Jones from Holland, where he had gone to enlist aide from the Dutch, "to such a degree that I think there will be no peace for some time. Indeed, if I could see a prospect of having half a dozen line-of-battle ships under the American flag, commanded by Commodore Jones, engaged with an equal British force, I apprehend that the event would be so glorious for the United States and lay so sure a foundation for their prosperity, that it would be a rich compensation for a continuation of the war."

This was the sort of praise and encouragement that went directly to the head of the Chevalier Jones. So often stymied by venality and shortsightedness, Jones was eternally grateful to hear, from time to time, from those rare figures who, like Adams, shared his larger sense of purpose. Jones was all for peace, he wrote Morris, but "if this war should continue, I wish to have the most active part in it."

Jones had been on the beach too long. He rented a phaeton and headed to Philadelphia to prospect for a ship. He did not come back entirely empty-handed. Congress finally paid him $20,705.27 in unpaid wages and expenses (Jones had been living off of prize money from his early cruises aboard *Providence* and *Alfred*). But a ship remained elusive. Incredibly, the *Indien* was once more dangled before him and snatched away. The Dutch-built heavy frigate first promised Jones in 1777 (and about once a year thereafter) was sitting in Philadelphia harbor when Jones arrived in December. She had been chartered by a wealthy South Carolinian adventurer, Alexander Gillon, who accomplished nothing for the rebel cause. Congress considered giving the frigate to Jones, with orders to attack the British colony of Bermuda. But Gillon stole away on the frigate and "was captured," Jones wrote disgustedly, "without resistance by a much inferior force."

Jones was by now philosophical about the mirage of the *Indien*. He had another idea, to seize an opportunity to continue his naval education and hopefully see a fleet action. With Congress's permission, he signed on as a volunteer on a French fleet sailing from Boston to invade Jamaica with 10,000 men. Jones dashed back to Boston in a rented horse-drawn sleigh (it was the dead of winter) and offered himself to the French as a pilot: he knew the local Jamaican waters from his days as a slave ship captain. Ever the self-improver, Jones had been reading tracts on naval tactics and architecture in between quarreling with Langdon and attending entertainments in Portsmouth. Here was a chance to get a firsthand tutorial, in preparation for his own destiny, he continued to dream, as the first fleet admiral in the United States Navy. Jones was genuinely humble about acquiring expertise. He later wrote Robert Morris that he had much to learn, since "there is now perhaps as much difference between a single battle between two ships and an engagement between two fleets as there is between a single duel and a ranged battle between two armies."

By joining a fleet of seventy French ships, "I hoped to find myself in the best military school in the world," Jones wrote. Jones was given a comfortable cabin aboard Admiral Vaudreuil's flagship, *Le Triumphant*, and—always critical to Jones—treated with respect by the French officers. The patronizing tones he had heard during his humiliating purgatory in Brest during the fall of 1778 had been silenced by the guns of the *Bonhomme Richard*. But the French had nothing to teach Jones about navigation or seamanship. After a confused rendezvous in the Gulf of Maine, the French fleet apparently miscalculated the tides in the Caribbean and spent weeks beating back to the jumping-off point for the invasion near Puerto Cabello, where they were supposed to join up with a Spanish fleet. No Spanish fleet appeared. Meanwhile, a French seventy-four-gun ship of the line hit a rock and foundered, with a loss of 200 men. By the time the French had pulled themselves together, word reached the fleet that the war was over. The British, French, and Americans had agreed to cease hostilities in American waters on April 7, 1783. America had won its independence.

Jones was happy about the "glorious and agreeable news," but his hopes for personal glory were now on hold. He sailed for America, where a recurring tropical fever laid him low. He was so sick that he was unable to sit in the courts-martial of Captains Nicholson and Manley for losing their ships in the war. It must have pained Jones to miss this opportunity to sit in judgment on two of the men who stood between him and flag rank. But accompanied by Samuel Wharton, the wealthy merchant who had praised Jones for his courage and seamanship in the tempest off the Penmarchs, Jones was forced to take the cure at a retreat in the mountains of Pennsylvania. It's doubtful that Jones was helped by the treatment prescribed—cold baths and probably bleeding, the eighteenth-century quackery by which patients purged ill humors from their blood, a pint or two at a time. But he recovered nonetheless, and even showed some quarterdeck swagger when an inn at the town of Bethlehem, Pennsylvania, was terrorized and a guest beaten by some robbers. "There being no magistrate in Bethlehem, Capt. Jones took matters into his hands and made arrangements to hold and guard the ruffians," a local account reported. According to a Bethlehem church diary, Jones told the thugs to be quiet, or he would "clear the decks for action."

Jones was a Hero of the Revolution. He was inducted into the Society of Cincinnati, a new fellowship of American army and navy officers that took its name from Cincinnatus, the citizen-soldier who had come off his farm to save Rome in the fifth century B.C. On his membership certificate, Jones was honored to see the signature of General George Washington, President. Though Ben Franklin was leery of this "order of hereditary knights," Jones was unperturbed by the Old World connotations of inherited nobility.

Jones was not ready to beat his sword into a plowshare. Forsaking his old wish to become a Virginia squire, he did inquire about buying a farm in New Jersey ("as New York will probably be one of our first naval ports") and contemplated, for another brief instant, domestic tranquillity. "I wish to establish myself on a place of my own and to offer my hand to some fair daughter of Liberty," he wrote his friend John Ross. But, at age thirty-seven, he was still too much the restless glory-seeker to settle down. To Morris, he drafted a twenty-three-page letter, nursing old wounds ("will posterity believe," he demanded, "that . . . the *sloop* of war *Ranger* was the best I was ever enabled, *by my country*, to bring into active service?"); thinking ahead about the future of the navy (he suggested starting "little academies" aboard warships where officers would be taught "the principles of mathematics and mechanics, when off duty"); extolling naval power ("In time of peace, it is necessary to prepare, and be always prepared for war by sea"); and angling for a job. He proposed "sending a proper person to Europe in a handsome frigate to display our flag in the ports of different Marine powers." The proper person for such a job, naturally, was Jones.

He was restless and frustrated. He was at the height of his powers. The nation he had fought to create was now fully born but in need of securing its future. Jones believed, not unreasonably, that he was the man to build the new nation's first navy, not the hodgepodge of the Continental Navy, but a true blue-water fleet of battleships to rival those of Great Britain and France.

But Congress was not interested. The strapped lawmakers were trying to sell off the few frigates that remained in the Continental Navy. They could not look ahead to see the need to protect America's commercial and security interests at sea. Jones was entirely right about the need to establish a naval academy, to train an officer corps, to build a fleet, to make America a maritime power. But he had a way of sounding preachy and presumptuous even when he was giving sound advice. His farsightedness was so couched in special pleading that it is easy to see why even his congressional patron, Robert Morris, brushed it off. Indeed, it is not clear that Jones even sent his most salient proposals to Morris. Though Jones's letter is often quoted as proof of his vision for the American navy, he may not have shared that vision with his most important congressional patron, at least in writing. The letter Morris actually received has not survived, and Jones's draft bears the notation, in Jones's handwriting, "Omit to H.R. Morris," in the margin of bracketed sections recommending a more professional sea service. Morris's diary refers only to Jones's "letter of complaint."

Jones tried a more modest proposal to Congress. He suggested that he be sent back to Paris to extract the prize money from the voyage of his "little squadron" under the *Bonhomme Richard*, as well as money still owing the officers and crew from the cruise of the *Ranger*. The money was tied up in diplomatic tangles, and Jones was now free to follow Poor Richard's maxim that, if you want something done correctly, go yourself. Congress consented, agreeing to pay Jones's expenses and captain's salary. On November 10, 1784, the Chevalier Paul Jones, as he now sometimes signed his formal correspondence, embarked on a packet boat for Europe. "Because this ship was very old and damp," Jones wrote in his memoir to Louis XVI, "I did not want to risk taking the sword with which His Most Christian Majesty had honored me, so I left it at Philadelphia." He did not expect to stay long in Paris.

CHAPTER THIRTEEN

"Cover Him With Kisses"

$\mathcal{J}$ONES'S FELLOW PASSENGERS on the packet boat to France were convivial company, brother officers from the French army returning home after their adventures abroad. Among them was Major L'Enfant, described as "everyone's favorite," a "gay and gallant officer," a member of the Society of Cincinnati and the urban planner who would later lay out the broad avenues of Washington, D.C. For most of the wintery voyage, the French officers stayed below, playing cards and dice. Captain Jones, however, preferred to walk the quarterdeck, his cloak wrapped tight against the November gales, as he moodily watched the gray sea rise and fall.

Often, his companion as he paced back and forth was Captain Joshua Barney, the commander of the packet boat, the *General Washington*. Barney, though twelve years younger, was a kindred soul. With jet black hair and a raffish manner, he was a ladies' man and, rare among Continental Navy officers, a brave and ambitious commander. Barney shared Jones's contempt for the craven and inept captains who had outranked them. Barney recounted his experiences with the hopeless Captain William Hallock of the *Hornet*, a sloop that had dropped out of the New Providence expedition in the winter of 1776 after colliding with the sloop *Fly*. Barney was then sixteen years old, a master's mate eager for combat. He described standing by his cannon with a lit match in his hand as a lightly armed British tender approached the *Hornet* off Chesapeake Bay. Naturally timorous, given to prayer and reflection, Captain Hallock ordered Barney to hold his fire because, the captain explained to his incredulous mate, he had "no inclination of *shedding blood!*" The British ship escaped. Barney entertained Jones with the even more ludicrous tale of James Nicholson, the captain at the top of the seniority list who had lobbied to deny Jones flag rank by smearing his character to Congress. In April 1778, with his brand-new frigate, the *Virginia*, caught on a sandbar and a British warship fast approaching, Nicholson had run from his cabin in his nightshirt, jumped in a small boat, and rowed for shore. While Barney, then a lieutenant, pleaded with the men to fight, the crew, in the pusillanimous spirit of their captain, broke into the liquor stores. They were thoroughly drunk by the time the British arrived to take their prize without a shot fired. Captain Nicholson slunk back on board the next day and pitifully asked if he could have his clothes and his books. This was too much for Barney, who called his captain a coward in front of the enemy. Given command of his own sloop, the *Hyder-Ally*, in the last year of the war, Barney won a rare American victory in a ship-to-ship action, taking a twenty-gun British sloop, the *General Monk*.

Jones, who regarded himself as a "voice crying in the desert" about the sorry state of America's young navy, must have taken some pleasure in knowing that there were officers like Barney coming up the ladder. Jones may have shared a mordant laugh or two as he listened to the description of Nicholson in his nightshirt, deserting his crew for safety. But as the two men paced the quarterdeck in the November gloom, Jones said little himself. Barney observed that Jones seemed reserved, even morose.

He was understandably low about his career and future prospects. "After my return to America in 1780," he wrote in his memoir, "my services were less brilliant and less useful than I would have desired." He missed war and the planning for war. Jones had a fertile mind, and he was usually able to keep it churning. In April, as he had cruised with the French, he had been thinking hard about "the future of our marine," as he put it to his friend Captain Hector McNeill. "I have not been idle since I saw you, but have collected many ideas on the subject." But even Jones's persistence and inventive zeal flagged in the face of constant disappointment and inaction. Reflecting on his frustrations over getting the *America* ready for sea, Jones had written John Brown, "In such a situation the labouring mind loses by degrees its fine edge and glowing energy; and becomes less and less fitted for great thoughts and glorious actions." Jones's fire had dimmed. He needed a spark of danger to reignite it.

That may explain why, to Captain Barney's surprise and consternation, Jones insisted on being put ashore in England. The *General Washington* had encountered head winds off the coast of France, so Jones told Barney to steer for England and drop him off in a fishing village near Portsmouth, on Britain's southern coast. Jones explained that he had secret dispatches to deliver to the American minister (John Adams) in London. Barney spluttered that Jones was a wanted man and would be hanged if he was caught wandering around the English countryside. Jones shrugged off the caution. He was accustomed, he said, to being chased by "British blood hounds."

Barney dutifully put Jones ashore, where he found a coach to London. He traveled, as he had once put it in an earlier context, "incog." The caricatures of the Pirate Paul Jones in the British press made him look dark and menacing. No one glanced twice at the weather-beaten, somewhat haggard sea captain swathed against the December chill in a boat cloak. Jones must have enjoyed this latest ruse—sailing, as it were, right into his former enemy's home port without arousing so much as a blink of an eye. Jones did not tarry in London. After he had come and gone, the British newspapers, excited to belatedly discover that the elusive Jones had been right under their noses, calculated that he had arrived in the capital at 9 P.M. on December 5 and departed at 3 A.M. on December 6. He had presumably met Adams at midnight and passed the dispatches, then caught a coach for Dover and the Channel boat to France.

Back on safe ground in Paris, Jones went favor-seeking at the royal court. On December 20, he had an audience with Louis XVI, who received him graciously at dinner at Versailles. The Marechal de Castries, who had succeeded Sartine as Minister of Marine and then become chief of all France's armed forces, told Jones that he had been instructed to say "that His Majesty had been pleased to see me again, and would always be glad to further my interests," Jones recorded in his memoir. Jones resumed his ties to the Lodge of the Nine Sisters, "that illustrious and learned society" he had been privileged to join, and picked up some of his old friendships with the ruling class of the old regime. But he no longer stayed at Passy. The Hôtel de Valentinois had become inhospitable since Jones began quarreling with its owner, Chaumont. Even Franklin was cool to Jones. A formality crept into their correspondence. Franklin, aging and gout-ridden, worn by his years shaking the tin cup for America, may have just run out of patience with the demanding sea captain. Jones, possibly, felt that Franklin had not been vigorous enough in his defense in his battles with Landais.

Extracting the prize money owed the American men of the *Bonhomme Richard* and *Alliance* proved to be a "difficult and disagreeable task," Jones wrote. The French had sold the *Serapis* and the *Countess of Scarborough* for a fraction of their worth, for less than $100,000, and then gouged out more than half that in deductions. Jones protested: why should American sailors be charged a 1.67 percent fee to support Les Invalides, a soldiers and sailors hospital that no American would ever visit? Why should Jones be charged for the care and feeding of British prisoners of war for three months—especially when, to his fury and disgust, he discovered that the prisoners had not been exchanged for Americans, as promised, but for Frenchmen in English jails? It took Jones more than two years of haggling to settle the accounts and another year after that to get paid in cash (Jones's share was roughly $2,500). The French government, as it tottered toward revolution, was nearly bankrupt in 1785.

While he dickered with French bureaucrats and waited, Jones cast about for opportunities. He contemplated going on a voyage to the South Seas with one of Captain Cook's lieutenants. He pondered a trip to India as a merchant. He blew £1,800 on a failed scheme by his old friend Dr. Bancroft to import bark that could be used for yellow dye for clothiers.

He warned—correctly—that the Barbary pirates were a problem that America would have to deal with sooner or later.

Piracy in the Mediterranean, an age-old scourge, was becoming a hazard to America's growth as a global trader. Claiming that the Koran entitled them to do as they pleased with infidels, ruthless corsairs in fast galleys were striking out from Algiers and Tunis, seizing and enslaving Christian sailors, and demanding that their countries pay tribute. The outrage touched Jones's compassion for Americans cast in chains and reminded him why America needed a strong navy. But he could not get Congress, still strapped for funds and celebrating independence from Britain, to pay much attention.

He did, to his satisfaction, accomplish one bit of unfinished business. At the end of 1784, he finally succeeded in returning Lord Selkirk's silver. The Earl had reconsidered his earlier haughty refusal to accept anything from a brigand such as Jones. Through intermediaries, he had sent word to Jones that he would like his silver back after all. Jones sent the silver plate to Selkirk's sister-in-law in London and received a gracious reply from his lordship. "I intended to have put an article in the newspapers about your having returned it," Selkirk wrote Jones, but apparently Jones had already seen to that, arranging through friends to have his gallantry announced in the English and Scottish press. Still, Selkirk wrote, he had mentioned Jones's chivalrous action to "many people of fashion" and tried to correct "confused accounts" in the London newspapers. "On all occasions, Sir, both now and formerly, I have done you the justice to tell that you have made an offer of returning the plate . . . and that you had your officers and men in . . . extraordinary good discipline."

During his long stay in Paris, Jones went looking for romance and, with at least one woman, found it. He did not reunite with Countess Lowendahl or Delia. Before coming to Paris, Jones asked to be remembered to the alluring and artful Lowendahl, but she had no further use for him, since there was no more point in trying to obtain a commission for her husband in the American army. Delia did plead to see Jones, desperately writing him not long after his arrival in Paris in the winter of 1784:

Is it possible that you are then so near me and that I am deprived of the sight of the mortal who has constituted the misery of my life for four years? O, most amiable and ungrateful of men, come to your best friend who burns with the desire of seeing you. You ought to know that it was but eight days since your Delia was at the brink of the grave. Come, in the name of heaven!

But Jones did not come. He moved on, possibly to a succession of mistresses. One stands out. For years, little was known about her, not even her real name, until that at last turned up in the papers of Thomas Jefferson, who acted as a reluctant intermediary in the romance. Jones called his lover "Madame T——." Her real name was Townsend. She was the widow of an Englishman who has been lost to history. Jones believed that she was the illegitimate daughter of the late king, Louis XV, a well-known sire of bastards. Her mother was a "lady of quality." Only two letters from Jones to Madame Townsend survive, and their tone is quite different from the flowery pap Jones usually sent his lovers. In one letter, Jones genuinely shared Mme. T——'s grief over the death of her protector, the Marquise de Marsan: "She was a true friend, and more than a mother to you! She would have been a mother to me also had she lived! We have lost her!"

Jones was feeling familial toward Madame T—— for another, perhaps more personal reason. Madame T—— was mother to a baby boy. Jones wrote that he hoped she would "cover him all over with kisses from me, they come warm *to you both* from the heart." Who was the father of this child? John Paul Jones is a good guess. Perhaps Jones meant to make an honest woman of her, but he was distracted again by ambition.

In 1786, Jones presented a long memoir of his career to Louis XVI. The document, bound in red leather and preceded by a fawning poem,*

---

*Prosecutor of fair Freedom's Rights
Louis, thy virtues suit a God!
The good Man in thy praise delights
And Tyrants Tremble at thy nod!

was no doubt intended to further Jones's career. Jones's friends in Paris speculated that he was plumping for flag rank in the French navy. But England and France were once more at peace, and Louis had no money in his Treasury with which to create more admirals and the fleets for them to command. Jones was flailing about for ways to keep his famous name alive. He had copies made of Houdon's bust of himself and sent them to various luminaries including Jefferson and Washington. He was indignant when a customs inspector imposed a duty on the busts. "They are not merchandise, and I flatter myself that my zeal and my exertions for the cause of America will not be requited with such a mark of dishonor," he huffed. "I would rather hear that the busts were broke to pieces than consent that they should be subject to a duty." At the same time, he was thrilled to get back a letter from Washington that he had received the bust "and shall place it with my own." Jones was not forgotten in America. But if he was to have any chance of professional advancement, he needed to return to his adopted country.

He arrived in New York, the young nation's capital for the time being, in the hot summer of 1787. He extracted from Congress a gold medal, of which he was exceedingly proud, but no flag or fleet—just permission to seek a French commission, the stratagem that had already failed. He had an unpleasant encounter with his old nemesis, Pierre Landais, who was now living in reduced circumstances in New York and still seeking the "satisfaction" of a duel with Jones. As Jones stood talking to another man in the street, Landais approached from behind, spat in the dust, and declared, "I spit in your face!" In the elaborate rites of gentlemanly honor, spitting in a man's face would normally demand a duel, which Jones was eager to avoid. Jones put a statement in the *New York Journal and Weekly Register* insisting that reports of the spitting incident were "an absolute falsehood." Landais then placed a letter "to the impartial public" in the newspapers: "I do hereby certify, to the public, that I really, and in fact, spit all the spittle I could spare out of my mouth then, out of contempt, in the face of John Paul, or Paul Jones. . . . Were I not more afraid of a law suit than I was of him, I would have caned him, showing him my cane at the same time." An impartial witness—the man to whom Jones was talk-ing—resolved the public standoff by swearing that Landais had indeed spoken the insulting words, but not delivered the spittle, and that in any case Jones had neither heard Landais nor noticed him as the mad captain passed six or seven yards behind.

Jones escaped Landais's épée, but he was thwarted and frustrated in New York. Restlessly, in November 1787—a few days after his encounter with Landais—he sailed again for Paris.

He was beginning to behave in a skittish, if not paranoid fashion. He declined to sail in a French packet because he had heard rumors of a British fleet on the prowl. What if war broke out between England and France and he was seized by the British? He waited several days for an American ship instead, but then tempted fate by going to London to de-liver dispatches to John Adams. In spite of, or perhaps because of, the dan-ger of recognition and capture by an angry mob, he strolled to Covent Garden to enjoy an evening at the theater. Traveling on to Paris, he was extremely secretive with Thomas Jefferson, who had succeeded Ben Franklin as the American Minister or plenipotentiary to the court of Louis XVI. From a hotel, Jones sent the ambassador a note: "I would have waited on you immediately instead of writing, but I have several *strong reasons* for desiring that no persons should know of my being here till I have seen you and been favored with your advice on the steps I ought to pursue. . . . I shall not go out until I hear from you. And as the people in this hotel do not know my name, you will please to ask for the gentleman that just arrived, who is lodged in No. 1."

What were the "strong reasons"? Was Jones ducking a romantic entan-glement or paternal obligations? He had already drafted Jefferson as an intermediary in his affair with Madame T——. From New York in Sep-tember, Jones had sent his tender letter to Madame T——, wishing to cover her child with kisses, in care of Jefferson. In an accompanying letter to the American ambassador, he had asked Jefferson to look up Madame T—— for him and to please help her, perhaps by arranging an audience with the King. Coping with Jones's mistresses was above and beyond Jefferson's call of duty. Madame T—— herself wrote Jefferson and asked his indulgence: could the American ambassador make her a small loan, to allow her to travel to England and sell some stock? Jefferson gracefully demurred. He was "infinitely distressed," he wrote back, but financial straits made him "incapable" of lending money.

Whatever "strong reasons" Jones had for sneaking about Paris, Jefferson apparently managed to resolve or finesse. Jefferson had his own agenda for seeing Jones on the night he arrived in Paris, a prospect that promised to divert Jones away from his romantic intrigues and restore him to duty and possibly glory at sea. Catherine, the Tsarina of Russia, was interested in hiring Jones to command a fleet in the Black Sea against the Turks. Was Jones interested in joining the Russian navy?

This was a startling gust in Jones's becalmed career. It may seem peculiar that Thomas Jefferson, of all people, was willing to rent out America's greatest naval hero to a famously cruel despot. But Jefferson shrewdly calculated that American interests would be served in the long run. Jones needed to be kept gainfully employed at sea until America could afford its own fleet. By permitting Jones to become a Russian admiral, America would be providing on-the-job training for a potential future naval commander-in-chief. The Russians, who were about to go to war with the Turks and quickly needed to organize a Black Sea navy, had sent feelers about Jones's availability though secret diplomatic channels. Jefferson was receptive to the idea, though, canny observer that he was, he had some well-considered advice for the Russians: "Mr. Jefferson, who knows the character of the said Chevalier, pointed out," wrote the Russian ambassador to France, "that on great and dangerous missions this officer, who is as spirited as he is disinterested, will be better employed as chief than under the orders of a superior."

Jones himself did not instantly leap at the chance to serve in Catherine's navy. "I regarded this as a castle in the air," he recounted in a memoir. His natural reluctance to sail under a new flag was prudent. America had just adopted its Constitution. Surely, Jones reasoned, a military establishment could not be far behind. Perhaps he would get his flag and his fleet after all. Russia was a mysterious and rather forbidding country without any naval tradition to speak of. "A man of very high rank at Paris," Jones recorded, counseled him to stay away from the tangled court politics of Catherine the Great. "He would advise me to go to Constantinople at once rather than enter the service of Russia," Jones wrote—in other words, anything, even fighting for the Turks, would be preferable to the Tsarina's intrigues.

Jones equivocated, intending to go ahead to Denmark to recover prize money from the cruise of the *Bonhomme Richard* (under pressure from Britain, the Danes had set free three of Jones's prizes when they arrived in Danish ports in September 1779). But the night before he left, Jones was approached by an American soldier of fortune, Lewis Littlepage, who urged him to meet with the Russian ambassador, M. de Simolin, in the morning. Over breakfast, Catherine's emissaries laid on the flattery and the proper inducements. As supreme commander of the Empress's Black Sea Fleet, Jones would have carte blanche. In less than a year, he would make Constantinople tremble. Jones liked to be flattered and wooed. He began to picture himself in the striking, all-white uniform of a Russian admiral.

From Denmark, where he dined with the royal family, Jones negotiated with Catherine personally. He was honest with her: "Loving glory," he wrote, "I am perhaps too attached to honors." He wanted no joint commands—no more *concordats*. "Being an entire stranger, I have more to fear from a joint authority than any officer in Her Majesty's Service. But I cannot conceive that Her Majesty could deem it expedient to *divide the command* in the Black Sea." Jones should have demanded ironclad guarantees. But his wariness had been replaced with impatience, his judgment clouded by ambition tinged with desperation. Catherine's navy may have been a sorry boatload of intriguers, but it was the only navy offering him a job and a chance for action. The alternative was to wait for America to awaken to the need for a true navy, possibly a very long wait. In a great rush for glory, he set out for St. Petersburg and opened the last and most bizarre chapter of his career.

*   *   *

JONES HAD NOT COMMANDED a ship of war at sea for more than eight years. He was forty years old and no longer in the best of health. The month-long journey from Paris to Copenhagen in late winter had been taxing. Exhausted, shivering when he arrived at the Danish court, Jones had been forced to bed with a lung infection. On April 8, he wrote Jefferson, "My sufferings, from the inclemency of the weather and my want of proper means to guard against it on the journey, were inexpressible; and I believe, from what I yet feel, will continue to affect my constitution." Jones was accustomed to extreme discomfort at sea, yet his frequent complaints were very rarely physical. He must have been sick indeed to write such a letter.

Neither illness nor the elements slowed him. Within a fortnight of bemoaning his health to Jefferson, he attempted a voyage that would have tested the constitution of the hardiest young sailor. He did not pause, as he headed north and east, for the usual honors and pleasures. "At Stockholm I stayed but one night . . . want of time prevented me from appearing at Court," Jones wrote. Jones had hoped to reach St. Petersburg by taking a packet boat across the Gulf of Bothnia to Finland, but the ice was still heavy in mid-April, and no one was willing to risk the passage. So Jones took matters into his own hands. He chartered a thirty-foot open-decked boat and a small skiff to tow behind. His plan was to get as far as he could in the larger vessel, and then drag the smaller one across the ice, or use it to hop from ice floe to ice floe. "The enterprise was very daring," Jones recalled, "and had never before been attempted. But by the far north [up the east coast of Sweden, down the west coast of Finland], the roads were impracticable." The longer southern route to Russia by land, back down into Germany and across Poland, was the safer way to go, but Jones could not have delayed an instant, he wrote, because, "the Empress expected me day to day."

Jones hired some Swedish boatmen for the voyage, but he did not tell them where they were going. Had he been honest about his destination,

Jones believed, they would have refused to make the trip. From Grissle-hamn, a port just north of Stockholm, Jones set out into the frozen waters of the Gulf of Bothnia. At first, Jones told the boatmen to steer to the south, skirting along the Swedish coast. But then, toward nightfall, he pulled out his pistol and gave a different order: steer due east—toward Finland, more than fifty miles across ice-choked, wind-tossed waters.

Jones's only light was the lantern from his traveling carriage, which he used as a binnacle light so he could read the compass in the dark. The night was raw and the wind high but fair for Finland, pushing Jones's boat and the smaller skiff at a fast clip toward their destination. Jones drew himself into his cloak and dreamed perhaps of leading a fleet into action, but he did not sleep. He was familiar with mutinous crews.

Dawn brought disappointment. In the far distance, Jones's little party could see the rise of the pine-forested Finnish coast—but miles of hard-packed ice blocked the way. Returning to Sweden was impossible. The strong west wind meant they could only sail south, hoping to circle around the ice and enter the Gulf of Finland, which divides Finland from the Baltic states.

The sailing conditions were appalling. Air and water temperatures in those northern waters in mid-April hovered around the freezing mark. The open boat offered no shelter from the knifelike wind or the needles of spray. Ropes became stiff and slippery; hands grew numb and clumsy. Floating ice was a constant hazard. In the middle of the second night, "we lost the small boat," wrote Jones, "but the men saved themselves in the large one, which with difficulty escaped the same fate." Hour after chilling hour, day after frozen day, Jones struck south, looking for a gap in the ice, while his men wondered how many toes they would have left when the frostbite healed. Cradling his pistol, Jones dozed intermittently, if at all. Finally, he recorded, "at the end of four days we landed at Reval [in Estonia], where our enterprise was regarded as a kind of miracle." Jones's men were grateful to be alive. Jones thanked them by hiring a pilot and giving them money to replace the boat they lost, "with the provisions necessary for making their homeward voyage, when the weather should become more favorable." Jones, who had sailed off Nova Scotia in a blizzard in December, remembered the experience as one of his most miserable at sea.

The canals were still frozen when Jones reached St. Petersburg in the first week of May. Russia's magnificent gateway to the west, built out of a bog by Peter the Great at the beginning of the eighteenth century, was designed to rival the grandeur of London and Paris. With its classical columns and graceful arches and bridges, St. Petersburg offered a splendid facade. Court life was a glittery succession of dinners and balls "enhanced," noted a diarist, "by Asiatic luxury." Veneers were misleading in this strange land suspended between East and West. Jones, who prided himself on speaking plainly, was entering the bazaar.

Russia imported Western ideas, manners, inventions; the court language was French, but the underlying ethos was universal suspicion and Oriental despotism. Under Catherine "le Grand," St. Petersburg was permeated by a feel of decadence, if not wickedness, that smacked more of late Byzantium than late European Enlightenment. Mannish and predatory, Catherine held transvestite balls, at which the men dressed as women and the women dressed as men. Catherine appeared to many courtiers to be not quite man nor woman, but somehow more than both. Intelligent and curious, she had, in her youth, befriended philosophers like Voltaire and affected liberal attitudes. She had talked about, someday, freeing the serfs and abolishing torture. She welcomed the Masons for their liberalism—and then banished them as potential rivals. Her real interest was in power.

As a young woman, she had arranged to have her aging husband strangled and her eldest son confined and watched. She intrigued abroad as well as at home, bribing Swedish nobles to conspire against their crown and installing a former lover as King of Poland. Her territorial ambitions to the south were signaled by the name she chose for her youngest son, Constantine. He would become the ruler of Constantinople and extend Eastern Christendom all the way to Greece. But first Catherine had to liberate Constantinople from the Muslim Ottoman Turks who had occupied it for the past 300 years.

In 1786, Catherine had made her famous progression down the Dnieper, Russia's Mississippi, accompanied by fawning foreign ministers who marveled at the flower-bedecked villages and grottos along the way (some of them fake, erected by Catherine's great lover and still friend, the Prince Potemkin). The procession of gilded carriages (the Empress's was drawn by thirty horses) and imperial barges passed signs, written in Greek, that read, "the Road to Constantinople." At the end of the mighty river on the north coast of the Black Sea stood, inconveniently, a Turkish fort and a Turkish fleet. Catherine needed a navy to liberate the Black Sea from the Sublime Porte, as Westerners called the government of the crumbling but still vast Ottoman Empire. Unfortunately, Russia's navy was slack and feeble. A much celebrated Black Sea victory over the Turks in 1770, at Tchesme, had really been the work of British officers imported as mercenaries. A Scotsman, ex–Royal Navy, had been imported to run Catherine's Baltic Fleet. The Tsarina needed an able foreigner to command her Black Sea Fleet, such as it was, a collection of galleys and a few battleships of doubtful seaworthiness.

Catherine had first heard about Jones from her ambassador to France. "He is, in the opinion of everyone, one of the greatest sailors of the time," Simolin had written one of Catherine's ministers on February 3, 1788. "To rare boldness, valour, and intelligence, he adds a great deal of prudence, circumspection, and disinterestedness, and seeks nothing but glory. . . . In the Black Sea, this officer will make the Seraglio [the Ottoman Palace] tremble." Catherine excitedly exclaimed, "He will get to Constantinople!"

At the age of fifty-nine, Catherine was fat and thick-browed, with swollen legs and false teeth, but she exuded an undeniable charm, certainly over Jones. "I shall never be able to express how much greater I find her than fame reports. With the character of a very great man, she will always be adored as the most amiable and captivating of the fair sex," Jones wrote the French minister to Russia, Count de Segur. To Lafayette, Jones recounted: "I presented the Empress with a copy of the new American Constitution. Her majesty spoke to me often about the United States, and is persuaded that the *American Revolution cannot fail to bring about others and to influence every other government."*

Catherine was shrewd about the contagiousness of revolution. What she did not tell Jones was that she was determined to keep it from spreading to her empire. Jones was such a romantic patriot that he seemed naive about his new employer. "I can never renounce the glorious title of a *citizen of the United States!"* he had written Thomas Jefferson, seeking formal permission to join the Tsarina's navy. He wanted to believe that Russia and America, flanking the Old World, enjoyed some kind of New World kinship. Jones was to be bitterly disillusioned by the Empress. But, as he admitted, he was seduced by Catherine. "Her Majesty gave me such a flattering reception, and up to the period of my departure, treated me with so much distinction, that I was overcome with her courtesies (*je me laissai seduire*)." Jones later recounted, with chagrin, that he put himself "into her hands without making any stipulation for my personal advantage. I demanded but one favor, that I should never be condemned unheard." Even that favor was too much to ask.

The Empress invited Jones to her magnificent Baroque palace at Tsarskoe Selo ("Tsar's Village"), on a hill overlooking the broad Neva plain, twelve miles from St. Petersburg. The English gardens were filled with towering columns to her military triumphs. "If this war continues," she told Voltaire during the first Russo-Turkish war, "my garden . . . will resemble a game of skittles." (Catherine was a memorializer: she had also erected imposing monuments to her three deceased English greyhounds.) Jones was eager to head for the sound of the guns, "but I was detained against my will a fortnight," he wrote Lafayette, "and continually feasted at court and in the highest society." "Pavel Dzhones," as he was known in St. Petersburg, was now a kontradmiral, a rear admiral. Catherine gave him a generous allowance, 2,000 ducats (about $1,000), to buy uniforms, and Jones looked dashing in the white coat with gold braid and blue stripes and facings. "He has made a good impression on the Empress," wrote a diarist of the time, and was "welcomed everywhere, except among the English, who cannot bear him." Out-of-work English naval officers had flocked to Catherine's employ after peace reduced the size of the Royal Navy. They remembered the upstart Jones for his defeat of the *Drake* and the *Serapis* and chose to describe him as a pirate. Jones was delighted to see British scowls as he was feted by the Russian nobility. "This was a cruel grief to the English," Jones wrote Lafayette, "and I own that their vexation . . . gives me no pain."

Catherine was well pleased with her new acquisition. "I saw him today," she wrote her adviser Baron Grimm. "I think he will suit our purposes admirably." She understood the power of Jones's reputation for bold strokes. "This man is extremely capable of multiplying fear and trembling in his foe," she wrote Prince Potemkin, informing him that she was sending "one more bulldog for the Black Sea."

Therein lay the seeds of misfortune: Jones was not the only bulldog, nor was he the top one. He did not have the unified command he had requested or the carte blanche he had been promised. When, in late May, he arrived at Russian military headquarters near the mouth of the Dnieper on the north coast of the Black Sea, after a twelve-day journey of a thousand miles, he reported to the ornately decorated tent of Prince Potemkin. The Prince in turn had three other rear admirals on the scene, none in a mood to defer to Jones.

Potemkin was a monster to be remembered among the many who ill-served the tsardom through the centuries. The favorite of Catherine's official line of lovers (at least thirteen of them), His Most Serene Highness Prince of the Holy Roman Empire, Grigory Alexandrovich Potemkin, Prince of Taurida, Field Marshal, Grand Hetman of the Black Sea and Ekaterinoslav Cossacks, Grand Admiral of the Black Sea and Caspian Fleets, President of the College of War, Viceroy of the South, was the Tsarina's supreme military commander in the new war against the Turks. He was a joke of a soldier. In military deportment and just about every other way, he stood in stark contrast to Jones. A sensualist and a glutton, he was flabby with indulgence and slovenly in dress and manner. He sometimes startled foreign ambassadors by greeting them wearing nothing but an open dressing gown. He was deceitful and corrupt on an epic scale. Yet, like Catherine, he exuded a kind of cunning magnetism, and Jones, after one meeting, persuaded himself that Potemkin was not a bad sort. "You would be charmed with the Prince de Potemkin," Jones wrote Lafayette. "He is a most amiable man, and none can be more noble-minded."

Jones would revise this estimate, along with most of his first impressions of the Russian elite. He was, to an unfortunate degree, susceptible to flattery by the great and too easily impressed by the decorations and ribbons of nobility. Too often, he had been blinded by rank and status and then, after the inevitable letdown, left feeling betrayed and bitter. True, he had been matured by his stormy and frustrating relations with the French navy, the court at Versailles, and the U.S. Congress. Jolted by Ben Franklin's letter criticizing his self-absorption, he vowed to show some of the "cheerful ardor" he knew to be essential to command. As ever, he was determined to try to rise above instinct. Older, wiser, and chastened by experience, he vowed to be on his best behavior, to follow the advice of his "philosopher" Franklin and show forbearance. Yet he was, at heart, a walking refutation of the Enlightenment ideal that passions could be tamed by reason and order. He could forbear only so long.

His patience was tested right away. Rear Admiral Mordwinoff, commander of the Russian naval arsenal at Kherson, near the mouth of the Dneiper, "did not affect to disguise his displeasure at my arrival," wrote Jones. The reception was worse aboard Jones's new flagship, the *Vladimir*, the next morning. Jones was used to sullen quarterdecks, but the one he mounted aboard the Russian ship of the line was openly defiant. The *Vladimir*'s captain, Brigadier Panaiotti Alexiano, was on deck conducting a meeting with the other ship captains in the fleet "to draw them into a cabal against my authority," Jones wrote. Jones suspected that Alexiano, a Greek, had begun his career as a Mediterranean pirate who cut the throats of his prisoners. Wisely, Jones made no attempt to confront Alexiano or the others, but instead departed for a few days to reconnoiter the battlefield, "to give time to those angry spirits to become calm, and to be able to decide on the part I should take."

Determining what part to take in the coming military campaign was a delicate and vexing question. He would be operating in waters hardly suited to fleet actions by a deep-water navy. Sailing in a small boat along the muddy estuary in the rising heat of early summer, waving away the clouds of mosquitoes, Jones could quickly see the obstacles. The Liman is a thirty-mile-long enclosed estuary, created by the merger of the Dnieper and Bug Rivers as they reach the Black Sea. On the south side is the Kinburn Peninsula, a long sandspit. On the north side is the mouth of the Bug and the southern rim of Russia. At the mouth of the Liman, at Ochakov on the north side, the Turks had built a powerful fort. The Russians controlled the tip of the Kinburn Peninsula, directly opposite, two miles across the water. A Turkish fleet was amassing in the Black Sea, just outside the Liman. Jones's job was to defeat that fleet and clear the way for Russian forces to lay seige to the Turkish fort at Ochakov.

The Liman is never more than eight miles wide, and in many places less than twenty feet deep. Since a frigate draws at least fifteen feet, full-size warships were in constant danger of running aground on the shifting mud banks. The winds in the river were fluky and erratic. Jones had under his command eight frigates and four other armed ships. They were built with green wood and armed with cannons that were as much a threat to their own gunners as the enemy. Cast too small for the gun barrels, the cannon-balls had been thickened by a coat of tar. The *Vladimir* was pierced for sixty-six guns but carried only twenty-four, to reduce the ship's weight and allow it to float higher in the shallow water. The flagship's rotten beams probably could not have withstood the recoil of a full broadside. Spit and polish was not even a concept to the peasant crews and their polyglot officers, many of whom had been corsairs in an earlier career.

Jones was informed that he was up against a larger and more powerful Turkish fleet. The Russians did have one advantage: a flotilla of some twenty-five galleys and assorted other small craft, some bearing only one large gun. Manuevered by oars, the galleys (many of them leftover gilded barges from Catherine's pleasure cruise down the Dnieper in 1786) could go straight into the wind, unlike the square-rigged frigates, and skim across shoals and sandbars because of their shallow draft. Jones could instantly see they were the keys to victory. Jones began to mold a strategy born of necessity. He needed to draw the more heavily armed but more ponderous Turkish fleet inside the Liman and then destroy it with a combined force of frigates and swift galleys.

A sound plan, but there was a catch: Jones did not command the galleys. That honor belonged to Charles, Prince of Nassau-Siegen. Handsome, in a rakish, indolent sort of way, Nassau-Siegen was a junior-grade version of Potemkin. The illegitimate heir to a penniless principality in Germany, the so-called Prince was a showy adventurer, oily, rash, untrustworthy, incompetent, except as a courtier. Jones knew him slightly from Paris. Nassau-Siegen had been commissioned by the French government to procure the frigate *Indien* for Jones, but the Prince had failed at that, like most of his undertakings. As a military commander, he had been a blundering amateur. His two combat missions for the French, a raid on the isle of Jersey and an attack on Gibraltar with fireships, had been fiascos, in part because of the prince's sloppy preparation. His résumé was exotic: he had sailed around the world with the French explorer Bougainville and boasted that he had seduced the Queen of Tahiti. But he didn't know enough seamanship, Jones quickly discovered, to identify the points of a compass. He married a Polish noblewoman, who seems to have encouraged his adventuring and philandering from afar. In 1786, he washed up on Catherine's shore and shrewdly befriended Potemkin. "Strange that you have taken a fancy to Nassau," the Empress wrote her Prince. "He had everywhere the reputation as a crazy fellow (*un cerveau brule*)."

Potemkin had a job for Nassau-Siegen. "Almost a sailor, is he?" he inquired as he was preparing for war against the Turks in the winter of 1788. Potemkin gave Nassau-Siegen almost a fleet—the galleys and gunboats in the Liman. Nassau-Siegen regarded his new command as a larksome opportunity for self-promotion. "Although my undertaking may not be very dangerous, yet I will make enough noise to get the attention of the world," he wrote his wife. He planned, he told her, to "stand up to . . . this 'sieur Jones.'"

When Nassau-Seigen greeted his co-commander and fellow rear admiral Paul Jones at the end of May, he oozed, "You know my esteem and friendship. It will end only with my life." Then he offered some practical advice for the acquisition of glory, titles, land, etc., in the court of Catherine le Grand. He explained to Jones, "that if we gained any advantage over the Turks, it was necessary to exaggerate it to the utmost." Jones icily replied that he had "never adopted this method of heightening my personal importance." Jones meant to get along, but his sense of honor, prickly and stiff, stood in the way.

CHAPTER FOURTEEN

"Conquer or Die"

*T*HE TURKS had their own imported naval hero. Known as the Capitan Pasha, the Algerine Renagado, and the Crocodile of Sea Battles, Ghazi Hassan-Pasha was a Barbary pirate who had become commander of the Sultan's navy in the Ottoman Empire. For his defense of Istanbul and his ruthless suppression of Egyptian rebellions, he had been favored with a palace and showered with diamonds. As a pet, the Capitan Pasha kept a lion, who lay down at his command. He terrorized his enemies and his own crews. He thought nothing of firing on his own ships if they retreated prematurely, and he once made an example to timid firefighters by ordering four of them thrown into the fire. Jones respected his adversary, whom he described as "brave." Jones would come close enough to the Capitan Pasha in battle to admire his great white mustache.

Jones did not wish to encounter the Capitan Pasha's fleet, not in open water. The Turkish fleet hovering outside the Liman consisted of over 100 vessels, including eighteen ships of the line and forty frigates. Marshaling his far smaller forces inside the estuary, Jones was careful to advocate a shrewd, defensive strategy, to play the odds and the angles and not put his entire fleet at risk. After many hours studying French fleet evolutions, Jones wanted to employ a measured, scientific approach to war. Nassau-Siegen, on the other hand, was interested only in flashy lunges.

Jones had no regard for Nassau-Siegen as a strategist. "The Prince . . . talked a great deal of projects of descents, surprises, and attacks, but without any rational plan," Jones later recalled.

Still, Jones dutifully tried to work with Nassau-Siegen. On June 4, invoking the custom of Peter the Great, Admiral Jones summoned his captains to a council of war. Pacing the great cabin of the *Vladimir,* resplendent in his white coat despite the oppressive damp heat, he made an urgent appeal for selflessness and unity. "We must be determined to win! Let us therefore join our hands and hearts! Let us show our noble sentiments, and throw away from ourselves any personal consideration," Jones declared, according to notes taken by his Russian secretary. Seeking to be collegial, Jones posed a series of nine questions to be considered by his fellow captains. The council of war had disposed of only three of them when Nassau-Siegen and the surly Alexiano broke up the meeting. They had apparently heard enough.

Before the meeting collapsed, the captains did agree to a rudimentary plan: to draw up Jones's heavy ships ("the Squadron") and Nassau-Siegen's galleys and lighter craft ("the Flotilla") in a line across the Liman, just beyond the mouth of the Bug River but short of the Turkish fort at Ochakov, a citadel bristling with heavy guns that could fire red-hot shot. Jones wanted to protect the mouth of the Bug because Potemkin and his army were supposed to ford the river before marching on Ochakov. Jones repeatedly asked Potemkin for orders and guidance, but he received only silence in return. The commander-in-chief was at once meddlesome and a hedger. He wanted to see how Jones would perform before he attached his own reputation to the American mercenary's.

On June 5, the first two of the Capitan Pasha's ships were seen entering the Liman. The next day, a small number of Turkish galleys crept up the north shore, toward the mouth of the Bug. It was agreed that Nassau-Siegen and part of the Flotilla would slip down the estuary in the dead of night and try to cut off the enemy from behind. The Prince set out shortly after 1 A.M., but the mission was a botch; the Turks opened fire and Nassau-Siegen retreated in disarray.

On the morning of June 7, Jones could see scores of the Capitan Pasha's ships sweeping down the estuary. The Turkish fleet was a kaleidoscope of sails, Western-style square-riggers and Mediterranean lateens and galleys. Nassau-Siegen, who saw battle as costume drama, wrote his wife that the spectacle of the enemy fleet was "better than a ball at Warsaw." Aboard the *Vladimir,* Jones strapped on his sword, put a brace of pistols in his belt, and readied himself for action. He had heard that the Turks did not take prisoners.

At 8 A.M., the admiral climbed into his barge and ordered his men to row along the line of Russian ships. The sight was not quite what he may have dreamed about as he had pored over naval texts on snowy nights in Portsmouth. Jones's two ships of the line were only half-armed, and his poorly built frigates were manned by impressed serfs. Jones could barely communicate his commands. He knew no Russian and had no signaling system. Accompanied by a translator, he had to shout his orders, ship by ship. From his barge, he stared up at swarthy Slavic faces, which stared dumbly back.

Jones returned to witness a pathetic spectacle. As the morning brightened and the two fleets drew close, Brigadier Alexiano, the *Vladimir*'s captain, suddenly appeared on deck in his night clothes. For some time, he had been "indisposed" below. Now he cried out, "like a frantic man," recalled Jones, "in French and Russian, that the Turks were going to attack and board us, and that we would be blown to pieces for having been so foolish as to leave our former position." Jones told him to get dressed and put him to work shoring up Nassau-Siegen's flank.

Jones wanted to catch the Turks in a vise by creating a large V out of his line of battle. But the wind was against Jones, forcing him to commandeer galleys to tow the left flank of the Squadron to windward, a ponderous manuever. As slow-footed peasant crewmen fumbled with tow ropes and their officers shouted confused commands, the Turks opened up a brisk fire on Nassau-Siegen's Flotilla on the right flank. The galleys were easily galled by shot, and, rather than stand and fight, their captains began to row for safety. Jones could see the Capitan Pasha's ship, a very sleek, fast fourteen-gun galley called a *kirlangitch*, leading the enemy thrust. To Jones's disgust, Nassau-Siegen, whose flagship was a large yacht, fled the heat of battle to take cover under the guns of the *Vladimir*.

A wind shift allowed Jones to spring his trap. The breeze, which had been blowing out of the west, favoring the Turks, swung around to the east. With his square-rigged ships able to run before the wind, Jones was able to create his V-shaped nutcracker, forming a wedge of two lines of ships to catch the Turks in an enfilade, a cross fire. The Russian gunnery was neither efficient nor accurate, but the Russians had cruder and more devastating weapons for close-in action. The Russian gunboats began lobbing brandcougles, incendiary bombs that were lethal to vessels made of wood, tar, and canvas. Two Turkish warships caught fire and burned. Seeing that his position was untenable, the Capitan Pasha ordered his ships to withdraw.

Jones watched from his quarterdeck as the smoke cleared to show Turkish warships and galleys flying before the wind to escape the cross fire. Russian casualties were not severe: about fifty men, including one officer. Jones permitted himself a tiny gloat. "I do not think Captain Pasha who commanded in person will dine with pleasure. He had 57 boats with him," Jones wrote the Prince Potemkin that night from his cabin aboard the *Vladimir*.

The victory was not smashing, but it was a victory nonetheless. A *Te Deum*, the traditional Russian Orthodox thanksgiving, was sung aboard the *Vladimir* the next day. Jones was in a magnanimous mood. Determined to follow Franklin's advice to bestow more credit on his subordinates, Jones decided to play up the role of Nassau-Siegen in his official dispatches to Potemkin. Jones was feeling brotherly toward the Flotilla's commander. As the last Turkish galley had fled down the estuary, the Prince embraced Jones and declared, "We should always make but one!" Heartened (and deceived) by this show of comradeship, Jones wrote Potemkin, generously if a trifle condescendingly:

The Prince conducted himself with a great deal of composure and intelligence. I had the honor of serving him as aide-de-camp and he took all of my advice in the best of spirits. Monsieur Alexiano came in another cutter and helped us to maintain good order.

Nassau-Siegen rewarded Jones's graciousness by maligning him. He convinced Potemkin that the glory was all his and that Jones had timidly hung back from the battle. Potemkin, who had favored Nassau-Siegen to begin with, was not hard to convince. "It is to you alone," Potemkin wrote his fellow prince, "I attribute this victory." Potemkin repeated this misjudgment to Catherine: "Nassau was the real hero and to him belongs the victory." Nassau-Siegen made sure that all the courts in Europe heard his version of the battle. With feigned sorrow, he put down his rival. "Paul Jones has changed very much. Fortune has taken from him that intrepidity which people said that he possessed." Nassau-Siegen wrote his wife. "I am greatly dissatisfied. You see what three-quarters of a reputation is!" To a fellow courtier, he wrote, "The corsair Paul Jones was very famous, but I fear greatly that at the head of a squadron is not his place."

Jones heard or sensed Nassau-Siegen's calumnies and labored to stay on the high road. "He is too jealous to be content with my self-denial," Jones lamented to Littlepage, the Virginia cavalier who had helped recruit him to Catherine's navy and now served in his fleet. "Perhaps he is ill-advised, without knowing it. There is nothing, consistent with my honor, that I would not do to make him easy. . . . If he now becomes my enemy, I will not imitate his example."

But the whispering was getting to Jones. He knew he was being watched at all times by his subordinates, Russian and British officers who were just waiting for him to misstep. "My situation here is very delicate and critical," he had confided to Don José de Ribas, his liaison officer to Potemkin, on May 31. "I have people around me who appear to be on their guard, and if I make the slightest mistake, even when following their advice, I was given to understand today that they would consider themselves only as passengers."

By June 11, Jones was sick in bed, exhausted and depressed. His usual post-battle letdown was deepened by suspicions about his fellow com-

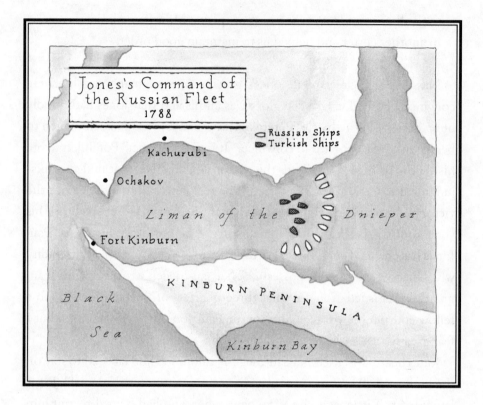

mander. Nassau-Siegen "seems to wish me to go to the devil," Jones wrote Ribas, the only officer he really trusted, "for no other reason, as far as I know, except that I faithfully extricated him from his confusion and danger during the affair of the 7th, for which he assumed so much credit." Jones gritted his teeth and vowed to swallow his bile. "I will do my best to go along with his temper," he wrote Ribas.

Jones wore graciousness like a hairshirt. In his stiffly self-abnegating dispatches to Potemkin, Jones couldn't resist little digs at Nassau-Siegen that were none too subtly intended to show that Jones had rescued his comrade from peril. Jones had heard of Nassau-Siegen's boasting, and he wrote Potemkin in a left-handed attempt to set the record straight. "I can assure you that I had no intentions whatsoever of putting myself forward personally during the engagement; my only object was the welfare of Russia; inasmuch as I saw the first division of her Majesty's flotilla in disorder and in a critical situation." The first division of her Majesty's flotilla, of course, was Nassau-Siegen's; the "disorder" was all his. Jones stopped short of taking credit for rescuing Nassau-Siegen and remembered to praise his subordinates instead. "Monsieur Alexiano helped to establish good order, during the last phase of the engagement so that, if there are any favors to be given. I solicit them for him; as for me, I do not as yet have any claims to them." Later, as he was reading over his correspondence on the Liman campaign, Jones attached a bitter footnote at the bottom of the page: "I always, but vainly, hoped to be able to attach this man [Alexiano] to my service by giving him more credit than he deserved, but he from the beginning has indignantly allied himself against me with all Prince de Nassau's cabal."

One can see, in Jones tortured correspondence with Potemkin and in his angry marginalia, his desire for glory clashing with his self-image as a noble-minded man who is above interest and pettiness. Jones kept tripping over his pride. His honor would not permit him to allow Nassau-Siegen to trample on his good name. His old self-defeating habits reasserted themselves. Unable to conceal his true feelings, he let his pridefulness corrode his already strained ties with Nassau-Siegen and Potemkin. The two courtiers were no match for Jones at war, but they were far superior at the back-stabbing politics of the Tsarina's entourage.

By sniping at Nassau-Siegen in his letters to Potemkin, Jones was just digging himself in deeper, because Potemkin showed the correspondence to Nassau-Siegen or told his protégé of Jones's condescending tone. Jones wrote one more conciliatory letter. "We will gain more honor and give him [Potemkin] more pleasure if we live together in harmony," he wrote Nassau-Siegen on June 14. But the split was irrevocable. In the letter, Jones reminded Nassau-Siegen that he had declared, "We should always be one!" But then, in another angry asterisk to himself, he wrote on a copy for his files, "I have been well duped by it."

The only remedy for Jones's anguish was battle. He nursed his fever in the rising heat of the Liman, a miasma in summer, and imagined stratagems that could be used to leverage the less powerful Russian fleet against the fearsome, but crude, Turk. He consoled himself with the certainty that the Capitan Pasha would return for a second round. Constantinople wanted the Russians driven back from the Black Sea, and the Capitan Pasha did not wish to return home having to explain how he was defeated by an American pirate.

The attack came on the morning of June 16, and it looked monstrous from the quarterdeck of the *Vladimir.* The Capitan Pasha had decided to go all-out. He had sailed into the Liman with his entire fleet, ships of the line as well as galleys. Henry Fanshawe, a young British adventurer who had joined the Russian navy, watched in awe as the Turkish fleet surged down the estuary, line abreast, their white sails gleaming in the brutal noonday sun. Fanshawe counted ninety-six craft, stretched from shore to shore: square-riggers, lateen-rigged gunboats, fast galleys. They were making a fierce commotion, banging on drums, clashing cymbals, blowing bugles. Across the water, the Russian crews could hear the Turks, who jammed the galleys gunwale-to-gunwale, crying to Allah, vowing death to the infidel, shouting, "No prisoners!"

The Capitan Pasha meant to use terror and overwhelming force to shock the Russians into submission. He did not intend to stand off and bombard the Russian fleet. The Turkish ships were ordered to drive right at the Russian ships and take them by boarding. Some of the Turkish ships were to be sacrificed on suicide missions, turned into burning hulks to set the Russian ships ablaze and strike fear in the hearts of the swine-eaters.

But Jones had been wise to position his ships well inside the estuary. A severe drought had lowered the water level in the Liman. The Capitan Pasha was forced to manuever his fleet through the sandbanks in the narrowed channel. His flagship was aimed straight for the *Vladimir* when it suddenly lurched, slewed, and stuck. The too heavy man-of-war had run aground. Without the Capitan Pasha leading the charge, the other Turkish captains hesitated, bore up in confusion, and began anchoring their ships.

Jones had at least a brief reprieve. At about 3 P.M., he summoned his captains to a council of war. Standing before his sulky charges, Jones was full of melodrama. "I see in your eyes the souls of heroes!" he exclaimed. This could be the battle that decided the war, he said. It was time to "conquer or die." Jones proposed taking the offensive. He suggested the tactic that had paid off in the last engagement against the Capitan Pasha. Jones wanted to swing the Russian fleet's left flank around to create a V. If the Turks regrouped and advanced, they would be sailing into a cross fire, a nutcracker of shot and shell. The procedure, he acknowledged, would be difficult. The wind was against the Russian fleet, so the ships would have to be towed or kedged, laboriously pulled to windward by advancing their anchors, a few yards at a time. Careful to play the democratic commander, Jones put his plan to a vote. The captains, who had no better idea, went along.

While the Turks struggled to pull the Capitan Pasha's flagship off the mud bank, about a mile away, the Russian ships on Jones's left flank slowly crept forward through the night. After midnight, the wind, which had been strong in the Russians' face from the west, swung around to the northeast. Now Jones had the advantage. Meeting with his captains again before dawn, Jones proposed to seize the initiative and launch an all-out attack at daybreak.

As the sun came up over the marshy waters of the Liman on the morning of June 17, Jones gave the signal and along the Russian line anchors weighed and sails billowed in the fresh morning breeze. The Turks, so fearsome just the day before, panicked. Capitan Pasha's flagship had been floated off the mud bank, but his captains fled in disarray, pulling up anchors or "cutting cables with the greatest precipitation," recorded Jones. "Not a shred of discipline remained" in the Turkish fleet. The *Vladimir* plunged ahead. Jones ordered the helmsman to make for the Capitan Pasha's flagship.

The *Vladimir* was "within pistol shot" when she suddenly swung up short. Jones looked, aghast, to see a flurry of activity on the flagship's forecastle. The *Vladimir*'s crew had dropped anchor. Captain Alexiano, speaking in Russian, so that Jones would not understand him, had given the order. Alexiano claimed that he was saving the *Vladimir* from running onto a sandbar, but Jones did not believe him. The Greek ex-pirate had tried to undermine Jones's authority each step of the way. Jones suspected that Alexiano had halted the ship because he feared close action or boarding the Capitan Pasha's ship.

Alexiano was not wrong to worry about sandbars. The ship of the Capitan Pasha's deputy commander ran aground, then the flagship of the Capitan Pasha himself, for the second time in two days. Two fat prizes lay exposed in the mud before Jones—but the Prince of Nassau-Siegen suddenly appeared with his Flotilla of galleys to claim them. According to Jones's acccount of the battle, Nassau-Siegen had dawdled at the beginning of the attack. Twice, Jones wrote, he had been compelled to slow his Squadron by heaving to in order to wait for Nassau-Siegen's lagging Flotilla. But now that the Turkish command vessels were helplessly aground, Nassau-Siegen swept in to grab the glory. His galleys "swarmed . . . like a hive of bees," pouring in shot and firebombs on the stranded Turkish warships, which were heeled over and unable to bring their guns to bear. The Turkish deputy commander's ship blew up, "a magnificent spectacle," recorded Fanshawe. Some seamen, Russian Cossacks, had recovered the Capitan Pasha's flag, which had been shot away from its halyard and fallen into the water. They were presenting the flag to Jones when Nassau-Siegen, who had come aboad the *Vladimir* from his yacht, reached over and plucked it out of their hands. The opportunistic prince wished to be the one to present the spoils of war to Catherine. Jones swallowed his anger, for the time being.

The Turks were not done. The Capitan Pasha had escaped the grounded flagship in his *kirlangitch*, his fast galley. He had formed a line of gunboats in the shallows of the north shore of the Liman, and they began to pepper Jones's squadron. The *Aleksandr Malyi*, a small frigate floating right next to the *Vladimir*, was battered and holed, caught fire, and sank. The quarterdeck of the *Vladimir* grew warm. Jones's friend, the liaison officer Ribas, was badly wounded in the hand, probably by a splinter or shell fragment, as he stood beside Jones. With men falling around him, the admiral needed reinforcements.

He set out in a skiff to persuade Nassau-Siegen to send some of his galleys and gunboats after the Turks lined up along the shore. Jones's frigates were too deep-draft to venture into the shallows. Nassau-Siegen coldly rebuffed Jones. He was too busy piling shot into the grounded Turkish flagship. Disgusted, Jones was finally able to persuade a Russian officer, Captain Korsakov, to counterattack. Jones had respect for the Russians under his command. They were not great seamen, but they were not timid about combat. Korsakov was "a brave and intelligent man," Jones wrote.

The counterattack succeeded. The Russians had lost scores of men killed or wounded as well as a small frigate, but the Turks were in retreat. By dusk, the Turkish gunboats were driven back all the way down the coast to Ochakov, where they took shelter under the great guns mounted on the Turkish ramparts. Jones was surprised at the alacrity of the Turkish flight. What had happened to the fearsome, take-no-prisoners holy warriors of the Ottoman horde? "How imbecile does the human mind become under the influence of sudden panic!" he wrote in his memoir of the Liman campaign. The Turks seemed dazed and confused, stupid with fear.

One strongly feels in Jones's account of the Liman campaign his disappointment in the unworthiness of his foe. Jones wanted to win against the odds, or in a fair fight. He took no satisfaction in one-sided slaughter. His responsibility as a fleet commander dictated strategic prudence, a caution not to overcommit against superior force. But his personal pride demanded boldness. He longed for an opportunity to show his gallantry. As the battle wound down in the late afternoon, Jones was still surging with the exuberance of action, the euphoria that filled him in combat. Jones decided, in his old way, to taunt the enemy by sailing right under their noses.

An hour after the fighting ended, as darkness settled over the Liman, Jones set out on an expedition so bold that it verged on the foolhardy. "The Rear Admiral," Jones wrote about himself in the third person, "advanced in his boat, took soundings all along the Turkish line, opposite the walls of Ochakov, and within reach of case shot, and not a single gun was fired upon him."

An old Russian sailor named Ivak later gave a colorful rendition of this daring reconnaissance mission. His version was probably slightly exaggerated but, given Jones's past exploits, not implausible. Climbing aboard a Cossack gunboat, Jones introduced himself simply as "Pavel." The admiral was dressed as an ordinary seaman, but his "weapons were better." He had "some grey hair," but appeared strong and confident. Characteristically, as soon as he stepped aboard, Jones began to inspect and fiddle, arranging and rearranging the arms and sails to his liking. He had a small boat pulled aboard for his reconnaissance and the oars muffled.

It had grown dark, and Jones sat down to share a meal with the men. He ordered a double round of spirits for the sailors, and the Cossacks began to sing, at first gaily, then a sad song. "Our Pavel listened very attentively as though he were trying to understand the meaning of the song; yet it seemed that clouds of sadness passed over his face, though he tried very hard to conceal his mood," recalled the sailor.

Suddenly, Jones jumped to his feet. "It is time," he said. After peering intently into his face, Jones chose the sailor Ivak as his oarsman. They descended into the small boat with muffled oars and pulled for the Turkish fleet, about a mile off.

The moon was full. The battlements of Ochakov loomed, a ghostly castle on the far shore. The Turkish fleet "looked like an entire town as it lay at anchor, a whole forest of masts" recalled Ivak. Silently, stealthily, the boat rowed in amongst the galleys and larger men-of-war. Jones ordered Ivak to pull under the stern of a large warship. Ivak called up to the sentry on the quarterdeck: did the Turks wish to buy some salt? Apparently, a Russian speaker was found (the Turkish crews were a mix of Turks, Greeks, and impressed Russians), and Ivak and the Turks palavered for a while. Meanwhile, Jones had an inspiration, a bit of cocky impishness not unlike his saucy single-gun salutes to British men-of-war aboard the *Providence*. As Ivak distracted the sentry with chatter, Jones took a piece of chalk from his cloak, reached up to the stern, and wrote, in French:

TO BE BURNED. PAUL JONES.

Jones was gleeful, drunk with daring, when Ivak rowed him back to Nassau-Siegen's yacht to report on the size, strength, and disposition of the Turkish fleet. (Jones later gave the sailor a dagger inscribed with his name, "From Pavel Jones to his friend the Zaporzhye Ivak, 1788.")

The scene aboard the Prince's yacht, as the commanders gathered sometime after midnight, was deflating to Jones. In the distance, cannon-fire rumbled along the shore. The Capitan Pasha had tried to remove some of his larger ships from the Liman under cover of night, but they had sailed within range of a Russian battery on the Kinburn Peninsula (presciently placed there by Jones). Veering out of range, the Turkish ships—all nine of them—ran aground on a sandbar. Standing on the deck of Nassau-Siegen's yacht, Jones and the other officers of the Flotilla and Squadron could see, in the moonlight, the Turkish ships at sixes and sevens in the mud on the distant shore.

Impulsive for glory, Nassau-Siegen wanted to rouse the Flotilla and head for the beached ships, to burn them where they lay. Jones tried to restrain him. The shallow-draft and swift Turkish galleys were still gathered close by under the guns of Ochakov. What if they attacked Jones's Squadron while Nassau-Siegen's Flotilla was downriver enjoying a bon-fire? Nassau-Siegen swelled up and denounced Jones for timidity. The Prince complained that he was always having to protect Jones's ships. He boasted that it was he who had taken the two Turkish ships the day before. Fatigued, coming down from his high, Jones allowed his sarcasm to get the better of him. It is not hard, he told Nassau-Siegen, "to capture a ship that is aground." Now it was the Prince's turn to bristle. Like a teacher's pet threatening to tattle, he told Jones that he would write Prince Potemkin to tell him of Jones's insolence. Fully worked up, he insisted to Jones that he knew how to take ships better than Jones. Jones retorted, contemptuously, that he had proved his ability to "take ships which *were not Turks.*"

"This ridiculous dispute," as Jones later described it, continued to go downhill, with Nassau-Siegen threatening to write the Empress Catherine herself. As dawn broke, the Prince did as he pleased. Leaving Jones with just a few small craft as a screen against the Turkish galleys, Nassau-Siegen set off with almost the entire Flotilla to wreak carnage on the grounded Turkish men-of-war. The Flotilla had no order or plan, aside from slaughter. "We had about as much discipline as a London mob," recalled one of Nassau-Siegen's mercenary captains, the British scientist and shipbuilder Samuel Bentham.

His cheeky "To be burned" message notwithstanding, Jones was in favor, whenever possible, of boarding and capturing, not burning and destroying. He had suggested that Nassau-Siegen close in and take the Turkish ships, which would be useful prizes. Instead, Nassau-Siegen stood off and lobbed brandcougles, incendiary devices, onto the decks of the helpless ships. Flames quickly shot up the sails and riggings. Screams of fear and pain could be heard across the water. The spectacle was "beautiful" to Nassau-Siegen, horrifying to Jones. Many of the Turkish sailors were slaves, kept in chains. "Vainly the wretched Turks made the sign of the cross and begged for quarter on their knees," Jones wrote. Some were Christians, captured by pirates and sold as slaves, others were just begging for Christian mercy. Nassau-Siegen gave none. More than 2,000 men burned to death. For days afterward, reported Bentham, their blackened corpses were seen floating by.

THE SECOND BATTLE of the Liman was a lopsided victory for Russia. The Turks lost ten warships, five galleys, and more than 1,500 prisoners, in addition to the thousands burned to death. The Russians lost only a single frigate and eighteen dead and sixty-seven wounded. At Ochakov, the Capitan Pasha was reportedly hanging his captains. As usual, Nassau-Siegen claimed all the credit. "Our victory is complete—my flotilla did it!" he declared to his wife: "I am, in short, content with myself." He sneered at Jones as a mere straggler on the march to victory. "Oh! What a poor man is Paul Jones! He has surely made a mistake to come here on such a day. I am master of the Liman." Jones, by contrast, swallowed his ego in his official reports, praising his subordinates though he could not refrain from a dig or two at Nassau-Siegen: "It is well known not to be difficult to take ships when they are aground."

Potemkin was thrilled with the news of victory. "I've gone mad with joy!" he exulted. "Isn't it amazing? I am the spoilt child of God!" He gave Nassau-Siegen the glory and the Prince and his cronies the rewards. Nassau-Siegen was awarded a gold sword encrusted with diamonds, a large estate served by thousands of peasants, and the promise of a vice admiral's flag as soon as Ochakov fell. His henchman Alexiano also received an estate, serfs, and a promotion to rear admiral. The officers of the Flotilla were all given extra pay and promotions. In an obvious snub, Catherine and Potemkin bestowed on Jones only a minor medal, the Order of St. Anne. His officers received nothing, and Jones burned with their humiliation. Catherine had not given up on Jones. But she was exasperated by his inability to get along with his colleagues. "I regret that Paul Jones drove everyone crazy," she wrote Potemkin. "Pray god they stop acting crazy, we need him."

The Capitan Pasha had withdrawn his larger ships outside the Liman, but his galleys and gunboats still remained anchored under the guns of the fortress at Ochakov. At the end of June, Potemkin ordered Nassau-Siegen to attack with his Flotilla. Jones's Squadron was essentially cut out of the operation, since the square-rigged men-of-war were too heavy to take into the shallows near the fort. Nonetheless, Jones wanted to be in the thick of battle. He observed that Nassau-Siegen and Alexiano always kept swift galleys nearby for a quick escape, should the Turks suddenly gain the upper hand and counterattack. Jones was much too proud to hedge his personal fortunes in war. For him, he recorded in his journal, it was "conquer or die." For the attack on the Capitan Pasha's galleys, Jones took command of a chaloupe, a small, fast-sailing vessel that was easy to manuever, and loaded it with Russian sailors whose courage he did not doubt.

At 1 A.M. on July 1, the Flotilla began to move toward the Turkish fleet, very slowly. By dawn it was still too far from the enemy to open fire. Jones brought his chaloupe alongside Nassau-Siegen's luxurious yacht. Wasn't it time to begin the assault? Jones asked. Nassau stared haughtily at him. "Is it of me you thus inquire?" he sniffed. "I have nothing to say to you on the subject." Jones shrugged and pushed off. He would give up any pretense of playing grand strategist and become a front-line combat officer instead.

Heavy rain clouds gathered over the muddy, dull Liman. While the Flotilla dawdled in the oppressive heat, Jones's chaloupe made for the nearest Turkish galley. The Russian crew did not ready brandcougles or stand to their cannon. Jones meant to attack and board. With a grinding crash, the two vessels collided; with shouts and yells, the Russians clambered over the side, Jones in the midst of the rush. Muskets popped, steel clanged. Eyes wild, pistol and cutlass in hand, Jones probably looked a little like the cartoon of the Pirate Paul Jones in the British chapbooks.

The Turks, shocked by the attack, quickly surrendered. Jones towed the captured galley to safety and set out again, this time after a bigger prey, the galley of the Capitan Pasha. By now Jones was caught in a cross fire between the slowly advancing Russian Flotilla and the guns of the Turkish ships and battlements. Men were falling around Jones when he clambered over the side and onto the deck of the Turkish galley. The Crocodile of Sea Battles was nowhere to be seen. His galley crew, terrified of the Cossacks and their ferocious commander, surrendered, apparently without much of struggle. Most of the Turkish sailors were slaves, kept in chains.

Jones wanted to tow his captured prize back to the *Vladimir*. But a junior officer cut the anchor cable before Jones was ready, and the galley began to drift into shore. Jones and his men scrambled to find some ropes to try to anchor the galley to the hulk of a burnt-out frigate, but no cable was long enough. Jones dispatched another officer in a small boat to return to the *Vladimir* for rope and anchor. Meanwhile, he cast off in his chaloupe to look for another target. A few minutes later, he was "mortified" to see smoke and flames shooting up from the Capitan Pasha's galley. He thought at first that the slaves chained on board had somehow escaped and set fire to the vessel. He later learned, to his greater consternation, that the perfidious Alexiano had sent a small boat to burn the captured galley, lest Jones receive credit for taking such a valuable prize. As Jones watched helplessly, the Capitan Pasha's galley went up in flames. He could hear the screams of the Turkish slaves as they burned to death.

Aside from Jones's foray, which captured fifty men and burned three galleys, the July 1 attack on the Turkish fleet was a failure. Nassau-Siegen withdrew without taking any ships. "Our flotilla never came up within the range of grape shot," Jones wrote contemptuously in his journal. Jones and Nassau-Siegen were compelled by Prince Potemkin and his retinue to embrace and make up a few days later, but by then Nassau-Siegen was no longer Jones's biggest problem. Potemkin had arrived on the scene.

Catherine's commander-in-chief, after marching his army at a leisurely pace toward Ochakov for the final siege, had at last crossed the Bug River and encamped near the Russian fleet's anchorage on the Liman's north shore, a few miles from the Turkish citadel. The "Serenissimus," as His Serene Highness Prince Potemkin preferred to be called, had brought his harem, including two nieces who were his "favorites." To avoid the heat of day, he stayed up all night playing billiards in his dressing gown and eating sorbet. For the rest of the summer and into the fall, Potemkin ran Jones ragged with nonsensical missions. After the Turks captured a Russian ship loaded with watermelon, Potemkin flew into a rage and ordered Jones to attack the Turkish fleet under the guns at Hassan Pacha, a fort at the end of the Kinburn Peninsula. Jones's nighttime surprise attack fizzled when a Greek lieutenant prematurely opened fire. Potemkin's headquarters were situated on a bluff overlooking the Turkish fleet, and it somehow irked the Prince to see a large cannon on the bow of a large Turkish galley anchored near the shore. Jones was ordered to throw the offending cannon into the sea. He dutifully launched a raid against the well-defended position on a dark and rainy night against a strong current, but that mission, too, failed when the Russian boats were unable to reach their target by daybreak. Without the element of surprise, Jones withdrew rather than have his men uselessly slaughtered.

Potemkin wrote Jones that if he did not fight *"courageously"* he risked standing accused of *"negligence."* This was too much for Jones. His attempt to heed Benjamin Franklin's advice and play the "philosopher," already wobbly, collapsed altogether. Jones wrote the Prince an intemperate letter, objecting to the insinuation that he was shy in battle. With a sideswipe at Nassau-Siegen, Jones angrily declared, "Since I did not come here as an adventurer, or as a charlatan to mend a broken fortune, I hope in the future to suffer no further humiliation."

That did it. For all practical purposes, Jones was finished in the Russian navy. Prince Potemkin allowed only sycophants to serve under him. Jones was permitted one last audience, and, with nothing to lose, told His Serenissimus exactly what he thought. "I spoke very freely," Jones recalled. "I told him he had played a very unfair game at the opening of the campaign by dividing the command in the Liman." Maybe so, Potemkin wearily allowed, but "it was too late to think of this now." Jones pressed on, telling him that he had been deceived by Nassau-Siegen. Potemkin protested that he had never been deceived, that he had known Nassau for what he was. "Don't think that I am being manipulated," he told Jones. "No one manipulates me." Potemkin rose to his full height and stamped his foot. "Not even the Empress!"

As a fig leaf, Jones was given a command with the Northern Fleet, but no one was fooled. It was winter in the Baltic. No ships were sailing. In a private letter to Catherine, Potemkin described Jones as "sleepy" and claimed, falsely, that no one wanted to serve under the American "pirate." (To the contrary, Jones's Russian men and officers remained notably loyal.)

Traveling in an open galley up the Dnieper River in November, Jones became very sick on the passage north to St. Petersburg. He was still suffering from pneumonia when he was granted a private audience with the Empress shortly after Christmas. Catherine was bland and noncommittal about Jones's future, but any good that Jones did with her was quickly undone by Nassau-Siegen, who had his own private audience two days later with the Tsarina. (Characteristically, the Prince boasted to his wife that Catherine received him in her bedroom.) Jones was not likely to be rehabilitated. Still, he hung on. Taking an apartment in the First Admiralty District with his retinue (a translator, a seaman, and a German manservent), he churned out plans and ideas, including a proposal that Russia and America join forces against the Algerian pirates in the Mediterranean.

He wrote Thomas Jefferson, sending the letter privately with the Virginian adventurer Littlepage. By Jefferson's return post, Jones discovered that, since his arrival in Russia, all of his letters abroad had been intercepted and not delivered. His mail had all been confiscated by Catherine's secret police, presumably so that only Potemkin's version of the Turkish war would reach foreign capitals. Forlornly, Jones wrote Jefferson for any news of Madame T——. He had not heard from her for a year.

Jones was isolated and lonely. He did not speak more than a few words of Russian, and the Englishmen in St. Petersburg, mostly former Royal Navy officers, would not speak to him. His only reliable friend was the French ambassador to Russia, the Comte de Segur, who had fought with the Americans in the Revolution and was Jones's brother officer in the Society of Cincinnati. Jones would need Segur's friendship. Before the end of the long Russian winter, the Kontradmiral Pavel Dzhones was swept up in a scandal.

In early April, St. Petersburg society was shocked, which is to say delighted, by a police report detailing a sordid episode. A ten-year-old German girl claimed that she had been raped by Jones. As the little girl described the incident, she had been selling butter in the Admiralty District when she was summoned to an apartment to see a man wearing a white uniform with gold braid and a red ribbon. The man punched her in the jaw, bloodying her mouth. He locked the door, threw off his uniform, and while holding the girl with one hand, threw a mattress on the floor. He pinned her down and penetrated her. Unable to call for help with a handerkerchief across her mouth, the girl fainted, woke up, and ran crying into the street.

The police had witnesses. Jones's manservant or "lackey" described peering through the keyhole to Jones's bedroom and seeing Jones, dressed in a gown, not his uniform. Later, the servant said, he had found blood on the floor. A midwife testified that the girl had indeed been raped, while a doctor testified that her "child bearing parts were swollen," her lip was cut, and her jaw bruised.

Under Russian law, anyone convicted of rape was "to have his head cut off or be sent to the galleys for the rest of his days." Jones had some idea what it might be like chained to an oar as a galley slave. He hired a lawyer—only to have the lawyer quit his case, feebly informing Jones that he had been ordered by the Russian government not to "meddle." Jones seemed defenseless and desperate. The Comte de Segur called on his friend and found him in a suicidal state. Jones's pistols were on the table in front of him. "I would have faced death a thousand times," he declared, "but today I desire it." Segur pleaded with him not to despair, and began pulling diplomatic strings.

Before long, the girl's story began to fray. She was twelve years old, not ten, and she had been "selling butter" for quite a while. Her customers included Jones's manservant. The girl's mother admitted that she had been given money by "a man with decorations" in return for telling a damaging story about Jones.

What really happened? Jones himself probably told the truth in his statement, written in French, to the chief of police three days after the incident. He called the girl depraved (*une fille perdue*). Jones admitted that he had often *badine* (sported, teased, played) with her and given her money, but that he had "positively" not taken her virginity. Rather, each time she came to see Jones, she lent herself *de la meilleur grace* (very amiably) "to do all that a man would want of her." She had left Jones that day appearing *contente et tranquille*. Jones delivered much the same message to Potemkin: "I love women, I confess, and the pleasures that one only obtains from that sex; but to get such things by force is horrible to me."

While not as sordid as the crime originally charged, Jones's account is tawdry. The kontradmiral's taste for twelve-year-old girls left him vulnerable to scandal. The Tsarina's courtiers were adept at exploiting the weaknesses of rivals through innuendo and stronger means, such as blackmail. It is more than likely that Jones was set up by his political enemies, with Nassau-Siegen the most obvious suspect. Jones was never obliged to stand trial, but he was ostracized by society, including the Empress. Though she deferred to no one in the intensity and, if legend is to be believed, the originality of her sexual appetites, Catherine referred to Jones's episode as "nasty." Hoping against hope, Jones continued to write the Empress fawning letters and proposing new schemes, like taking a squadron into the Mediterranean to attack shipping between Egypt and Constantinople. But Catherine was finished with him. The Turkish war was over for the time being (Ochakov had been captured by Potemkin, its 10,000 occupants put to the sword), and in the Baltic, all the English officers in Catherine's employ refused to serve under the Pirate Jones. The kontradmiral was put "on leave" for two years, allowed to keep his pay and emoluments so that he wouldn't turn right around and join the Swedish navy. In July, Jones was permitted to see Catherine long enough to kiss her hand. She bestowed upon him a curt and no doubt chilly "bon voyage." In late summer of 1789, Jones left Russia, still resplendent in his beribboned white uniform, but shunned and disgraced.

CHAPTER FIFTEEN

"The Ghost of Himself"

For a year, Jones wandered. He drifted to Poland, Austria, Amsterdam, and London. He toyed with the idea of joining the Swedish navy, if only to get a crack at Nassau-Siegen, who had been made commander of Russia's Baltic Fleet. At the same time, he continued to write fawning letters to Catherine, hoping to climb back into her good graces. He sent the Empress a long journal of his battles in the Liman, so that she would better understand the "mortifications" he had endured. He proposed new schemes, like sending a small squadron around the Cape of Good Hope to attack the Ottoman Empire's southern flank. Just give him "two ships of 50 guns, a couple of frigates, and *carte blanche*," he implored, and he would put all of Arabia "under contribution" to the Tsarina.

He had not forgotten America. He continued to send his bust to statesmen like John Adams, and he wrote the new nation's new President, George Washington, to explain how he had fallen victim to "dark Asiatic intrigue." He contemplated, in several letters, buying a "small farm" in Pennsylvania. But he could not bring himself to retire, as long as there was a chance of returning to active service, somewhere, anywhere. His health was not robust, but he was still only forty-two years old, and his ambition was undimmed. He still longed to command a blue-water fleet in an ocean battle, preferably against a worthy foe, like the Royal Navy. The memory of his depredations was still fresh in Britain. When he arrived in England, at the port of Harwich in April 1790, wearing the uniform of a Russian naval officer, he was nearly killed by a mob out to get the "Pirate Paul Jones." (He had traveled to England to try to settle a debt with Edward Bancroft; the ex-spy had lured him into a dubious investment in experimental dyes.) No longer a rake, he was spry enough for a certain kind of courtship. He wrote a friend in Hamburg to say that he might come in spring to "pay court to some of your rich, kind old ladies."

By May, he was back in Paris. The gardens were flowering, just as they had a decade earlier, in May of 1780 when he had passed from one fete in his honor to the next. But Jones's Paris, the convivial society of the *ancien régime*, had been swept away by revolution. Many of the nobles and courtiers had fled into exile (including Madame Townsend, along with her child). Jones wrote that he was "alarmed" by the "disturbances" in the capital. Louis XVI and his Queen were living under a kind of gilded house arrest; the French Revolution was more vengeful than America's, though it had not yet begun to devour its own. Jones's aristocratic former comrade-in-arms, the Marquis de Lafayette, was a great favorite of the crowd. Jones sent him some Russian furs and offered to stop by, but Lafayette apparently had no time for Jones. Salons that once vied for the brave Paul Jones were now shuttered. On one of his first nights in Paris, Jones dressed to attend a midnight masquerade. But when he arrived at the ball, he was told that "the house was full."

Jones tried to maintain a social life. At one dinner party, he chanced to meet the heir of the Earl of Selkirk, Basil Lord Daer, who had been fifteen years old at the time Jones's men raided his home and appropriated his family's silver plate. Lord Daer thanked Jones for returning the plate and chatted amiably with his father's would-be kidnapper for an hour or two. Later, he wrote his father that Jones "seems a sensible little fellow. He is not as dark as I had heard." Daer had expected to meet the scowling blackguard of the chapbooks. He was surprised to find a soft-spoken, hazel-eyed man whose brown hair was turning gray and whose manner was benign, even delicate.

Jones took a fine apartment near the gardens of the Palais du Luxembourg, right around the corner from St. Sulpice and the Lodge of the Nine Sisters. He wore his decorations and left his calling card, but his cough was hacking and his visage gray and fatigued. The English writer Thomas Carlyle, in Paris to observe the Revolution, painted a forlorn figure:

In faded naval uniform, Paul Jones lingers visible here; like a wine skin from which the wine is drawn. Like the ghost of himself! Low is his once loud bruit, scarcely audible, save with extreme tedium, in ministerial ante-chambers; in this or that charitable dining room, mindful of the past.

To Gouverneur Morris, the American minister in Paris, Jones was a burden and a bore. Morris, a lawyer and financier who had lived in New York and Philadelphia, was an aristocratic snob, and his disdain drips through his diary entries:

November 14, 1790: Paul Jones calls on me. He has nothing to say but is so kind as to bestow on me the hours which hang heavy on his hands.

November 16: Paul Jones calls. He has nothing to say.

November 18: Paul Jones calls and gives me his time but I cannot lend him mine.

December 19, 1791: Paul Jones comes in but I neglect him perforce so that he goes away.

And yet, Morris's diary also shows that Jones was dreaming on, still agitating for a war to fight. On February 1, 1791, Morris wrote: "Jones calls me and wishes to have my sentiments on a plan for carrying on war against Britain in India should she commence hostilities against Russia."

Jones missed the quarterdeck. Command in battle had afforded him his one true joy, and he would do almost anything to recapture it.

Incredibly, and a bit pathetically, Jones continued to court Catherine and Potemkin. "I await the orders of your majesty," he wrote the Tsarina in March 1791, almost two years after she put him "on leave." He proposed leading an expedition against the English in India and tried to sell the Empress on the improbable design for a newfangled warship that could sail close to the wind without any ballast in its keel. Catherine sniffed at Jones's strategic advice, "India is a long way off," the Tsarina wrote to her German friend, Baron Grimm, "and before we reach it, peace would be made." As for the miracle boat, "Let him propose it to England." Catherine wearied of Jones's dogged flattery. "I think I have nothing more to say of Jones," she wrote Grimm. "I have already emptied my bag regarding him."

Jones could hardly be blamed for indulging in self-pity as he waited, day after day, for orders that never came from Catherine—or Lafayette—or President Washington. Jones lived in deepening gloom, lit with flickers of self-awareness. When a lady acquaintance gently chastised him for preferring "love to friendship," Jones did not argue. Romantic love, however fleeting, helps mortals "digest the nauseous draft of life," Jones wrote. Feelings of betrayal reinforced his isolation. "Sad experience generally shows," he wrote, "that where we expect to find a friend, we have only been treacherously deluded by false appearances." He was generalizing, but he meant his own experience. Jones had enjoyed some genuine friendships with fellow sea captains like Hector McNeill, and he had played the faithful protégé to the great and good like Ben Franklin, but he had been financially burned by his "dear friend" Edward Bancroft and other seedy pretenders. In drawing rooms and houses of ill-repute, he had had many lovers, but no true love, with the possible exception of Mme. Townsend, now fled.

One hopes that Jones remembered his exultation in combat, his "hair-breadth scapes" and defiance of the odds at sea. More likely, he brooded. He blamed everyone for his misfortunes and unrealized potential—corrupt and self-interested politicians, narrow-minded commanders, balky crews, insubordinate officers. But he undoubtedly faulted himself as well, if not in his self-serving memoirs, then in the recesses of his own mind. All through his life, Jones struggled to put forth his more virtuous, Addisonian self, his capacity for self-sacrifice and noble-mindedness. But his anger and insecurity eventually showed through. He would have had faster and better ships to sail in harm's way if he had followed Franklin's advice and shared credit more generously and if he had been less prickly and pushy with his superiors. Jones was sufficiently self-aware to know what to do, but tragically incapable of doing it.

His ambition rendered him both gullible and self-absorbed. His sarcastic asides and demanding perfectionism often defeated his efforts to show "cheerful ardor" and reach out to colleagues. And yet, his pride masked sensitivity and a longing to be loved and forgiven. Jones's gentler side showed in some touching letters to his sister Janet Taylor, with whom he had stayed in touch over the years. Jones took an interest in the careers of his nephews, desiring that they should have what he had sorely missed on his upward climb: a university education. (His nieces, he said with his era's sensibility, "require an education suited to the delicacy of character that is becoming in their sex.") He wrote his sister, "I wish I had a fortune to offer to each of them; but though this is not the case, I may yet be useful to them." It pained Jones that his two sisters had fallen out. He had learned, by his own trying experience, that nursing a prideful grudge brought only more bitterness. He urged his sisters to read Pope's Universal Prayer:

> Teach me to feel another's woe,
> To hide the fault I see;
> That mercy I to others show,
> Such mercy show to me!

If only Jones had been able to take his own advice and hide his contempt toward others, they might have forgiven him. But he could not, and they did not.

Jones was sick. He was worn by care and the exposure of too many years, staying awake for days at a time, standing alert on the quarterdeck of troubled ships in troubled seas. His lungs were weakened by "dropsy," frequent bouts of pneumonia, and his kidneys were failing. In the brutally hot summer of 1792, as the French Revolution rushed toward chaos and terror on the cobblestones outside, Jones withered and shrank in his apartment at 52 rue de Tournon. He began to lose his appetite and his skin yellowed. Jaundice swelled his legs, then his belly, until he could no longer button his waistcoat. He could breathe only with difficulty.

On July 18, 1792, less than two weeks after Jones's forty-fifth birthday, Gouverneur Morris laconically noted in his diary, "A Message from Paul Jones that he is dying. I go thither and make his will." He found Jones sitting up, gasping for breath but able to give instructions to leave his estate—some shares in the Bank of North America, worth about $6,000, some land in Vermont and shares in the Ohio and Indiana Companies, some uncollected debts and unpaid back wages—to his two sisters. Morris finished with this lugubrious business, came home to "dine *en famille*," went to an official meeting at the Louvre, and stopped in to visit his mistress. When he returned to Jones's apartment later that evening, he found a corpse. Jones was facedown on the bed, with his feet on the floor. Had he been kneeling? This disciple of Mars and Neptune had never gone to church, or, despite the occasional plea to the Almighty, showed much interest in faith or religion, but, judging from the position of his body, he may have been praying at the end.

A few days after he died, a packet arrived in Paris bestowing the kind of recognition that Jones so craved during his life. For years, Jones had been corresponding with Thomas Jefferson about the fate of "our poor countrymen" imprisoned by the Dey of Algiers. Jones had been all for raising a fleet to put down the Barbary Coast pirates (hearing of Jones's agitation and employment with the Russian infidels, the Dey had put a price on Jones's head). Lacking the will or funds, Congress had dawdled. But now some thirteen American prisoners, sailors seized from merchantmen and thrown in the grim cells of Algiers, were writing pleading letters, saying they would have to convert to Islam if help did not come soon. In the late spring of 1792 Congress was at last moved to create a delegation to negotiate with the Dey. Remembering Jones and his deep concern for the fate of prisoners, Jefferson, the first American Secretary of State, appointed Jones to lead the American delegation. But Jones was dead by the time his commission and instructions reached Paris at the end of July.

The American minister, Gouverneur Morris, did not wish to waste public funds on a grand or even decent burial for the tiresome Jones. But the French National Assembly rescued the Chevalier from a pauper's grave. The French government placed Jones's body, pickled in alcohol, in a lead-lined coffin, should more enlightened American governments seek to reclaim and properly honor their hero's remains. On the sultry evening of July 20, 1792, a motley funeral cortege formed outside Jones's apartment near the Palais du Luxembourg. There were delegates from the National Assembly in their Republican finery, some gendarmes shouldering muskets, a smattering of Masons from the Nine Sisters, and a small gaggle of friends and common folk. Minister Morris could not attend. He had a dinner engagement.

Through the steamy, fretful streets of Paris they trudged, to a Protestant cemetery at the outskirts of the city. The gendarmes' drums beat a slow, mournful cadence; thunder rumbled in the distance; lightning flashed. (Morris, a bit guilty perhaps, reported that a bolt struck nearby as he went to dinner.) An official made a windy political speech about popular will and religious tolerance. Jones's plain coffin was lowered into a grave. Not a month later, the bodies of Swiss Guards who had been slaughtered trying to protect Louis XVI and Marie Antoinette, after they were wrested from their palace in the Tuileries by the mob, would be tossed into graves nearby.

Europe's royalists sneered at Jones's demise. "This Paul Jones was a wrongheaded fellow; very worthy to be celebrated by a rabble of detestable creatures," wrote the Empress Catherine. The *London Times* dismissed the annoying corsair: "The man possessed the mind of a modern French Jacobin. He rebelled against his lawful King, and raised his arm against the nation that gave him birth, and nursed him to his years of maturity. . . . He was a man of mean birth, and without education; naturally ferocious in his mind, and when possessed of power, savage and cruel."

Morris was amused that Jones had been honored by the ever more radical National Assembly, since, Morris wrote, Jones had "detested the French Revolution" and been "much vexed by its democracy." It is true that Jones had no great love of democracy. He remembered too well the surly officers and hands of the *Ranger*, insisting on taking a vote before going into battle. Jones loved hierarchies, as long as he could climb them. But Jones did cherish *freedom*. He did not much philosophize about it, save for his ritual devotions to "the universal rights of mankind." But he was willing to fight to the death for freedom from despotism. He had seen enough of tryanny, in the fate of American seamen left to die in British prison hulks, and in his own surreally twisted treatment by Catherine and her henchmen. Russia under the Tsars made Jones appreciate America all the more. Before coming to Russia, Jones wrote, he had spent the past "fifteen years among an enlightened people, where the press is free, and where the conduct of every man is open to discussion, and subjected to the judgment of his fellow citizens."

Jones cherished above all the freedom that had allowed him to create himself as he pleased. Though he had many models, from philosophers like Franklin to stoic soldiers like Washington to dashing nobles like Lafayette, Jones was essentially self-made. From the name he chose to the style of uniform he wore, he was a product of his own creation. While he often felt wronged or badly used, and tiresomely complained about it, he also knew the exhilaration of making his own destiny, of standing on a ship he alone commanded, for a cause that perfectly squared with his own ambition. His War of Independence was personal. He came of age at a time when the old social strictures were beginning to slip, when the Great Chain of Being was showing cracks, and he broke free of his place as a servant's son to be his own master. He used his wit, his sword, his Masonic connections, any tool of advancement he could grasp, but he was also bound by honor.

John Paul Jones may not have said, "I have not yet begun to fight," but on that night, and on all days before and after, he never stopped fighting. He was a lonely man, but not unique in his single-minded determination. The same refusal to quit was true of Washington and Adams and other Founding Fathers, who complained, bitterly at times, about the lassitude and incompetence of their comrades, but who never flagged in their devotion to a cause. Jones's true cause, one might argue, was his own advancement. But he was never narrow-minded or purely materialistic. He passed by many chances for profit and easy pleasure. He fought for a world in which men might advance by their merits and drive, and not be pegged by their birth or place. His pride would not allow him to see that, as most men measure success, he won.

EPILOGUE

"Envy of the World"

I N 1913, Jones was finally reunited with his most prized possession, the gold sword presented to him by Louis XVI as the "valiant avenger of the rights of the sea," in his crypt beneath the Naval Academy Chapel in Annapolis. The tomb, built in the high Beaux Arts style of the early 1900s, is magnificent beyond Jones's most grandiose dreams. Just as Nelson was buried beneath the transept of St. Paul's Cathedral, Jones was at last given the respect he craved in the spiritual heart of the professional navy he had worked to create.* The academy was not established until 1845, and it took another century for America to realize Jones's vision of a navy that is "the wonder and envy of the world." But Jones has been memorialized as the navy's founding spirit, the inspiration for its traditions and success. After Pearl Harbor, the Chief of Naval Operations, Admiral Ernest King, sent the U.S. fleet to war by quoting a letter from Jones to the congressional Marine Committee at the beginning of the American Revolution, calling on the navy to "do the best we can with what we have."

---

*In 1794, two years after Jones died, Congress finally commissioned the construction of six frigates to deal with the Barbary pirates. Three—*United States, Constitution,* and *Constellation*—were eventually built. This was the true beginning of the U.S. Navy.

After having been under-appreciated, Jones has been over-mytholo-gized. He never said or wrote the words quoted by Admiral King. They were imagined by Augustus Buell, a charlatan who wrote a best-selling bi-ography of Jones in 1900. For years, Naval Academy midshipmen were required to memorize a letter, supposedly written by Jones, on the proper qualifications for a naval officer, which were deemed to include a knowl-edge of French and Spanish, law and diplomacy. Jones never wrote that, either. To this day, *Reef Points*, the manual for Midshipmen, begins with a quote from Jones, fabricated by Buell, that a naval officer should be a "gentleman of liberal education, refined manners, punctilious courtesy, and the nicest sense of personal honor." Jones did write that officers should be gentlemen as well as seamen, but his determination to be seen as the former interfered with his ability to be the kind of leader the Naval Academy wishes to produce, a leader of broad vision and deep human un-derstanding.

Jones was a strategic seer. He understood, alone among his fellow navy officers, the need to take the battle to the enemy, to counter the Royal Navy's superiority by waging psychological warfare against the British homeland. He was the first to suggest sending a French fleet to cut off the British in American waters—the strategy that ultimately won the war. His outpourings to Morris and Hewes seemed whiny at times, but they laid out a blueprint for a professional naval service, chosen by merit, schooled in science, held to a high standard of honor. Jones tried hard to meet his own high standards, and suffered terribly that he could not tame his de-mon pride.

Truth be told, Jones was not qualified to be a great fleet commander. He lacked the temperament. He may have been unlucky never to have commanded a true blue-water fleet, but he was in no sense a Nelson, or even an Admiral Nimitz, the commander of the U.S. Pacific Fleet in World War II. He was too suspicious and self-defeating to be a gifted leader.

If he was not exactly a model of maritime greatness, he was a most fasci-nating and protean figure. Despite deep and almost crippling flaws, he invented himself. He wanted to be something far greater and grander than the position assigned to him by birth and chance, and so he was. His drive and energy were of enormous use to his adopted country. He did not possess the political vision of the Founders, but they were lucky to have a few men like Jones—and there were precious few—to chase the dream of liberty with a drawn sword and indomitable courage. Jones, in his life, did not win the glory he sought. But he did help win a nation's freedom.

ACKNOWLEDGMENTS

*I*T IS POSSIBLE to retrace at least some of the steps taken by John Paul Jones more than two centuries ago. In Scotland my wife, Oscie, and I visited the small white cottage, overlooking the Firth of Solway, where Jones was born. With our knowledgeable and intrepid host, David Lockwood, the curator of the Dumfries Museum, we walked the gardens of Arbigland, laid out by Jones's father 250 years ago. In Kirkcudbright we visited the jail cell where Jones, charged with flogging a man to death, was imprisoned in November 1770. On St. Mary's Isle, we walked down the wooded path to the beach where Jones and the men of *Ranger* landed, planning to kidnap the Earl of Selkirk. Across the Firth of Solway, we visited Whitehaven, the English town that Jones raided before dawn in April 1778. The battlements he climbed that morning still exist.

In the United States, I was able to sail through a beautiful June night in Block Island Sound aboard the *Providence*, a replica of the seventy-foot sloop that was Jones's first command. My thanks to Robert Hofmann of the Providence Maritime Heritage Foundation and the sloop's able captain, Austin Becker. In Fredericksburg, Virginia, I was given a tour of the Rising Sun Tavern, preserved as it was from the era when Jones arrived there, on the lam for murder, in the winter of 1774. My thanks to the docent, Dr. Gloria Atkins, and historian Paula Felder for her help getting an accurate picture of eighteenth-century Fredericksburg.

Jones's papers, painstakingly collected and expertly annotated by

Professor James C. Bradford of Texas A & M, are in the Library of Congress. I am grateful to Peter Reaveley, a lively and very well informed John Paul Jones afficianado who aimed me in the right direction in my researches and who closely read and corrected my manuscript; to Captain Richard Bailey of the *Rose*, who talked to me about the challenges of sailing an eighteenth-century three-master; and to John Hattendorf of the U.S. Naval War College, William Gilkerson, the marine painter, and Jeff Bolton of the University of New Hampshire, all of whom graciously took my calls seeking their expert advice on Jones and the Age of Sail in general. Thanks, too, to Joanne Freeman of Yale University for helping me to better understand notions of eighteenth-century honor.

There have been numerous Jones biographies over the past two centuries. The first scholarly one was *John Paul Jones*, by Lincoln Lorenz, published in 1943; the best was the biography of Jones by naval historian Samuel Eliot Morison, published in 1959. I was informed as well by Thomas Schaeper's revisionist monograph on the Battle at Flamborough Head and his biography, *France and America in the Revolutionary Era: The Life of Jacques-Donatien Leray de Chaumont.*

My greatest help came from Mike Hill, my endlessly resourceful researcher. I rely on his judgment, skill, good humor, and great friendship. It was Mike who found the proof of betrayal by the spy Bancroft in the Admiralty Archives in London. Mike and I would like to thank his former student, Curtis Tucker; Suzanne Houyoux for her French translations; Bryson Clevenger, Jr., at the University of Virginia; and, at the Library of Congress, Jeffrey Flannery, Bruce Kirby, Patrick Kerwin, Ahmed Johnson, Fred Bauman, and Harold Leich (Russian Area specialist) and Vera de Buchananne (for her Russian translations). At the U.S. Naval Academy, James Cheevers offered his expertise on Jones and his help finding illustrations. Thanks, too, to Dolly Pantelides at Annapolis and Andrea Ashby Leraris of the Independence National Historic Park for their photo research. In Scotland, we were greatly aided by Ralph Coleman and James Williams of the Dumfries and Galloway Natural History and Antiquarian Society. On Martha's Vineyard, Nat Benjamin helped me understand square-rigged sailing. For my glossary of terms, I drew from Dean King's excellent lexicon, *A Sea of Words*, and my own experiences sailing small boats and cruising boats in Long Island Sound and off the New England Coast.

I received invaluable editing from my old friends Matthew Hall, Ann McDaniel, Jon Meacham, Tod Sedgwick, Stephen Smith, Steve Tuttle, and Steve Wrage. I count on their sharp eyes and good judgment. Peter Drummey and William Fowler, Jr., of the Massachusetts Historical Society gave the manuscript a careful read. At the MHS, Fowler, the director and naval historian of Jones's era (*Rebels Under Sail*), and his colleagues Drummey and Celeste Walker were early sources of encouragement and guidance. Thanks, too, to Gerard Gawalt, a historian at the Library of Congress, and Michael Crawford of the U.S. Naval Historical Center, who lent their expertise to the manuscript.

This is my fifth book with the great Alice Mayhew at Simon & Schuster, the best book editor there is. As always, I was well cared for by Alice's associate Anja Schmidt, and everyone at S&S: Jonathan Jao and Roger Labrie in Alice's office; President Carolyn Reidy, Publisher David Rosenthal, Deputy Publisher Walter Weintz, Publicity Chief Victoria Meyer, Art Director Jackie Seow, and copy editor Fred Chase.

My agent, Amanda Urban, has made it possible for me to write books for the past twenty years; I rely on her shrewd and unvarnished advice.

My wife, Oscie, was as always a clear-eyed editor and wonderful exploring companion.

My daughters Louisa and Mary asked, with their usual cheerful skepticism, "Dad, why are you writing this book? Who *is* John Paul Jones?" I have tried to keep their questions in mind as I took what has been, through squalls and calm, an exhilarating voyage.

Evan Thomas
Washington, D.C.
November 3, 2002

GLOSSARY

Aft: behind or toward the back of the ship.

Aloft: up the ship's mast.

Astern: at the back of or behind the ship.

Ballast: heavy material—usually gravel or lead—placed in the bottom of the ship for greater stability.

Beam ends: a ship on her beam ends is lying so far over she is in danger of capsizing.

Beat to Quarters: drummer's signal to men to report to their duty stations for battle.

Bilge: lowest depths of the ship's hold. Usually foul with wastewater.

Boatswain or Bos'n: a petty officer, usually a good sailor, who inspects ship's sails and rigging.

Boom: a long *spar* that extends perpendicular to the mast.

Bow: front of the ship.

Bowsprit: a long *spar* sticking out from the *bow* of the ship.

Broach: suddenly and uncontrollably veering around when running before the wind. Very hazardous; the ship can roll over or lose a mast or *spars*.

Bulkhead: partition inside a ship. Best if watertight.

Clewed-up: pulled up to the *yards* by lines attached to lower corners of the square sails.

Close-hauled: sails pulled in as tight as possible to allow ship to sail close to the wind.

Collier: ship carrying coal.

Con: to give directions on sailing the ship.

Course: the lowest and largest sail on the mast of a square-rigged ship.

Coxswain or cox'n: helmsman of a small boat.

Fall off: steer away from the direction of the wind.

Fantail: overhang on the end or *stern* of the ship.

Fore-and-aft rig: the sails are set up to run the length of the ship, as opposed to *square-rigged*.

Forecastle or fo'c'sle: Raised deck at front of the ship. Also used to describe crewmen—fo'c'sle hand—whose quarters were below this deck.

Foremast: the mast farthest forward on a ship.

Furl: to roll or fold sails on a *spar* or *boom*.

Futtocks: iron plates attached to the mast to secure the *shrouds* or *stays* that run down to the sides of the ship.

Gaff rig: a *fore and aft* sailing rig that runs up the mast and extends out along a *spar* at the top and a *boom* at the bottom.

Gallant: on a *square-rigged* ship, the third highest sail, above the *course* and *top sail*.

Galley: where meals are prepared aboard ship.

Halyards: ropes used to pull up sails.

Heel: when the ship leans over in the wind.

Helmsman: the sailor who steers the ship.

Jibe: when a ship is running before the wind and changes direction, the *booms* and *spars* have to be swung from one side of the ship to the other. If badly performed, the ship will *broach*.

Knot: a measurement of speed over the water, slightly faster than miles per hour. Derived from knots tied in a line at fixed intervals (every forty-seven feet, three inches). Streamed over the side, timed against a twenty-eight-second sand glass, the line measures "knots," or nautical miles per hour.

Lateen: a type of *fore and aft* rig, a triangular-shaped sail hung from a diagonal *yard*.

Lee shore: a shore that is downwind. A ship can be pushed down on a lee shore by a gale.

Leeward: the side of a ship that is away from the wind.

Mainmast: in a three-masted ship, the center mast.

Mainsail: The main *course*.

Main topmast: the mast of a *square-rigged* ship was often built in three pieces, each fixed on top of the other (a lower mast, then a top-mast, then a *topgallant* mast).

Main topsail yard: the *spar* fixed across the mast from which hangs the main top sail, the second highest sail (above the *course* and below the *topgallant*).

Mizzenmast: on a three-masted ship, the rear mast.

Nor'easter: wind out of the Northeast. A Nor'easter on the Atlantic coast is often gusty and accompanied by clouds and rain.

Poop deck: on a large man-of-war, the furthest *aft* deck, behind the *quarterdeck*.

Privateer: a privately owned warship given permission—a so-called letter of marque—by the government to capture enemy ships and keep any prizes they seize.

Quarterdeck: raised deck at the back of the ship, from which the captain and officers give orders. On bigger ships, in front of and lower than the *poop deck*.

Ratlines: small ropes, attached lengthwise, that seamen use as steps to climb the rigging.

Reef: a ship in a strong wind will roll up, or reef, a portion of its sails to reduce windage.

Royal: in a *square-rigged* ship, the topmost sail, above the *course*, the *topsail*, and the *gallant*.

Rudder: a swinging fin hanging off the rear of the ship that guides the direction of the vessel. The rudder is attached by ropes and pulleys to the *helm*.

Run before the wind: to sail with the wind coming over the stern.

Ruse de guerre**:** trick played in wartime to fool the enemy. Typically, sailing under a false flag of another country.

Schooner: a *fore-and-aft-rigged* ship, usually with two masts, built for speed.

Scupper: an opening cut through the ship's bulwark, allowing water that comes in over the side to flow overboard.

Shallop: a boat powered by oars used close to shore. Sometimes has a small mast.

Sheets: ropes attached to the sail used to pull in or let out the sail depending on the direction of the wind.

Shrouds: ropes that help hold up the mast, attached to the sides of the ship.

Sloop: a smaller ship-of-war than a frigate.

Slops: rough, ready-made clothing worn by the ship's men.

Spars: the poles in the ship's rigging—*masts, booms, yards, bowsprits, gaffs*.

Squall: a brief, severe storm of wind, usually accompanied by rain and lowered visibility.

Square-rigged: a vessel with *yards* set across the mast.

Staysail: small *fore-and-aft* sail hoisted on a stay running between or in front of the mast.

Stern: back of the ship.

Strike: take down, as in "strike the flag" or "strike a sail."

Studding sails: small sails extended on *booms* sticking out from the *yards* to provide more sail area.

Tack: the course of a ship sailing close to the wind. Since a sailing ship cannot get closer than 45 degrees off the wind, she sails against the wind by "tacking" or "beating," sailing on one tack, then coming about on to the other tack.

Taffrail: the rail on the *fantail*.

Tarry ropes: ropes used as *stays* or *shrouds* were often covered with tar to make them stronger and not fray.

Tiller: a long wooden bar or pole attached to the head of the rudder, used to steer the ship.

Topgallant: the mast above the *topmast*.

Topsail: the second highest sail above the deck, set above the *course*.

Trim: pulling on the *sheets* to adjust the angle of the *spars* to the direction of the wind.

Windward: on the side or direction from which the wind is blowing.

Yard: long, narrow pole or *spar* slung across the mast on a *square-rigged* ship. Sails hang from yards.

NOTES

ABBREVIATIONS USED

ADM   Admiralty Records, Public Records Office, Kew
Gardens, England

AHP   Alexander Hamilton Papers

BFP   Benjamin Franklin Papers

JPJ   John Paul Jones

JPJP   John Paul Jones Papers

LOC   Library of Congress

LP   Lafayette Papers

NDAR   Naval Documents of the American Revolution,
Naval Historical Center, Washington, D.C.

PRO   Public Record Office, Kew Gardens, England

TJP   Thomas Jefferson Papers

Introduction: "My Desire for Fame Is Infinite"

PAGE

1   *John Paul Jones:* JPJ to Benjamin Franklin, Oct. 3, 1779, BFP vol. 30, p. 453;
Log of the *Bonhomme Richard*, p. 45.

1   *The ship was cleared:* See, generally, Rodgers, *Wooden World*, pp. 54–57; Pope, *Life in Nelson's Navy*, p. 58 (splinters); Miller, *Broadsides*, p. 54 (tubs); Rider, *Valour*, p. 53 (rum ration).

3   *On a brilliant summer's:* Described in "JPJ Commemoration at Annapolis," pp. 11–13, 75, *New York Times*, July 7, 1905, July 23, 1905.

4   *The young President:* New York Times, Feb. 14, 1905.

4   *"My desire for fame":* JPJ to Sartine, Sep. 13, 1778, JPJP, LOC.

4   *He craved—too much:* JPJ to Krudener, Mar. 23, 1788, JPJP, LOC. ("I am perhaps too much attached to honors. . . .")

4   *During his life:* Morison, "The Arms and Seals of John Paul Jones," *American Neptune,* Oct. 1958, vol. XVIII, no. 4.

4   *He spent hours:* "Uniforms Recommended by a Group of Continental Navy Captains," Feb. 27, 1777, NDAR, vol. 7, p. 1303.

5   *He was very pleased:* Gerard Gawalt, ed., *John Paul Jones' Memoir of the American Revolution: Presented to King Louis XVI of France,* p. 47.

5   *Angry when Congress:* Journal of the Campaign of the Liman, JPJP, LOC.

5   *In cheap penny chapbooks:* Oxford Companion to English Literature, p. 189. The Naval Academy Museum has a collection of chapbooks about Jones.

5   *Throughout the nineteenth century:* Alexandre Dumas (*Le Capitaine Paul*), James Fenimore Cooper (*The Pilot*), Rudyard Kipling ("The Rhyme of the Three Captains"), William Thackeray (*Denis Duval*).

5   *"an audacious Viking":* Herman Melville, *Israel Potter,* p. 116.

5   *In the mid-1920s, FDR:* FDR Family, Business, and Personal Papers, Writing and Statements File, Box 109, Scenario on John Paul Jones, 1923 Franklin D. Roosevelt Library. FDR also wrote a five-page book proposal.

5   *"I have not yet begun to fight!":* See Chapter 9.

6   *His boldness and resourcefulness:* See, J. R. Dull, "Was the Continental Navy a Mistake?"; William S. Dudley and Michael A. Palmer, "No Mistake About It: A Response to Jonathan R. Dull," *The American Neptune,* XLIV (1984) pp. 167–70; XLV (1985), pp. 244–48.

6   *Herman Melville saw the identification:* Melville, *Israel Potter,* p. 120.

6   *"in defense of the violated rights of mankind":* JPJ to Robert Morris, Jan. 21, 1777, JPJP, LOC.

6   *At his first meeting:* JPJ to Marquis de Lafayette, June 15, 1788, JPJP, LOC.

6   *He was proud:* Gawalt, p. 5.

6   *"Our marine," he wrote:* JPJ to Thomas Bell, Nov. 15, 1778, JPJP, LOC.

7   *General George Washington:* JPJ to George Washington, Dec. 20, 1789; Washington to JPJ, May 19, 1781, JPJP, LOC.

7   *Benjamin Franklin was an:* JPJ to Benjamin Franklin, Aug. 31, 1778, JPJP, LOC ("I have need of some of your philosophy").

7   *(On one occasion, Jones:* JPJ to Thomas Jefferson, Sep. 4, 1787, JPJP, LOC.

7   *"I consider this officer":* Thomas Jefferson to William Carmichael, Aug. 12, 1788, TJP, vol. 12, p. 503.

7   *"This is the most ambitious":* Diary and Autobiography of John Adams, vol. 2, p. 370.

7   *Adams's wife, Abigail:* Adams Family Correspondence, vol. 6, pp. 5–6.

8   *Jones may have been part "abigail":* From *The Scornful Lady* by Beaumont and Fletcher (c. 1613), *Webster's New College Dictionary,* 3rd ed.

8   *Admiralty records:* See Lord Sandwich to Capt. Cooper, HMS *Stag,* "By express at 3/4 past 11 p.m.," Aug. 21, 1778 (this was a false alarm) PRO/ADM 2-104. Minutes of Admiralty Board, Sep. 20, 22, 23, 24, 25, 26 (Sunday), Oct. 3 (Sunday), 8, 11, 12, 22, 28, 29, Nov. 22, 1779, PRO/ADM 3-89.

8   *In the eighteenth century:* Duffy, *The Military Experience in the Age of Reason,* pp. 11–14.

8   *Naval commanders:* King, *Every Man Will Do His Duty*, p. 170. Nelson's doctor had wished that Nelson "cover the stars on his coat with a handkerchief."

8   *Yet an unwritten code:* Rodger, *The Wooden World*, p. 55.

8   *Of the fifty-seven ships:* Coggins, *Ships and Seamen of the American Revolution*, pp. 203–5, and information provided by Peter Reaveley from Hepper, *British Warship Losses in the Age of Sail, 1650–1859*.

9   *When one of Jones's:* Memoirs of Nathaniel Fanning (hereinafter Fanning's Narrative), p. 45.

9   *He understood the power:* JPJ to the American Commissioners, May 27, 1778, JPJP, LOC.

9   *"Without a respectable Navy":* JPJ to Robert Morris, Oct. 17, 1776, JPJP, LOC.

9   *"I wish to have no connection":* JPJ to Chaumont, Nov. 16, 1778, JPJP, LOC.

10   *"leprous with vanity":* De Koven, vol. I. p. 84.

10   *But then so were Lord:* King, p. 169.

10   *Jones's temperament:* Robert Harvey, *Cochrane: The Life and Exploits of a Fighting Captain*, p. xix. C. S. Forester's Horatio Hornblower series also borrowed from Cochrane's exploits. O'Brian acknowledges his debt to Cochrane in *The Far Side of the World*, p. 7. See also O'Brian, *Master and Commander, passim*.

10   *John Paul Jones's ambition:* See Douglass Adair, *Fame and the Founding Fathers*.

11   *It is more than an interesting:* Gordon Wood, *The Radicalism of the American Revolution*, p. 197.

11   *He could quote Pope:* "When jove from high Olympus goes," Feb. 1782. See Bradford's note 1, JPJP, LOC.

11   *His friends included:* JPJ to Hector McNeill, Oct. 31, 1777, JPJP, LOC.

11   *A bastard immigrant:* Alexander Hamilton to Edward Stevens, Nov. 11, 1769, AHP, vol. 1, p. 4.

12   *He was traveling "incog.":* JPJ to Benjamin Franklin, Mar. 6, 1779, BFP, vol. 29, p. 63.

Chapter One: "You Meet a Gentleman"

13   *John Paul Sr.:* Interview with David Lockwood, director of Dumfries Museum and trustee of John Paul Jones cottage.

13   *He had been hired:* Author's tour.

13   *Abandoning the constrained:* Edward Hymans, *Capability Brown and Humphrey Repton*, p. 36.

13   *"fine feelings":* JPJ to Benjamin Franklin, Mar. 6, 1779, JPJP, LOC.

14   *The world was still stratified:* Woods, *The Radicalism of the American Revolution*, p. 21.

14   *William Craik, the master:* G. W. Shirley, "Two Pioneer Galloway Agriculturalists—Robert Maxwell of Arkland and William Craik of Arbigland," *Transactions and Journal of Proceedings*, 1925–26, Dumfriesshire and Galloway Natural History and Antiquarian Society, pp. 129–61.

15   *"for the sake of symmetry":* Morison, John Paul Jones, p. 8.

15   *For many years after John:* Ibid., pp. 6–7; Lorenz, p. 18; author's tour of Kirkbean parish graveyard. Morison scoffs at the suggestion that Jones was a bastard and calls Craik "an amiable gentleman," Morison, pp. 7–10. That is not the impression left by contemporary accounts.

16 *Mr. Craik's son:* Morison, pp. 10–11.

16 *John Paul turned twelve:* Peter Padfield, *Maritime Supremacy and the Opening of the Western Mind*, p. 208.

16 *Hawke's flagship captain:* Oliver Warner, "The Action off Flamborough Head," *American Heritage*, August 1963.

16 *"I had made the art":* JPJ to Benjamin Franklin, Mar. 6, 1779, JPJP, LOC. Some earlier biographers suggest that Jones actually served in the British navy, but the evidence is exceedingly thin. See Morison, p. 418.

16 *The navy could be a social:* N. A. M. Rodger, *The Wooden World*, pp. 252–54.

17 *If they waited any longer: Johnson's England*, p. 56. See also Marcus Redicker, *Between the Devil and the Deep Blue Sea*, p. 211.

18 *The* Friendship *was:* William Gilkerson, *The Ships of John Paul Jones*, p. 5.

18 *"that dreadful thing":* Herman Melville, *Redburn*, p. 87.

18 *"that most disheartening, dispiriting malady":* Abigail Adams to Mrs. Cranch, July 6, 1784, Letters of Mrs. Adams, p. 3.

18 *A wooden ship rigged:* See John Adams's Journal, Feb. 21–22, 1778, *Autobiography of John Adams*, p. 14.

18 *Belowdecks in all weathers:* Peter Kemp, *The British Sailor*, p. 44; Dudley Pope, *Life in Nelson's Navy*, p. 181.

18 *Aboard the* Friendship: Kemp, pp. 44, 81; Pope, p. 70.

18 *Drunkenness:* Kemp, p. 44; James Valle, *Rocks and Shoals*, p. 185; McKee, *An Honorable and Gentlemanly Profession*, pp. 450–52.

19 *John Paul didn't develop:* Fanning's Narrative, p. 116.

19 *Like all new hands:* Miller, p. 5.

19 *Creeping out along:* Rodger, p. 46; Lewis, pp. 391–94; William Fowler, *Rebels Under Sail*, p. 254.

19 *The* Friendship *carried:* Rodger, pp. 40–41, 116–17.

19 *The most common medical:* Lewis, pp. 394–94.

20 *Navigation was still crude:* Dava Sobel, *Longitude*, pp. 12–13, 90.

21 *"the awful majesty":* JPJ to Madam D'Ormoy, Oct. 16, 1780, JPJP, LOC.

21 *He must have learned:* Morison, pp. 9–10; A. E. Truckell, Walter Duncan, Rev. Thomas Scott, *Kirkbean Parish and Kirk* (Dumfries: privately printed, 1976). Jones's geometry book is preserved at the Dumfries Museum, Dumfries, Scotland.

22 *Released from his apprenticeship:* Morison, pp. 14–15.

22 *"middle passage:"* Melville, *Redburn*, p. 107. See William Katz, *Eyewitness*, p. 44.

22 *On the voyage:* Kemp, p. 142; Pope, pp. 131, 134–37; Brian Lavery, *The Arming and Fitting of English Ships of War, 1600–1815*, p. 201 (between 1793 and 1815, 80 percent of fatalities were caused by disease and accident, only 7 percent by enemy action). Jones himself was not immune. See JPJ to Robert Craik, Aug. 5, 1770, JPJP, LOC.

22 *John Paul was not:* Gilkerson, pp. 6–7; Customs Document, Aug. 30, 1769, JPJP, LOC.

23 *On John Paul's second:* Mungo Maxwell Case: Information and Complaint of Robert Maxwell against John Paul, Nov. 10, 1770; Warrant for Apprehension of John Paul, Nov. 10, 1770; Application and Obligation of Robert Maxwell, Nov. 13, 1770; Petition for Bail by John Paul, Nov. 13, 1770; Statement of James Simpson, June 30, 1772 ("mortal nor dangerous"); Statement of James Eastmont, Jan. 30, 1773 ("taken ill of a fever"), JPJP (Judicial Proceedings), LOC.

23   *It has been said that ship:* Miller, *Broadsides*, p. 41; Pope, p. 219; Kemp, p. 90. For a comprehensive overview, see Eugene Resor, *The Problem of Discipline in the Mid-19th Century Royal Navy*, pp. 74–131.

23   *The age was violent:* Rodger, p. 212.

25   *At the quay, Captain Paul:* Alastair Penman, *Old Kirkcudbright*, p. 22; author's tour of Kirkcudbright and the Tolbooth.

25   *The Maxwells were a powerful:* Sir William Fraser, *The Book of Caerlaverock: Memoirs of the Maxwells, Earls of Nithsdale, Lords Maxwell and Herries*, 2 vols. (Edinburgh: privately printed, 1873). The anti-Jones feeling among the Maxwells lived on: "Paul Jones was a fine sailor, no doubt, but never was there a rogue should have swung more properly than from a yard arm," Sir Herbert Maxwell, *A History of Dumfries and Galloway* (London: William Blackwood & Sons, 1896), p. 335; author's tour of Caerlaverock Castle (Maxwell family seat), Galloway, Scotland.

26   *"Mr. Craik's nice feelings":* To His Mother and Sisters, Sep. 24, 1772, JPJP, LOC.

26   *On November 27, 1770:* Petition to Masons of the Lodge of Saint Bernard, undated, JPJP, LOC. Jones was admitted on Nov. 27, 1770. Interestingly, he was accepted by the Masons only three weeks after he was jailed in the Mungo Maxwell incident. Presumably, the rising classes, the merchants and shopkeepers and sea captains of Kirkcudbright, were more sympathetic to Jones than the local gentry.

26   *Freemasonry was an essential:* Steven Bullock, *Revolutionary Brotherhood*, pp. 1–50.

27   *"he approved himself":* Statement of Currie, Beck & Co., Apr. 1, 1771, JPJP, LOC.

27   *Armed with this praise:* Gilkerson, pp. 7–8.

27   *London was then the largest:* Kirstin Olsen, *Daily Life in 18th Century England*, pp. 57–69; Roger Hart, *English Life in the Eighteenth Century*, pp. 7–18; Dorothy George, "London and the Life of the Town," *Johnson's England*, pp. 159–96.

28   *"speak fluently, though not elegantly":* George, p. 176.

28   *Pall Mall and St. James:* Amanda Foreman, *Georgianna, Duchess of Devonshire*, pp. 36 (hair), 45 (drawl), 56 (macaronis).

28   *A certain languor:* Pope, p. 13.

29   *"intimacy with many officers:"* JPJ to Robert Morris, Sep. 4, 1776, JPJP, LOC.

29   *"Even masters, though generally":* Rodger, pp. 264, 237.

29   *With a social lesser:* Allen Taylor, *William Cooper's Town*, p. 143.

29   *In the early 1700s:* Philip Mason, *The English Gentleman*, pp. 10–11.

Chapter Two: "That Great Misfortune"

30   *"calm contemplation":* JPJ to Benjamin Franklin, Mar. 6, 1779, JPJP, LOC.

30   *Making his way from:* JPJ to John Leacock, Apr. 15, 1773, JPJP, LOC.

30   *Arriving at the island:* JPJ to Benjamin Franklin, Mar. 6, 1779, JPJP, LOC.

34   *Legend says that:* "The Jones Connection," *Vineyard Gazette*, July 13, 2001.

34   *"America was my favorite country:"* JPJ to Benjamin Franklin, Mar. 6, 1779, JPJP, LOC.

34   *With 3,000 inhabitants:* English, *General Hugh Mercer*, p. 47; Oscar Darter, *Historic Fredericksburg*.

34   *William Paul, like his sibling:* *Virginia Gazette*, Sep. 20, Oct. 25, 1770; "John Paul

Jones As a Citizen of Virginia," *Virginia Magazine of History and Biography*, Jan. 1907, vol. 7, no. 8, p. 286; Oct. 1907, vol. 15, no. 2, p. 215. It is possible that Jones lived for a time at his brother's house.

35 *At the age of twenty-six:* The best source is the bust by Jean-Antoine Houdon (see photo insert). Houdon worked from life and followed exact proportions and dimensions. Morison, p. 201. There is some dispute over Jones's height. The report on the recovery of his body says he was five foot seven (General Horace Porter, "The Recovery of the Body of John Paul Jones," *Century Magazine*, Sep. 1905, p. 953), but Morison contends that the doctors were just following the unreliable Buell. Citing John Hancock and John Adams, who describes Jones as "little," Morison guesses that his height was five foot five. Morison, p. 17. Midshipman Fanning says he was five foot six. Fanning's Narrative, p. 117.

35 *There still stands:* Author's tour of the Rising Sun. See also English, *Hugh Mercer*, p. 51, and John T. Goorick, *Historic Fredericksburg*, p. 76.

35 *"prey to melancholy":* JPJ to Stuart Mawey, May 4, 1777, JPJP, LOC.

36 *All men were not created:* Wood, *The Radicalism of the American Revolution*, pp. 21–32.

36 *A squirearchy of some forty:* Ibid., pp. 114–15, 122, 131.

36 *Strangers were openly gawked at:* Ibid., p. 60.

36 *The landed gentry looked down:* Felder, *Fielding Lewis and the Washington Family*, p. 204.

36 *"maccocracy":* Charles Lee to Robert Morris, June 16, 1781, Lee Papers, p. 457.

36 *Even the Scottish faith:* The Journal of John Harrower, pp. 7, 47.

36 *Jones was welcomed:* The Lodge at Fredericksburg, *A Digest of the Early Records*, pp. 4–13; Alvin Embrey, *History of Fredericksburg*, p. 89. George Washington joined the lodge in the 1750s as a struggling planter, but after he married "up" to a wealthy widow, who was a member of a prominent local family, he ceased to attend Masonic meetings. Bullock, p. 104.

37 *Dr. John K. Read:* S. A. Ashe, "Some New Light on John Paul Jones," *South Atlantic Quarterly*, Jan. 1918.

37 *"the many sentimental hours":* John Read to JPJ, Oct. 13, 1775, JPJP, LOC.

37 *"You once more taste":* John Read to JPJ, Feb. 28, 1778, JPJP, LOC.

37 *"Any young gentleman":* Wood, p. 33.

37 *"The learning he obtained":* Fanning's Narrative, p. 106.

38 *There was a recognized canon:* Thomas Jefferson to Robert Skipwith, July 17, Aug. 3, 1771, TJP vol. 1, pp. 74–81.

38 *He quotes Shakespeare's Othello:* JPJ to Robert Morris, Dec. 11, 1777, in NDAR, vol. 10, p. 1092.

38 *Jones avidly read James Thomson:* Peter Padfield, *Maritime Supremacy and the Opening of the Western Mind*, p. 185. "I have spoken to you several times of the beautiful poems called *The Seasons*, written by the delicate author," Jones wrote a friend years later. "There is nothing in the English language that surpasses his thoughts, and his happy elegance of expression." JPJ to Mme. and Mlle. La Comtesse de Walery a Versoire, Nov. 23, 1789, JPJP, LOC.

38 *"The happiest he":* James Thomson, *The Seasons*, "Autumn," p. 174.

38 *"You'll never be alone":* David McCullough, *John Adams*, p. 19.

39 *He imagined himself in* The Poems of Ossian: Paul de Gategno, *James Macpherson*, pp. 1–2, 11, 39; *The Poems of Ossian*, translated by James Macpherson.

39   *"We cannot insure success"*: McCullough, p. 91.

39   *"To make man mild"*: Wood, pp. 217–18.

39   *"natural aristocrats"*: Gordon S. Wood, "The Greatest Generation," *New York Review of Books*, Mar. 29, 2001, p. 20.

39   *Jones often used the word "liberal"*: See JPJ to Benjamin Franklin, Sep. 14, 1778 ("I think a liberal minded man ought not to take offense at liberal sentiments"), JPJP, LOC.

39   *"a citizen of the world"*: JPJ to Lady Selkirk, May 8, 1778, JPJP, LOC.

39   *Dorothea Spottswood Dandridge*: Felder, p. 64.

39   *"Miss Dandridge is no more"*: John Read to JPJ, Feb. 28, 1778, JPJP, LOC.

40   *"neighborhood gossip"*: Norine Dickson Campbell, *Patrick Henry*, p. 324.

40   *On April 22, 1775*: Oscar Darter, *Colonial Fredericksburg and Neighborhood in Perspective*, pp. 23–24.

41   *One of the Master Masons*: English, *Hugh Mercer*, pp. 1–6; 56–57.

41   *"prospects for domestic happiness"*: JPJ to Lady Selkirk, May 8, 1778, JPJP, LOC.

41   *"the more danger"*: Wood, *Radicalism of The American Revolution*, 40

Chapter Three: "Proof of Madness"

42   *Philadelphia, with 30,000*: Sylvester Stevens, *Pennsylvania, Birthplace of a Nation*, p. 96.

42   *"martial spirit"*: Harold E. Gillingham, "Dr. Solomon Drowne," *Pennsylvania Magazine of History and Biography*, vol. 48, 1924, p. 242 (diary from Oct. 16, 1775).

42   *"Oh that I was a soldier!"*: John Adams to Abigail Adams, May 29, 1775, Adams Family Correspondence, vol. 2, p. 207.

42   *The green behind the State*: McCullough, *John Adams*, pp. 88, 78–79.

43   *(Benjamin Franklin suggested*: Nathan Miller, *Broadside*, p. 19.

43   *Josiah Quincy*: William Fowler, *Rebels Under Sail*, p. 48.

43   *"It is the maddest idea"*: Miller, p. 20.

43   *In October, a seven-man*: Fowler, p. 58; McCullough, p. 100.

43   *They discussed Roman*: "Rules for the Regulation of the Navy of the United Colonies of North America," 1775, Articles 3 (collar), 4 (flogging), 17 (fishing tackle), Massachusetts Historical Society; Morison, p. 37; McCullough, p. 141.

43   *In 1775, the British Navy*: Kemp, pp. 136–37. The British navy was somewhat weakened by corruption, and it missed an opportunity to choke off the colonies. See Daniel Baugh, "The Politics of British Naval Failure, 1775–1777," *American Neptune*, July 1982, p. 227. See also William James Morgan, "American Privateering in America's War for Independence, 1775–1783," *American Neptune*, Apr. 1976, and Charles Oscar Paullin, "The Conditions of the Continental Naval Service," *U.S. Naval Institute Proceedings*, vol. 32, Mar. 1906.

44   *He buoyantly prophesied*: Fowler, pp. 55–56.

44   *By the time the Naval*: Miller, p. 21.

44   *Meanwhile, Lord Dunmore*: Fowler, p. 52.

44   *To find them, they*: Ibid., pp. 58–59.

45   *Through the network*: John Paul's sponsor in the Kirkcudbright Lodge in Scotland had been a local merchant, James Smith. Smith's brother, Joseph, was the junior partner of Hewes, a prosperous North Carolina merchant. Hewes and

Jones apparently stayed at the same Walnut Street house in Philadelphia owned by another Scottish merchant from Kirkcudbright, David Sproat. Morison, p. 31; JPJ also had a connection with Dr. Read's father, who was in Philadelphia working with the Continental Congress. John Read to JPJ, Oct. 13, 1775, JPJP, LOC.

45   *"the angel of my happiness"*: JPJ to Joseph Hewes, Aug. 17, 1777, JPJP, LOC. See Rev. Charles A. Goodrich, "Joseph Hewes," *Lives of the Signers of the Declaration of Independence*, p. 427; T. R. Fehrenbach, "Joseph Hewes," *Greatness to Spare*, pp. 182–86.

45   *On December 7, 1775:* JPJ to Robert Morris, Oct. 10, 1783, JPJP, LOC.

45   *Four days before he:* Lorenz, pp., 58–59.

45   *She was a slab-sided:* Gilkerson, p. 18; JPJ to Continental Marine Committee, Jan. 11, 1777, JPJP, LOC.

46   *"Was it proof":* JPJ to Robert Morris, Oct. 10, 1783, JPJP, LOC.

46   *The American flotilla:* Gerard Gawalt, ed., *John Paul Jones' Memoir of the American Revolution*, p. 5.

46   *Smallpox broke out:* Fowler, p. 256.

46   *He worked his men:* Morison, pp. 40–42.

46   *Working with the gun crews:* JPJ to Joseph Hewes, May 19, 1776, JPJP, LOC. Captain Biddle called him "morose." William Bell Clark, ed., *The Letters of Captain Nicholas Biddle*, p. 380 (Biddle also called him "sensible and indefagitable," however). Hopkins's background: Morison, p. 43; Lorenz, p. 51; Fowler, p. 241; Officers of Continental Frigate *Warren* to Robert Treat Paine, Feb. 11, 1777 ("oftener guilty of profane swearing than any Jack Tar that belongs to the ship"), NDAR, vol. 7, p. 1167.

48   *An ancient, profane figure:* Darold Wax, "The Browns of Providence and the Slaving Voyage of the Brig *Sally*, 1764–1765," *American Neptune*, July 1972, pp. 175–79.

48   *He seized on a loophole:* Coggins, p. 44.

48   *Hopkins figured that with smallpox:* Hope Rider, *Valour Fore and Aft*, p. 57.

48   *The squadron had trouble:* JPJ to Joseph Hewes, Apr. 14, 1776, JPJP, LOC.

49   *"It was I who developed the plan":* Gawalt, p. 6. Naval scholars were dubious, see n. 3.

49   *While they slept:* "Journal Prepared for the King of France by John Paul Jones," NDAR, vol. 3, p. 133.

49   *"the Americans had conquered":* Fowler, p. 92.

49   *"part of a cask of spirits":* Morison, p. 46.

50   *"She had all the appearance":* Nicholas Biddle to Charles Biddle, May 2, 1776, in Clark, p. 385.

50   *"At 2 a.m. cleared ship for action":* JPJ to Joseph Hewes, Apr. 14, 1776, JPJP, LOC.

50   *Pipes shrilled and drummers:* Rodger, pp. 55, 53; Pope, p. 60; Miller, pp. 13, 54.

51   *"away we all went helter skelter":* Nicholas Biddle to James Biddle, May 10, 1776, in Clark, p. 286.

51   *The brig* Cabot *was the first:* JPJ to Joseph Hewes, Apr. 14, May 19, 1776, JPJP, LOC. See also Report of *Glasgow*'s captain, Tyringham Howe, NDAR, vol. 4, pp. 679–82; Fowler, pp. 93–94; Morison, pp. 47–53; Ridley, pp. 65–68; Coggins, pp. 27–30.

51   *"an unlucky shot":* JPJ to Joseph Hewes, Apr. 14, 1776, JPJP, LOC.

52   *"Good News for America!":* Morison, p. 51.

52 *"the shameful loss"*: Nicholas Biddle to Charles Biddle, May 2, 1776, in Clark, p. 384.

52 *The captain of the* Columbus: NDAR, vol. 4, pp. 1419, 1458.

52 *Jones later wrote that:* JPJ to Joseph Hewes, Apr. 14, 1776, JPJP, LOC. In single-ship actions during the Age of Sail, casualty rates were often surprisingly low. The cannons were inaccurate and their balls could not penetrate thick oak at long range. By unwritten custom, a captain could break off the action or strike to avert a bloodbath. For casualty rates and courage issues generally: McKee, pp. 398–99 (comparing engagements in the War of 1812); Rodger, pp. 55–56, 59, 247; Kemp, pp. 60, 127; interview with John Hattendorf, U.S. Naval War College, Newport, Rhode Island. The British were considered more bloody-minded, firing on the downroll into the enemy ship while the French supposedly fired on the uproll, into the rigging to dismantle (but not kill) the enemy. There were many, many exceptions to this rule. See, Rodger, p. 57. The real difference between the British and French was discipline. British gun crews fired faster. Kemp, p. 127.

52 *"I formed an exercise"*: JPJ to Joseph Hewes, May 19, 1776, JPJP, LOC.

53 *A week after the battle:* Gunner James Thomas to Lieutenant John Paul Jones, Apr. 15, 1776, NDAR, vol. 4, p. 836.

53 *Sitting in his tiny:* JPJ to Joseph Hewes, Apr. 14, May 19, 1776, JPJP, LOC.

55 *When Captain Jones was piped:* Esek Hopkins to JPJ, May 10, 1776, JPJP, LOC.

55 *"We are used like dogs"*: Crew of the Continental Sloop *Providence* to Commodore Esek Hopkins, May 1, 1776, NDAR, vol. 4, p. 1360.

55 *"a stout man"*: Clark, p. 380.

56 *Close in age:* Frank Rathbun, "Rathbun's Raid on Nassau," *U.S. Naval Institute Proceedings*, Nov. 1970; Amalia Atkinson, "Captain Rathbun's Last Voyage," *New England Historical and Geneological Register*, vol. 115, no. 115, July 1961.

56 *He compelled the lieutenant:* Lt. Alpheus Rice to Capt. John Paul Jones, Aug. 9, 1776; John McNeal to Capt. John Paul Jones, NDAR, vol. 6, pp. 131, 314.

56 *The* Providence *was lightly armed:* Gilkerson, pp. 10–12. The author sailed on a replica of the sloop from Newport, Rhode Island, to Fishers Island, New York, in June 2001.

57 *Jones spent most of the summer:* Journal of JPJ, NDAR, vol. 6, p. 210.

57 *In a letter sent:* Rider, p. 77. Whipple was a tough-minded salt, unusual in the Continental Navy, one of the few captains Jones respected. See Horace Mazet, "The Navy's Forgotten Hero," *U.S. Naval Institute Proceedings*, Mar. 1937, pp. 342–52; Proceedings of Court Martial of Abraham Whipple, May 6, 1776, NDAR, vol. 4, p. 1419.

57 *"You are to proceed"*: Continental Marine Committee to Capt. John Paul Jones, Aug. 6, 1776, JPJP, LOC.

57 *Although Jones always insisted:* Morison, pp. 66–69.

57 *Before weighing anchor:* Rider, p. 83.

58 *The city was in an uproar:* McCullough, pp. 128, 138–39.

58 *As he sailed from Boston:* Journal of JPJ, NDAR, vol. 6, p. 210.

59 *He had seventy-three officers:* Jones says he had seventy men (Gawalt, p. 8), but Muster Roll, Sloop *Providence*, NDAR, vol. 6, p. 1372, shows 73.

59 *The men slept belowdeck:* Brian Lavery, *The Arming and Fitting of English Ships of War, 1600–1815*, pp. 178, 181–82.

59   *The* Providence *cleared:* JPJ to Continental Marine Committee, Sep. 4, 1776, JPJP, LOC.

62   *Jones wrote a second:* JPJ to Robert Morris, Sep. 4, 1776, JPJP, LOC.

64   *Jones had just allowed:* JPJ to Continental Marine Committee, Sep. 30, 1776, JPJP, LOC.

64   *Jones had not misjudged: Whitehall Evening Post,* Nov. 19, 1776, NDAR, vol. 7, p. 749.

65   *Jones suspected he might:* Ibid; Journal of JPJ, NDAR, vol. 6, p. 114.

66   *When she sailed safely: Newport Mercury,* Oct. 11, 1776, NDAR, vol. 6, p. 1214.

Chapter Four: "Determined at All Hazards"

67   *The Revolution was not:* McCullough, pp. 151–53, 158–59.

67   *At Harlem Heights:* David Eyenon, "Foxhunting and the American Revolution," *Pennsylvania Horseman,* Dec. 1970.

67   *Would Jones mount:* Esek Hopkins to JPJ, Oct. 22, 1776, NDAR, vol. 6, p. 1362.

67   *"All my humanity":* JPJ to Robert Morris, Oct. 17, 1776, JPJP, LOC.

68   *"Hell Afloat":* Coggins, p. 79.

68   *Sailing on a privateer:* Ernest Eller, "Seapower in the American Revolution," *U.S. Naval Institute Proceedings,* June 1936, p. 781.

68   *"Privateers entice men":* JPJ to Robert Morris, Oct. 17, 1776, JPJP, LOC.

68   *"inveigled away":* Muster Roll of Sloop *Providence,* NDAR, vol. 6, p. 1372.

69   *"sly, smooth tongued fellow":* Advertisement for a deserter from the Continental sloop *Providence,* Nov. 23, 1776, NDAR, vol. 7, p. 263.

69   *"never become respectable":* JPJ to Robert Morris, Oct. 17, 1776, JPJP, LOC.

69   *"The noble captain":* JPJ to Joseph Hewes, Jan. 12, 1777, JPJP, LOC.

69   *"our infant navy":* Ibid.

70   *His provisions for the cruise:* Provisions on board the Continental ship *Alfred,* Nov. 1, 1776, NDAR, vol. 7, p. 7.

70   *As the* Alfred *cruised:* JPJ to Esek Hopkins, Nov. 2, 1776; JPJ to Robert Morris, Jan. 21, 1777, JPJP, LOC; see account from Trevett's Journal and Deposition of Justin Jacobs, NDAR, vol. 7, p. 16, n. 2.

70   *He tried to send money:* Lorenz, pp. 715–20; Last Will and Testament, Oct. 29, 1777, JPJP, LOC.

71   *"The prize is, I believe":* JPJ to Continental Marine Committee, Nov. 12, 1776, JPJP, LOC.

71   *"This will make Burgoyne":* JPJ to Robert Smith, Nov. 12, 1776, JPJP, LOC.

71   *Burgoyne's march down:* JPJ to President of Congress, Dec. 7, 1779, JPJP, LOC; see Journal of Lt. John Trevett, Nov. 3–Nov. 30, 1777, NDAR, vol. 7, pp. 329–30. But see Gawalt, p. 10, n. 2, quoting General Washington that the clothes were not distributed until late January.

72   *"Stormy and contrary winds still prevail":* JPJ to Continental Marine Committee, Nov. 16, 1776, JPJP, LOC. For chronology, see "Notes on Alfred's Cruise, Nov.–Dec. 1776," JPJP, LOC.

72   *"an unaccountable murmurring":* JPJ to Continental Marine Committee, Jan. 12, 1777, JPJP, LOC.

73   *Sailing in winter:* Interview with Captain Richard Bailey of the *Rose.*

73   *On November 24, Jones:* JPJ to President of Congress, Dec. 7, 1779, JPJP, LOC.

74 *On December 7:* JPJ to Continental Marine Committee, Jan. 12, 1777; JPJ to President of Congress, Dec. 7, 1779, JPJP, LOC; Gawalt, p. 10. Morison examined the *Milford*'s log and notes the captain at first thought Jones was another British ship. Morison, pp. 81–83.

75 *"My success hath indeed fallen":* JPJ to Continental Marine Committee, Jan. 12, 1777, JPJP, LOC.

75 *As he walked down:* Morison, p. 85.

75 *Still smarting over the impressment:* Owners of Privateer *Eagle* to William Ellery, Dec. 3, 1776, NDAR, vol. 7, p. 357 ("an act of piracy"); Daniel Tallinghast to JPJ, Jan. 17, 1777; Esek Hopkins to JPJ, Feb. 11, 1777, JPJP, LOC.

76 *Any good humor vanished:* Esek Hopkins to JPJ, Jan. 14, 1777, JPJP, LOC.

76 *On October 10:* Journal of the Continental Congress, Oct. 10, 1776, NDAR, vol. 6, p. 1200.

76 *Next was John Manley:* Lorenz, pp. 82, 97.

77 *He described Thomas Thompson:* JPJ to Joseph Hewes, Aug. 17, 1777, JPJP, LOC.

77 *"a gentleman who will do honor":* JPJ to Joseph Hewes, Jan. 12, 1777, JPJP, LOC.

77 *"That such despicable characters":* Ibid.

77 *Jones did not blame Hewes:* JPJ to Joseph Hewes, Sep. 1, 1777, JPJP, LOC.

77 *"You have herein":* Congressional Committee in Philadelphia to John Hancock, Jan. 16, 1777 (signed by Morris), NDAR, vol. 7, p. 972.

78 *"I admire the spirited":* John Hancock to Robert Morris, Jan. 17, 1777, in Lorenz, p. 104.

78 *"always entertaining":* Robert Morris to JPJ, Feb. 5, 1777, JPJP, LOC.

78 *It has long been clear to me:* Ibid.

79 *"wretched condition":* JPJ to Robert Morris, Feb. 10, 1777, JPJP, LOC.

79 *Jones was harsh:* Esek Hopkins to JPJ, Oct. 28, Dec. 18, 1776; JPJ to Continental Marine Committee, Jan. 21, 1777; JPJ to Esek Hopkins, Jan 20, 1777; JPJ to Commodore Hopkins Continental Marine Committee, Nov. 8, 1776; JPJ to John Bradford, Feb 8, 1777; JPJ to Robert Morris, Feb. 28, 1777, NDAR, vol. 7, pp. 85, 1142, 1319; Gawalt, p. 10 (paid wages from his own purse). For the best explanation of this tangled affair, see Morison, p. 92.

81 *"The best way is to cooperate":* JPJ to Robert Morris, Feb. 28, 1777, JPJP, LOC.

81 *As the heavy snows:* JPJ to President of Congress, Dec, 7, 1779, JPJP, LOC.

81 *Grand and unctuous:* JPJ to Robert Morris, Oct. 3–4, 1783, JPJP, LOC.

82 *The city was as desolate:* William Robinson, *Phillis Wheatley and Her Writings,* p. 51.

82 *She had been named:* William Fowler, "The Business of War: Boston As a Navy Base, 1776–1783," *American Neptune,* Jan. 1984, pp. 27–28.

83 *"who keeps us at awful":* JPJ to Joseph Hewes, Jan. 12, 1777, JPJP, LOC.

83 *A fellow Scotsman:* "Captain Hector McNeill, Continental Navy," *Massachusetts Historical Society Proceedings,* Oct. 1921–June 1922, vol. 55, pp. 46–48.

83 *The St. Andrew's Lodge:* Elizabeth Steblecki, *Paul Revere and Masonry,* pp. 1–3, 11, 33; Bullock, pp. 86, 91, 96, 107, 110–11, 113; *Centennial Memorial: Lodge of St. Andrew and the Massachusetts Grand Lodge,* pp. 160–85; Elbridge Goss, "Masonic History," *The Life of Col. Paul Revere,* pp. 466–73. Jones was a member of the Ancient Masons, the more middle-class Masonic lodge. The elite belonged to the St. John's Lodge. It is possible that Jones also sought to patronize the more aristocratic St. John's Lodge; he may have later visited a St. John's Lodge

in Portsmouth. See Lorenz, p. 394. Morison (p. 87) writes that Jones's companionship included "solid men of Boston."

84 *Small-boned and frail:* John Shields, "Phillis Wheatley (Peters) (ca. 1753–1784)," *Black Women in America*, Darlene Clark, ed., vol. 2, pp. 1251–55; Henry Lewis Gates, Jr., "In Her Own Write," pp. vii–xxii, in John Shields, ed., *The Collected Works of Phillis Wheatley.*

85 *"into the hands of the celebrated":* JPJ to Hector McNeill, undated (probably summer-fall 1777), JPJP, LOC.

85 *"Pity So Excellent a Face":* Undated, in Poetry section, JPJP, LOC.

85 *Jones decided to ignore:* See "Plan for Regulation and Equipment of the Navy," Apr. 7, 1777, JPJP, LOC.

85 *"I have determined that":* JPJ to Robert Morris, Feb. 10, 1777, JPJP, LOC.

85 *Jones did agree with his:* Minutes of the Marine Committee, Sep. 5, 1776, NDAR, vol. 6, p. 715; Uniforms Recommended by a Group of Continental Navy Captains, Feb. 27, 1777, NDAR, vol. 7, p. 1303; Morison, p. 72.

86 *"You young bachelors":* William Grinnell to JPJ, Jan. 17, 1777, JPJP, LOC.

Chapter Five: "Delicate Notions of Honor"

87 *In the spring of 1777:* Capt. John Manley to JPJ, Apr. 23, May 3, 1777; Hector McNeill to JPJ, May 7, 1777, NDAR, vol. 8, p. 924.

87 *He despaired over the illiteracy:* JPJ to Robert Morris, July 28, 1777, JPJP, LOC.

87 *Jones was ordered to proceed:* Secret Committee to JPJ, May 9, 1777, JPJP, LOC.

87 *He could sail to glory:* JPJ to President of Congress, Dec. 7, 1779, JPJP, LOC.

87 *But the French captain:* JPJ to American Commissioners in France, June 3, 1777, JPJP, LOC.

88 *His joy was quickly restored:* Journal of the Continental Congress, June 14, 1777, NDAR, vol. 9, p. 109.

88 *"I ardently wish":* JPJ to American Commissioners in France, June 3, 1777, JPJP, LOC.

88 "under contribution": JPJ to Robert Morris, July 28, 1777, JPJP, LOC.

88 *"GREAT ENCOURAGEMENT":* NDAR, vol. 9, p. 208.

89 *"scarcely half-rigged":* JPJ to Continental Marine Committee, July 21, Aug. 30, 1777, JPJP, LOC.

89 *"in a shorter space of time":* JPJ to American Commissioners, Aug. 30, 1777, JPJP, LOC.

89 *"laden as deep as a merchant ship":* JPJ to Joseph Hewes, Aug. 17, 1777, JPJP, LOC.

89 *"dull inactive genius":* Ibid.

89 *"art of war":* JPJ to Robert Morris, Aug. 24, 1777, JPJP, LOC.

89 *"I dread such dishonor":* JPJ to Joseph Hewes, Sep. 1, 1777. See JPJ to Joseph Hewes, Aug. 17, 1777; JPJ to Robert Morris, Aug. 24, 1777, JPJP, LOC.

89 *"I am not under a childish pet":* JPJ to Joseph Hewes, Sept. 1, 1777, JPJP, LOC.

89 *As usual the privateers:* JPJ to New Hampshire Committee of Safety, Aug. 29, 1777; Journal of New Hampshire House of Representatives, Sep. 22, 1777, NDAR, vol. 9, pp. 846, 948. (The cannoneers were called "matrosses.")

89 un parfait bijou: JPJ to Continental Marine Committee, Feb. 28, 1777, JPJP, LOC.

90 *About 110 feet long:* Gilkerson, pp. 22–25.

90 *Jones partly resolved this problem:* JPJ to Continental Marine Committee, July 21, 1777, JPJP, LOC.

90 *So Jones understandably questioned:* JPJ to John Langdon, Sep. 11, 1777, JPJP, LOC.

90 *"he thinks himself my master":* JPJ to John Brown, Oct. 31, 1777, JPJP, LOC.

90 *Langdon had been the master:* Morison, p. 106.

90 *The two men squabbled:* JPJ to John Brown, Oct. 31, 1777, JPJP, LOC (expense account: NDAR, vol. 10, p. 367).

90 *Instead of canvas:* JPJ to Joseph Hewes, Oct. 30, 1777, JPJP, LOC.

91 *Jones also complained bitterly:* JPJ to Continental Navy Board of the Eastern Department, Oct. 30, 1777, JPJP, LOC.

91 *It later turned out that:* David Sawtelle, ed., *John Paul Jones and the Ranger*, p. 6.

91 *Jones had high standards:* JPJ to Lt. George House, June 26, 1777; JPJ to Robert Morris, July 28, 1777, JPJP, LOC.

91 *The first lieutenant, Thomas Simpson:* JPJ to American Commissioners, undated (ca. June 1778), JPJP, LOC; Morison, p. 107.

91 *Jones fared better in Portsmouth:* Wood, p. 121.

91 *In Portsmouth, Jones stayed with:* Sawtelle, p. 4.

92 *He had made $3,000:* JPJ to Joseph Hewes, Aug. 17, 1777, JPJP, LOC.

92 *He wrote Robert Morris:* JPJ to Robert Morris, Oct. 30, 1777, JPJP, LOC.

92 *As a squire, he would:* Morison, "The Arms and Seals of John Paul Jones," *American Neptune*, Oct. 1958, vol. XVIII, no. 4, p. 301.

92 *Jones had heard that Fox's Ferry:* JPJ to Joseph Hewes, Oct. 30, 1777, JPJP, LOC; John G. Frazer to JPJ, Sep. 1, 1777, JPJP, LOC.

92 *"a frolic together":* JPJ to Hector McNeill, Aug. 24, 1777, JPJP, LOC.

92 *"The thought distracts":* JPJ to Robert Morris, Oct. 30, 1777, JPJP, LOC.

93 *"I would lay down my life":* JPJ to Joseph Hewes, Oct. 30, 177, JPJP, LOC.

93 *"Honor was the core":* Joanne Freeman, *Affairs of Honor*, p. xvi.

93 *"When it clears up":* JPJ to Joseph Hewes, Oct. 30, 1777, JPJP, LOC.

93 *At 9 A.M. on November 1:* Diary of Ezra Green for Nov. 1–2, 1777, p. 17.

93 *Jones's mood had improved:* JPJ to Continental Marine Committee, Oct. 29, 1777, JPJP, LOC.

93 *Her tiller rope parted:* Diary of Ezra Green, Nov. 16, 1777, p. 17.

94 *Ranger had chanced upon a fleet:* JPJ to Continental Marine Committee, Dec. 10, 1777, JPJP, LOC; Diary of Ezra Green, Nov. 26, 1777, p. 18.

94 *"Our captain took a very":* Extract of a letter from an officer on board the *Ranger*, dated Dec. 5, 1777, NDAR, vol. 10, p. 1069.

94 *"the continued alarms":* JPJ to William Whipple, Dec. 11, 1777, JPJP, LOC.

94 *"I have had agreeable proofs":* JPJ to Robert Morris, Dec. 11, 1777, JPJP, LOC.

95 *("When lo! This Halcyon":* JPJ to John Wendell, Dec. 11, 1777, JPJP, LOC.

95 *He made his compliments:* John Wendell to Benjamin Franklin, Oct. 30, 1777, BFP, vol. 25, p. 128; John Wendell to JPJ, Oct. 29, 1777, JPJP, LOC.

95 *Major Frazer turned out:* JPJ to Robert Morris, Dec. 11, 1777, JPJP, LOC.

95 *The "fine frigate":* JPJ to Continental Maritime Committee, Dec. 10, 1777, JPJP, LOC.

96 *"Traitors & pirates":* JPJ to Robert Morris, Dec. 11, 1777, JPJP, LOC.

96 *Shortly before Christmas 1777:* JPJ to Continental Marine Committee, Dec. 22, 1777; to American Commissioners, Dec. 23, 1777, JPJP, LOC.

96   *The metropolis he saw:* Susan Mary Alsop, *Yankees at the Court*, pp. 65 (barbers), 66 (*la boue*), 126, 133–34 (prostitutes); Claude-Anne Lopez, *Mon Cher Papa: Franklin and the Ladies of Paris*, p. 141 (water).

97   *His destination was the Hôtel:* Alsop, pp. 111–31; Thomas Schaeper, *France and America in the Revolutionary Era: The Life of Jacques Donatien Leray de Chaumont, 1725–1803*, pp. 96–103; Lopez, pp. 12, 124.

97   *"princely residence":* Schaeper, p. 102.

97   *John Adams, who arrived:* Adams, *Diary and Autobiography*, vol. 4, p. 109.

97   *A merchant prince:* Schaeper, pp. 28–29; Lopez, pp. 126–29 (titles).

98   *His aid was a godsend:* Jonathan Dull, *A Diplomatic History of the American Revolution*, pp. 3–96; Schaeper, pp. 52–56.

98   *"I tremble, I shake":* Alsop, p. 35.

98   *His foreign minister:* Ibid., p. 37.

98   *Before the French government:* H. W. Brands, *The First American*, pp. 523–35; Schaeper, pp. 45–51.

99   *"It is with great pleasure":* JPJ to Unknown, Dec. 22, 1777, JPJP, LOC.

99   *The three American:* "Arthur Lee," *Sibley's Harvard Graduates*, vol. 13, pp. 245–55; Alsop, p. 88 (bilious); Schaeper, pp. 137–40.

99   *Lee refused to sign:* American Commissioners to JPJ, with Arthur Lee's Dissent and Their Rejoinder: Three Documents, BFP, vol. 25, pp. 479–87.

100   *He had been recruited to spy:* Edward Bancroft to Lord North, Aug. 8, 1783, PRO (Bancroft's payment by the British government) Adams Papers, Massachusetts Historical Society, Reel # 361. S. F. Bemis, "British Secret Service and the French American Alliance," *American Historical Review*, Apr. 1924, pp. 474–95; Julian P. Boyd: "Silas Deane: Death by a Kindly Teacher or Treason?," *William and Mary Quarterly*, Apr. 1959, pp. 165–85, 319–42, 515–50.

100   *For the payment of £400 to £500:* Alsop, p. 87.

101   *It was probably Bancroft:* Lorenz, p. 128. Jones says the British ambassador to The Hague "obtained possession of the papers of an American minister," Gawalt, p. 12.

101   *"I have long observed one rule":* Benjamin Franklin to Juliana Ritchie, Jan. 19, 1777, in Edward Hale, *Franklin in France*, p. 87.

102   *Praised by Voltaire:* Brands, pp. 2–3.

102   *Medallions and snuff boxes:* Alsop, p. 75.

102   *He often remained enigmatically:* Alsop, p. 135; Lopez, p. 19.

102   *During his fortnight:* Alsop, p. 142.

102   *Franklin liked music:* Lopez, p. 22.

102   *Eager to improve his manners:* Ibid., p. 19.

103   *"only one service":* Ibid., p. 131.

103   *The French upper classes:* Antonia Fraser, *Marie Antoinette*, pp. 139 (foreskin), 182, 287 (penalty for adultery).

103   *"caca dauphin":* Lopez, p. 21.

103   *"a faithful husband":* Ibid., p. 66.

103   *"I soon saw and heard":* *Diary and Autobiography of John Adams*, vol. 4, p. 47.

104   *The hostess at that dinner:* Alsop, pp. 116–17; Lopez, pp. 29–121.

104   *"the pleasures which Paris affords:* Thomas Thompson to JPJ, Dec. 26, 1777, JPJP, LOC.

104   *Some biographers have asserted:* Alsop, p. 176; Morison, p. 123; Schaeper, pp. 240–42. See photo insert after p. 121 for her likeness.

105 *"infested with vermin":* Thomas Simpson to JPJ, Dec. 26, 1777, JPJP, LOC.

105 *The ship's log shows:* Sawtelle, pp. 97–98.

105 *In retrospect, Jones would:* Morison, p. 114. Frazer later wrote Jones, "Your friendship appears like the Vernal snow's, but of a very short duration indeed." John Frazer to JPJ, Dec. 30, 1777, JPJP, LOC.

106 *"Everyone was seized":* JPJ to American Commissioners, undated (ca. June 1778), JPJP, LOC.

106 *"good and gallant behavior:"* American Commissioners to JPJ, Jan. 15, 1778, JPJP, LOC.

106 *He sent Captain Matthew Parke:* Thomas Simpson, Elijah Hall, and David Cullam to JPJ, Feb. 14, 1778; Matthew Parke to JPJ, Feb. 19, 1778; JPJ to Eastern Navy Board, Feb. 23, 1778, JPJP, LOC.

106 *On January 16:* American Commissioners to JPJ, Jan. 16, 1778, JPJP, LOC. The commissioners may have pushed Jones to cruise for prizes off the coast of France. Jones wrote, "I ask the Commissioners . . . whether it is not inexpedient for a ship that is crank, that sails slow, and that is of trifling force, to pursue a tract where there is almost a certainty of meeting with the enemy's fast sailing ships of superior force." JPJ to American Commissioners, undated (1778), JPJP, LOC.

106 *On February 10:* See JPJ to Benjamin Franklin, Feb. 9, 1778, JPJP, LOC; Gawalt, pp. 12–13.

106 *A force of no more than:* JPJ to American Commissioners, Feb. 10, 1778, JPJP, LOC.

107 *Deane took Jones's brainstorm:* Gawalt, p. 14.

107 *In mid-February:* JPJ to American Commissioners, Jan. 27, 1778, JPJP, LOC.

107 *He had ordered Simpson:* Gilkerson, p. 24.

107 *In one knock-down squall:* Diary of Ezra Green, p. 19.

108 *"Strange! That nothing can remain secret":* JPJ to American Commissioners, Feb. 10, 1778, JPJP, LOC. Jones may have been foiled when the British Admiralty ordered merchant fleets in France not to leave port until further orders. James Moylan to JPJ, Mar. 24, 1778, JPJP, LOC.

108 *The French navy encouraged:* JPJ to Silas Deane, Mar. 25, 1778, JPJP, LOC ("tate a tate," "masque").

108 *"very well bred men":* JPJ to Marine Committee, Feb. 22, 1778, JPJP, LOC.

108 *Ever conscious of marks:* JPJ to William Carmichael, Feb. 13, 14, 1778; William Carmichael to JPJ, Feb. 13, 1778; Adm. Picquet de la Motte to JPJ, Feb. 13, 1778; JPJ to Marine Committee, Feb. 22, 1778; JPJ to Silas Deane, Feb. 26, 1778, JPJP, LOC.

108 *About 85 percent:* Duffy, p. 37.

109 *An even more splendid reception:* JPJ to John Ross, Mar. 25, 1778, JPJP, LOC; Gawalt, p. 15.

109 *With its paneling:* Boudriot, *The 74 Gun Ship,* pp. 77–150.

109 *He could remember:* Gawalt, p. 16 ("horrors that ravaged Scotland in 1745").

109 *"I resolved," he later wrote:* JPJ to President of Congress, Dec. 7, 1779, JPJP, LOC.

109 *"The commissioners did not":* JPJ to Marine Committee, Feb. 22, 1778, JPJP, LOC.

109 *Wickes and Conyngham:* Fowler, pp. 118–131.

112 *"As Milton said of Adam":* JPJ to John Ross, Apr. 8, 1778, JPJP, LOC.

Chapter Six: "A Rash Thing"

113 *"Fresh gales": Ranger* log for Apr. 15, 1778; Sawtelle, p. 137.

114 *One of the crew:* JPJ to Silas Deane, Mar. 25, 1778, JPJP, LOC.

114 *"A slow and half obedience":* JPJ to American Commissioners, undated (c. June 1778), JPJP, LOC.

114 *He was alerted by:* Statement of Jean Meijer, Apr. 14, 1780, JPJP, LOC. It is not clear from Meijer's statement exactly when the mutiny happened. Morison, p. 140, places it on the night of the Whitehaven raid, but I read the statement to place the time earlier in the voyage. Jones's report to the commissioners suggests he learned of the plot before even leaving Brest. JPJ to American Commissioners, undated (c. June 1778), JPJP, LOC.

115 *The crews of the* Fly: Fowler, p. 240.

116 *"As they were 'Americans'":* JPJ to Edward Bancroft, Aug. 14, 1780, JPJP, LOC.

116 *Those roots ran deep:* Daniel Vickers, *Farmers and Fishermen*, p. 151.

116 *Abroad privateers:* B. R. Burg, "Legitimacy and Authority: A Case Study of Pirate Commanders in the Seventeenth and Eighteenth Centuries," *American Neptune*, 1977–78, p. 48.

116 *Lord Loudoun:* Wood, pp. 163–64.

116 *He would later say:* De Koven, vol. I p. 273.

117 *"wooden wall":* Morison, p. 142.

117 *On the night of April 17:* JPJ to American Commissioners, May 27, 1778, JPJP, LOC; the *Ranger*'s log does not mention the attempt but places the ship off St. Bees Head.

117 *A British revenue cutter:* Statement from Capt. Gurley's relation, Whitehaven, Apr. 18, 1778, PRO/ADMI-3972.

118 *Jones's sullen crew:* Diary of Ezra Green, Apr. 19, 1778, p. 21.

118 *"to prevent intelligence":* JPJ to American Commissioners, May 27, 1778, JPJP, LOC.

119 *"cut her out":* Diary of Ezra Green, Apr. 21, 1778, p. 21.

119 *As a rising wind:* Gawalt, p. 17; JPJ to American Commissioners, May 27, 1780, JPJP, LOC.

120 *He gathered his balky crew:* Gawalt, pp. 17–18; JPJ to American Commissioners, May 27, 1780, JPJP, LOC; Examination of David Freeman, Apr. 24, 1778, PRO/SP 371-12.

121 *"Nothing could be got by burning":* JPJ to President of Congress, Dec. 7, 1779, JPJP, LOC. It is not clear whether Jones intended to set fire to the town as well as the shipping. There are conflicting accounts.

121 *Seizing the moment:* Gawalt, pp. 17–18; JPJ to American Commissioners, May 27, 1780, JPJP, LOC; Don Seitz, *Paul Jones*, pp. 3–18 (contemporary newspaper accounts). See Morison, pp. 139–42; Lorenz, pp. 143–47. Jones recalls going in with thirty-one men; the log puts the number at forty. Sawtelle, p. 142.

123 *The seaman was a traitor:* Examination of David Freeman, Apr. 24, 1778, PRO/SP 371-12.

124 *"watching the night":* Diary of Ezra Green, Apr. 24, 1778, p. 23.

124 *Jones later grumbled:* JPJ to President of Congress, Dec. 7, 1778, JPJP, LOC.

124 *"haste, haste":* Samuel Martin to Philip Stephen, Admiralty Office, Apr. 19, 1778, PRO/ADMI-3972.

125 *Though he had barely rested:* Author's tour of St. Mary's Isle.

125 *The day was brightening: Ranger* log, April 24, 1778; Sawtelle, p. 143.

125 *Lugging their muskets:* Gawalt, p. 19; JPJ to Lady Selkirk, May 8, 1778, JPJP, LOC.

126 *Fortunately, the Earl's formidable:* Lady Selkirk to Lord Selkirk, Apr. 24, 1778, in De Koven, vol. I, p. 309.

127 *In the nearby village:* Robert Malcolmson's notebook, Stewartry Museum, Kirkcudbright.

127 *An ancient cannon:* De Koven, vol. I., p. 311.

127 *As the ship rocked:* Gawalt, p. 20; JPJ to American Commissioners, undated (c. June 1778), JPJP, LOC.

128 *"The tide and what little wind":* Diary of Ezra Green, Apr. 24, 1778, p. 20.

129 *Finally, the* Drake's *boat:* JPJ to American Commissioners, May 27, 1778, JPJP, LOC.

129 *"exhilerating [sic] effect":* Gawalt, p. 20.

130 *No American navy ship:* A privateer took the British sloop-of-war *Lynx* in 1776, and two American frigates, *Boston* and *Hancock,* combined to take HMS *Fox,* twenty-four guns, in 1777. Morison, p. 161.

131 *The moment had come:* JPJ to American Commissioners, May 27, 1778, JPJP, LOC; Gawalt, pp. 20–21. See Morison, pp. 157–9; Mark Halliday, "'An Agreable Voyage,'" *American Heritage,* June 1970.

133 *He recorded the particulars:* Diary of Ezra Green, Apr. 24, 1778, p. 25.

133 *Sponges were dipped:* Coggins, p. 185. JPJ wrote Lieutenant Dobbs's agent, "His hurt exceeded the art of the surgeon and the skill of the physician." JPJ to John Black & Co., May 28, 1778, JPJP, LOC.

133 *"the rebel privateer":* Philip Stephen to William Fraser, May 5, 1778, PRO/Letters to Secretary of State, ADM 3-4135.

133 *The Admiralty sent more ships:* Seitz: p. 23.

133 *Jones still had on board:* Gawalt, p. 21.

134 *"truly gallant":* JPJ to American Commissioners, undated (c. June 1778), JPJP, LOC.

134 *The men on the* Drake: Ibid.; JPJ to Thomas Simpson, Apr. 26, 1778, May 7, 1778, JPJP, LOC.

134 *Jones's fitful attempts:* JPJ to American Commissioners, undated (c. 1778), JPJP, LOC.

135 Ranger *entered the French harbor:* JPJ to American Commissioners, May 9, 1778, JPJP, LOC.

135 *"What was done, however":* JPJ to American Commissioners, May 27, 1778, JPJP, LOC.

135 *The real impact:* Simon Lutnick, *The American Revolution and the British Press, 1775–1783,* pp. 150–51 ("While Britons worried about the rumored invasion of their homeland, their press introduced them to an American sea captain who would strike more fear into their hearts than probably any other foreigner had done in centuries.")

135 *"When such ravages":* London *Public Advertiser,* May 2, 1778.

135 *"very weak and bad":* Seitz, p. 20.

135 *"In our engagements":* Ibid., p. 22.

136 *The countryside in the spring:* De Koven, vol. I. p. 290. See Amanda Foreman, *Georgianna: Duchess of Devonshire*, p. 62.

136 *"You have heard o' Paul Jones?":* Morison, p. 163.

Chapter Seven: "Officer of Fine Feelings"

137 *"Madam," he began:* JPJ to Lord Le Despencer, May 8, 1778; JPJ to Lady Selkirk, May 8, 1778, JPJP, LOC.

140 *Lady Selkirk's husband:* Selkirk to JPJ, June 9, 1778, JPJP, LOC (see annotation for Lord Le Despencer).

140 *Though it took him:* JPJ to Barren Vander Capellen, Nov. 29, 1779; JPJ to the Earl of Selkirk, Feb, 12, 1784; De Calonne to JPJ, Sep. 24, 1784; JPJ to Lady Selkirk, Nov. 8, 1784; Earl of Selkirk to JPJ, Aug. 4, 1785, JPJP, LOC.

140 *The tea leaves:* De Koven, vol. 1, p. 324.

141 *Instead, Jones's draft:* JPJ to American Commissioners, May 16, 1778, JPJP, LOC.

141 *"I know not where":* JPJ to American Commissioners, May 27, 1778, JPJP, LOC.

141 *"I am so ashamed":* JPJ to Jonathan Williams, May 29, 1778; JPJ to Edward Bancroft, May 27, 1778, JPJP, LOC.

141 *Adept at managing:* Benjamin Franklin to JPJ, May 27, 1778. Arthur Lee's draft had curtly begun, "We have heard your arrival at Brest with a prize, and are surprised that you have not given us an account of that." American Commissioners to JPJ, May 17, 1778, JPJP, LOC.

141 *Jones's pride was further assuaged:* Gawalt, p. 22.

142 *The French navy had attempted:* Padfield, p. 254; Lambert, pp. 42–43. For Nelson's approach, see Keegan, "Trafalgar," *The Price of Admiralty*, pp. 9–95.

142 *One of d'Orvilliers's commanders:* Fraser, pp. 66, 392, 441; JPJ to Chartres, Sep. 21, 1778, JPJP, LOC.

143 *"I have the pleasure of informing you":* Benjamin Franklin to JPJ, June 1, 1778, JPJP, LOC.

143 *Jones was to captain:* JPJ to Robert Morris, Nov. 13, 1778, JPJP, LOC. The ship's name was variously spelled *L'Indienne, L'Indien,* or by Jones, "the Indian." (See JPJ to Chaumont, Nov. 18, 1778, JPJP, LOC.)

143 *Jones was instructed:* Benjamin Franklin to JPJ, June 10, 1778, JPJP, LOC.

143 *By the end of June:* Alsop, pp. 21, 83, 108, 110, 122, 124.

143 *Jones had written him:* JPJ to Sartine and the American Commissioners, July 5, 1778, JPJP, LOC.

144 *Jones could not even tell:* JPJ to American Commissioners, July 3, 1778, JPJP, LOC.

144 *He celebrated his rising:* Morison, p. 174. Morison, "The Arms and Seals of John Paul Jones," *American Neptune*, Oct. 1958, vol. XVIII, no. 4.

144 *"twelve silver plates":* JPJ to Henry Grand, July 12, 1778, JPJP, LOC.

144 *Jones decided he needed:* Ibid.

145 *Jones sought to solidify:* JPJ to George Washington, Aug. 6, 1778, JPJP, LOC.

145 *Seeking entrée into Paris:* JPJ to Genlis, Sep. 21, 1778, JPJP, LOC; Lorenz, p. 209.

145 *"The cry of Versailles":* Autobiography of John Adams, June 3, 1778, vol. 4, p. 125.

145 *Jones was in a rare state:* Alsop, p. 148.

146 *"navigated without ballast"*: JPJ to Grimm, July 9, 1791, JPJP, LOC.

146 *Jones remained leery:* Schaeper, p. 230.

146 *"Jovial Tars"*: *Ranger* crew members to the Commissioners, June 1778, in Sawtelle, pp. 180–85.

146 *"The true source"*: *Autobiography of John Adams,* July 16, 1778, vol. 2, p. 166.

146 *"Lt. Simpson has certainly"*: JPJ to American Commissioners, July 4, 1778; JPJ to Abraham Whipple, Aug. 19, 1778, JPJP, LOC.

147 *Sartine was offering him:* American Commissioners to JPJ, June 16, 1778, JPJP, LOC.

147 *"I have reason"*: JPJ to Sartine, July 17, 1778, JPJP, LOC.

147 *He was severely disappointed:* JPJ to Edward Bancroft, Aug. 21, 1778; JPJ to Nassau-Siegen, Sep. 9, 1778 ("This whole business is a deep mystery to me"), JPJP, LOC.

147 *The* Indien *once more:* JPJ to Robert Morris, Nov. 13, 1778, JPJP, LOC.

148 *While Jones was away:* JPJ to Jonathan Williams, Aug. 23, 1778, JPJP, LOC.

148 *"shameful inactivity"*: JPJ to Nassau-Siegen, Aug. 24, 1778, JPJP, LOC.

148 *Shockingly, the* Drake: JPJ to John Ross, Aug. 23, 1778, JPJP, LOC.

148 *Neither the American:* JPJ to Jean B. De La Porte, Aug. 30, 1778, JPJP, LOC.

148 *"to the last degree unhappy"*: JPJ to Nassau-Siegen, Sep. 9, 1778, JPJP, LOC.

148 *Jones had grown close:* See, for instance, JPJ to Edward Bancroft, Sep. 9, 1778, Sep. 23, 1778 ("my dear friend"), JPJP, LOC.

148 *British Admiralty records:* Intelligence reports, Mar. 4, Aug. 6, 7, 13, 1778, Papers of King George III, PRO.

149 *"I have been in the most"*: JPJ to Sartine, Sep. 13, 1778, JPJP, LOC.

149 *He held Sartine:* JPJ to Jonathan Williams, Sep. 11, 1778; JPJ to Edward Bancroft, Oct. 4, 1778, JPJP, LOC.

149 *"The Minister to my infinite"*: JPJ to La Rochefoucauld-Liancourt, Oct. 9, 1778, JPJP, LOC.

150 *"une bonne voiture"*: JPJ to Edward Bancroft, Oct. 7, 1778, JPJP, LOC.

150 *"By earth, air, and sea"*: JPJ to Jonathan Williams, Oct. 13, 1778, JPJP, LOC.

150 *Franklin stepped in:* JPJ to Louis XVI, Oct. 19, 1778, JPJP, LOC.

150 *It is doubtful:* JPJ to Benjamin Franklin, Oct. 19, 1778, JPJP, LOC. The letter may have been shown Louis by the Duchesse de Chartres. JPJ to Duchesse de Chartres, Oct. 19, 1778, JPJP, LOC. See William Franklin to JPJ, Oct. 22–24, 1778, JPJP, LOC.

150 *"I need not tell you"*: JPJ to Edward Bancroft, Aug. 21, 1778, JPJP, LOC.

150 *"I have need of some of your philosophy"*: JPJ to Benjamin Franklin, Aug. 31, 1778, JPJP, LOC.

150 *"His silence has hurt me"*: JPJ to Jonathan Williams, Dec. 16, 1778, JPJP, LOC.

150 *"agitated and torn to pieces"*: JPJ to Jonathan Williams, Oct. 20, 1778, JPJP, LOC.

150 *"have no connection"*: JPJ to Chaumont, Nov. 16, 1778, JPJP, LOC.

151 *"an old Indiaman"*: Melville, *Israel Potter,* p. 115.

151 *Well worn after sailing:* Gilkerson, p. 31; James Boudriot, *John Paul Jones and the Bonhomme Richard,* pp. 8–51.

151 *He had learned that the old:* James Moylan to JPJ, Nov. 3, 1778; JPJ to Chaumont, Nov. 18, 1778, Nov. 30, 1778, JPJP, LOC.

151 *"The frame is now thought"*: JPJ to Chaumont, Dec. 11, 1778, JPJP, LOC.

152 *"If you want your affairs to prosper"*: Gawalt, p. 24.

152 *"Let them place round me"*: JPJ to Benjamin Franklin, Mar. 6, 1779, JPJP, LOC.

152 *Jones even supplied Bancroft:* See JPJ to Edward Bancroft, Aug. 14, 1778, Sep. 23, 1778, JPJP, LOC.

152 *"the great misfortune"*: JPJ to Benjamin Franklin, Mar. 6, 1779; JPJ to Edward Bancroft, Mar. 9, 1979, JPJP, LOC.

153 *"The old gardener and his wife"*: Benjamin Franklin to JPJ, Mar. 14, 1779, JPJP, LOC.

154 *Given Jones's tendency:* JPJ wrote her what Morison (p. 186) calls a "love 'em and leave 'em" letter that seems more neutral and respectful to the author. JPJ to Mme. de Chaumont, June 13, 1779, JPJP, LOC.

156 *Jones had not been entirely:* James C. Bradford, "John Paul Jones: Honor and Professionalism," James C. Bradford, ed., *Command Under Sail,* p. 27.

156 *"in raptures"*: Thomas Bell to JPJ, Nov. 3, 1778, JPJP, LOC.

156 *"Tho' I am no prophet"*: JPJ to Thomas Bell, Nov. 15, 1778, JPJP, LOC.

157 *"Jones enjoyed fitting out"*: Morison, p. 187.

157 *His goal was to put together:* Gawalt, p. 24.

157 *Finding the cannon:* Boudriot, *John Paul Jones and the Bonhomme Richard,* pp. 53–58.

157 *Jones's spirits were boosted:* Marquis de Lafayette to Vergennes, Apr. 1, 1779, LP, vol. 2., p. 251.

157 *Marie Joseph Paul Yves Roch Gilbert:* Brands, pp. 574–77.

158 *"the best of London society"*: Lafayette to Comte de Maurepas, Mar. 23, 1779, LP, vol. 2, p. 244.

158 *"in accordance with"*: Lafayette to Sartine, Apr. 16–20, 1779, LP, vol. 2, p. 255.

158 *Jones and Lafayette:* See LP, vol. 2, p. 260, n. 4.

158 *It has been observed:* Benjamin Franklin to JPJ, Apr. 27, 1779, JPJP, LOC.

159 *"Where men of fine feeling"*: JPJ to Lafayette, May 1, 1779, JPJP, LOC.

159 *"I'll be happy to divide"*: Lafayette to JPJ, Apr. 27, 1779, JPJP, LOC.

159 *"As many of your officers"*: Instructions to JPJ, Apr. 28, 1779, LP, vol. 2, p. 262.

160 *Lafayette was assigned:* Lafayette to JPJ, May 22, 1779, LP, vol. 2, p. 267; JPJ to Benjamin Franklin, May 26, 1779, JPJP, LOC. Jones attributed the cancellation to a leak of the plan to raid Liverpool. Gawalt, p. 26.

161 *As he stood on the quay:* Lorenz, p. 256.

161 *"sensible, well-informed man"*: JPJ to Benjamin Franklin, May 14, 1779, JPJP, LOC.

161 *"L[andais] is jealous"*: *Diary and Autobiography of John Adams,* May 12, 1779, vol. 2, p. 368.

162 *On one "agreeable evening"*: Ibid., May 13, 14, 1779, pp. 370–71.

163 *"I am to be made the sport"*: Ibid., May 12, 1779, vol. 2, p. 369.

163 *"I had an entire distrust"*: Ibid., July 2, 1779, vol. 2, p. 397.

163 *Someone, quite possibly:* Morison, p. 188.

163 *Bancroft's spying was selective:* Francis Wharton, *The Revolutionary Diplomatic Correspondence of the United States,* vol. 1, pp. 637–41; Boyd, "Silas Deane", pp. 326–27. JPJ wrote Bancroft on the eve of his departure, "I am under apprehensions that the enemy will too soon discover our destination, as I find it is but too well known to every captain here. . . . We now however have the satisfaction to know that the enemy have all their eyes on one great object, so that we may perhaps be able to escape their notice." JPJ to Edward Bancroft, Aug. 13, 1779, JPJP, LOC.

164 *The* Alliance *was riding out:* JPJ to Benjamin Franklin, July 1, 1779; Court-martial of Robert Robinson, Aug. 8, 1779, JPJP, LOC.

165 *His crew was a virtual:* Lorenz, p. 268; Schaeper, p. 238 (Virgin Mary).

165 *"They were generally so mean":* Gawalt, p. 29.

165 *The worst were a group:* JPJ to Benjamin Franklin, July 18, 1779; Court-martial Records of Robert Towers, Aug. 9, 1779, JPJP, LOC.

165 *A seaman named John Kilby:* Narrative of John Kilby, p. 28.

165 *In late July:* JPJ to Robert Finlay, July 28, 1779, JPJP, LOC.

166 *After months of wheedling:* JPJ to Benjamin Franklin, July 28, 1779, JPJP, LOC.

166 *"smooth tongue":* Fanning's Narrative, p. 117.

166 *Fanning also recalled:* Ibid., pp. 24, 28.

166 *"Commodore Paul Jones":* Testimony of Captain Wybert, Nov. 28, 1781, Charges and Proofs Respecting the Conduct of Peter Landais, JPJP, LOC.

166 *Wybert was one of the soldiers:* Boudriot, *John Paul Jones and the Bohomme Richard,* pp. 61–62.

166 *Most of the officers:* Fanning's Narrative, p. 124.

167 *On the morning of August 14:* Log of *Bonhomme Richard,* Aug. 14, 15, 1779, p. 24.

Chapter Eight: "Lay It in Ashes"

168 *The battle and the invasion:* Morison, p. 192; Lambert, p. 134.

168 *Jones would later write:* Gawalt, p. 47.

168 *Even before the* Bonhomme Richard: Narrative of John Kilby, p. 29.

169 *"hot and sultry":* Log of *Bonhomme Richard,* Aug. 25, 1779, p. 28.

169 *They were accompanied:* JPJ to Benjamin Franklin, Oct. 3, 1779, JPJP, LOC.

169 *Off the Irish coast:* Ibid; Narrative of John Kilby, p. 29.

169 *A gale came up:* Fanning's Narrative, p. 26.

169 *Jones had been understandably:* Memorial to Justify Peter Landais' Conduct in the Late War, p. 29. JPJ to Benjamin Franklin, Oct. 3, 1779, JPJP, LOC; Statement of Antoine Felix Wybert, Nov. 28, 1781, JPJP, LOC. Wybert testified that Jones said, "It is an untruth," not, "you lie."

170 *To an eighteenth-century:* See Freeman, pp. 167–71; Charles Oscar Paullin, "Du-elling in the Old Navy," *U.S. Naval Institute Proceedings,* vol. 35, 1909, pp. 1155, 1158.

171 *"spoke of Capt. Jones":* Sherburne, pp. 174–75.

171 *Jones sent written instructions:* JPJ to Pierre Landais, Sep. 5, 1779; Landais to JPJ, Sep. 2, 5, 1779, JPJP, LOC.

171 *The concordat was designed:* JPJ to Benjamin Franklin, Aug. 13, 1779. See Alfred Mahan, "John Paul Jones in the American Revolution," *Scribner's Magazine,* July 1898, p. 34. Schaeper, *France and America in the Revolutionary Era,* pp. 260–61, argues that the document was perfectly fair, and Jones was mostly concerned with its distribution of prize money.

171 *Jones's overall orders:* JPJ to Benjamin Franklin, July 4, July 25, 1779; Benjamin Franklin to JPJ, July 8, 19, 1779, JPJP, LOC.

172 *Jones had planned:* Gawalt, p. 29.

172 *The country was in an "uproar":* London Evening Post, Sep. 6, 1779, in Seitz, pp. 29–30.

172 *Back in London:* Ibid., Sep. 15, 1779.

172 *The American Revolution:* Morison, pp. 214–15; *London General Advertiser and Morning Intelligencer,* Sep. 24, 1779; Seitz, p. 52.

173 *By interrogating seamen:* JPJ to Benjamin Franklin, Oct. 3, 1779; Plan for Attack on Leith, Sep. 14, 1779, JPJP, LOC; Gawalt, pp. 30–31.

173 *Captains Denis Cottineau:* Ibid; Log of *Bonhomme Richard,* Sep. 15, 1779, pp. 39–40.

174 *Then Colonel Paul Chamillard:* JPJ to Paul Chamillard, Sep. 14, 1779, JPJP, LOC.

174 *"I do not wish to distress":* To the Provost of Leith; Articles of Capitulation, Sep. 14, 1779, JPJP, LOC.

175 *"I am Paul Jones":* Narrative of John Kilby, p. 30; Morison, p. 218.

175 *All that day:* Lorenz, pp. 283–84.

175 *To Jones's immense chagrin:* JPJ to Benjamin Franklin, Oct. 3, 1779, JPJP, LOC; Log of *Bonhomme Richard,* Sep. 17, 1779.

176 *Sailing in close to the isle:* Morison, p. 221.

176 *Jones summoned Ricot:* JPJ to Benjamin Franklin, Oct. 3, 1779, JPJP, LOC.

177 *At 11 P.M. on Wednesday:* Log of *Bonhomme Richard,* Sep. 23, 1779, JPJP, LOC.

Chapter Nine: "We've Got Her Now!"

178 *Richard Pearson was a formidable:* John Evangeline Walsh, *Night on Fire,* pp. 8–9.

178 *On the morning of September 23:* The best overall narratives are Peter Reaveley, "The Battle," in Boudriot, pp. 63–89, *John Paul Jones and the Bonhomme Richard* and Walsh, *passim.* Reaveley's account is very detailed and precise, Walsh's slightly more novelistic, but lively, and seeks to be accurate. A clear and thoughtful analysis can be found in James C. Bradford, "The Battle off Flamborough Head," in *Great American Naval Battles* (ed., Jack Sweetman), pp. 27–47. See also Mahan, "John Paul Jones in the Revolution," *Scribner's Magazine,* July-August, 1898, pp. 22–36, 204–19. Thomas J. Schaeper, *John Paul Jones and the Battle off Flamborough Head,* is a strong revisionist account that defends the role of Captain Landais and makes good use of overlooked documents. The exact sequence of events is difficult to determine, and historians have offered varied interpretations. All battle narratives rely on these primary sources: Fanning's Narrative, which is the most colorful though not wholly reliable, as Fanning was an "embroiderer" (Morison, p. 170); Narrative of John Kilby; Jones's battle report to Benjamin Franklin and his Memoir to Louis XVI; the log of *Bonhomme Richard* (including remarks by Lieutenant Henry Lunt, which were ripped from the log and kept by JPJ in his papers); Richard Dale's Narrative in Sherburne; Captain Pearson's Action Report; the court-martial of Captain Pearson; the various testimonies of seamen and officers in Charges and Proofs Respecting the Conduct of Peter Landais, and Memorial to Justify Peter Landais in the JPJP, LOC.

179 *They had let fly their topsail:* Richard Pearson to Philip Stevens, Oct. 6, 1779, PRO/ADM-2305.

179 *Aboard the* Bonhomme Richard: JPJ to Benjamin Franklin, Oct. 3, 1779, JPJP, LOC; Fanning's Narrative, p. 32 ("We could count 37 sail of vessels in that quarter").

179 *"As soon as Jones":* Fanning's Narrative, p. 33.

180 *"appeared to be impatient"*: Ibid.

180 *At 5 P.M., the marine:* Log of *Bonhomme Richard*, Sep. 24, 1779, p. 45.

181 *On the quarterdeck:* Fanning's Narrative, pp. 35, 37.

181 *"The captains of the tops"*: Ibid.

182 *Jones brought around:* JPJ to Benjamin Franklin, Oct. 3, 1779, JPJP, LOC. Fanning claims Jones actually spoke to Landais, ordering him to be ready to lie alongside the *Serapis* and board. Fanning's Narrative, p. 34.

182 *(Landais, ever the contrarian:* Memorial to Justify Peter Landais, p. 35, JPJP, LOC.

182 *Surveying the quarterdeck:* Fanning's Narrative, p. 36.

183 *"The surface of the great deep"*: Ibid., p. 39.

183 *Captain Pearson's voice:* Ibid., Log of *Bonhomme Richard*, Sep. 24, 1779, p. 46; Dale's Narrative, Sherburne, p. 126; Narrative of John Kilby, p. 31; Richard Pearson to Philip Stephens, Oct. 6, 1779, PRO/ADM-2305.

183 *"The battle thus begun"*: JPJ to Benjamin Franklin, Oct. 3, 1779, JPJP, LOC.

183 *In the gun room:* Gawalt, p. 33; JPJ to Benjamin Franklin, Oct. 3, 1779, LOC. Most accounts say two guns, but Boudriot, an authority on the French navy, suggests only one gun burst. Boudriot, *John Paul Jones and the Bonhomme Richard*, p. 53.

184 *As the two ships glided:* Richard Pearson to Philip Stephens, Oct. 6, 1779, Admiralty/PRO; Fanning's Narrative, p. 39; Dale's Narrative, in Sherburne, p. 126.

184 *On the poop deck:* JPJ to Benjamin Franklin, Oct. 3, 1779, JPJP, LOC.

186 *"She made a dreadful havoc"*: Fanning's Narrative, p. 40.

186 *In the cockpit, Surgeon Brooke:* Ibid., p. 58.

186 *"by two feet to one"*: Ibid., p. 40.

186 *"I must confess"*: JPJ to Benjamin Franklin, Oct. 3, 1779, JPJP, LOC.

186 *"A true-blooded Yankee"*: Fanning's Narrative, p. 40.

187 *"Well done my lads"*: Ibid.

188 *He called for Sailing Master:* Gawalt, p. 33; JPJ to Benjamin Franklin, Oct. 3, 1779, JPJP, LOC; Fanning's Narrative, p. 41.

188 *"Mr. Stacey, it's no time"*: Fanning's Narrative, p. 41.

188 *The British captain ordered:* Gawalt, p. 33.

188 *"at least 50 of them"*: Narrative of John Kilby, p. 31.

188 *They were literally muzzle-to-muzzle:* JPJ to Benjamin Franklin, Oct. 3, 1779, JPJP, LOC.

189 *When one of them was smashed:* Gawalt, p. 33; JPJ to Benjamin Franklin, Oct. 3, 1779, JPJP, LOC.

190 *At about 9:15 P.M.:* JPJ to Benjamin Franklin, Oct. 3, 1779; Proofs Respecting the Conduct of Peter Landais, Oct.–Nov., 1779, JPJP, LOC (testimony of witnesses). Most historians have followed Jones's argument that Landais was evil, mad, or both. See Morison, p. 235. But see Schaeper, *John Paul Jones and the Battle off Flamborough Head*, pp. 43–55, for a strongly argued case that Landais did not intentionally fire into the *Bonhomme Richard*. Schaeper also suggests Jones molded the testimony of his men.

190 *He ordered his men to hang:* JPJ to Benjamin Franklin, Oct. 3, 1779, JPJP, LOC.

190 *The carpenter, John Gunnison:* Narrative of John Kilby, p. 32; JPJ to Benjamin Franklin, Oct. 3, 1779, JPJP, LOC.

191 *"Who are those rascals"*: Fanning's Narrative, p. 45.

192   *"in the most determined negative"*: JPJ to Benjamin Franklin, Oct. 3, 1779, JPJP, LOC. Pearson claimed that Jones did not reply at all. Richard Pearson to Philip Stephens, Oct. 6, 1779, PRO/ADM-2305.

192   *"I have not yet begun to fight!"*: Dale's Narrative, in Sherburne, p. 127. Dale places the exchange early in the battle, but the stronger evidence indicates that it came in the sequence described. See Walsh's note, Walsh, pp. 155–57. Morison argues that it "makes no sense" that Jones would say "I have not yet begun to fight" toward the end of the battle, but that seems to miss the point of Jones's defiance and, in any case, the evidence is slender that Jones spoke those words. Two or three years after the battle, Jones may have told a small dinner party that he had replied to Pearson, "No sir, I will not—we have had a small fight as yet." Dr. Benjamin Rush recorded this version nearly twenty years later. Morison, pp. 140–41.

192   *"Je ne songe point"*: Gawalt, p. 35. Earlier accounts translate it, "I do not dream of surrendering, but I am determined to make you strike." A contemporary account quotes Jones as responding to Pearson's demand, "No sir, I have not yet thought of it, but am determined to make you strike." *London Evening Post*, Oct. 12, 1779, Seitz, p. 88. See note, Morison, pp. 241–42.

192   *"I may sink"*: See Boudriot, p. 82; *John Paul Jones and the Bonhomme Richard*, Lorenz, p. 304. The earliest account may be from Thomas Berry, a British volunteer who deserted the *Bonhomme Richard* the morning after the battle, stealing a boat in the confusion and rowing ashore. Berry reported that "the captain of the *Serapis* called out to Jones to strike, else he would sink him. To which the latter replied 'that he might if he could; for whenever the Devil was ready for him, he would rather obey his summons than strike to anyone.'" *London Evening Post*, Sep. 30, 1779, in Seitz, p. 55. The less convoluted version would be something like, "I may sink, but I'll be damned if I'll strike."

192   *The master-at-arms, John Burbank*: Narrative of John Kilby, p. 32.

192   *Jones and Dale were able*: Gawalt, p. 38.

193   *The last assault came from*: Fanning's Narrative, 46; Gawalt, p. 37.

193   *In the maintop*: Fanning's Narrative, pp. 43–47.

193   *"The coat on my back"*: Ibid. p. 55.

193   *As the battle entered*: Ibid., p. 47; Narrative of John Kilby, p. 32.

194   *But during the course*: Dale's Narrative, Sherburne, p. 128.

194   *Pearson walked, stiff-backed*: Ibid.

195   *He ordered Lieutenant Dale*: Ibid.

195   *"Have you struck, sir?"*: Ibid.

195   *With a grinding, wrenching crash*: JPJ to Benjamin Franklin, Oct. 3, 1779, JPJP, LOC.

195   *His calf had been badly cut*: Dale's Narrative, Sherburne, p. 128.

195   *Captain Jones may have been*: Boudriot, p. 83. He later wrote about the flag "for which I have shed some of my blood." See, for example, JPJ to Arthur Lee, Feb. 10, 1784, JPJP, LOC.

196   *Mostly Americans*: Morison, p. 205.

196   *"Then it was diamond cut diamond"*: Narrative of John Kilby, p. 32.

196   *"has a halter around his neck"*: Fanning's Narrative, p. 48.

196   *According to Fanning*: Ibid., p. 49.

196 *"I found her in the greatest"*: Richard Pearson to Philip Stephens, Oct. 6, 1779, PRO/ADM-2305.

196 *"A person must have been"*: JPJ to Benjamin Franklin, Oct. 3, 1779, JPJP, LOC.

196 *"Only an old timber here and there"*: Gawalt, 37.

197 *"One might have drove"*: Fanning's Narrative, p. 54.

197 *"the dead lying in heaps"*: Ibid., p. 53.

197 *"only the collars of their shirts"*: Dale's Narrative, in Sherburne, p. 128.

197 *"The flesh of several of them"*: Ibid., p. 59.

197 *The number of dead:* Walsh, pp. 121–32.

197 *"within a few inches of the powder"*: Gawalt, p. 40.

197 *A human chain was formed:* Fanning's Narrative, p. 50.

197 *"The leak still gaining"*: Log of *Bonhomme Richard*, Sep. 24, 1779, p. 47.

198 *Jones was determined to save:* JPJ to Benjamin Franklin, Oct. 3, 1779, JPJP, LOC.

198 *By nightfall on the 24th:* Gawalt, p. 40.

198 *At the last minute:* Fanning's Narrative, p. 56.

198 *"with inexpressible grief"*: JPJ to Benjamin Franklin, Oct. 3, 1779, JPJP, LOC.

Chapter Ten: "No Sooner Seen than Lost"

199 *At least eight Royal Navy:* London Sunday Post, Sep. 30, 1770, in Seitz, p. 57. The Minutes of the Admiralty Board show considerable concern before Flamborough Head. See September 20, 22, 1779. By the 23rd, Jones was the lead item on the agenda and ships were being dispatched. At a meeting on Sunday, September 26, the board has learned of the engagement and is sending ships to intercept Jones. Minutes of Admiralty Board. Sep.–Oct 1779, PRO/ADM 3-89.

199 *"Paul Jones resembles"*: London Morning Post and Daily Advertiser, Oct. 1, 1779, in Seitz, p. 61.

200 *"During the engagement"*: London Evening Post, Sep. 30, 1779, in Seitz, pp. 54–55.

200 *"Jones flings us all"*: Lutnick, *The American Revolution and the British Press, 1775–1783*, p. 154.

200 *"blockhead"*: London Morning Post and Daily Advertiser, Oct. 29, 1779, in Seitz, p. 118.

200 *But the poems and ballads:* John Paul Jones Collection, U.S. Naval Academy. (For example: *The Life and History of Paul Jones, the English Corsair: Giving an Account of the Extraordinary Perils, Escapes, & Voyages, of That Bold and Determined Pirate & Smuggler.*)

200 *The more abuse: Gentleman's Magazine,* Sep. 1779 ("desperado"); *London Gazetteer and New Daily Advertiser,* Sep. 28, Oct. 2, 1779 ("good seaman but a bad man"; "vile fellow"); *London Morning Chronicle,* Oct. 8, 1779 ("daring pirate").

200 *He was teaching:* For examples of alarms over Jones being cited in Parliamentary debate, see *Parliamentary History of England,* vol. 20 (Dec. 1778–Jan. 1780), pp. 1030–31, 1107–8. ("The coast of Scotland being left naked and defenceless, the people of Dumfries had petitioned for arms to defend themselves. To my certain knowledge, Paul Jones might have destroyed Glasgow, Leith, Greenock, and Edinburgh at the same time.")

200 *"A gentleman in the city"*: London Morning Chronicle, Oct. 4, 1779.

201 *Jones and his prizes:* Jones had wanted to make for the French port of Dunkirk but the other captains insisted on the Texel, where he had been originally ordered to end his cruise in order to convoy a stranded fleet of French merchantmen. Jones was unenthusiastic but did hope that he might at last pick up the *Indien* in Amsterdam. Jan Willem Schulte Nordholt, *The Dutch Republic and American Independence,* pp. 71–72.

201 *The sight of the Stars:* Chaumont and Franklin to Dumont, Sep. 2, 1779, JPJP, LOC.

201 *"My telescope":* Charles Dumas to Benjamin Franklin, Oct. 30, 1779, BFP, vol. 30, p. 442.

201 *In a small cabin:* JPJ to Benjamin Franklin, Oct. 3, 1779, JPJP, LOC.

201 *It was a detailed:* Schaeper, *John Paul Jones and the Battle off Flamborough Head, passim.* Schaeper (pp. 81–85) has turned up an overlooked letter from Cottineau to Chaumont, Nov. 15, 1779, and memoir that are very critical of Jones.

201 *He had returned Pearson's:* Fanning's Narrative, pp. 62–63. See exchange of letters, Richard Pearson to JPJ, Oct. 19, 1779; JPJ to Pearson, Oct. 20, 1779, JPJP, LOC.

202 *Jones wanted to swap:* JPJ to La Vauguyon, Oct. 5, 1779, JPJP, LOC. Jones wanted to use Pearson as a hostage to secure the release of Gustavus Conyngham, a very successful privateer imprisoned in England. Conyngham later escaped. JPJ to Benjamin Franklin, Oct. 11, 1779, JPJP, LOC.

202 *As he was rowed away:* Fanning's Narrative, p. 61.

202 *He was mobbed by crowds: London Evening Post,* Oct. 12, 1779, in Seitz, pp. 87–90.

203 *"he is a very different man": London Gazetteer and New Daily Advertiser,* Oct. 22, 1779, in Seitz, p. 113.

203 *"A great hue and cry":* Abigail Adams to James Lovell, Dec. 13, 1779, *Adams Family Correspondence,* vol. 3, p. 248.

203 *"little taste":* Benjamin Franklin to Jane Mecom, Oct. 25, 1779, BFP, vol. 30, p. 582.

203 *"immortalizes you":* Paul Chamillard to JPJ, Oct. 9, 1779, JPJP, LOC.

203 *"made our hair stand on end":* Chaumont to JPJ, Oct. 11, 1779, JPJP, LOC.

203 *"Congratulations for the commander":* Charles Dumas to JPJ, Oct. 10, 1779, JPJP, LOC.

203 *"We already smelt the fire":* De Koven, vol. 2, p. 4.

204 *He courted the ladies:* JPJ to John de Neufville, Nov. 26, 1779, JPJP, LOC. In a letter to Edward Bancroft, JPJ wrote, "I have seen a 'fine lady' of this country which I came to Europe to espouse. She is really a fine woman. Yet I have seen a second sister equally belle who will soon fit for a man; and I should think I prefer this younger because one might prevent some little errors from taking root in her mind which this other seems to have contracted. It is a great pity that two such lovely lasses should be watched with so much jealousy; for they are not as comeatable here as they might be in France. I have left to me only Dr. Franklin's remedy, 'patience.'" Morison suggests Jones is a "coarse, cold-blooded" seducer here (p. 260), but Bradford notes that all this refers to ships, not women—Jones has been over to look at the *Indien,* the Amsterdam-built frigate he had long coveted, but now desired a ship still being built that might be closer to his specifications. See Bradford's note to JPJ to Edward Bancroft, Oct. 26, 1779, JPJP, LOC.

204 *Were I dear Maid "the King of Sea"*: JPJ to Charles Dumas, Jan. 16, 1780, JPJP, LOC.

205 *"the Virgin Muse has snatched"*: Dumas to JPJ, Mar. 2, 1780, JPJP, LOC.

205 *"The Virgin Muse had my Virgin Thanks"*: JPJ to Charles Dumas, Nov. 8, 1779; Dumas to JPJ, Nov. 3, 1779, JPJP, LOC.

205 *The two men encountered each other:* Memorial to Justify Peter Landais' Conduct in the Last War, pp. 45–47; JPJP, LOC. JPJ to Chaumont, Oct. 24, 1779, JPJP, LOC. Ben Franklin worried about this "mortal quarrel" but did not believe Landais intentionally fired into the *Bonhomme Richard*. Benjamin Franklin to Eastern Navy Board, Mar. 15, 1780, BFP, vol. 32, p. 107. Franklin wrote Sartine that a formal "enquiry" had served to head off a duel in Holland "which might have proved fatal to one or both of them." Benjamin Franklin to Sartine, Mar. 20, 1780, BFP, vol. 32, p. 141.

205 *According to Fanning:* Fanning's Narrative, p. 62. Schaeper doubts they dueled, says there is no other evidence. Schaeper, *John Paul Jones and the Battle off Flamborough Head*, p. 60. There is a letter to Jones from Phillippe Ricot, Oct. 23, 1779, JPJP, LOC. suggesting that Landais wished to duel: "Just at the time I was going to come aboard your ship, I was informed from ashore that Mr. Landais is there with the American Lieutenant Colonel and they insist that they want to speak with Mr. Cottineau. Since he is not in a state to be able to bear such a visit, I am going promptly to his side. Landais is a madman of whom much is to be feared, which is what I am hurrying to prevent."

205 *"Paul Jones frequents"*: London Gazetteer and New Daily Advertiser, Oct. 22, 1779, in Seitz, p. 113.

205 *The American agent:* Schaeper, *John Paul Jones and the Battle off Flamborough Head*, p. 77.

206 *"Their feeling is that"*: Charles Dumas to JPJ, Oct. 18, 1779, JPJP, LOC.

206 *"People employed cleaning"*: Logs of *Serapis-Alliance-Ariel*, Oct. 19, 22, 1779. Schaeper (*John Paul Jones and the Battle off Flamborough Head*, pp. 74–78) suggests Jones neglected the wounded. He quotes Cottineau (p. 85) that Jones "neglected the means of putting the wounded on land and gave no more attention to them than if they had been strangers." But see JPJ to John de Neufville & Son, Oct. 5, 1779, JPJP, LOC. ("As the necessary arrangement of my wounded and my prisoners require my attendance here at present I send this by post, but will follow it with M. Dumas, I hope tomorrow.")

207 *The prisoners schemed:* Dumas to Benjamin Franklin, Nov. 5, 1779, BFP, vol. 31, p. 35; JPJ to John de Neufville, Nov. 3, 1779, JPJP, LOC.

207 *The log shows entry:* Logs of *Serapis-Alliance-Ariel*, Oct. 5, 14, 26–Nov. 8, pp. 29–37.

207 *"The bread that has been"*: JPJ to La Vauguyon, Nov. 4, 1779, JPJP, LOC.

207 *But he was caught:* Gawalt, p. 42; JPJ to Benjamin Franklin, Oct. 11, 1779, BFP, vol. 30, p. 520 (arrest of Jones: see n. 5). For an excellent analysis, see Nordholt, pp. 70–91. For a sympathetic view of the French role, see Schaeper, *France and America in the Revolutionary Era*, pp. 255–56.

208 *In mid-November:* Logs of *Serapis-Alliance-Ariel*, Nov. 21, 1779, p. 41; Fanning's Narrative, p. 66.

208 *Under pressure from Sir Joseph:* JPJ to John de Neufville, Nov. 26, 1779, JPJP, LOC; Fanning's Narrative, p. 71.

208 *"They have done me the honor"*: JPJ to John Bondfield, Nov. 2, 1779, JPJP, LOC.

208 *"For God's sake"*: Minutes of Admiralty Board, Nov. 22, 1779, PRO/ADM 3-89; Lorenz, p. 347.

208 *a letter of marque:* JPJ to La Vauguyon, Dec. 13, 1779, JPJP, LOC.

209 *"dirty piece of parchment"*: JPJ to Benjamin Franklin, Dec. 13, 1779, JPJP, LOC.

209 *"I do not much fear"*: Ibid.

209 *"escape this Purgatory"*: JPJ to Charles Dumas, Dec. 27, 1779, JPJP, LOC.

209 The Alliance *was a fast ship:* Logs of *Serapis-Alliance-Ariel*, Dec. 25–30, 1779, pp. 48–49.

209 *"Our thirteen stripes"*: Fanning's Narrative, p. 73.

210 *The morning was very clear:* Narrative of John Kilby, p. 34. The log shows the weather was "windy and cloudy" but it confirms shaking out the reefs. Kilby recalled a chase by British ships, but the log makes no mention.

210 *At 9 A.M. the next morning:* Logs of *Serapis-Alliance-Ariel*, Dec. 29, 31, 1779, p. 50.

210 *"We have made our way"*: JPJ to Charles Dumas, Jan. 16, 1780, JPJP, LOC.

210 *"I have made my passage safe"*: JPJ to Benjamin Franklin, Jan. 16, 1780, BFP, vol. 31, pp. 388–89.

210 *Jones had such difficulty:* Logs of *Serapis-Alliance-Ariel*, Apr. 2, 1780, p. 78.

211 *In the fall, the sailors:* Fanning's Narrative, p. 76.

211 *Jones wanted the crew:* Narrative of John Kilby, p. 35.

211 *(Fanning remarked on the length:* Fanning's Narrative, p. 77.

211 *"All the people refused"*: Logs of *Serapis-Alliance-Ariel*, Jan. 19–20, 1780, p. 59.

211 *Fanning wrote that Jones:* Fanning's Narrative, p. 70.

211 *But the* Alliance's *first officer:* JPJ to Benjamin Franklin, Feb. 25, 1780, BFP, vol. 31, p. 525.

211 *A delegation confronted:* Narrative of John Kilby, p. 35.

212 *"stamped his foot"*: Fanning's Narrative, p. 79.

212 *"I am almost blind"*: JPJ to Gourlade & Moylan, Feb. 10, 1780, JPJP, LOC.

212 *"appeared much agitated"*: Fanning's Narrative, p. 80.

212 *"old man"*: JPJ to Alexander Smith, Nov. 2, 1779, JPJP, LOC.

212 *"It is very probable"*: JPJ to Thomas Scott, Dec. 3, 1779, JPJP, LOC.

212 *"So great is the respect"*: JPJ to John de Neufville, Nov. 26, 1779, JPJP, LOC.

213 *Benjamin Franklin was eager:* Benjamin Franklin to Marquis de Lafayette, Mar. 2, 1780, LP, vol. 2, p. 360.

213 *Jones was also asked:* Arthur Lee to JPJ, Feb. 20, 1780, JPJ to Lee, Feb. 28, 1790, JPJP, LOC.

213 *Before he left for America:* Morison, p. 358. Jones did get a month's pay for the men to ward of mutiny. See JPJ to Benjamin Franklin, Apr. 4, 1780, BFP, vol. 32, p. 213.

214 *Jones, in his paranoid way:* See, for example, JPJ to La Vauguyon, Mar. 28, 1780, JPJP, LOC. For the best sorting out of this complicated dispute, see Schaeper, *France and America in the Revolutionary Era*, pp. 269–82.

214 *"My mind is torn to pieces"*: JPJ to Edward Bancroft, Apr. 10, 1780, JPJP, LOC.

Chapter Eleven: "Caressed by All the World"

215 *Jones arrived at Passy:* Edward Bancroft to Benjamin Franklin, Apr. 17, 1780, BFP, vol. 32, p. 260.

216 *"received me coldly":* Gawalt, p. 47.

216 *But the next day:* Ibid.

216 *Louis XVI smiled blandly:* Lorenz, p. 392; Fanning's Narrative, p. 78.

216 *That fall, a ballet:* Fraser, p. 171.

216 *He went to the theater:* Michelle de Bonneuil to JPJ, May 10, 1780, JPJP, LOC.

216 *"Since the public":* De Bachaumont, *Memoires Secrets,* May 18, 1780, p. 180.

216 *On May 1, 1780:* Ibid., July 18, 1780, p. 250.

217 *Named after the nine muses:* Brands, p. 563.

217 *He was informed by the Prince:* Nassau-Siegen to JPJ, May 10, 1780, JPJP, LOC.

217 *Madame d'Ormay, the widow:* Montplaisir to JPJ, May 10, 1780; Madame La Présidente d'Ormay to JPJ, May 23, 1780, JPJP, LOC.

217 *"the ladies are practicing":* Madame La Présidente d'Ormay to JPJ, May 16, 1780, JPJP, LOC.

217 *Jones was formally honored:* Gawalt, p. 47; JPJ to Charles Dumas, Sep. 8, 1780, JPJP, LOC. He did not actually receive the sword until June when he was back at his ship. Sartine to JPJ, June 28, 1780, JPJP, LOC. Jones fished for these awards: "I should be happy to carry with me to the Congress of the United States such testimony of his Majesty's approbation as my conduct may be thought to have merited during my absence from the country." JPJ to Benjamin Frankin, Apr. 20, 1780 (BF forwarded to Vergennes), BFP, vol. 32, p. 274.

218 *Such recognition was occasion:* Morison, "The Arms and Seals of John Paul Jones," *American Neptune,* Oct. 1958, vol. XVIII, no. 4.

218 *The brethren of the Nine:* Ibid.

218 *"I have never met so modest":* Lorenz, p. 399.

218 *The Marshal Duc de Biron:* De Bachaumont, May 20, 1780, p. 181.

219 *Insulted freedom bled: London General Advertiser and Morning Intelligencer,* Sep. 7, 1780, in Seitz, p. 159.

219 *"This brave corsair":* De Koven, vol. 2, p. 75.

219 *John Adams reported:* Joseph Ellis, *American Sphinx,* pp. 90–91.

220 *"regrets very much":* Madame de St. Julien to JPJ, May 17, 1780, JPJP, LOC.

220 *"It is quite a pity":* Madame de St. Julien to JPJ, May 28, 1780, JPJP, LOC.

220 *"The good Madam":* "Angelique" to JPJ, undated (May 1780), JPJP, LOC.

221 *The famous Paul Jones: London General Advertiser and Morning Intelligencer,* Sep. 7, 1780, in Seitz, p. 158.

221 *On June 1, the captain:* Benjamin Franklin to JPJ, June 1, 1780, BFP, vol. 32, p. 458.

221 *He had pressed Sartine:* JPJ to Sartine, May 25, May 30, 1780, JPJP, LOC.

221 *tried to interest the French government:* Gawalt, p. 50.

221 *But Jones was dilatory:* Jones may have felt that he did not have to rush back right away. He was able to free up some money to pay the crew's wages. "The people of the Alliance are very easy since the distribution you ordered of the cash." James Moylan to JPJ, May 3, 1780, JPJP, LOC.

221 *"Nothing short of my duty":* JPJ to Comtesse de Lowendahl, June 7, 1780, JPJP, LOC.

222 *Since my last, Paul Jones: London General Advertiser and Morning Intelligencer,* Sep. 7, 1780, in Seitz, p. 159.

223 *I am touched by the feelings:* Comtesse de Lowendahl to JPJ, undated (June 1780), JPJP, LOC.

223   *The Countess decided to put Jones:* Comtesse de Lowendahl to JPJ, undated (June 1780), JPJP, LOC.

223   *"I have carefully examined":* JPJ to Comtesse de Lowendahl, July 14, 1780, JPJP, LOC.

224   *She wrote him a final:* JPJ to Comtesse de Lowendahl, Sep. 21, 1780, JPJP, LOC.

224   *The Chevalier de Pontgibaud:* Robert B. Douglas, ed., *A French Volunteer of the War of Independence: Chevalier de Pontgibaud,* pp. 83–87.

225   *While Jones was emjoying:* Pierre Landais to James Degge, June 12, 1780, JPJP, LOC; Comte de Vergennes to Lafayette, Aug. 7, 1780, LP, vol. 3, p. 129; Gawalt, p. 51.

225   *As they bided their time:* Arthur Lee to JPJ, June 13, 1780, JPJP, LOC.

225   *This sea-lawyer's argument:* Morison, p. 294. Jonathan Williams, Franklin's nephew, described Lee as "an industrious genius . . . who . . . would disturb the tranquility of heaven." JW to Benjamin Franklin, June 14, 1780, BFP, vol. 32, p. 526.

225   *On May 31, seventeen officers:* Officers of the *Alliance* to Benjamin Franklin, May 31, 1780, BFP, vol. 32, p. 454.

225   *"that Captain Jones loved close fighting":* Benjamin Franklin to Officers of the *Alliance,* June 7, 1780, BFP, vol. 32, p. 491.

225   *"I see you are likely":* Benjamin Franklin to JPJ, June 12, 1780, BFP, vol. 32, p. 508.

226   *On the morning of June 12:* JPJ to Edmé Genet, June 8, 1780; JPJ to Jean Marie Thevenard, June 13, 1780, JPJP, LOC; Logs of *Serapis-Alliance-Ariel,* June 12, 1780, p. 89.

226   *Landais quickly culled:* Crew of the *Bonhomme Richard* to JPJ, June 21, 1780, JPJP, LOC.

226   *"Open your eyes"* Matthew Parke to JPJ, June 20, 1780, JPJP, LOC.

226   *Instead Jones headed back:* JPJ to Robert Morris, June 27, 1780, JPJP, LOC; JPJ to Benjamin Franklin, June 21, 1780, BFP, vol. 32, p. 565.

227   *"poised to hold the ship":* Steps Taken to Pevent the *Alliance* from Leaving Port, June 20, 1780, JPJP, LOC.

227   *Instead, he chose:* JPJ to President and Board of Admiralty, June 27, 1780, JPJP, LOC; Morison, pp. 297–98.

227   *"My humanity would not suffer":* JPJ to Robert Morris, June 27, 1780, JPJP, LOC.

227   *"I sent word surreptitiously":* Comte de Rochambeau to Lafayette, July 16, 1780, LP, vol. 3, p. 97.

227   *"I . . . confess it is":* Lafayette to George Washington, July 21, 1780, LP, vol. 3, p. 103.

227   *"acted rather like women than men":* JPJ to Edward Bancroft, June 27, 1780, JPJP, LOC.

228   *If you had stayed aboard:* Benjamin Franklin to JPJ, July 5, 1780, BFP, vol. 33, p. 28.

229   *"a plan for future":* JPJ to Sartine, July 28, 1780, JPJP, LOC.

229   *At the end of May:* Charlary to JPJ, May 15, 1780, JPJP, LOC.

229   *Delia arrived in L'Orient:* See letters from Delia (July–August 1780), JPJP, LOC.

229   *Delia's letters to Jones:* There are six undated letters from July to August and one dated August 22, 1780. No letters from Jones survive, but Bradford cites "Thus

when thy Warrior . . ." as a poem to Delia—and shows that it could be recycled for a woman on the other side of the Atlantic. JPJ Poems, JPJP, LOC.

231 *According to Fanning:* Fanning's Narrative, pp. 112–14.

231 *Undated, written in Latin:* JPJ poems, JPJP, LOC.

232 *Sodomy in the navy:* Rodger, p. 227; Valle, p. 174; McKee, p. 438.

232 *"Though the Ariel":* JPJ to Edmé Genet, Aug. 9, 1780, JPJP, LOC.

232 *King Louis's ministers:* Vergennes to JPJ, Aug. 13, 1780; Maurepas to JPJ, Aug. 13, 1780, JPJP, LOC.

232 *"Had a grand entertainment":* Logs of *Serapis-Alliance-Ariel*, Sep. 2, 1780, p. 109.

233 *"Neither cash nor pains":* Fanning's Narrative, p. 99.

234 *"I have been detained":* JPJ to Edmé Genet, Sep. 21, 1780, JPJP, LOC.

234 *"that wicked and conceited upstart":* JPJ to William Carmichael, Aug. 22, 1780, JPJP, LOC.

234 *"that hairbrained [sic] man":* JPJ to Sartine, Sep. 22, 1780, JPJP, LOC.

234 *"As human nature is imperfect":* JPJ to Silas Deane, Sep. 21, 1780, JPJP, LOC.

234 *"my dearest friend":* JPJ to Edward Bancroft, Sep. 23, 1780, JPJP, LOC.

Chapter Twelve: "The Gale Still Increasing"

235 *At 2 P.M., on October 7:* There are three contemporaneous accounts and two memoirs. The most detailed and reliable record is Lieutenant Dale's report, Declaration of the Officers of the *Ariel*, Oct. 13, 1780, JPJP, LOC. Fanning's (written in 1805) is, as usual, the most vivid, marred by his usual small inaccuracies (about time of departure, wind direction, etc.). Fanning's Narrative, pp. 87–90. Jones gave his account in his memoir to Louis XVI, Gawalt, pp. 53–54, and the log is reasonably detailed about courses, weather, and sail changes. (Logs of *Serapis-Alliance-Ariel*, pp. 117–19—the logs are always one day ahead; the maritime day begins with the noon observation, twelve hours before the calendar day.) Wharton's report is Samual Wharton to Benjamin Franklin, Oct. 14, 1780, BFP, vol. 33, pp. 420–21. For conditions in the Bay of Biscay, I consulted maritime expert William Gilkerson; for the sounds of a sailing ship in a storm, Captain Richard Bailey of the *Rose*, a replica of a British frigate. ("The sound scares the hell out of me," said Bailey). Jones made a few more contemporaneous references: "Enclosed I send you a copy of the declaration of my officers [Dale's report] respecting the storm; but no language can describe the tremendous scene that contending elements then presented. You will have some idea of our danger by comparing the [latitude] and soundings with the chart." JPJ to Jonathan Williams, Nov. 20, 1780, JPJP, LOC.

241 *In the Great Storm of 1703:* Daniel Defoe, *The Storm*, p. 406.

243 *"The crew and passengers":* Morison, p. 306. ("The heavens have rightly desired to keep alive one of the most courageous defenders of freedom," Barbantane Hunolstein to JPJ, Nov. 14, 1780, JPJP, LOC.)

243 *"I will only add that the tempest":* JPJ to Edmé Genet, Oct. 13, 1780, JPJP, LOC.

243 *"I can give you no just idea":* JPJ to Madame La Présidente d'Ormay, Oct. 16, 1780, JPJP, LOC.

243 *"Pray, have you seen":* JPJ to Edward Bancroft, Oct. 17, 1780, JPJP, LOC.

244 *With the* Ariel *still:* Memorandum [enclosed in letter to Silas Deane, Nov. 1, 1780], c. Oct. 17, 1780; JPJ to Castries, Oct. 25, 1780; to Vauban, Oct. 27, 1780;

to Silas Deane, Nov. 1, 1780; Castries to JPJ, Nov. 6, 1780; Silas Deane to JPJ, Nov. 14, 1780, JPJP, LOC.

244   *"Everyone here thinks"*: William Nicolson to JPJ, Nov. 18, 1780, JPJP, LOC. ("My sister in law having set to work the nobility the most in credit at court to carry it through." He seems to be referring to his sister, Countess de Nicolson, not a sister-in-law.)

244   *"My friends tell me"*: JPJ to Robert Morris, Nov. 8, 1780, JPJP, LOC.

244   *Aggrieved, the lieutenant*: Fanning's Narrative, pp. 89–97; *London Gazetteer and New Daily Advertiser,* Dec. 1, 1780, in Seitz, p. 160.

245   *He slipped along*: Gawalt, pp. 55–56; Sands, pp. 300–302; JPJ to Edmé Genet, June 20, 1781, JPJP, LOC.

246   *A pair of British frigates*: Gawalt, p. 56.

246   *Philadelphia had been transformed*: Brands, p. 652.

247   *He was able to hire*: Pennsylvania Evening Post, Oct. 19, 1779, Dec. 22, 1779, Jan. 23, 1780.

247   *Jones always loved*: Gawalt, p. 56. "The Ariel frigate, commanded by the gallant John Paul Jones, fired a *feu de joie*, and was beautifully decorated with a variety of streamers in the day, and ornamented with a brilliant appearance of lights in the night." *Pennsylvania Evening Post,* Mar. 5, 1781.

247   *The* Ariel *delivered*: JPJ to John Brown, Mar. 13, 1781, JPJP, LOC.

247   *Still, even Jones's friends*: See Virginia Delegates to Thomas Jefferson, Dec. [12], 1780, James Madison to Edmund Pendleton, Dec. [12], 1780, *Letters of Delegates to Congress,* Paul Smith, ed., vol. 16, pp. 439–40.

247   *Almost a year earlier*: Vergennes to Lafayette, Aug. 7, 1780, LP, vol. 3, p. 129.

247   *When the* Alliance: Lafayette to Chevalier de Luzerne, Sep. 10, 1780, LP, vol. 3, p. 168.

247   *"All Paris runs"*: Ibid., p. 170.

247   *"How disappointed"*: Lafayette to George Washington, Feb. 23, 1781, LP, vol. 3, p. 340.

247   *Jones's rival had gone mad*: Richard Morris, "The Revolution's Caine Mutiny," *American Heritage,* June 1960, p. 11.

248   *On February 20*: Board of Admiralty to JPJ, Feb. 20, 1781, JPJP, LOC.

248   *Jones skillfully finessed*: JPJ to John Brown, Mar. 13, 1781, JPJP, LOC. See No. 34.

248   *In Congress's final report*: Report of the Board of Admiralty, Mar. 28, 1781, JPJP, LOC.

249   *"The Chevalier ever since"*: Nicholson to John Barry, June 24, 1781, in De Koven, vol. 2, pp. 211–14.

249   *All but two of the*: Gawalt, p. 58.

249   *In August he rented*: Lorenz, p. 488.

250   *Over 220 feet long*: Gilkerson, p. 64.

250   *"I have had her bottom opened"*: JPJ to John Barry, Sep. 7, 1781, JPJP, LOC.

250   *"there was neither wood, nor iron"*: Gawalt, p. 60.

250   *Jones immediately suspected*: JPJ to John Brown, Apr. 21, 1782, JPJP, LOC.

250   *"What has been done"*: JPJ to John Brown, Dec. 9, 1781, JPJP, LOC.

250   *An important exception*: Joseph Gura, *John Barry, Father of the American Navy,* pp. 174–84.

251   *"Coldness begets difference"*: Robert Morris to JPJ, Feb. 18, 1782, JPJP, LOC. See Robert Morris to John Langdon, Feb. 18, 1782, JPJP, LOC.

251 *Jones, who venerated Morris:* JPJ to John Brown, Apr. 21, 1782, JPJP, LOC.
251 *"bickering and uneasiness":* JPJ to Robert Morris, Feb. 25, Mar. 12, 1782, JPJP, LOC. See Robert Morris to JPJ, Mar. 26, 1782, JPJP, LOC.
251 *"I should have been with the fleet":* JPJ to Benjamin Franklin, Dec. 13, 1781, JPJP, LOC.
251 *"Your coming to the army":* Lafayette to JPJ, Dec. 22, 1781, JPJP, LOC.
252 *"my most lovely Delia":* JPJ to "Delia," Dec. 25, 1781, JPJP, LOC.
252 *"of medium height and square built":* Morison, p. 319.
252 *No longer the lithe:* Boudriot, *John Paul Jones and the Bonhomme Richard,* p. 98.
252 *"a good piece of linen":* JPJ to John Brown, Apr. 4, 1782, JPJP, LOC.
252 *"good hair powder":* JPJ to Hector McNeill, Mar. 21, 1782, JPJP, LOC.
252 *"I reached Portsmouth":* JPJ to John Brown, Mar. 25, 1782, JPJP, LOC.
252 *Just as he had aboard* Ariel: Gawalt, p. 61.
253 *"an affair of the heart":* JPJ to John Brown, Mar. 25, 1781, JPJP, LOC.
253 *"Your silence, I fear":* JPJ to John Brown, Sep. 7, 1782, JPJP, LOC.
253 *"It is all over":* John Brown to JPJ, Oct. 1, 1782, JPJP, LOC.
253 *"Will* America *ever be finished?":* JPJ to John Brown, Apr. 21, 1782, JPJP, LOC.
253 *Rumors reached him:* JPJ to John Langdon (Jan. 30, 1782); JPJ to Mesach Weare, June 11, 1782, JPJP, LOC.
253 *In August, a French ship:* JPJ to Gouverneur Morris, Sep. 2, 1782; Congressional Resolution, Sep. 3, 1782, JPJP, LOC.
253 *"It is a sacrifice I shall make with pleasure":* JPJ to Robert Morris, Sep. 22, 1782, JPJP, LOC.
253 *"voluntary contribution":* JPJ to Gouverneur Morris, July 19, 1782, JPJP, LOC.
254 *"The command of the America":* John Adams to JPJ, Aug. 12, 1782, JPJP, LOC.
255 *"if this war should continue":* JPJ to Robert Morris, Sep. 2, 1782, JPJP, LOC.
255 *He rented a phaeton:* Salary and Expense Account, 1781–1782, JPJP, LOC.
255 *Congress finally paid him:* Morison, p. 317.
255 *Incredibly, the* Indien: Gawalt, p. 64; JPJ to Edward Bancroft, Feb. 28, 1783; to Marquis de Castries, Feb. 28, 1782, JPJP, LOC. (*Indien* was renamed *South Carolina.*)
255 *With Congress's permission:* JPJ to Robert Morris, Nov. 29, 1782; Robert Morris to JPJ, Dec. 5, 1782, JPJP, LOC.
255 *Jones dashed back:* JPJ to Hector McNeill, June 11, 1783, JPJP, LOC.
255 *"there is now perhaps as much":* JPJ to Robert Morris (Oct. 3–4, 1783), JPJP, LOC.
256 *"I hoped to find myself":* Gawalt, p. 64.
256 *Jones was given a comfortable:* Ibid, pp. 64–65; JPJ to Robert Morris, Feb. 28, 1783, JPJP, LOC.
256 *"glorious and agreeable news":* JPJ to Hector McNeill, Apr. 26, 1783, JPJP, LOC.
256 *He sailed for America:* Robert Morris to JPJ, June 18, 1783; JPJ to Hector McNeill, July 18, 1783; JPJ to John Sherburne, Aug. 1, 1783; Samuel Wharton to JPJ, Aug. 18, 1783, JPJP, LOC.
256 *But he recovered:* "Capt. John Paul Jones at Bethlehem, Pa. 1783," *Pennsylvania Magazine of History and Biography,* vol. 34, p. 1915; De Koven, vol. 2, pp. 229–31.
257 *He was inducted into:* JPJ to Arthur St. Clair, Nov. 10, 1783, JPJP, LOC.
257 *On his membership:* Certificate of Membership in the Society of Cincinnati, Oct. 31, 1785, JPJP, LOC.

257   *"order of hereditary knights"*: Brands, p. 668.

257   *"I wish to establish myself"*: JPJ to John Ross, Mar. 16, 1783, JPJP, LOC.

257   *To Morris, he drafted:* JPJ to Robert Morris (Oct. 3–4, 1783), JPJP, LOC. See notation by James C. Bradford.

258   *On November 10, 1784:* Gawalt, p. 66.

258   *"Because this ship was very old"*: Ibid., p. 67. The sword now rests in Jones's crypt at Annapolis.

Chapter Thirteen: "Cover Him With Kisses"

259   *"everyone's favorite"*: Louis A. Norton, *Joshua Barney*, p. 96.

259   *Often, his companion:* Ibid., pp. 21 (*"shedding blood!"*), 37 (Nicholson), 47 (Barney's appearance), 95–97; Hulbert Footner, *Sailor of Fortune*, pp. 149–52. As captain of the thirty-two-gun frigate *Trumbull*, Nicholson did redeem himself somewhat in a single-ship action against a thirty-two-gun British letter of marque, the *Watt*, in 1780. Badly battered, the British ship withdrew.

260   *"After my return to America"*: Gawalt, p. 72.

260   *"the future of our marine"*: JPJ to Hector McNeill, Apr. 26, 1783, JPJP, LOC.

261   *"In such a situation"*: JPJ to John Brown, Apr. 21, 1782, JPJP, LOC.

261   *"British blood hounds"*: Footner, p. 152.

261   *After he had come and gone:* Lorenz, p. 515. The British papers would later report rumors that Jones was in London: "The famous Paul Jones is likewise in this metropolis and often parades on the public walks." *London Times*, Mar. 3, 1786.

261   *On December 20:* Gawalt, p. 67.

262   *"that illustrious and learned society"*: JPJ to Edward Bancroft, Feb. 28, 1783, JPJP, LOC.

262   *But he no longer:* JPJ to Joshua Barney, Dec. 16, 1783, JPJP, LOC.

262   *The Hôtel de Valentinois:* JPJ to Castries, Feb. 18, 1784, JPJP, LOC.

262   *Even Franklin was cool:* Morison, p. 338. See, for example, JPJ to Franklin, Mar. 25, 1784, JPJP, LOC.

262   *"difficult and disagreeable"*: JPJ to Thomas Jefferson, July 29, 1785, TJP, vol. 8, p. 326.

262   *The French had sold:* Gawalt, pp. 67–72; JPJ to Castries, Feb. 1, 1784; Prize Money Apportionment, Feb. 10, 1784; JPJ to Franklin, Mar. 4, 1784; JPJ to Castries, Apr. 13, 1784 (Invalides, care of prisoners); JPJ to Robert Morris, Dec. 17, 1784; Prize Money Receipt, Aug. 18, 1785, JPJP, LOC.

262   *While he dickered:* Lorenz, p. 534; Morison, pp. 341–43.

263   *He warned—correctly:* JPJ to John Jay, Aug. 6, 1785, July 18, 1787, JPJP, LOC; JPJ to Thomas Jefferson, July 31, 1785, TJP, vol. 8, p. 334. The British press, which tracked the Pirate Jones closely, picked up reports that Jones would lead a fleet against the Algerines. *London Times*, Nov. 4, Dec. 28, 1785, Feb. 12, 1788.

263   *At the end of 1784:* JPJ to Selkirk, Feb. 12, 1784; JPJ to Countess of Selkirk, Nov. 8, 1784; Selkirk to JPJ, Aug. 4, 1785, JPJP, LOC.

264   *"Is it possible that you are then"*: Delia to JPJ (Dec. 1783), JPJP, LOC.

264   *Her real name was Townsend:* JPJ to Thomas Jefferson, Sep. 4, 1787, JPJP, LOC; Morison, pp. 343–45.

264   *"cover him all over with kisses"* JPJ to Mme. T——, Sep. 4, 1787, JPJP, LOC.

264   *In 1786, Jones presented:* JPJ to Louis XVI, Jan. 1, 1786, JPJP, LOC; Lorenz, p. 542 (wishes to become French admiral).

265   *He had copies made of Houdon's:* JPJ to John Jay, Feb. 8, 1787; JPJ to George Washington, July 25, 1787, JPJP, LOC.

265   *"They are not merchandise":* JPJ to Robert Morris (April/May? 1787), JPJP, LOC.

265   *"and shall place it with my own":* George Washington to JPJ, Sep. 2, 1787, JPJP, LOC.

265   *He had an unpleasant encounter:* See, note, Jones–Pierre Landais Exchange, Oct. 29–31; JPJ "To the Public," Oct. 29, 1787; Landais, "To the Impartial Public," Oct. 31, 1787; James Milligan Statement, Oct. 31, 1787, JPJP, LOC.

266   *He declined to sail:* JPJ to Thomas Jefferson, Oct. 24, 1787, JPJP, LOC.

266   *In spite of, or perhaps because:* Journal of the Campaign of the Liman, p. 5, JPJP, LOC.

266   *"I would have waited on you":* JPJ to Thomas Jefferson, Dec. 19, 1787, JPJP, LOC.

266   *He had already drafted:* JPJ to Thomas Jefferson, Oct. 24, 1787; Thomas Jefferson to Madame Townsend, Oct. 15, Nov. 7, 1787 ("infinitely distressed"); Madame Townsend to Thomas Jefferson, Oct. 13, 1787, TJP, vol. 12, pp. 243, 331, 357.

267   *Catherine, the Tsarina:* Journal of the Campaign of the Liman, pp. 5–7, JPJP, LOC.

267   *But Jefferson shrewdly:* Thomas Jefferson to Edward Carrington, May 27, 1788, TJP, vol. 13, p. 209.

267   *"Mr Jefferson, who knows":* Simolin to Count Besborodko, Jan. 23/Feb. 3, 1788, F. A. Golder, *John Paul Jones in Russia*, p. 149. The Russian (Julian) calendar was eleven days earlier than the Gregorian calendar, used by the rest of Europe. I have used the Russian dates in the narrative.

268   *From Denmark, where he dined:* JPJ to Thomas Jefferson, Mar. 11, 1788, TJP, vol. 12, p. 659.

268   *He was honest:* JPJ to Krudener, Mar. 13, 1788, JPJP, LOC.

269   *"My sufferings":* JPJ to Thomas Jefferson, Apr. 8, 1788, TJP, vol. 13, p. 44.

269   *"At Stockholm I stayed":* Journal of the Campaign of the Liman, p. 8, JPJP, LOC.

269   *Jones hired some Swedish:* Ibid., pp. 8–10.

271   *Russia's magnificent gateway:* Simon Montefiore, *Prince of Princes*, pp. 327–28.

271   *Her territorial ambitions:* Lorenz, *The Admiral and the Empress*, pp. 35–42.

272   *In 1786, Catherine had made:* The legend of the Potemkin villages is probably an exaggeration. See Montefiore, pp. 364, 380–81.

272   *"He is, in the opinion":* Simolin to Count Besborodko, Jan. 23/Feb. 3, 1788, Golder, p. 149.

272   *"He will get to Constantinople!":* Golder, p. 38.

272   *"I shall never be able":* JPJ to Segur (May 18–20), 1788, JPJP, LOC.

272   *"I presented the Empress":* JPJ to Lafayette [and Thomas Jefferson], June 15, 1788, JPJP, LOC.

273   *"I can never renounce":* JPJ to Thomas Jefferson, Apr. 8, 1788, TJP, vol. 13, p. 45.

273   *"Her majesty gave me":* Journal of the Campaign of the Liman, p. 10, JPJP, LOC.

273   *The Empress invited Jones:* Montefiore, pp. 317–19.

273   *"If this war continues":* John Alexander, *Catherine the Great*, p. 132.

273 *"but I was detained"*: JPJ to Lafayette [and Thomas Jefferson], June 15, 1788, JPJP, LOC.

273 *Catherine gave him a generous:* Statement of Salary and Expenses, Journal of the Campaign of the Liman, annex, JPJP, LOC.

273 *"He has made a good impression"*: Golder, p. 40. The British officers all theatened to resign. Christopher Lloyd, ed., *A Memoir of James Trevenen*, p. 122. The British papers closely tracked Jones in Russia. "Paul Jones (who is not blind, nor retired, as some papers announced) has likewise entered the Russian service." *London Times*, Apr. 24, 1788. See also *London Times*, Apr. 17, May 1, May 19, June 3, 11, 12, 19, 25, July 3, 9, 10 (reporting that the Dey of Algiers had put a bounty on Jones's head), 12, Aug. 6, 1788.

274 *"This was a cruel grief"*: JPJ to Lafayette [and Thomas Jefferson], June 15, 1788, JPJP, LOC.

274 *"I saw him today"*: Golder, p. 40.

274 *"This man is extremely capable"*: Catherine to Potemkin, Feb. 13, 1788, in V. S. Lopatin, ed., Catherine II and G. A. Potemkin: Personal Correspondence, 1769–1791, p. 268.

274 *Potemkin was a monster:* Lorenz, *The Admiral and the Empress*, pp. 45–46; Montefiore, *passim*.

275 *"You would be charmed"*: JPJ to Lafayette [and Thomas Jefferson], June 15, 1788, JPJP, LOC.

275 *"did not affect to disguise his displeasure"*: Journal of the Campaign of the Liman, p. 12, JPJP, LOC.

275 *"to draw them into a cabal"*: Ibid., p. 13.

275 *"to give time to those angry"*: Ibid., p. 14. Alexiano threatened to Potemkin to quit. Lopatin, pp. 823–24.

276 *Jones had under his command:* Ibid., p. 18. A Russian account states that Jones had two ships of the line, four frigates, and eight smaller craft. IU.L. Korshunov, Kogda okean soediniaet: iz istorii druzhestuennykh otuoshenii flotov Russii i SSLA, p. 28.

277 *Handsome, in a rakish:* Montefiore, p. 352; Lorenz, *The Admiral and the Empress*, p. 51.

277 *"Strange that you have taken"*: Ibid. "Prince Nassan arrived three days ago. Filled with zeal to serve. Asks relentlessly for the most dangerous commission that presents itself. Potemkin to Catherine, Feb. 15, 1788, in Lopatin, pp. 268–69.

277 *"Almost a sailor"*: Lorenz, *The Admiral and the Empress*, p. 53.

277 *"Although my undertaking"*: Golder, p. 44.

278 *"You know my esteem"*: Nassau-Siegen to JPJ, May 28, 1788, JPJP, LOC.

278 *"that if we gained"*: Journal of the Campaign of the Liman, p. 14, JPJP, LOC.

Chapter Fourteen: "Conquer or Die"

279 *Known as the Capitan Pasha:* Montefiore, p. 399. A Russian account states that the Turkish fleet consisted of ten line-of-battle ships, six frigates, forty-seven galleys, and many smaller vessels. Korshunow, p. 22.

279 *Marshaling his far smaller:* JPJ to Potemkin, May 30, 1788; JPJ to Nassau-Siegen, June 1, 1788, JPJP, LOC; Golder, pp. 47–48.

280 *"The Prince . . . talked"*: Journal of the Campaign of the Liman, p. 16, JPJP, LOC.

280 *"We must be determined"*: Speech to Council of War, June 4, 1788, JPJP, LOC.

280 *Jones repeatedly asked:* JPJ to Don José de Ribas, June 1, 1788, JPJP, LOC.

280 *The Prince set out shortly:* JPJ to Potemkin, June 6, 1778 (Jones was diplomatic, in his way: "The Turks have fired on him from a distance, but he had the prudence not to reply"), JPJP, LOC.

281 *"better than a ball"*: Montefiore, p. 400.

281 *At 8 A.M., the admiral:* JPJ to Potemkin, June 7, 1788, JPJP, LOC.

281 *Accompanied by a translator:* Journal of the Campaign of the Liman, p. 21, JPJP, LOC.

281 *"like a frantic man"*: Ibid., p. 20.

281 *Jones wanted to catch the Turks:* Ibid., pp. 21–24; JPJ to Potemkin, June 7, 8, 1788, JPJP, LOC; Ian Christie, *The Benthams in Russia, 1780–1791*, pp. 220–22; Ian Christie, "Samuel Bentham and the Russian Dnieper Flotilla, 1787–1789," *Slavonic and East European Review*, Apr. 1972, pp. 187–88. See Lorenz, *The Admiral and the Empress*, pp. 66–72; De Koven, vol. 2, pp. 330–31. There is no good single description of the battle, and accounts vary. I have relied mostly on Jones's contemporaneous accounts in his dispatches to Potemkin and letters to friends. Jones's Journal was probably colored by his later anger.

282 *"I do not think Captain Pasha"*: JPJ to Potemkin, June 7, 1788, JPJP, LOC.

282 *A Te Deum:* JPJ to Potemkin, June 8, 1788, JPJP, LOC.

282 *"We should always make but one!"*: JPJ to Lewis Littlepage, June 11, 1788, JPJP, LOC.

282 *"The Prince conducted himself"*: JPJ to Potemkin, June 7, 1788, JPJP, LOC.

283 *"Nassau was the real hero"*: Golder, p. 53. Potemkin gave much credit to Alexiano in his correspondence with Catherine. Far from picturing Alexiano as a coward, he wrote that the Greek captain was merely upset that Jones was given the command Alexiano had coveted. Potemkin to Catherine, June 14, 1788, in Lopatin, pp. 292–94.

283 *"Paul Jones has changed"*: Lorenz, *The Admiral and the Empress*, p. 68.

283 *"He is too jealous"*: JPJ to Lewis Littlepage, June 11, 1788, JPJP, LOC.

283 *"My situation here is very delicate"*: JPJ to Don José de Ribas, May 31, 1788, JPJP, LOC.

284 *"seems to wish me to go to the devil,"* JPJ to Ribas, June 11, 1788, JPJP, LOC.

284 *"I can assure you"*: JPJ to Potemkin, June 11, 1788, JPJP, LOC.

285 *"We will gain more honor"*: JPJ to Nassau-Siegen, June 14, 1788, JPJP, LOC.

285 *The attack came on the morning:* JPJ to Potemkin, June 17, 18, 20, 1788; JPJ to Lewis Littlepage, June 20, 1788; JPJ to Admiralty of the Black Sea at Kherson, June 21, 1788; JPJ to Don José de Ribas, Aug. 1, 1788, JPJP, LOC; Journal of the Campaign of the Liman, pp. 24–30; JPJP, LOC Christie, *The Benthams in Russia*, pp. 224–27; Christie, "Samuel Bentham," pp. 188–94 ("as much discipline as a London mob"). Again, there is no solid, dispassionate history of this battle. The Bentham account is more generous to Nassau-Siegen than Jones's version.

287 *"I see in your eyes"*: Speech to Squadron Commanders, June 16, 1788, JPJP, LOC.

289 *An old Russian sailor:* De Koven, vol. 2, pp. 323–25; Morison, p. 377. Morison puts the mission on the night of July 16, but it appears from Jones's journal that it occurred on the night of July 17. Journal of the Campaign of the Liman, p. 31, JPJP, LOC.

291 *Impulsive for glory:* JPJ to Lewis Littlepage, June 20, 1788, JPJP, LOC. A Russian account states that JPJ was ordered to destroy the ships on the sandbar by Gen. Suvorov, Potemkin's field commander. Korshunov, p. 22, citing Russian naval documents.

292 *He had suggested:* Journal of the Campaign of the Liman, p. 34, JPJP, LOC; JPJ to Don José de Ribas, Aug. 1, 1788, JPJP, LOC.

292 *"Our victory is complete":* Lorenz, *The Admiral and the Empress,* p. 80.

293 *"I've gone mad":* Montefiore, p. 402; Golder, pp. 57–58.

293 *Nassau-Siegen was awarded:* Journal of the Campaign of the Liman, p. 41, JPJP, LOC.

293 *"I regret that":* Catherine to Potemkin, June 25, 1788 in Lopatin, pp. 297–98.

293 *At 1 A.M. on July 1:* JPJ to Potemkin, July 6, 1788, July 24, 1790; Lewis Littlepage to Branizsky, Sep. 3, 1788, JPJP, LOC; Journal of the Campaign of the Liman, pp. 35–39, JPJP, LOC.

295 *Potemkin wrote Jones that:* Lewis Littlepage to JPJ, Sep. 15, 1788; certificate of Bibicov, Oct. 26, 1788; JPJ to Potemkin, Oct. 11, 12, 14, 16, 18, 1788; Potemkin to JPJ, Oct. 11, 1788; Potemkin to JPJ, Oct. 13, 1788, JPJP, LOC ("Hold yourself in readiness to receive him [Pasha] *courageously and drive him back*" Jones wrote at the bottom, "A warrior *is always ready,* and I had not come there as an apprentice." Then when Potemkin wrote him again to be "courageous," Jones wrote at the bottom, "It will be hard to believe that Prince Potemkin addressed such words to John Paul Jones.")

296 *"I spoke very freely":* Journal of the Campaign of the Liman, p. 92, JPJP, LOC.

296 *"Not even the Empress!":* Note by JPJ on bottom of page, JPJ to Potemkin, Oct. 20, 1788, JPJP, LOC.

296 *As a fig leaf:* JPJ to Potemkin, Oct. 25, 1788, JPJP, LOC.

296 *"sleepy":* Potemkin to Catherine, Oct. 18, 1788, in De Koven, vol. 2, pp. 344–45. Potemkin also wrote Catherine that Jones had a "black soul." Potemkin to Catherine, Oct. 17, 1788, in Lopatin, pp. 320–22.

296 *Traveling in an open gallery:* Journal of the Campaign of the Liman, p. 95, JPJP, LOC.

296 *He was still suffering:* Ibid., p. 96.

296 *Taking an apartment:* JPJ to Ivan Osterman, Jan. 31, 1789, JPJP, LOC.

297 *He wrote Thomas Jefferson:* JPJ to Thomas Jefferson, Jan. 20, 1789, JPJP, LOC.

297 *By Jefferson's return post:* JPJ to Krudener, Dec. 20, 1789, JPJP, LOC.

297 *A ten-year-old German girl:* The police charge from April 6, 1789, and the witness accounts are under "Russian Scandal" in the Judicial Proceedings section of JPJP, LOC.

298 *He hired a lawyer:* JPJ to Potemkin, Apr. 13, 1789, JPJ to Catherine, May 17, 1789, JPJP, LOC.

298 *The Comte de Segur:* De Koven, vol. 2, p. 351 (quoting from Segur's "Memoirs").

298 *Segur pleaded with him:* Count Segur to Count Montmorin, July 21, 1789, with enclosures, JPJP, LOC.

298 *Jones himself probably:* JPJ to Mr. Rileef, Apr. 2, 1789, JPJP, LOC. See Morison, p. 388, for French usage.

298 *"I love women":* JPJ to Potemkin, Apr. 13, 1789, JPJP, LOC.

299 *"nasty":* Catherine to Grimm, Mar. 1791, in De Koven, vol. 2, p. 360.

299 *Hoping against hope:* JPJ to Bezborodko, June 6, 1789, JPJP, LOC.

299 *The kontradmiral was put:* JPJ to Bezborodko, June 14, 1789, JPJP, LOC.

299 "bon voyage": Jones note, June 26, on letter to Bezborodko, June 13, 1789, JPJP, LOC.

Chapter Fifteen: "The Ghost of Himself"

300 *He toyed with the idea:* JPJ to Bourgoing, Dec. 29, 1789, JPJP, LOC; Gouverneur Morris, *Diary of the French Revolution,* Mar. 8, 1790, vol. 1, p. 443.

300 *"mortifications":* JPJ to Catherine, Sep. 25, 1789, JPJP, LOC.

300 *He proposed new schemes:* JPJ to Simolin, May 21, 1790, JPJP, LOC.

300 *He continued to send his bust:* JPJ to William Short, Dec. 10, 1789; JPJ to John Adams, Dec. 20, 1789; JPJ to Gouverneur Morris, Dec. 21, 1789, JPJP, LOC.

300 *"dark Asiatic intrigue":* JPJ to George Washington, Dec. 20, 1789, JPJP, LOC.

300 *He contemplated, in several:* JPJ to Charles Thomson, Dec. 20, 1789; JPJ to John Ross, Dec. 27, 1789, JPJP, LOC.

300 *He still longed to command:* JPJ to Thomas Jefferson, Mar. 20, 1791, JPJP, LOC.

301 *When he arrived in England:* JPJ to Madame d'Altigny, Dec. 27, 1790, JPJP, LOC; Morris, *Diary of the French Revolution,* May 3, 1790, vol. 1, p. 502.

301 *(He had traveled to England:* JPJ to John Ross, Dec. 27, 1789; JPJ to Edward Bancroft, Apr. 30, 1792, JPJP, LOC.

301 *"pay court to some":* JPJ to John Parish, Dec. 29, 1789, JPJP, LOC.

301 *Many of the nobles:* William Short to JPJ, Mar. 7, 1790, JPJP, LOC.

301 *"alarmed":* JPJ to Mme. d'Altigny, Dec. 27, 1790, JPJP, LOC.

301 *Jones sent him some Russian:* JPJ to Marquis de Lafayette, Dec. 7, 1791, JPJP, LOC.

301 *"the house was full":* Morris, *Diary of the French Revolution,* Mar. 7, 1790, vol. 1, p. 442.

301 *At one dinner party:* Ibid., Apr. 20, 1791, vol. 2, p. 166; Lord Daer to Lord Silkirk, Apr. 20, 1791, in De Koven, vol. 1, p. 325.

302 *"In faded naval uniform":* Morison, p. 395.

302 *Morris, a lawyer:* Morris, *Diary of the French Revolution,* vol. 2, pp. 59, 61, 64, 113.

303 *"I await the orders":* JPJ to Catherine, Feb. 25, 1791, JPJP, LOC.

303 *He proposed leading:* JPJ to Grimm, July 9, 1791, JPJP, LOC.

303 *"India is a long way":* Catherine to Grimm, Sep. 2, 1791, in Golder, p. 217.

303 *"I think I have nothing":* Catherine to Grimm, Sep. 1, 1791, in Golder, p. 217.

303 *"digest the nauseous draft of life":* JPJ to Mesdames La Grande & Rinsby, Feb. 25, 1791, JPJP, LOC.

304 *He wrote his sister:* JPJ to Janet Taylor, March 26, 1790, and undated (three months before death), JPJP, LOC.

304 *"Teach me to feel":* JPJ to Janet Taylor, Dec. 27, 1790, JPJP, LOC.

305 *Jones was sick:* JPJ to St. Legere, June 23, 1790; JPJ to Gouverneur Morris, June 24, 1790, JPJP, LOC.

305 *"A Message from Paul":* Morris, *Diary of the French Revolution,* July 18, 1792, vol. 2, p. 468.

305 *Jones was facedown:* Colonel Blackden to Janet Taylor, Aug. 8, 1792, in De Koven, vol. 2, p. 410; John Paul Jones, Commemoration at Annapolis, pp. 69–71, 87–92.

305 *For years, Jones had been:* JPJ to William Carmichael, Feb. 28, 1791, to Thomas Jefferson, Mar. 20, 1791, JPJP, LOC.

306 *Remembering Jones and his deep:* Thomas Jefferson to JPJ, June 1, 1792, JPJP, LOC.

306 *The American minister:* Gouverneur Morris to Robert Morris, May 26, 1793, in Morris, *Diary of the French Revolution,* vol. 2, p. 469; De Koven, vol. 2, pp. 417–18.

306 (*Morris, a bit guilty:* Morris, *Diary of the French Revolution,* July 20, 1792, vol. 2, p. 471.

306 *"This Paul Jones was":* Catherine to Grimm, Aug. 15, 1792, in Golder, p. 220.

306 *"The man possessed the mind":* London Times, July 28, 1792.

307 *"detested the French":* Morris, *Diary of the French Revolution,* July 5, 1791, vol 2, p. 213.

307 *"fifteen years among":* Journal of the Campaign of the Liman, p. 102, JPJP, LOC.

Epilogue: "Envy of the World"

309 *The academy was not established:* "On board I would have a little academy where the officers should be taught the principles of mathematics and mechanics, when off duty. When in port, the young officers should be obliged to attend at the academies established at each dockyard, where they should be taught the principles of every art and science that is necessary to form the character of a great sea officer." JPJ to Robert Morris, Oct. 3–4, 1783, JPJP, LOC.

309 *"do the best we can":* Morison, p. 429.

310 *They were imagined:* See L. H. Bolander, "Two Notes on John Paul Jones," *U.S. Naval Institute Proceedings,* July 1928, pp. 546–48.

310 *"gentleman of liberal education":* Reef Points, p. 2. Inaccurately, *Reef Points* credits "a composite letter of John Paul Jones' phrases and clauses compiled by Augustus C. Buell." Jones did write, "None other than a Gentleman, as well as a Seaman, both in theory and in practice, is qualified to support the character of a commission officer in the navy, nor is any man fit to command a ship of war, who is not also capable of communicating his ideas on paper in language that becomes his rank." JPJ to Marine Board, Jan. 21, 1777, JPJP, LOC.

310 *He was the first to suggest:* Bradford, "John Paul Jones," p. 40.

BIBLIOGRAPHY

Manuscript Collections

Admiralty Records, Public Record Office, Kew Gardens, England
Papers of King George III, Public Record Office, Kew Gardens, England
Peter Force Papers, Library of Congress, Washington, D.C.
F. A. Golder Papers, Library of Congress, Washington, D.C.
John Paul Jones Papers, Library of Congress, Washington, D.C.

Books

Adair, Douglass. *Fame and the Founding Fathers*. Indianapolis: Liberty Fund, 1974.
Adams, Charles Francis. *Letters of Mrs. Adams*. Boston: Little Brown, 1840.
Adams, John. *Diary and Autobiography of John Adams*. vols. II, IV. L. H. Butterfield, ed. Cambridge, Massachusetts: Belknap Press, 1961.
Adams Family Correspondence. vols. II, III, and VI. L. H. Butterfield and Richard Alan Ryerson, eds. Cambridge, Massachusetts: Belknap, 1963 and 1993.
Addison, Joseph. *The Works of Joseph Addison*. New York: Harper and Brothers, 1845.
Alexander, John T. *Catherine the Great*. New York: Oxford, 1989.
Alsop, Susan Mary. *Yankees at the Court: The First Americans in Paris*. Garden City, New York: Doubleday, 1982.
Bangs, Edward, ed. *Journal of Lieutenant Isaac Bangs*. Cambridge, Massachusetts: John Wilson and Son.
Banning, Lance. *The Jeffersonian Persuasion: Evolution of a Party Ideology*. Ithaca, New York: Cornell University Press, 1978.
Barnes, John S., ed. *The Logs of the* Serapis, Alliance *and* Ariel. New York: Naval History Society, 1896.
Black, Jeremy. *The Grand Tour in the Eighteenth Century*. New York: St. Martin's, 1992.
Boudriot, Jean. *John Paul Jones and the* Bonhomme Richard. Annapolis: Naval Institute Press, 1987.
———. *The Seventy-Four Gun Ship*. vol. II. Annapolis: Naval Institute Press, 1986.
Brands, H. W. *The First American: The Life and Times of Benjamin Franklin*. New York: Doubleday, 2000.
Bridenbaugh, Carl. *Cities in Revolt: Urban Life in America, 1743–1776*. New York: Knopf, 1955.
Buell, C. Augustus. *Paul Jones*. New York: Scribner's, 1900.

Bullock, Steven C. *Revolutionary Brotherhood.* Chapel Hill: University of North Carolina Press, 1996.

Butterfield, L. H., ed. *Diary and Autobiography of John Adams.* vols. II, III, and IV. Cambridge, Massachusetts: Belknap Press, 1961.

Campbell, Norine Dickson. *Patrick Henry: Patriot and Statesman.* New York: Devin-Adair, 1969.

Catherine II and G. A. Potemkin: Personal Correspondence, 1769–1791. V. S. Lopatin, ed. Moscow: Nauka, 1997.

Chapelle, Howard I. *The History of the American Sailing Navy.* New York: Bonanza, 1949.

Christie, Ian R. *The Bethams in Russia, 1780–1791.* Oxford: Berg, 1993.

Claudy, Carl H. *Introduction to Freemasonry.* Washington, D.C.: Temple Publishers, 1957.

Coggins, Jack. *Ships and Seamen of the American Revolution.* Harrisburg, Pennsylvania: Stackpole, 1969.

Cordingly, David. *Women Sailors and Sailors' Women: An Untold Maritime History.* New York: Random House, 2001.

Darter, Oscar H. *Colonial Fredericksburg and Neighborhood in Perspective.*
———. *Historic Fredericksburg.* New York: Bookman, 1957.

De Bachaumont, Louis Petit de. *Memoires Secrets.* Farnborough, Hants: Gregg Federation, 1970.

DeFoe, Daniel. *The Storm.* London: G. Sawbridge, 1704.

De Gategno, Paul J. *James Macpherson.* Boston: G.K. Hall, 1989.

De Koven, Mrs. Reginald. *The Life and Letters of John Paul Jones.* vols. I and II. New York: Scribner's, 1930.

Duffy, Christopher. *The Military Experience in the Age of Reason, 1715–1789.* New York: Barnes & Noble, 1987.

Dull, Jonathan. *A Diplomatic History of the American Revolution.* New Haven: Yale University Press, 1985.

Ellis, Joseph J. *American Sphinx: The Character of Thomas Jefferson.* New York: Knopf, 1998.

Embrey, Alvin J. *History of Fredericksburg.* Richmond: Old Dominion Press, 1937.

English, Frederick. *General Hugh Mercer.* Lawrenceville, New Jersey: Princeton Academic Press, 1975.

Fanning, Nathaniel. *Fanning's Narrative: Being the Memoirs of Nathaniel Fanning An Officer of the Revolutionary Navy, 1778–1783.* John S. Barnes, ed. New York: Naval History Society, 1912.

Fehrenbach, T. R. *Greatness to Spare.* Princeton: D. Van Nostrand, 1968.

Felder, Paula S. *Fielding Lewis and the Washington Family: A Chronicle of Eighteenth Century Fredericksburg.* Fredericksburg, Virginia: American History Company, 1998.

Flexner, James Thomas. *George Washington: The Forge of Experience.* Boston: Little Brown, 1965.

Footner, Hulbert. *Sailor of Fortune: The Life and Adventures of Commodore Barney, USN.* Annapolis: Naval Institute Press, 1940.

Forbes, Esther. *Paul Revere and the World He Lived In.* Boston: Houghton Mifflin, 1942.

Foreman, Amanda. *Georgiana: Duchess of Devonshire.* New York: Modern Library, 1998.

Fowler, William M. Jr., *Rebels Under Sail: The American Navy During the Revolution.* New York: Scribner's, 1976.

Franklin, Benjamin. *Papers of Benjamin Franklin.* vols. 25, 29–33. William B. Wilcox and Barbara B. Oberg, eds. New Haven: Yale University Press, 1986, 1992–97.

Fraser, Antonia. *Marie Antoinette*. New York: Nan. A Talese, 2001.

Fraser, Sir William. *The Book of Caerlaverock: Memoirs of the Maxwells, Earls of Nithsdal, Lords Maxwell and Herries*. vols. I and II. Edinburgh: Privately printed, 1873.

Freeman, Joanne B. *Affairs of Honor*. New Haven: Yale University Press, 2001.

Gawalt, Gerard W., ed. *John Paul Jones' Memoir of the American Revolution Presented to King Louis XVI of France*. Washington, D.C.: Library of Congress, 1979.

Gilkerson, William. *The Ships of John Paul Jones*. Annapolis: Naval Institute Press, 1987.

Golder, F. A. *John Paul Jones in Russia*. Garden City, New York: Doubleday, 1927.

Goodrich, Reverend Charles A. *Lives of the Signers of the Declaration of Independence*. Hartford: H. E. Robins, 1848.

Goolrick, John T. *Historic Fredericksburg*. Richmond, Virginia: Whittet & Shepperson, 1922.

Goss, Elbridge Henry. *The Life of Colonel Paul Revere*. vol. II. Boston: Howard W. Spurr, 1912.

Green, Ezra. *Diary of Ezra Green, M.D.* George Henry Preble and Walter C. Green, eds. Boston: 1875.

Gurn, Joseph. *John Barry: Father of the American Navy*. New York. P. J. Kennedy and Sons, 1933.

Hale, Edward E., and Edward E. Jr. *Franklin in France*. Boston: Roberts Brothers, 1887.

Hamilton, Alexander. *Papers of Alexander Hamilton*. vol. I. Harold C. Syrett, ed. New York: Columbia University Press, 1961.

Hamilton, Frederick, and Earl Taylor. *The Grand Lodge of Massachusetts, 1733–1933*. Boston: Grand Lodge of Masons in Massachusetts, 1945.

Hart, Roger. *English Life in the Eighteenth Century*. New York: G. P. Putnam's Sons, 1970.

Harvey, Robert. *Cochrane: The Life and Exploits of a Fighting Captain*. New York: Carroll & Graf, 2000.

Hibbert, Christopher. *The Days of the French Revolution*. New York: Morrow Quill, 1981.

Hunt, John Dixon, and Peter Willis, eds. *The Genius of the Place: The English Landscape Garden 1620–1820*. Cambridge, Massachusetts: MIT Press, 1997.

Hyams, Edward. *Capability Brown and Humphrey Repton*. New York: Scribner's, 1971.

Ireland, Bernard. *Naval Warfare in the Age of Sail: War at Sea 1756–1815*. New York: Norton, 2000.

Jefferson, Thomas. *Papers of Thomas Jefferson*. vols. I, VIII, XII, and XIII. Julian P. Boyd, ed. Princeton, New Jersey: Princeton University Press, 1950, 1953, 1955, 1956.

Jefferson, Thomas. *Writings*. New York: Library of America, 1984.

Katz, William Loren. *Eyewitness: A Living Documentary of the African American Contribution to American History*. New York: Touchstone, 1995.

Keegan, John. *The Price of Admiralty: The Evolution of Naval Warfare*. New York: Viking.

Kemp, Peter. *The British Sailor: A Social History of the Lower Deck*. London: J. M. Dent, 1970.

Kennedy, Roger. G. *Burr, Hamilton and Jefferson: A Study in Character*. New York: Oxford, 1999.

King, Dean, with John Hattendorf and J. Worth Estes, *A Sea of Words*. New York: Henry Holt and Co., 1995.

King, Dean, and John B. Hattendorf, eds. *Every Man Will Do His Duty: An Anthology of Firsthand Accounts from the Age of Nelson*. New York: Henry Holt, 1997.

Korshunov, IU. L. *When the Ocean Unites: From Stories of Friendly Relations Between the Russian and American Fleets.* St. Petersburg: St. Petersburg University, 1996.

Lafayette, Marquis de. *Lafayette in the Age of the American Revolution: Selected Letters and Papers.* vols. II and III. Stanley J. Idzerda, ed. Ithaca: Cornell, 1979, 1980.

Lambert, Andrew. *War at Sea in the Age of Sail 1650–1850.* London: Cassell, 2000.

Langley, Harold D. *Social Reform in the United States Navy, 1798–1862.* Chicago: University of Illinois Press, 1967.

Lavery, Brian. *The Arming and Fitting of English Ships of War.*

Leamon, James S. *Revolution Downeast.* Amherst: University of Massachusetts, 1993.

Lewis, Michael. *A Social History of the Navy 1793–1815.* London: George Allen, 1960.

Lloyd, Christopher, ed. *A Memoir of James Trevenen.* London: Naval Records Society, 1959.

Lodge of St. Andrew and the Massachusetts Grand Lodge. Boston: Lodge of St. Andrew, 1870.

Log of the Bon Homme Richard. Mystic, Connecticut: Marine Historical Association, 1936.

Lopez, Claude-Anne. *Mon Cher Papa: Franklin and the Ladies of Paris.* New Haven: Yale University Press, 1966.

Lorenz, Lincoln. *The Admiral and the Empress.* New York: Bookman Associates, 1954.

———. *John Paul Jones: Fighter for Freedom and Glory.* Annapolis: Naval Institute Press, 1943.

Lucas, Stephen E. *Portents of Rebellion.* Philadelphia: Temple University Press, 1976.

Lutnick, Solomon. *The American Revolution and the British Press 1775–1783.* Columbia, Missouri: University of Missouri Press, 1967.

MacPherson, James, trans. *The Poems of Ossian.* Boston: Phillips, Sampson and Co., 1852.

Malcomson, Robert. *Notebook.* Stewartry Museum, Kirkcudbright, Scotland.

Malins, Edward. *English Landscaping and Literature, 1660–1840.* London: Oxford, 1966.

Malone, Dumas. *Jefferson the Virginian.* Boston: Little Brown, 1948.

Mason, Philip. *The English Gentleman: The Rise and Fall of an Ideal.* New York: William Morrow, 1982.

Massie, Robert K. *Peter the Great: His Life and World.* New York: Ballantine, 1980.

Maxwell, Sir Herbert. *A History of Dumfries and Galloway.* London: William Blackwood & Sons, 1896.

May, Henry F. *The Enlightenment in America.* New York: Oxford, 1976.

McCullough, David. *John Adams.* New York: Simon and Schuster, 2001.

McKee, Christopher. *A Gentlemanly and Honorable Profession: The Creation of the U.S. Naval Officer Corps, 1794–1815.* Annapolis: Naval Institute Press, 1991.

Melville, Herman. *Israel Potter.* Evanston, Illinois: Northwestern University Press, 1997.

———. *Redburn.* London: Penguin, 1976

Memorial to Justify Peter Landais Conduct During the Late War. Boston: Peter Eades, 1784.

Miller, Nathan. *Broadsides: The Age of Fighting Sail, 1775–1815.* New York: John Wiley, 2000.

Montefiore, Simon Sebag. *Prince of Princes: The Life of Potemkin.* London: Weidenfeld & Nicholson, 2000.

Morison, Samuel Eliot. *John Paul Jones: A Sailor's Biography.* Boston: Northeastern University Press, 1959.

Morris, Gouverneur. *A Diary of the French Revolution.* vols. I and II. Beatrix Cary Davenport, ed. Boston: Houghton Mifflin, 1939.

Neill, Peter, ed. *American Sea Writing*. New York: Library of America, 2000.

Norton, Louis Arthur. *Joshua Barney: Hero of the Revolution and 1812*. Annapolis: Naval Institute Press, 2000.

O'Brian, Patrick. *Far Side of the World*. New York: Norton, 1984.

———. *Master and Commander*. New York: Norton, 1970.

Olsen, Kirstin. *Daily Life in Eighteenth Century England*. Westport, Connecticut: Greenwood, 1999.

Padelford, Philip, ed. *Colonial Panorama, 1775: Dr. Robert Honeyman's Journal for March and April*. San Marino, California: Huntington Library, 1939.

Padfield, Peter. *Maritime Supremacy and the Opening of the Western Mind*. Woodstock, New York: Overlook Press, 1999.

Penman, Alastair. *Old Kirkcudbright*. United Kingdom: Stenlake, 1998.

Pontgibaud, Chevalier de. *A French Volunteer in the War of Independence*. Robert B. Douglas, ed. Paris: C. Carrington, 1987.

Pope, Dudley. *Life in Nelson's Navy*. London: Chatham, 1981.

Rasor, Eugene Latimer. "The Problem of Discipline in the Mid-19th Century Royal Navy," Dissertation, University of Virginia, June 1972.

Rediker, Marcus. *Between the Devil and the Deep Blue Sea: Mercant Seamen, Pirates, and the Anglo-American Martime World 1700–1750*. Cambridge: Cambridge University Press, 1987.

Renfro, G. Herbert. *Life and Works of Phillis Wheatley*. Freeport, New York: Books for Libraries Press, 1970.

Rider, Hope S. *Valour Fore & Aft*. Annapolis: Naval Institute Press, 1978.

Riley, Edward Miles. *The Journal of John Harrower: An Indentured Servant in the Colony of Virginia, 1773–1776*. Williamsburg, Virginia: Holt, Rinehart and Winston, 1963.

Robinson, William H. Critical Essays on Phillis Wheatley. Boston: G.K. Hall & Co., 1982.

Rodger, N.A.M. *The Wooden World. An Anatomy of the Georgian Navy*. London: Fontana Press, 1988.

Sawtelle, Joseph G., ed. *John Paul Jones and the* Ranger. Portsmouth, New Hampshire: Peter Randall, 1994.

Schaeper, Thomas J. *France and America in the Revolutionary Era: The Life of Jacques-Donatien Leray de Chaumont, 1725–1803*. Providence, Rhode Island: Berghahn, 1995.

———. *John Paul Jones and the Battle off Flamborough Head: A Reconsideration*. New York: Peter Lang, 1989.

Seitz, Don C. *Paul Jones: His Exploits in English Seas During 1778–1780*. New York: Dutton, 1917.

Shackelford, George Green. *Thomas Jefferson's Travels in Europe, 1784–1789*. Baltimore: Johns Hopkins, 1995.

Sherburne, John Henry. *Life and Character of John Paul Jones*. New York: Wilder & Campbell, 1825.

Shields, John C. *The Collected Works of Phillis Wheatley*. New York: Oxford, 1988.

Shipton, Clifford K. *Sibley's Harvard Graduates*. vols. XIII and XIV. Boston: Massachusetts Historical Society, 1965, 1968.

Smith, Paul, ed. *Letters of the Delegates to Congress*. vol. XVI. Washington, D.C.: Library of Congress, 1989.

Sobel, Dava. *Longitude*. New York: Penguin, 1995.

Sparrow, Elizabeth. *Secret Service: British Agents in France 1792–1815*. Woodbridge, England: Boydell, 1999.

Steblecki, Edith J. *Paul Revere and Freemasonry*. Revere Memorial Association, 1985.

Stevens, Sylvester K. *Pennsylvania: Birth of a Nation.* New York: Random House, 1964.

Stewart, Charles W. *John Paul Jones: Commemoration at Annapolis, April 24, 1906.* Washington, D.C.: GPO, 1966.

Sweetman, Jack, ed. *Great American Naval Battles.* Annapolis: Naval Institute Press, 1998.

Taylor, Alan. *William Cooper's Town.* New York: Knopf, 1995.

Taylor, Earl and Robert Beach. *Historical Sketch of the Grand Lodge of Masons in Massachusetts.* Boston: Grand Lodge of Masons in Massachusetts, 1973.

Taylor, Janette. *Life and Correspondence of John Paul Jones, including his Narrative of the Campaign of the Liman.* New York: A. Chandler, 1830.

Thomson, James. *The Seasons.* New York: R. & W. A. Bartow, 1819.

Truckell, A. E., Walter Duncan and Reverend Thomas Scott. *Kirkbean Parish and Kirk.* Dumfries, Scotland: Grieve, 1976.

Turberville, A. S., ed. *Johnson's England.* Oxford: Clarendon, 1933.

Tuchman, Barbara. *The First Salute.* New York: Knopf, 1988.

Valle, James F. *Rocks & Shoals: Order and Discipline in the Old Navy 1800–1861.* Annapolis: Naval Institute Press, 1980.

Vickers, Daniel. *Farmers & Fisherman: Two Centuries of Work in Essex County, Massachusetts, 1630–1850.* Chapel Hill: University of North Carolina Press, 1994.

Walsh, John Evangelist. *Night on Fire: The First Complete Account of John Paul Jones' Greatest Battle.* New York: McGraw-Hill, 1978.

Washington, George. *The Writings of George Washington.* vol. 28. Fitzpatrick, John C., ed. Washington, D.C.: GPO, 1931.

Wharton, Francis. *The Revolutionary Diplomatic Correspondence of the United States.* vol. I. Washington, D.C.: GPO, 1889.

Winthrop, William. *Military Law and Precedents.* vol. II. Boston: Little Brown, 1896.

Wood, Gordon. *The Radicalism of the American Revolution.* New York: Vintage, 1991.

ARTICLES

Allen, Jane E. "Lying at the Port of Philadelphia Vessel Types 1725–1775." *American Neptune,* vol. 53, no. 3, summer 1993.

Ashe, S. A. "Some New Light on John Paul Jones." *South Atlantic Quarterly,* vol. XVII, no. 1, January 1918.

Atkinson, Amalia. "Captain Rathbun's Last Voyage." *New England Historical and Geneological Register,* vol. CXV, no. 115, July 1961.

Barnett, Richard C. "The View From Below Deck: The British Navy, 1777–1781." *American Neptune,* April 1978.

Baugh, Daniel A. "The Politics of British Naval Failure, 1775–1777." *American Neptune,* July 1982.

Bemis, Samuel. "British Secret Service." *American Historical Review,* April 1924.

Bolander, Louis H. "The Frigate *Alliance,* The Favorite Ship of the American Revolution." *U.S. Naval Institute Proceedings,* September 1937.

———. "Two Notes on John Paul Jones." *U.S. Naval Institute Proceedings,* July 1928.

Boyd, Julian P. "Silas Deane: Death by Kindly Teacher of Treason?" *William and Mary Quarterly,* April 1959.

Buell, Augustus C. "Narrative of John Kilby." *Scribner's,* July 1905.

Burg, B. R. "Legitimacy and Authority: A Case Study of Pirate Commanders in the Seventeenth and Eighteenth Centuries." *American Neptune,* vol. 38, 1977.

Clark, William Bell. "Letters of Captain Nicholas Biddle." *Pennsylvania Magazine of History and Biography,* vol. LXXIV, July 1950.

Christie, Ian R. "Samuel Bentham and the Russian Dnieper Flotilla, 1787–1788." *The Slavonic and East European Review*, vol. I, no. 119, April 1972.

Cullen, Joseph P. "John Paul Jones: A Personality Profile." *American History Illustrated*, vol. I, no. 1, April 1966.

Dean, Nicholas. "John Paul Jones Came Awfully Close to Being a Loser." *Smithsonian*, December 1980.

Dudley, William S. and Michael A. Palmer. "No Mistake About It: A Response to Jonathan R. Dull," *American Neptune*, fall 1985.

Fowler, William. "The Business of War: Boston as a Navy Base, 1776–1783." *American Neptune*, January 1982.

Frost, Holloway H. "Our Heritage From Paul Jones." *U.S. Naval Institute Proceedings*, October 1918.

"Deane Papers," *Collections of the New York Historical Society*. New York: New York Historical Society, 1886.

Eller, Ernest M. "Sea Power in the American Revolution." *U.S. Naval Institute Proceedings*, vol. 62, no. 6, June 1936.

Gillingham, Harrold E. "Dr. Solomon Drowne." *Pennsylvania Magazine of History and Biography*, vol. 48, 1924.

Halliday, Mark. "An Agreeable Voyage." *American Heritage*, June 1970.

"John Paul Jones as a Citizen of Virginia," *Virginia Magazine of History and Biography*, vol. VII, no. 3, January 1900.

"John Paul Jones at Bethlehem, Penna. 1783." Notes and Queries. *Pennsylvania Magazine of History and Biography*, vol. XXXIX, 1915.

Johnson, Major G. A. "John Paul Jones: Strategist and Tactician." *U.S. Naval Institute Proceedings*, vol. 54, no. 7, July 1928.

Litto, Frederic M. "Addison's *Cato* in the Colonies." *William and Mary Quarterly*, third series, vol. 23, no. 3, July 1966.

Mahan, Alfred Thayer. "John Paul Jones in the Revolution." *Scribner's*, July 1898.

"Captain Hector McNeill." *Massachusetts Historical Society Proceedings*, vol. LV. Boston: Massachusetts Historical Society, November 1921.

Mazet, Lieutenant Horace S. "The Navy's Forgotten Hero." *U.S. Naval Institute Proceedings*, March 1937.

Morgan, James. "American Privateering in America's War for Independence, 1775–1783." *American Neptune*, April 1976.

Morison, Samuel Eliot. "The Arms and Seals of John Paul Jones." *American Neptune*, vol. XVIII, no. 4, 1958.

———. "The Willie Jones–John Paul Jones Tradition." *William and Mary Quarterly*. third series, vol. 16, no. 2, April 1959.

Morris, Richard B. "The Revolution's Caine Mutiny." *American Heritage*, April 1960.

"List of Natucket Men Who Served Under John Paul Jones During the Revolutionary War." *Proceedings of the Nantucket Historical Society*, 1901.

Parker, T. D. "The Romance of Joshua Barney." *U.S. Naval Institute Proceedings*, vol. 42, 1916.

Paullin, Charles Oscar. "The Conditions of the Continental Naval Service." *U.S. Naval Institute Proceedings*, vol. 32, March 1906.

———. "Dueling in the Old Navy." *U.S. Naval Institute Proceedings*, vol. 35, 1909.

Porter, General Horace. "The Recovery of the Body of John Paul Jones." *Century*, September 1905.

Rathbun, Frank H. "Rathbun's Raid on Nassau." *U.S. Naval Institute Proceedings*, November 1970.

Seawell, Molly Elliot. "Paul Jones." *Century*, April 1895.

Shirley, G. W. "Two Pioneer Agriculturalists." *Transactions of the Dumfries and Galloway Natural History and Antiquarian Society*, vol. XIII, third series, 1925–1926.

Stark, Suzanne J. "Sailor's Pets in the Royal Navy in the Age of Sail." *American Neptune*, vol. 51, no. 2, spring 1991.

———. "Women at Sea in the Royal Navy in the Age of Sail." *American Neptune*, vol. 57, no. 2, 1997.

Warner, Oliver. "The Action Off Flamborough Head." *American Heritage*, August 1963.

Wax, Darold. "The Browns of Providence and the Slaving Voyage of the Brig *Sally*, 1764–1765. *The American Neptune*, July 1972.

Wood, Gordon. "The Greatest Generation." *New York Review of Books*, March 29, 2001.

Newspapers and Journals

Boston Gazette

Continental Journal

Gazette of the United States

Gentleman's Magazine

Gazetteer and New Daily Advertiser (London)

Morning Chronicle (London)

Public Advertiser (London)

Times (London)

Daily Gazette (New York)

New York Times

Virginia Gazette

INDEX

PHOTO CREDITS

ABOUT THE AUTHOR

EVAN THOMAS is the author of *The Wise Men: Six Friends and the World They Made* (with Walter Isaacson); *The Man to See: Edward Bennett Williams: Ultimate Insider; Legendary Trial Lawyer*; *The Very Best Men: Four Who Dared, the Early Years of the CIA*; and *Robert Kennedy: His Life*. He is an assistant managing editor of *Newsweek* magazine and lives with his wife and two daughters in Washington, D.C.